YOUTH HOSTELS A...

ACCOMMODATI...

CW00322803

Patron:
Her Majesty The Queen

President:
Dr David Bellamy

Vice Presidents:
Hedley Alcock
Chris Bonington CBE
Len Clark CBE
The Rt Hon The Lord Lovell-Davis
Alun Michael JP, MP
John Parfitt CBE
The Rt Hon The Lord Rippon of Hexham, QC
The Rt Hon The Lord Shackleton KG, AC, OBE, FRS

Chairman:
John Patten

Vice Chairman:
Ian Shaw

Treasurer:
Derek Hanson

Assistant Treasurer:
Alan Bourne

Chief Executive:
Andrew Chinneck

YHA is a registered charity founded in 1930. Its aim is "to help all, especially young people of limited means, to a greater knowledge, love and care of the countryside, particularly by providing hostels or other simple accommodation for them in their travels, and thus to promote their health, rest and education."

National Office:
Trevelyan House, 8 St Stephen's Hill, St Albans, Hertfordshire AL1 2DY.
Tel: (0727) 55215. Fax: (0727) 44126.

Trade Distribution by:
Moorland Publishing Co. Ltd., Moor Farm Road, Ashbourne, Derbyshire DE6 1HD. Tel: (0335) 44486. Fax: (0335) 46397.

This publication has been printed on environment friendly paper.

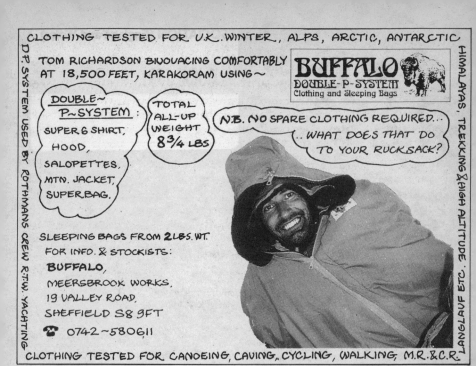

CONTENTS

Welcome to YHA

YHA opens up new horizons, whatever your age! With an exciting choice of 250 Youth Hostels, all providing excellent low-cost accommodation, YHA helps you discover the varied and beautiful landscapes of England and Wales. Above all, it's a fun organisation that cares for people and the environment and presents a great way to travel and meet friends.

The Association was originally set up in the early 1930s to provide accommodation for walkers and cyclists. Today, YHA has a much wider appeal, with over 320,000 members and over 2 million overnights spent each year. YHA attracts people with a whole range of interests, from climbing, caving and canoeing, to juggling, photography and wine-tasting.

You'll find Youth Hostels in cities, towns, the coast and countryside — in fact almost anywhere you choose to visit! Each Hostel has its own character and charm, for instance, you might choose to stay at a ghostly Norman castle situated on the edge of the Forest of Dean, a Victorian Carrstone house on the Norfolk Coast, or perhaps a former shepherd's bothy in the Lake District is more your style.

Youth Hostels provide an excellent base for exploring the countryside, enjoying an organised YHA activity holiday or why not travel from one Hostel to another while touring.

Come on your own, or with friends. Either way, you're sure to enjoy the lively atmosphere found at our Hostels.

YHA is affiliated to the International Youth Hostel Federation — the largest travel organisation in the world. This means that your YHA membership entitles you to stay at over 5300 Youth Hostels in more than 58 countries. So, wherever you decide to visit, you can always stay with YHA!

There are many benefits of being a YHA member — see page 5 for details of membership and how to join.

How to Use This Guide

This Guide will tell you all you need to know about youth hostelling, from how to join, to what to do when you arrive at the Hostel. There's information about our exciting Great Escapes activity holidays and short breaks, helpful hints for walking and cycling, plus details of how the Association is organised and how an individual Youth Hostel operates. Town maps are provided under each Youth Hostel entry.

To enable us to give you as much information as possible, several symbols and codes are used. These are explained on the useful bookmark which you will find within the Accommodation Guide and which may be used as an easy reference when you are planning your holiday. So — don't lose it! Information we are unable to squeeze onto that bookmark can be found in

other sections of the Guide, for example, public transport details are explained on page 9 and Youth Hostel daytime opening patterns on page 11.

To find out how to make the most of your YHA membership, just read on!

Membership and How to Join

Join YHA and you won't ever look back! Full of action and fun, the Association offers much more than just a place to stay. Activities, social events, conservation projects, worldwide travel and discounts — the opportunities are endless!

You need to be a member of YHA to stay at a Youth Hostel — you'll find out what it costs to join on the inside front cover. YHA membership is open to residents of England and Wales only, so if you are visiting the UK, please apply for membership at the Youth Hostels Association of your country.

Who Can Join?

Anyone aged 14 years or over can join and stay with YHA independently. Children between 5 and 13 can become members, but can only stay at Hostels if supervised by a parent or guardian (see page 15 for details of the under 5's).

Groups

Organisations sending a group of more than five people to a Youth Hostel can benefit from a special membership concession — only the leader needs to be a full YHA member! See page 13 for more details.

Family Membership

When parents (or parent in the case of single parent families) enrol at the normal fee, children aged between 5 and 15 are enrolled FREE! They will receive their own membership cards.

Parents of young hostellers travelling alone are advised that some Youth Hostels are isolated and/or do not have a resident Warden at certain times.

International Travel

One of the exciting benefits of YHA membership is that once you affix your photograph to your membership card you have access to the whole international Youth Hostel network!

How to Join

Becoming a member of YHA is simple — just complete the Membership Form on page 183 and send it with the appropriate enrolment fee (see inside cover) to: **YHA Membership Department, Trevelyan House, 8 St Stephen's Hill, St Albans, Herts. AL1 2DY** or you can contact your local YHA Enrolment Centre (see pages 172-175). Alternatively, you can join at the Hostel when you arrive.

Direct Debit

Paying for your membership by this method makes things easier for you and us! You will receive a validated membership card — ready to use — plus all the usual benefits, each year. Just contact the YHA Membership Department (as above) for details.

Covenanted Subscriptions

If you pay income tax at the basic rate on your earnings, you can make your subscription worth almost half as much again to YHA, at no extra cost! All you need to do is sign a Deed of Covenant. It's not complicated! Just write to us at National Office for details and the appropriate form.

This scheme applies to life membership by 5 annual payments. YHA is a registered charity and therefore does not pay tax on its income and reclaims from the Inland Revenue the tax which has already been deducted from your own income in respect of the amount covenanted.

Please help us in this way if you possibly can.

Renewing Your Membership

YHA membership is valid for one year upon joining. When your membership runs out, you will automatically be sent a Renewal Form that gives you the chance to pay by cheque, postal order or direct debit. This method of renewal will enable you to retain all the benefits of being a member and helps avoid any delay in processing your application during busy periods.

WHAT MEMBERSHIP INCLUDES:

▲ **Comfortable budget accommodation in 250 locations.**

▲ **FREE YHA Accommodation Guide.**

▲ **FREE touring map.**

▲ **FREE members' magazine, mailed out three times a year — including interesting travel articles, updates on Hostel-based activities and countryside issues, pen-pal and events sections.**

▲ **Discounts on many tourist attractions and selected items from YHA Adventure Shops.**

▲ **A wide selection of outdoor (and indoor) activities — all year round.**

▲ **Opportunities for involvement in practical conservation projects.**

▲ **The chance to make new friends and join a YHA Local Group.**

▲ **Access to over 5,300 Youth Hostels abroad.**

▲ **Lots more!**

SPECIAL RATES FOR UB40 HOLDERS

If You Have a UB40 Card

YHA offers you a special deal — membership at the Young rate (just £1.90) and discount rates at nearly all the Youth Hostels (well over 200) and for most of the year. Of course you can still use the others, but the normal rate will apply. To obtain your membership simply fill in the form on page 183 and send it to National Office with a photocopy of your current UB40 card and a cheque or Postal Order for £1.90. NB: refunds are not available if full membership has already been paid.

Special discount rates apply at all times except those listed below:

▲ Good Friday, Easter Saturday and Sunday
▲ Fridays and Saturdays in May and June
▲ Throughout July and August
▲ Fridays and Saturdays in Sept and Oct
▲ December 24th-January 1st inclusive

And at all Youth Hostels in England and Wales except those listed below:

Alfriston	Bath	
Alpheton	Birmingham	
Bangor	Bradenham	

Bretton
Brighton (Patcham)
Bristol
Cambridge
Canterbury
Cardiff
Chester
Dover
Exeter
Golant
Harlow
Langsett
Llangollen
London (all 8 Youth Hostels)
Newquay

Oxford
Penzance
Plymouth
Portsmouth
Salisbury
Shining Cliff
Southampton
Stratford-upon-Avon
Swanage
Tebay
Winchester
Windsor
Woody's Top
York

HOW TO BOOK

When planning a youth hostelling trip it is advisable to book in advance, especially if travelling to a popular area at Easter, Christmas, or in July or August.

Booking by telephone

If you telephone to check availability, please give your name and ask to have a bed reserved just in case the Youth Hostel fills up before you arrive. Please 'phone the Hostel during opening hours (normally before 10.00 and after 17.00 hours) and we'd be grateful if you also avoided mealtimes when the Warden is very busy.

You can pay by Access or Visa over the 'phone at most Hostels, otherwise please confirm your booking in writing, stating the date of your visit as well as your name and address, with payment within 7 days. If you book less than 7 days in advance, without payment, your bed will only be held until 6pm on your arrival date.

Hostels unable to accept Access/Visa payments:

Alpheton, Badby, Bellingham, Blaencaron, Bretton, Bryn Poeth Uchaf, Copt Oak, Cynwyd, Ellingstring, Epping, Glascwm, Harlow, Hartland, Hindhead, Langsett, Lockton, Maeshafn, Marloes Sands, Meerbrook, Penmaenmawr, Rowen, Shining Cliff, Telscombe, Trevine, Tyncornel, Wheathill, Woody's Top, Ystumtuen.

Booking by post

A Hostel Booking Letter is included in this Guide (pages 185-186) or they are available free from National Office and should be sent direct to the Warden unless another address is given in the Hostel details. Please state: date(s) of your visit; males and females in your party; senior, junior or young bookings; evening meals, breakfasts, packed lunches, and sheet sleeping bags required.

Full payment is required for bookings made by post. Cheques and postal orders are payable to Youth Hostels Association (keep the postal order counterfoil in case your payment has to be returned). Please — *no* stamps. You can book as far ahead as you like, but replies may be delayed when Hostels are closed. PLEASE send a stamped addressed envelope for the Warden's acknowledgement and confirmation of booking.

BOOK-A-BED-AHEAD SERVICE

Just to let you know that from 1991 onwards, a number of key Youth Hostels (including those in London) will be offering a service for YHA members to book their future Hostel overnights by fax — in this country and abroad!

▲ First, you fill in a request form to reserve the bed(s) you wish to book for the next night or beyond.

▲ Then, you hand in the form at Reception and pay the overnight charge(s) (plus a small administrative fee for the service).

▲ The Hostel staff will fax your request and a reply will be received within a couple of hours from the Hostel you wish to visit.

▲ If the accommodation you require is available, you simply take the faxed reply and hand it to the Hostel warden when you arrive as evidence of your payment and reservation. However, should the Hostel inform you that they cannot offer the accommodation you require, your payment will be refunded straight away.

▲ Your reserved bed will be held for you right up to the latest check-in time.

Watch out for the special Book-A-Bed-Ahead poster in participating Hostels and also the YHA magazine 'Triangle', for a full list of Hostels on the new fax network, both in this country and abroad.

CHECKLIST

If you are carrying your own luggage, don't spoil the enjoyment by taking too much! Remember that outdoor clothing will receive hard wear and even in summer you should carry adequate warm and waterproof clothing. Everyone has his/her own essential items list but here are some guidelines:

YHA membership card
YHA Guide
money
towel, toilet articles
basic personal first aid kit and any medicines
    you usually take
light shoes or slippers for Hostel wear
sheet sleeping bag (*these can be hired at the
    Hostel*) or 2 sheets and a pillowslip
nightwear
changes of underwear and socks
changes of shorts, trousers, skirts, shirts
woollen sweater
windproof cagoule
hood or woollen hat, gloves
plastic bags (*to keep clothes dry*)
torch, whistle
map and compass
emergency high energy food

Walkers only:

framed rucksack
suitable footwear for the terrain — well
    broken-in walking boots with good ankle
    support is best

Cyclists only:

saddle bag or panniers
appropriate footwear
tool kit
water bottle
cycle lock
cycle insurance

TRAVELLING BY RAIL AND BUS

This Guide offers appropriate detail on bus services to Youth Hostels, but in cases where many services exist, only the main, frequent, services are indicated, particularly those that link best with the 'outside world' or stations. Odd market-day services are not listed unless they are the only ones available. If no distance is quoted you can assume the bus passes close to the Hostel.

Where possible, telephone numbers are those of County Council Enquiry Lines that can offer detail about many operators — otherwise if several numbers appear they are in the order of the operators listed. No detail is offered about Sunday services for buses. Please note that "passing close ..." to a BR station may mean anything up to a mile's walk — this can only be a guide, so please make allowances for this.

BR Station details are shown separately so that you can see how far it is to walk or cycle and they are the closest but not necessarily those from which the buses depart. Details about Sunday rail services are shown. Please make enquiries with BR before you set out if you intend taking a cycle on the train — there is sometimes a need to reserve and/or pay a fee or even a ban on some routes or times of day.

All public transport information is provided by Barry S. Doe of Travadvice, 25 Newmorton Road, Bournemouth BH9 3NU, but please note that whilst he will be pleased to hear from readers who discover errors or who wish to make suggestions for improvements to this Guide, HE CANNOT ANSWER QUERIES FROM YHA MEMBERS, WHETHER BY PHONE OR BY POST, ABOUT TRAVEL TO YOUTH HOSTELS. Please use the phone Enquiry Lines quoted in the text.

However, he does publish a Guide giving times of buses from stations to some 285 places not on the BR network, many of which have Hostels. Published in January, May, July and October, a single copy is £4.50 post-free (within UK) or an annual subscription to any 4 consecutive copies £16.00 (£15.00 for YHA members). Cheques/POs to 'B S Doe' to the above address.

FINDING THE HOSTEL

You will find Hostel addresses, maps and directions listed under each Hostel entry.

Hostels are signposted and you may see a variety of signs. Two new signs are being introduced, a YHA green and white sign and a new brown and white international sign which features the words 'Youth Hostel'. The symbols to look for are those shown opposite, the International Youth Hostel sign (right) and the YHA England and Wales signs (left). Obviously some of the old signs are still in existence. These may show simply the letters YHA (centre) or just the international symbol.

The Hostels themselves carry the YHA triangle sign which may be in the new form (left) or the old form (centre). In many places, the local authority has erected road signs to the Hostel. These are usually a brown and white pointer carrying the International Youth Hostel Federation sign (right) and the words 'Youth Hostel'.

At the Hostel

Youth Hostels provide great opportunities for making new friends and joining in the fun, whatever your age! The following are some things to remember when staying at our Hostels, including some useful tips about how a Youth Hostel operates.

When You Arrive

At the Hostel Reception, the Hostel Warden will ask you to sign the housebook, make any payment due and leave your membership card. You should let the Warden know which meals you require and also ask for a *sheet sleeping bag* if you have not brought one along with you (see below).

Your Accommodation

Unless you have pre-booked special 'Family' accommodation (see page 15) you will stay in a comfortable bunk bedded room or dormitory, sharing with people of the same sex.

The Hostel will provide pillows and duvets (or blankets) for your use. Bed linen however, is *not* included in your overnight fee. We ask that you use either a *sheet sleeping bag* or two sheets and a pillow case.

You can hire a freshly laundered *sheet sleeping bag* from the Hostel Reception or if you wish to buy one they are available from many Youth Hostels, YHA National Office and YHA Adventure Shops (see page 163). Details are shown below if you wish to make your own. Sorry but down or synthetic filled sleeping bags are not acceptable for reasons of hygiene. (Please note that you may have to pay a laundry charge if you have the incorrect bedding.) The only exception to this is at unheated 'simple' Hostels during the winter months — but please check with the Warden first.

Please Be Considerate

Please only play radios where nobody minds and not in the dormitories. Smoking is prohibited in dormitories and the Members' Kitchen — and in the dining room when meals are being served. Other non-smoking areas will be marked and we ask that these be respected.

The Length of Your Stay

The length of your stay is normally unlimited, but Wardens have the discretion to restrict this if necessary in the interests of other hostellers.

Helping Us to Help You!

To help us keep prices as low as possible, Wardens may ask for help with simple household tasks like washing up and you are asked to clear up after yourself as much as possible. This is usually regarded as fun when joining with others!

Sorry, No Pets!

We are sorry that Youth Hostels cannot allow pets, although it is possible for special arrangements to be made with the Warden for Guide Dogs for the Blind.

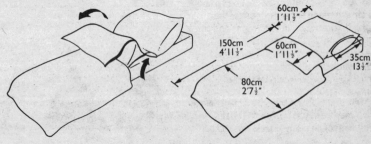

Alcohol

Some Hostels are licensed to sell beer, wine and cider with meals (see individual entries) but alcohol must not be brought into Hostels unless special arrangements have first been made with the Warden. Please also note that the use of illegal drugs and other substances is not allowed on Youth Hostel premises and the Warden may refuse admission to anyone under the influence of drugs.

Hostel Wardens

The Hostel Warden is there to ensure that you enjoy your stay. He or she can help with any problem and has the authority to take whatever action is necessary to ensure the proper running of the Hostel.

Camping Arrangements Ⓐ

YHA members who bring their own tents and bedding may camp at certain Hostels as shown under the Hostel entries.

The charge per person is half the senior overnight fee for the Hostel concerned, regardless of age.

This charge normally covers the use of Youth Hostel facilities, but no bedding, blankets or Hostel equipment may be taken to the tent.

The relieve pressure on Members' Kitchens, campers may prefer to use their own cooking equipment. Campers sign the housebook and hand their cards to the Warden in the same way as members staying in the Hostel.

HOSTEL HOURS

Most Youth Hostels are normally closed between 10.00-17.00 hours, but the chart below shows the facilities available during those hours.

The number shown eg ② on the Hostel entry gives the daytime access category of the Hostel. If no number is given, either it has not been possible to provide shelter, or the Hostel has no resident Warden and the key has to be collected by members when they arrive.

In the Evenings:

You can check in until 22.30 hrs. Hostels are open until 23.00 hours and "lights out" is usually at 23.30 hrs.

For security reasons and to avoid disturbing members the Hostel is closed until 07.00 hours, so even if it is a lovely morning please don't get up too soon!

Please bear in mind that Wardens and other Hostel staff have their 'time off' during the day, so try not to disturb them. Only category ④ Hostels have a member of staff available outside normal opening hours.

PLEASE REMEMBER THAT YOU MAY NOT BE ABLE TO GET IN IF YOU ARRIVE OR RETURN LATE.

Daytime Access Arrangements Between 1pm and 5pm (13.00-17.00 hrs)

HOSTEL OPENING CATEGORY	①	②	③	④
Simple shelter	▲			
Good simple shelter		▲	▲	▲
WC where possible	▲			
WC		▲	▲	▲
Luggage storage		▲		
Secure luggage storage			▲	▲
Booking facility		▲	▲	▲
Often drinks machine			▲	▲
Staff on duty				▲

WHAT'S COOKING?

When you've been out and about all day, you'll be glad to know that there's a good wholesome meal waiting for you at the Youth Hostel. Most of our Hostels offer a meals service and have qualified staff with considerable experience in catering for both individual hostellers and groups. Menus vary between Hostels, each offering their own specialities which often reflect the local cuisine.

Breakfast

Start the day with a full nutritious breakfast! Most Youth Hostels offer a choice of English or Continental-style at an all-inclusive cost of £2.30. Please ensure that you order your breakfast the night before.

Lunch Packs

Travel with ease and make use of our convenient packed lunches. These are available at most of our Hostels and they provide all the protein and goodness you need to keep you going during the day! The standard pack costs just £1.60 (including a vegetarian option if ordered in advance). Selected Hostels also offer a superior alternative at £2.50 or a 'pick and mix' for you to choose your own packed lunch — to suit your appetite and your pocket!

Evening Meals

An evening meal costs from £3.00. In addition to the standard evening meal, many Hostels now offer a wide variety of main courses and snack meals. These meals are individually priced to offer the same excellent value as the standard meals and are sure to tempt everyone's appetite — and meet all budgets! (If you have paid the standard meal charge in advance, any extras or alternatives requiring a further charge may be paid on the day.) **Cafeteria dining facilities** are now available at many Hostels, offering even greater flexibility in both menus and meal times. The Warden will let you know what the arrangements are.

Vegetarian Meals and Special Diets

For those who prefer not to eat meat, it's good to know that all catering Youth Hostels offer wholesome vegetarian meals. Some Hostels provide vegetarian options daily, but please let the Warden know sufficiently in advance that you require a vegetarian meal. Wardens are happy to cater for other special diets if required — but they do need full information in advance of your visit regarding the types of food you can eat.

Ordering Your Meals

You can order your meals when making your Hostel booking by post — include payment with your overnight charges. Alternatively, please let the Warden have as much notice as possible of your requirements at the Hostel — for example, most Hostels will need your evening meal booking by 18.00 hours and your breakfast booking the previous evening.

Self-Catering

For those who prefer to cook for themselves, all permanent Youth Hostels have a Members' Kitchen. These are equipped with cooking stoves, pots and pans, crockery and cutlery and food storage. Use of the Members' Kitchen is free but please do consider others by leaving everything clean and tidy. This includes doing your own washing up (yes, even the pots and pans!) and cleaning work surfaces that you have used.

Group Self-Catering [GSC]

Perhaps you are a teacher or a group leader planning a visit with a school, college, youth or community organisation group and you would like your group to self-cater. If so, please make sure that you select a Hostel showing the [GSC] symbol. It is essential that you contact the Warden to ensure that the Members' Kitchen is suitable for the numbers in your group.

BRING A GROUP

Your organisation can take a group hostelling — perhaps for a short break — and enjoy with them the freedom and adventure offered by YHA! Whether you take off into the hills on a 3-day hike, visit the local attractions, or study the geology of the area, Youth Hostels provide the perfect base.

Youth Hostels provide comfortable and spacious accommodation, together with excellent facilities which are ideal for party visits. A variety of groups stay with YHA, including schools, colleges, youth groups (such as Guides, Scouts and Venture Scouts) and community organisations.

Your visit can be action-filled, leisure or study orientated, with over 250 glorious locations to choose from. Many of our Hostels are ideally located for educational study, such as Literature, History, Geology and Ecology.

There's a special membership concession available to organisations sending a group of more than five people and who book in advance — only the leader needs to be a full YHA member! Groups taking full board may qualify for free leader places on a 1 for 10 ratio.

Information for Group Leaders

Those who are leading a group must be aged over 18 and mixed groups including under 18's must have both male and female leaders. A leader : group ratio of at least 1:15 is required (we recommend 1:10).

International Leader Cards

Venture out and take your group to Scotland, Ireland — and overseas! The International Leader Card allows a YHA member to take a group of non-members aged 10-21 years to over 5,300 Youth Hostels worldwide. Group numbers can range between 3-15 including the leader. The above Information for Group Leaders also applies. To obtain one of these cards, just write to National Office for an application form. The card costs £1.50.

Group Bookings

Please make initial enquiries with the Hostel of your choice regarding vacancies, your requirements and any special needs. The Warden will need to know the date(s) of your group visit with details of group numbers, ages, how many males and females, and which meals you will require. This information will need to be confirmed on our Group Booking Form (available at Hostels and National Office) which should be returned, together with a deposit, to the Hostel Warden.

Educational Facilities

28 of our Youth Hostels have extremely well-equipped Field Study Centres, with classroom(s), basic equipment, books and local OS maps. Just look for the special Field Study symbol **FS** in the individual Hostel entries. An inclusive price is offered to Field Study groups to include accommodation, breakfast, packed lunch, evening meal, sheet sleeping bag hire and use of the classroom. Teachers/leaders pay the same as the students and these prices can be found on the inside front cover. Further details are available from our Datapack which can be obtained from National Office.

Many other Hostels have classrooms available — watch for the special Classroom symbol **C** in the individual Hostel entries.

Groups Away Packages

Our inclusive **Groups Away** packages are designed especially for educational groups and include coach travel to cover a variety of exciting itineraries — in 40 scenic locations. Contact National Office for a free colour brochure.

Need Any Help?

If you feel you need more guidance regarding a group residential visit, YHA can help. We have an experienced team of YHA Regional Development Officers who will be delighted to discuss your requirements and guide you towards a suitable Youth Hostel. To contact the Officer in your area, for general group visit enquiries, or for 'Datapack' — our special publication for group visits, please contact YHA National Office (see page 1).

YHA AND THE DISABLED

YHA welcomes hostellers — young or old, individuals or groups — who need a wheelchair to get around or who have visual, hearing or other handicaps. We have many positive advantages to offer — above all, friendly companionship and inexpensive accommodation.

Some of our Youth Hostels are designed to cater for people with disabilities: Broad Haven, Manorbier, and to a more limited extent, Cardiff and Llwynypia. Other Hostels do vary greatly in terms of accessibility (particularly for wheelchairs); the amount of ground floor accommodation available; the width of doorways; and the number of downstairs loos. So, it really is important that you either write to the Hostel Warden, or ring him/her for a chat before booking.

Alternatively, especially if you are a leader of a party, you may prefer to write to YHA National Office or the appropriate Regional Office. Let us know the type and degree of disability and the number of people in your group, the area you would like to visit, whether meals are

required and so on, and we will help you choose a Hostel suitable for your party.

It is usually a good idea for the leader of a party to visit the Hostel in advance to discuss requirements in detail, noting any problems there may be and to plan activities.

There are other things which you may need to consider too. Not all Youth Hostels have car parks in the grounds. Hostellers are required to make their own beds — two-tier bunks in dormitories — and carry out a small duty such as washing up, so those who cannot manage alone really do need a friend who is willing to help.

Please remember that we are always here to help and advise. Just contact us at National Office, the Regional Office or the Hostel Warden direct.

STAY WITH THE FAMILY

More and more families are discovering the freedom and flexibility of YHA! Hostel Wardens are there to advise on activities and local attractions and will ensure that you have a comfortable stay. There are over 134 locations across England and Wales to choose from, all providing an ideal base for your family holiday! When planning your trip, please remember that all family accommodation must be booked in advance.

Family Rooms 👪

Family Rooms offer both a high standard of accommodation and the freedom to come and go as you please during the day. Families are provided with their own key and the facilities will vary between Youth Hostels; some have en suite facilities and all are equipped with wash basins together with adequate storage space. Wholesome meals are available from the Hostel, or if you prefer to cook for yourself, you can use the shared facilities in the self-catering kitchen. Families are charged per room; prices start from just £19.00 and vary according to the facilities offered. Please consult the Warden for details of availability and cost before you book.

The following Hostels contain Family Rooms, although more may become available during the year, so please check with the Warden.

Boswinger	Hawkshead
Bristol	Kirkby Stephen
Broad Haven	Matlock
Cambridge	Newquay
Hartington	Ridgeway (Wantage)

Family Annexes 🏠

There are now 11 Family Annexes available across the YHA network. These are separate self-contained units, providing you with access at any time of the day (key provided) and are also available to families with children under 5 years — not normally able to stay at Youth Hostels. The annexes are usually booked for 7 day periods — Saturday to Saturday — but shorter stays are possible during non-peak periods. When the main Hostel building is open, meals can be purchased at the Hostel at the usual prices (see page 12) — please remember that it is best to book meals in advance. Family Annexes are located at:

Bradenham	Knighton
Bryn Poeth Uchaf	Manorbier
Buttermere	Poppit Sands
Corris	St Davids
Cynwd Gwyndy Cottage	Welsh Bicknor —
Kirkby Stephen	Laundry cottage

See the main Hostel entry for further information and booking details. The cost to stay in a Family Annexe will vary according to the facilities available. Contact the Hostel Warden for details, or write to YHA for our Family Price List.

Family Dormitories 👪

A number of Youth Hostels offer small dormitories as Family Bunk Rooms for their exclusive use, often with wash basins but without the extras provided in Family Rooms. Watch out for the special symbol (as above). Families are charged only for beds occupied, at the standard rates.

Children Under 14

Under 14s can only stay at Hostels when accompanied by a responsible adult (over 18). Exception is made for under 14s from a recognised youth or educational organisation, in a party of at least 3, and who carry a letter of authority from their organisation. Under 5s may be accommodated in family rooms and dormitories at the warden's discretion — please check in advance.
Family Leaflet and Price List — Available from National Office (address on page 1).

LIKE TO WORK WITH YHA?

From Easter to September, we need Assistant Wardens at many of our Hostels throughout England and Wales.

There is a great deal of variety in the work, and locations range from castles in Cornwall to cottages in the Cotswolds.

"It beats working in an office"

If you are fit and like meeting people, you too could be a YHA Assistant Warden in the Region of your choice. If you choose to get stuck into the job during what promises to be one of our busiest summer seasons, we'll give you plenty of time off during the day, a good wage and free board and lodgings plus YHA benefits. What's more, there's always the chance of a permanent job with YHA later on!

"It's totally different from anything I've done before"

All you have to do is complete the coupon below making sure you tick the Region(s) where you would like to work and the box to indicate your preference for town or country, then hand it in at any Youth Hostel in England or Wales, or post it to the YHA.

I would like to apply for the position of Assistant Warden with the YHA. I am fit and available from
_____ to _____ 19____
(Give exact dates when you are available to work).
I have included my choices of Region(s) and town or country below. I would like to work in:

Northern England ☐
Central England ☐   Town ☐
South England ☐
Wales ☐   Country ☐

Name: Mr/Mrs/Miss/Ms_____
Address_____
_____
_____
Post Code_____
Contact Tel No. (Day)_____
(Evening)_____
Date of Birth_____
I am/Not a member

Hand this application to any Youth Hostel in England or Wales or post to: Personnel Department, YHA (England and Wales), Trevelyan House, 8 St. Stephen's Hill, St Albans, Herts AL1 2DY.

HOW YOU CAN HELP YHA

YHA is a registered charity, but the Association is not funded by the Government. Every member can help by recommending YHA to friends and colleagues or getting a group together to go on a YHA holiday.

You can join others in doing something practical for YHA such as conservation work, publicity, voluntary wardening and fund raising. To find out what is going on near you or to offer assistance, contact your Regional Office who can also supply publicity leaflets and posters.

YHA is a large organisation and has a team of full-time professional managers to run its operations. The policies they follow are decided by YHA members through the democratic structure shown below:

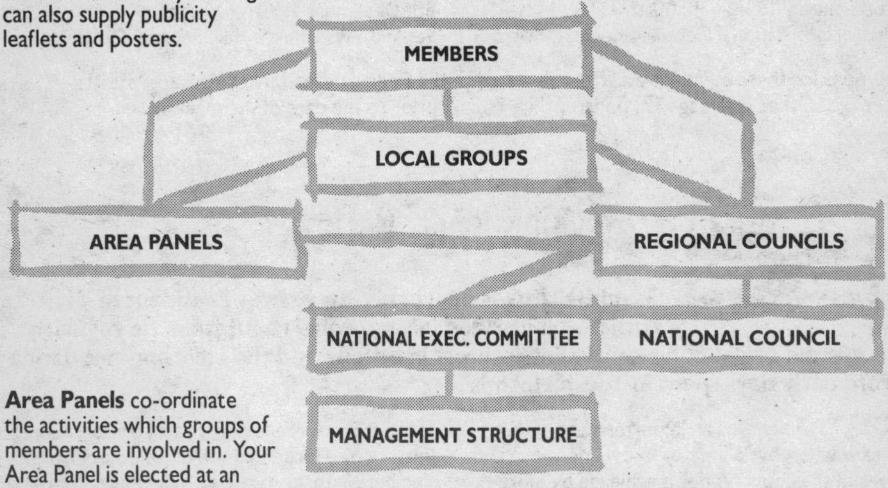

```
                    MEMBERS

                  LOCAL GROUPS

  AREA PANELS                    REGIONAL COUNCILS

            NATIONAL EXEC. COMMITTEE    NATIONAL COUNCIL

        MANAGEMENT STRUCTURE
```

Area Panels co-ordinate the activities which groups of members are involved in. Your Area Panel is elected at an open Area AGM announced in 'Triangle', our members' magazine. This meeting will be a good place to find out what is going on in YHA. Contact your Regional Office for more information (see map on page 179).

Regional Councils are involved in the development of policy, in encouraging members to participate in YHA activities and in monitoring the service provided to members.

There are four Regional Councils — Northern England, Central, Wales and South of England. They are elected at an open Regional AGM and are drawn from members nominated at the meeting, together with representatives of Area Panels and Local Groups.

You are welcome to come along to your Regional AGM and ask questions, express opinions, propose motions (with appropriate notice), stand for election, and vote. Details of your Regional AGM are on page 18 and will also be in 'Triangle'. Contact your Regional Office for more information.

National Council, which consists mainly of representatives of Regional Councils, meets annually and establishes the principles of YHA. It elects a National Executive Committee which determines policies within these principles. These policies are then implemented by the management and volunteers as appropriate.

The Regional Office addresses are:

Northern England
(Yorkshire, Border & Dales and Lakeland Areas)
D Floor, Millburn House, Dean Street, Newcastle upon Tyne NEI ILF. Tel: 091-221 2101

Central (Midland, East and Peak Areas)
P.O. Box 11, Matlock, Derbyshire.
Tel: (0629) 825850

Wales (North & South Wales Areas)
4th Floor, 1 Cathedral Road, Cardiff CF1 9HA.
Tel: (0222) 396766

South of England (South Areas 1-7)
Rolfes House, 60 Milford Street, Salisbury
SP1 2BP. Tel: (0722) 337515

1991 REGIONAL ANNUAL GENERAL MEETINGS

Don't forget, you are always welcome to attend your Regional AGM to express your opinions, ask questions, stand for election and vote — just what the YHA democracy is all about. So make a note of the following dates in your diary now!

Central Region
12th January 1991 — 2.00pm
County Offices, Matlock, Derbyshire.

South of England Region
26th January 1991 — 10.00am
Bristol International Centre, Prince St, Bristol.

Wales Region
26th January 1991 — 2.00pm
Llangollen Youth Hostel, Tyndwr Rd, Llangollen.

Northern Region
8th December 1990 — 1.30pm
St. Andrews Church Hall, Penrith, Cumbria.

Motions for these meetings must be submitted to the Regional Chairman at the appropriate Regional Office (see page 17) no later than 14 days prior to the date of the meeting.

COUNTRYSIDE MATTERS

David Bellamy is now in his 8th year as President of YHA. With a well-justified international reputation, he regularly recalls the origin of his continuing interest in botany and the environment dating from early days spent in Youth Hostels.

Today, YHA remains an important and unique means whereby "a greater knowledge, love and care of the countryside" is achieved by more than 320,000 people.

As part of its accommodation-providing and membership role throughout the country, YHA encourages and supports volunteers' involvement in both the policies and the practical work necessary to conserve the countryside and wider environment of England and Wales.

Countryside matters of relevance to Youth Hostels and Hostelling are handled by our full-time Countryside Officer, working in conjunction with National and Regional Countryside Committees of elected member-volunteers, as well as other staff within the Association. A range of practical conservation, amenity or educational activities are available to members in many localities. These include tree planting, rights of way projects and conservation weekends, often undertaken in conjunction with BTCV, the National Trust or County Wildlife Trusts.

What happens in and to the countryside is of great interest to our members. Accordingly, each issue of YHA's magazine, 'Triangle', continues to provide details of current or forthcoming environmental events and arguments, and the Association's relations with them. Your contribution to our Countryside work is welcome; if you'd like to get involved or simply learn more, please contact the Countryside Officer at YHA National Office.

Walking

Well worn-in walking boots with a cleated composition sole are essential for any walking tour. Smooth soled shoes without ankle support will not make for a comfortable walk.

Remember to take account of the unpredictability of the British climate and how changes in altitude can dramatically affect temperatures. Always wear or carry adequate clothing and equipment for the worst conditions you expect to encounter.

Obtain 1:50,000 or 1:25,000 OS maps for the area you are covering and learn to read them and use a compass.

Your high energy food should be in addition to any food you intend eating during the day and could be chocolate, glucose tablets, barley sugar, mint cake or dried fruit.

If you are in trouble and need to use your whistle, the distress signal is six blasts, repeated at minute intervals. However, you will find your walk most enjoyable if you always stay well within the limits of your own experience unless accompanied by a reliable leader.

Always ensure that someone knows your intended route and what to do if you do not arrive at your destination.

Hill walking is more fun and a lot safer if you team up with others or why not join one of our led walks and meet new friends.

Cycling

Bicycle sheds are provided at our Youth Hostels and if you like to ride in company you'll enjoy meeting other cyclists at Youth Hostels — or why not join a YHA Local Group (see page 21).

Your bike

Use a good quality saddlebag, panniers or handlebar bag. Waterproofs can be strapped on top and tools in side pockets. A sturdy support for these is essential. **Never** carry luggage on your back while cycling.

In an English climate, mudguards (with a front mudflap) are essential. They will prevent you and your companions getting covered with mud and will protect the cycle bearings and chain from grit and water.

It doesn't matter how many gears you have, provided they are low enough, they work properly, and you know how to use them.

Do not use worn tyres or ones with splits, cuts or cracks. Fit new ones if necessary before you start, and blow them up hard. Soft tyres make pedalling hard work, and can damage rims and tyres on pot-holes.

Pedal straps are not essential, but help smooth rhythmic pedalling on the flat and give more power on hills. You can leave the straps just loose enough to pull your feet out easily.

Brakes get more use during a tour because of longer hills and heavier luggage. Renew worn-out brake blocks before you start, and check for frayed brake cables; cables usually break where they are hidden inside the levers.

Dropped handlebars are not essential but provide a variety of riding positions to prevent aching wrists.

A low saddle will be hard work and a high saddle will be uncomfortable. Your leg should be just slightly bent with the pedal right down. Check by putting your heel on the back of the pedal: your leg should just be straight. Handlebars should normally be about level with the saddle.

You should carry a pump, two spare inner tubes, a puncture outfit, tyre levers and a spanner to remove the wheels; a rear brake cable (can be used on the front), gear cable, PVC insulating tape, screwdriver, pliers and spanner(s) for the small nuts. Don't forget a rear reflector and front and rear lights.

Your clothing

Proper cycling shoes or shoes with a sturdy sole will prevent the pedals from cutting into your feet. Shorts should be long enough to prevent the saddle from chafing your legs; thin shorts are unadvisable. In cooler weather a tracksuit or trousers (without thick lumpy seams) tucked into long socks are practical and braces will prevent them sagging and exposing your back. Take waterproofs but as they cause condensation avoid wearing them unless it is actually raining.

GREAT ESCAPES

ADVENTURE HOLIDAYS AND SPECIAL INTEREST BREAKS

Action, excitement, interest and fun — that's what's on offer with YHA's Great Escapes! Our all-year-round adventure programme brings new sparkle to the winter months and extra zest to summertime.

Activities range from two-week holidays to two-day breaks and there are over 25 varied and interesting locations to choose from. Week-long holidays range from horseriding in the Black Mountains, deep sea diving in Cornwall and sailing in North Wales, to a winter mountaineering course and learning how to fly a glider in the Lake District. Weekend breaks are as varied as caving in the Yorkshire Dales, sand yachting in Mid Wales, dry slope skiing in Kent and studying a 'Whodunnit' case in Lincoln.

Everything is included in our excellent value holiday packages: comfortable Hostel accommodation, all meals, expert instruction, specialist equipment and local transport where appropriate. Most of our holidays are for 16+ years although there are many options for different age groups, including special breaks for the under 16's, 30+ years and families.

Multi-Activity Holidays at Edale and Llangollen

Ever wanted to learn how to climb a crag, abseil, ride a horse over mountain tracks, take a canoe on the river, shoot a bow and arrow and relate map to compass — all in one week? Well now you can do just that. Our full-time Activity Centres — Edale in the heart of the Peak District and Llangollen in beautiful North Wales — specialise in action-packed Multi-Activity holidays, offering professional instruction in a wide variety of skills.

Both YHA Activity Centres have recently been refurbished, ensuring the comfort of your stay. They offer excellent accommodation, including smart new rooms and dormitories (many with en suite facilities), modern washrooms and showers and cafeteria-style dining facilities with a good choice of menu. The Centres also have their own specialist equipment and this is regularly up-dated to maintain high safety standards.

Edale and Llangollen both have resident instructors who are selected not only for their specialist experience, but also for their excellent social skills. They will be there to guide you safely through the day's activities and to ensure the action continues through to the evenings. Entertainments include barbecues, discos, treasure hunts, visits to local inns and perhaps a night abseil!

Exciting Activities Abroad!

For those wishing to travel further afield, YHA's Great Escapes Abroad programme offers a great variety of holidays in both popular and less visited destinations. Choose from a mystery tour of Holland, cycling holidays in Ireland and France, touring in Iceland, a cultural visit to the Soviet Union and many more.

If you like the sound of any of the above, write or telephone for a free colour brochure. You'll find us at: Reservations Department, YHA National Office, Trevelyan House, 8 St Stephen's Hill, St Albans, Hertfordshire AL1 2DY. Tel: (0727) 55215.

More Hostel-Based Activities and Events . . .

Those interested in activity and hobby weekends should also check 'Triangle', our regular members' magazine. This keeps you up-to-date with a fantastic array of Hostel-based activities and events and also keeps you in touch with other members.

LOCAL GROUPS

There are well over 100 YHA Local Groups in England and Wales so there's probably one near you. They are formed by YHA members and organise regular hostelling, special interest and social activities.

Your YHA Local Group will make new members welcome and you will soon make many new friends in the lively 'club' atmosphere that prevails.

Local Groups are YHA clubs who regularly go youth hostelling and take part in various social events and special interest activities. And with over 100 Local Groups in England and Wales, there's bound to be one near you!

Social evenings are held regularly, and may typically involve a talk by an expert on mountaineering, or a slide show by a member of exciting travels abroad. There are discos, folk nights, Halloween parties, country dancing, barbecues, short evening walks, or perhaps a visit to a local place of interest.

Weekend activities are regarded by many as the most fun. What you do depends on what members of your Local Group enjoy, but there are trips to Hostels near and far by 'pooled' transport; rambles; cycle trips; long distance walks; pony trekking; climbing; sailing; conservation — the list is as extensive as your imagination!

Local Groups will also welcome YOUR new ideas and contributions.

Many Local Group members help YHA by assisting with publicity at exhibitions, recruiting new members, distributing leaflets, or by organising working parties to decorate Hostels, or improve Hostel grounds. Members may also serve on Local or National YHA committees.

During the year, there are many opportunities to get together with other Local Groups for joint activities, for example, parties, 'It's-a-Knockout' competitions and other gatherings where Local Group members from all over the country can exchange ideas.

Each Local Group differs, because all are run for their members *by* their members — and that could easily include YOU!

Many colleges and universities have a YHA Local Group, with a social and outdoor programme organised by students *for* students, including many of the activities described above. All YHA Local Groups are part of a huge national club, and by joining one you can get even more out of your YHA membership!

Cost? Not a lot! Most Groups charge a small annual subscription, and there's usually a charge to cover the cost of the week's social meeting.

So why not find out what goes on near you? Just refer to pages 176-178 for the address of your nearest Group. 'Triangle' carries information on Local Groups in a special section. If you find there is not a Local Group near you, then why not start one with some friends? You will be offered advice and assistance by the National Local Groups Committee which is made up of Group members and also produces 'Group News', your own quarterly newsletter keeping Local Group members in touch with activities and ideas.

For more information on starting a YHA Local Group or to contact your Area's member of the National Local Groups Committee, please write to our Local Groups Officer at: YHA National Office, Trevelyan House, 8 St Stephens Hill, St Albans, Herts AL1 2DY.

Please see the list of Local Group contact addresses on pages 176-178.

OTHER YHA'S IN BRITAIN AND IRELAND

YHA (England and Wales) is separate from the other YHA's in Britain and Ireland, but your membership card is valid at all of them.

They are run on similar lines and offer the same friendly welcome. Full details are given in the national handbooks, available from the association concerned or from National Office. Please send a stamped addressed envelope for prices.

Youth Hostel Association of Northern Ireland (YHANI)

56 Bradbury Place, Belfast BT7 1RU.
Tel: (0232) 324733.
Fax: (0232) 439699.

Walking in some of the least spoilt hill country and coastal scenery in Europe, cycling over miles of quiet country roads, motoring with a superb new vista around every corner — that's Northern Ireland. It has a wonderfully varied landscape, short distances and a splendid array of opportunities for the outdoor enthusiast. Fishermen, photographers, birdwatchers and canoeists, joggers and nature trekkers, rock climbers and many more, can all find their own personal challenge in a new environment.

YHANI's comfortable Hostels offer a friendly welcome and their location offers easy access to many of the natural attractions. Hostels at Belfast and Ballygally (near Larne) are a good starting point for your stay in Ireland, then the Antrim Coast Road staying in Cushendall Hostel; the North Coast and the Giant's Causeway from Whitepark Bay Hostel; the Mourne Mountains from Newcastle Hostel; and Fermanagh and the Lakes from our Hostel in Castle Archdale Forest Park.

YHANI Hostel details can be found on pages 160-161.

Advance reservations for all Hostels can be made by 'phoning our central reservations on (0232) 324733.

Irish Youth Hostel Association (An Oige)

39 Mountjoy Square, Dublin 1.
Tel: (0001) 363111.
Fax: (0001) 365807.

An Oige, the Irish Youth Hostel Association has 50 Youth Hostels located countrywide to provide comfortable accommodation for those who like to travel and enjoy outdoor activities with a hint of adventure.

An Oige Youth Hostels vary in size and type of building — from a large mansion in 70 acres of lawns and woodland (Aghadoe House, Killarney), a converted Norman Castle (Foulksrath Castle, Co. Kilkenny), old coastguard stations and cottages, to very modern buildings.

The Youth Hostels, situated in the most beautiful parts of the country in mountains, beside beaches, lakes and rivers, provide excellent venues for all sorts of activity holidays. An Oige also has well-located and convenient Hostels in the major cities to enable you to enjoy the life and culture of the city.

Accommodation follows the same pattern in all Hostels. Each Hostel has self-catering facilities, dining room, common room, sleeping and washing facilities. Many of the Hostels will also provide food on request.

An Oige has a number of attractively priced packages which include a Rail/Cycle Holiday and a Rambler Package Holiday.

Details of these holidays, enquiries and advance reservations should be made through Head Office, 39 Mountjoy Square, Dublin 1.
Tel: (0001) 363111.

Scottish Youth Hostels Association (SYHA)

7 Glebe Crescent, Stirling, FK8 2JA.
Tel: (0786) 51181.
Fax: (0786) 50198.

Experience the magic of Scotland for yourself when you visit any one of the SYHA's 80 Hostels: whether it's in the remote highlands or the busy city centres you can be sure of a warm welcome.

Most Hostels are in excellent and scenic hillwalking areas and are within cycling distance of each other. For lovers of city life and entertainment our excellent Hostels in Glasgow, Edinburgh, Inverness and Aberdeen are open until 2am. City Hostels with their easy access to major public transport routes are ideal starting points for any tour.

SYHA have excellent ski schools at Braemar and Loch Morlich and SYHA Summer

Breakaway holidays include walking, golfing, pony trekking, canoeing, sailing and multi-sport holidays.

Hostel facilities, naturally, vary from place to place, but all offer fully equipped self-catering kitchens (however, bring your own cutlery and tea towel) and small stores. Many now provide continental quilts, central heating, T.V. or games rooms, hot showers and laundry facilities. Meals are provided at some larger Hostels during the main holiday period.

Family rooms are available for advanced booking at certain Hostels. Advance booking requirements vary with the Hostel and time of year and are detailed in the SYHA Handbook. Enquiries and bookings should be made direct to the Warden. Opening dates should be carefully checked for all Hostels especially those in the north. A Hostel availability list is obtainable from National Office, Stirling at the address above.

WORLD TRAVEL

Join the YHA and you join a worldwide organisation that gives you the freedom to travel all over the world. There are more than 5300 Hostels in over 58 countries, so whether you choose Europe, Australia or such exotic places as India or Peru, you can still stay with YHA!

All you need to do is attach a recent photograph of yourself to your membership card and voila! your passport to Hostels in:

Algeria	Cyprus	Hungary	Mexico	Spain
Argentina	Czechoslovakia	Iceland	Morocco	Sri Lanka
Australia	Denmark	India	Netherlands	Sudan
Austria	Egypt	Ireland (Republic of)	New Zealand	Sweden
(2 Associations)	Finland	Ireland (Northern)	Norway	Switzerland
Bahrain	France	Israel	Pakistan	Syria
Belgium	German	Italy	Peru	Thailand
(2 Associations)	Democratic	Japan	Philippines	Tunisia
Brazil	Republic	Kenya	Poland	United Arab
Bulgaria	German Federal	Korea (South)	Portugal	Emirates
Canada	Republic	Libya	Qatar	USA
Chile	Greece	Luxembourg	Saudi Arabia	Uruguay
Columbia	Hong Kong	Malaysia	Scotland	Yugoslavia

For details of useful guidebooks, see page 162.

YHA CAMPING BARNS

May 1990 saw the launch of an entirely new concept in YHA accommodation with the official opening of five Camping Barns in the Forest of Bowland Area of Outstanding Natural Beauty.

Chipping Barn

For more information (including a leaflet and booking form) please contact:
The Bowland Barns
Booking Office
1A New Market Street
Clitheroe
Lancashire
BB7 2JW
Tel: (0200) 28366
(24 hour answerphone service)

The YHA is also developing Camping Barns in other popular areas. In 1991 a network of barns will open in the North Pennines — described by Dr David Bellamy, YHA President, as "England's last wilderness". This Area of Outstanding Natural Beauty is home to some of the rarest alpine flora in Britain and has magnificent herb-rich meadows which are preserved by traditional farming practices. As well as walking and cycling, there are plenty of opportunities for outdoor pursuits in the area.

Camping Barns, sometimes known as 'stone tents', are farm buildings converted to provide simple accommodation for up to 12 or 15 visitors for only £2.00 per night. You may find yourself staying in a former barn, stable, or byre.

The barns have been converted with care to retain their original character. Facilities are basic: wooden sleeping platforms, tables and benches for eating and preparing food, a supply of cold running water and a flush toilet. At present, three have electric light and one has a wood burning stove.

The YHA Camping Barns provide an excellent base for exploring the superb countryside in the Forest of Bowland. Walkers are well served by several long-distance walks, while cyclists can enjoy the quiet minor roads and the North Lancashire Cycleway. There are also many other outdoor activities available in Bowland.

Look out for news about these Camping Barns, and a network due to open in North Yorkshire during 1992, in 'Triangle' magazine or phone Denis O'Connor on (061) 881 6228.

Hurst Green Barn

HOSTEL ENTRIES

Although we do our best to ensure that the Youth Hostel details in this Guide are accurate at the time of going to press, we reserve the right to change opening times, other Hostel details and prices if circumstances warrant. You are advised to check details with the Hostel when planning your trip. From time to time amendments to this Guide may appear in the YHA magazine 'Triangle' which is mailed to members 3 times a year.

In addition to the Youth Hostel entries for England and Wales, we have also included a special section on the Youth Hostels Association of Northern Ireland (YHANI), (see pages 160-161)

THANK YOU

YHA would like to thank all those who have kindly written to us with invaluable suggestions and comments to help improve the YHA Accommodation Guide.

We do all we can to get our facts right, but our eyes cannot be everywhere! Your information may well be more up-to-date than ours. Please write to us, at any time. If your letter reaches us early enough in the year it will be considered for the next edition, but suggestions will certainly be put forward for future improvements.

See the next page for our location map, indicating the tourist divisions used within this Guide.

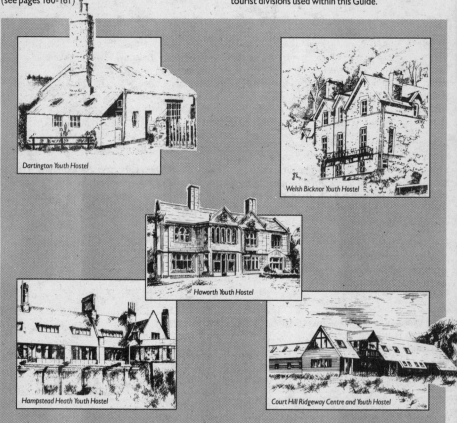

Dartington Youth Hostel

Welsh Bicknor Youth Hostel

Haworth Youth Hostel

Hampstead Heath Youth Hostel

Court Hill Ridgeway Centre and Youth Hostel

GENERAL HOSTEL MAP

This location map indicates the tourist divisions used within this Accommodation Guide.

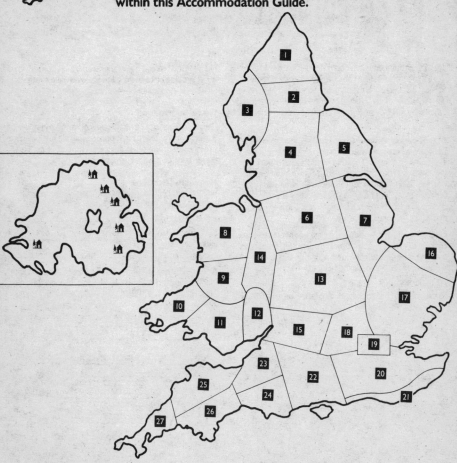

1. Northumberland and Roman Wall
2. North Pennines
3. Lake District
4. Yorkshire Dales
5. Yorkshire Wolds, Moors and Coast
6. Peak District
7. Lincolnshire
8. North Wales
9. Mid Wales
10. West Wales
11. Brecon Beacons and South Wales
12. Wye Valley and Forest of Dean
13. Heart of England
14. Shropshire and the Welsh Borders

15. Cotswolds
16. Norfolk Coast and Broads
17. East Anglia
18. Chiltern Hills and Thames Valley
19. London
20. North Downs Way and Weald
21. South Coast
22. New Forest and Isle of Wight
23. Avon and Mendips
24. Dorset Coast
25. North Devon, Exmoor and the Quantocks
26. South Devon and Dartmoor
27. Cornwall
    Ireland

NORTHUMBERLAND AND ROMAN WALL

Northumberland, a county that is both wild and beautiful is, for many, a holiday area yet to be discovered. Unspoilt and uncrowded with open views of magnificent countryside and coastline. Once seen it is a county which enchants and captivates visitors.

At the heart of the county lies Northumberland National Park, one of the last wilderness areas of Great Britain. The majestic Cheviot Hills and heather-clad moorland are all set in a landscape steeped in centuries of turbulent history. Opportunities for outdoor recreation abound, for example mountain biking, horse riding and water sports — particularly at Kielder Water, the largest man-made lake in Northern Europe.

Much of the Northumberland Coast has been designated an Area of Outstanding Natural Beauty and it is easy to see why; it has superb beaches, romantic castles, picturesque fishing ports and rich bird-life.

Hadrian's Wall, built by Legions of the Roman Army, lies to the south of the county. Many of the Roman forts have been excavated and the best preserved section, which is a most exciting place to visit, lies between our Youth Hostels at Acomb and Greenhead.

Useful Information

During Winter closed months, early Spring and late Autumn, many Youth Hostels are available for exclusive use by parties booked in advance. For further details please contact the appropriate Hostel.

Helpful Publications

Pennine Way Central Booking Service
Information Pack —
including postage and packing £1.50

Northumberland and Hadrian's Wall —
*leaflet describing inter-Hostel
cycling route* .... please send sae

Available from YHA Northern Regional Office, D Floor, Milburn House, Dean Street, Newcastle upon Tyne NE1 1LF. Tel: 091 221 2101.

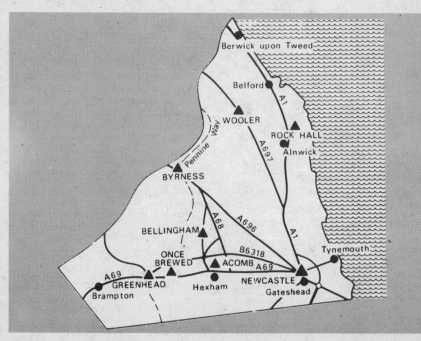

A COMB

40 BEDS

**Youth Hostel,
Acomb, Hexham,
Northumberland NE46 4PL**
☎ Hexham (0434) 602864

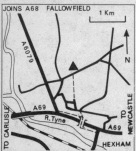

Overnight charge:
Young £2.60 Junior £3.50 Senior £4.40
🅰 🚻 🅰 ⊗ 🅶🅲 🍴 Small 🆂 Shop
and 🅿🅾 Acomb. 🅴🅾 Thu

Jan 1-Feb 28	Open Fri & Sat
Mar 1-31	Open (except Mon)
Apr 1-14	Open
Apr 15-May 5	Open (except Mon)
May 6-12	Open
May 13-26	Open (except Mon)
May 27-Jun 2	Open
Jun 3-Jul 6	Open (except Mon)
Jul 7-Aug 31	Open
Sep 1-Oct 31	Open (except Mon)
Nov 1-Dec 23	Open Fri & Sat
Dec 24-31	Closed
Jan 1-Feb 29 92	Open Fri & Sat

Advance bookings may be accepted
from parties during winter closed
period: enquiries welcome

Converted stable buildings in
pleasant village in Roman Wall
country. E end of village. 2m N of
Hexham

🆂 87 🅶🆁 934666 🗺 39, 42

Attractions: River walk 1m. Low
Warden Bird Sanctuary 1m. Disused
lead mines 1m. Hadrian's Wall 2m.
Hexham Abbey 2½m. Corstopitum
(nr Corbridge) Roman Camp 5m.
Northumberland National Park 5m.
🅰 ⛵ 🚲 Aydon Castle

🚌 Tyne Valley 880-2 from Hexham
(pass BR Hexham) (☎ 0434 602217);
otherwise Northumbria 685, X85
Carlisle — Newcastle-upon-Tyne,
alight Hexham, 2½m (☎ 0434
602061)

🚉 Hexham 2m

Next Youth Hostels: Once Brewed
15m. Bellingham 15m. Edmundbyers
16m. Newcastle 20m. Ninebanks
18m

B ELLINGHAM

34 BEDS

COMFORT IMPROVED

**Youth Hostel, Woodburn Road,
Bellingham, Hexham,
Northumberland NE48 2ED**
☎ Hexham (0434) 220313

Overnight charge:
Young £3.10 Junior £4.00 Senior £5.10
🚻 🅰 1 ⊗ 🍴 🅶🅲 Snack bar in village.
No 🆂 Shop nearby. 🅿🅾 Bellingham
½m. 🅴🅾 Thu and Sat. 🅿 🅻

Jan 1-Feb 28	Closed
Mar 1-25	Open (except Sun)
Mar 26-Apr 8	Open
Apr 9-29	Open (except Sun)
Apr 30-May 6	Open
May 7-20	Open (except Sun)
May 21-27	Open
May 28-Jul 5	Open (except Sun)
Jul 6-Aug 31	Open
Sep 1-Oct 31	Open (except Sun)
Nov 1-Feb 29 92	Closed

Open in closed months for advance
bookings from parties of 10 and over

Bellingham is in the heart of the
beautiful Border country of
Northumberland. The Youth Hostel,
a single storey building constructed
in Red Cedar wood, overlooks the
village and surrounding countryside

Bellingham Youth Hostel has been
completely modernised: A new
heating system has been installed
allowing comfortable year round use;
showers and drying room provided;
new self catering facilities and
completely refurbished dormitories

The choice of activities and places of
interest in the area are extensive.
The countryside nearby has fortified
houses and castles. Hadrian's Wall is
only a short drive to the south;
walking in the area is excellent; the
Hostel is on the Pennine Way and
there are many local walks. Cycling is
a pleasure, the roads are good and
traffic is light. Nearby Kielder Water
with its picturesque 27 mile shoreline
and numerous water based activities
is a major attraction for visitors.
Canoeing, Windsurfing and Sailing
are all available or you can hire a
Mountain Bike to explore the many
forest trails

Available for exclusive use by groups
and day time access can be arranged

🆂 80 🅶🆁 843834 🗺 42

Attractions: Northumberland
National Park. Pennine Way 1m.
River walks. 🚲 ⛵ 🅰 Mountain 🚴 at
Kielder Water 10m. 🎣 Hareshaw
Linn

🚌 Tyne Valley 880 from Hexham
(passes BR Hexham) (☎ 0434 602217)

🚉 Hexham 16m

Next Youth Hostels: Acomb 15m.
Byrness 15m by path. Once Brewed
18m (14m by path). Greenhead 22m
(by path)

Bellingham Youth Hostel

B YRNESS

28 BEDS

Youth Hostel,
**7 Otterburn Green, Byrness,
Newcastle upon Tyne NE19 1TS**
☎ **Otterburn (0830) 20222**

Overnight charge:
Young £3.10 Junior £4.00 Senior £5.10
🚻🧺②🍴② rooms only GSC 🔲 S
Shop ½m. PO nearby. 🔲 Wed and Sat.
P nearby

Jan 1-Feb 28	Closed
Mar 1-Apr 1	Open (except Wed)
Apr 2-15	Open
Apr 16-May 27	Open (except Wed)
May 28-Jun 3	Open
Jun 4-Jul 5	Open (except Wed)
Jul 6-Aug 31	Open
Sep 1-Oct 31	Open (except Wed)
Nov 1-Feb 29 92	Closed

Two adjoining houses in peaceful
Forestry Commission village 5m from
Scottish border, between
Northumberland National Park and
Border Forest. An ideal stepping
stone to and from Scotland and the
Borders. Well located for exploring
picturesque Jedburgh and Hawick. W
of A68 in Byrness village

OS 80 GR 764027 🚌 42

Attractions: Forest and moorland
country. National Park. Pennine Way
long distance footpath. High
Rochester Roman Camp 4m. Chew
Green 5m. Kielder Lake. Cheese
Farm. Otterburn Mill. Site of Battle
of Otterburn. Good access to
beautiful Northumberland Valleys 🚶

🚌 National Express 370/2/3 or
Scottish Citylink 170 Edinburgh —
Newcastle-upon-Tyne (pass close BR
Newcastle & Edinburgh) (☎ 091 261
6077 (National Express) or 031 557
5717 (Citylink))

🚂 Morpeth 34m; Newcastle 40m

Next Youth Hostels: Bellingham
15m by path. Kirk Yetholm (SYHA)
27m by path. Wooler 28m by path

G REENHEAD

40 BEDS

Youth Hostel,
**Greenhead, Carlisle,
Cumbria CA6 7HG**
☎ **Gilsland (06972) 401**

Overnight charge:
Young £3.50 Junior £4.40 Senior £5.50
🚻🧺②🍴 GSC 🔲 Evening meal 19.00
hrs. S Shop and PO nearby. 🔲 Tue. L

Jan 1-Feb 12	Closed
Feb 13-Mar 31	Open (except Mon & Tue)
Apr 1-Aug 31	Open
Sep 1-Nov 17	Open (except Mon)
Nov 18-Dec 27	Closed
Dec 28-Jan 2 92	Open

Advance bookings may be accepted
from parties during winter closed
period: enquiries welcome

Modern conversion of former
Methodist Chapel in small village
close to the most dramatic parts of
Hadrian's Wall and Carvoran Roman
Army Museum. 3m W of Haltwhistle
on the edge of Northumberland
National Park

OS 86 GR 659655 🚌 38

Attractions: Roman camps.
Milecastles. 13th & 14th C border
castles. Gilsland Spa 2½m. Lanercost
Priory 6m. River Irthing, good
walking and cycling routes. 🚶 Roman
Army Museum and Wall 1m. L
Pennine Way and Hadrian's Wall pass
close to village. Birdoswald Fort 🚩
U

🚌 Northumbria 685 Carlisle —
Newcastle-upon-Tyne (passes BR
Haltwhistle) (☎ 0434 602061)

🚂 Haltwhistle 3m

Next Youth Hostels: Once Brewed
7m. Ninebanks 16. Alston 17m by
path. Carlisle 19m. Bellingham 22m
by path

N EWCASTLE UPON TYNE

60 BEDS

Youth Hostel,
**107 Jesmond Road,
Newcastle upon Tyne NE2 1NJ**
☎ **Newcastle (091) 281 2570**

Overnight charge:
Young £3.50 Junior £4.40 Senior £5.50
🚻🧺 🔲①🍴 GSC Snack meals
available 17.30-21.30 hrs. Continental
breakfast 07.45-08.30 hrs. S PO ½m.
P Pool table. L

Dec 28-Jan 2 91	Open
Jan 3-31	Closed
Feb 1-28	Open (except Mon & Tue)
Mar 1-Oct 31	Open
Nov 1-30	Open (except Mon & Tue)
Dec 1-Jan 31 92	Closed
Feb 1-29	Open (except Mon & Tue)

Conveniently located town house
not far from centre of historic city
and a good starting point for
Hadrian's Wall. ½m east of civic
centre next to RAC on Jesmond
Road (A1058). Opposite cemetery.
Readily accessible by public transport

OS 88 GR 257656 🚌 39

Attractions: Historic City of
Newcastle, Museums, Theatres,
Excellent shops, Jesmond Dene Park
1m, Tourist Information Centre 1m
(☎ 091-261 0691), Coastline walks
8m, Washington Wildfowl Trust,
Hadrian's Wall, Beamish Museum.
Bede Monastery Museum Jarrow —
discounts for groups. Gateshead
Metro Centre — Europe's largest
shopping centre. Road; Rail; Airport
and ferry services offer excellent
links with city. Newcastle is a good
base for exploring the coast and
countryside of Northumbria

🚌 Frequent from surrounding areas
(☎ 091-232 5325)

🚂 Jesmond (Tyne & Wear Metro) ¼m;
Newcastle 1½m

Next Youth Hostels: Edmundbyers
18m. Acomb 20m. Bellingham 33m.
Rock Hall 40m. Durham 17m (Jul &
Aug only)

R OCK HALL

**Youth Hostel, Rock Hall,
Rock, Alnwick,
Northumberland NE66 3SB**
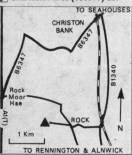 Charlton Mires (066579) 281

Overnight charge:
Young £3.50 Junior £4.40 Senior £5.50
〔〕 Evening meal
19.00 hrs (or at other times by prior
arrangement for groups). S PO Rock.
FS P for cars and coaches.

Jan 1-Feb 14	Open Fri & Sat
Feb 15-Mar 30	Open (except Sun)
Mar 31-Sep 30	Open
Oct 1-31	Open (except Sun)
Nov 1-30	Open
	(except Sun & Mon)
Dec 1-27	Open Fri & Sat
Dec 28-Jan 1 92	Open
Jan 2-Feb 14	Closed
Feb 15-29	Open (except Sun)

Advance bookings may be accepted
from parties of 20 or more during winter
closed period: enquiries welcome

Old manor house, originally 15th
century pele tower, set in quiet farmland
4m from Northumberland coast. In
Rock village. Entrance drive past
duckpond, near church. 5m NE of
Alnwick and only 2m from the A1

OS 75 GR 201203 Bar 42

Attractions: Sea and sandy beaches
4m. Alnwick Castle 4m. Warkworth
Castle 10m. Dunstanburgh Castle
4m. Howick Hall 4m. Seahouses
(boat to Farne Islands) 8m. Holy
Island and Lindisfarne Priory. Grace
Darling Museum and Bamburgh Castle
10m. Parachuting. Daytime
access by arrangement with warden

Northumbria 501 Newcastle-
upon-Tyne — Berwick-upon-Tweed
(passes close BR Morpeth &
Berwick-upon-Tweed) alight
Charlton Mires, 2m (0665 602182)

Chathill (very infrequent and not
Sun) 6½m; Alnmouth 9m

Next Youth Hostels: Wooler 17m.
Coldingham (SYHA) 38m.
Newcastle 40m

O NCE BREWED

COMFORT IMPROVED

**Youth Hostel, Once Brewed,
Military Road, Bardon Mill, Hexham,
Northumberland NE47 7AN**
 Hexham (0434) 344360

Overnight charge:
Young £4.40 Junior £5.40 Senior £6.60
〔〕 Evening meal 18.00-
19.00 hrs. Breakfast 07.45-08.30 hrs.
Small self catering kitchen. S PO
Bardon Mill 2½m. Thu. P
adjoining. Laundry facilities.
limited facilities.

Jan 1-31	Closed
Feb 1-28	Open (except Sun)
Mar 1-Oct 31	Open
Nov 1-30	Open (except Sun)
Dec 1-Jan 31 92	Closed
Feb 1-29	Open (except Sun)

Once Brewed offers excellent
residential accommodation. It has
small bedrooms and a superb range
of facilities. Fully inclusive package
available to groups including: full
board accommodation; return
transport from home; excursions and
site visits — full details available from
warden

Daytime access is available from 1.00
pm every day

Once Brewed is an excellent base for
any group studying Roman History.
Hadrian's Wall and many excavated
Roman Forts are nearby. There is
easy access from here to other parts
of the Northumberland National
Park and throughout the remainder
of the county for visitors who wish
to explore the beauty and rich
historical heritage of Northumbria

OS 86, 87 GR 752668 Bar 38, 39, 42

Attractions: Pennine Way. Roman
Wall ½m. Vindolanda Roman Fort
1m. Housesteads Roman Fort 3m.
Rock climbing 1m. Chesters 11m.
Binocular hire. next to Hostel.
Roman Army Museum — Carvoran
6m. Haltwhistle Leisure Pool —
discount for groups. Industrial
archaeology at Haltwhistle Burn.
Beamish-North of England Open Air
Museum

From Hexham, Haltwhistle
(passes BR Hexham & Haltwhistle),
peak summer only (043472 251);
otherwise Northumbria 685 Carlisle
— Newcastle-upon-Tyne, alight
Henshaw, 2m (0434 602061)

Bardon Mill 2½m

Next Youth Hostels: Greenhead
7m. Acomb 15m. Ninebanks 16m
(12m by path). Bellingham 18m (14m
by path). Edmundbyers 28m. Carlisle
23m

Once Brewed Youth Hostel.

Wooler

47 BEDS

COMFORT IMPROVED

**Youth Hostel,
30 Cheviot Street, Wooler,
Northumberland NE71 6LW**
☎ Wooler (0668) 81365

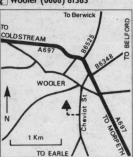

Overnight charge:
Young £3.50 Junior £4.40 Senior £5.50
🏠 🅰 ② 🔥 📵 Evening meal 19.00
hrs. Ⓢ P⊙ Wooler. 🍴 Thu. 🅿 Pool
table Ⓛ

Jan 1-Feb 28	Closed
Mar 1-30	Open Fri & Sat
Mar 31-Apr 8	Open
Apr 9-29	Open (except Sun)
Apr 30-May 6	Open
May 7-20	Open (except Sun)
May 21-Aug 31	Open
Sep 1-Oct 31	Open (except Thu)
Nov 1-Feb 29 92	Closed

Advance bookings for parties may be accepted during winter closed period

A single storey hostel located on the edge of the typical border town of Wooler, with its busy livestock market. Ideally placed for exploring the Scottish Borders, the Cheviot Hills and other remote areas of the Northumberland National Park

🆗 75 ᴳᴿ 991278 🚍 41, 42

Attractions: Cheviot Hills, Cheviot summit 8m. Chillingham Castle and Park (unique wild cattle) 7m. Holy Island and Lindisfarne Castle 15m. Berwick-upon-Tweed 16m. Viewpoints at Yeavering Bell and Ross Castle 8m. Ancient Battlefields, Prehistoric sites and Cup and Ring markings nearby. 🚲 Ⓤ Horseriding for experienced and novice riders. 🚲 Cycle hire at Hostel

🚌 Northumbria 464, 470/3, Taxibus, Goldleaf 710 from Berwick-upon-Tweed & Alnwick, with connections from BR Morpeth (pass close BR Morpeth) (☎ 0668 81359 or 0289 307588)

🚉 Berwick-upon-Tweed 16m

Next Youth Hostels: Kirk Yetholm (SYHA) 14m. Rock Hall 17m. Byrness 28m by path. Coldingham (SYHA) 30m

Administrative Region: Northern

Kirk Yetholm

38 BEDS

**Youth Hostel,
Kirk Yetholm, Kelso,
Roxburghshire TD5 8PG**
☎ (057382) 631

Overnight charge:
Please contact SYHA for 1991 charges
telephone SYHA ☎ (0786) 51181

🏠 Members' kitchen. No Ⓢ ② Shop
Yetholm 🍴 📵 Wed

Mar 23-Oct 1	Open

This Hostel, administered by the Scottish YHA, 7 Glebe Crescent, Stirling FK8 2JA, is included because it is at the end of the Pennine Way. It is a small modernised Hostel 50 yds down lane at W corner of village green

🆗 74 ᴳᴿ 826282 🚍 41 (H24)

Attractions: Kirk Yetholm is the northern end of the Pennine Way. Excellent centre for hill walking in the Cheviots. Kirk Yetholm was for long the home of the gipsies, and the "Gipsy Palace" cottage of the Faa family can be seen by the road leading to the Halter Burn Valley. In Kelso (8m) there is the Abbey, Rennies Bridge over the Tweed and Floors Castle. Nature Reserve Yetholm Loch. 🍴 locally. Mountaineering: Cheviot 2,676ft by Sourhope 12m or by Halter Burn and English boundary 9m

🚌 Tweed Valley/Lowland Scottish 81 from Kelso (☎ 0573 23504 & 24141) (Kelso is linked with BR Berwick-upon-Tweed by Swan/Northumbria 23 — ☎ 0573 24141)

🚉 Berwick-upon-Tweed 21m

Next Youth Hostels: Wooler 14m. Melrose 24m. Byrness 27m by path. N. Abbey St. Bathans 28m. Coldingham 29m

Administration: SYHA

NORTH PENNINES

2

As one of England's last areas of wilderness, the North Pennines has been designated an Area of Outstanding Natural Beauty. The scenery offers many contrasts — from the high bleak moorlands to the rich, fertile valleys dotted with tranquil stone-built villages. The beautiful riverside scenery includes the famous waterfalls of Low Force, High Force and Cauldron Snout.

The countryside offers many opportunities for a wide range of activities, from mountain biking to canoeing. One of the most scenic and least-used stretches of the Pennine Way passes through the area, linking up four Youth Hostels.

The North Pennines cater for those with an interest in industrial history. Old lead and fluorspar mine workings may be seen, and there is a living museum of lead mining at Killhope Wheel. Otherwise this is mainly hill farming country, with small market towns unspoilt by modern industry.

As the only area in Northern Europe where spring gentians are to be found, part of the North Pennines has been designated a National Nature Reserve and a Site of Special Scientific Interest. This means that during Spring, the landscape of unspoilt hay meadows still remains, covering the interesting limestone geology.

Useful Information

During Winter closed periods, early Spring and late Autumn, many Youth Hostels are available for exclusive use by parties booked in advance. For further details please contact the appropriate Hostel.

Helpful Publications

Pennine Way Central Booking Service
Information Pack —
including postage and packing £1.50

Available from YHA Northern Regional Office, D Floor, Milburn House, Dean Street, Newcastle upon Tyne NE1 1LF. Tel: 091 221 2101.

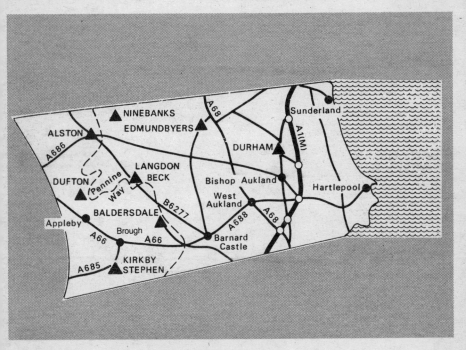

A LSTON

30 BEDS

**Youth Hostel,
The Firs, Alston,
Cumbria CA9 3RW**
☎ Alston (0434) 381509

Overnight charge:
Young £3.80 Junior £4.70 Senior £5.90
🏠🅰 2 🛏 🍽 Evening meal 19.00 hrs.
Small 🆂 Shop and 🅿 ½m in town. 🍴
Tue. 🅿 Cars and mini-buses only;
coaches 300 yds behind Hendersons
Garage. Ⓛ

Dec 28-Jan 5 91	Open
Jan 6-Mar 21	Open Fri & Sat
Mar 22-28	Open
Mar 29-Apr 11	Open (except Sun)
Apr 12-May 2	Open
May 3-9	Open
May 10-23	Open (except Sun)
May 24-30	Open
May 31-Jun 30	Open
Jul 1-Aug 31	Open
Sep 1-Oct 31	Open (except Sun)
Nov 1-Dec 27	Closed
Dec 28-Jan 4 92	Open
Jan 5-Feb 29	Open Fri & Sat

Advance bookings may be accepted
from parties during winter closed
period: enquiries welcome

Purpose-built Hostel, right beside
Pennine Way and overlooking South
Tyne River. On southern outskirts of
Alston, a fascinating old market
town, the highest in England

Ⓞ🆂 86, 87 ⒼⓇ 717461 Ⓑⓐⓡ 38, 39

Attractions: Pennine Way. Railway
museum in town. High moorland
country (Cross Fell 2930ft).
Waterfalls: Nent High Force 1½m,
Ashgill Force 6m. Industrial
archaeology and geology. 🚻 at old
railway station. Narrow gauge
railway. Killhope Wheel 15m

🚌 Wright Bros 681 from Haltwhistle
(passes BR Haltwhistle)
(☎ 0434 381200)

🚉 Haltwhistle 15m, Penrith 19m

Next Youth Hostels: Ninebanks
8m. Greenhead 17m (via Pennine
Way). 15m by road. Langdon Beck
15m. Dufton 22m (via Pennine Way)

Administrative Region: Northern

B ALDERSDALE

46 BEDS

**Youth Hostel, Blackton,
Baldersdale, Barnard Castle,
Co Durham DL12 9UP**
☎ Teesdale (0833) 50629

Overnight charge:
Young £3.50 Junior £4.40 Senior £5.50
🏠🅰 2 ❌ 🆂🆂🅲 🆂 Workroom.
Shop, 🅿 and Inn Cotherstone 6m.
🍴 Thu. Please order milk in advance.
🅿 No access by car via Clove Lodge.
Use road from Romaldkirk (not
Cotherstone) to Balderhead
Reservoir Ⓛ

Jan 1-Mar 21	Closed
Mar 22-Apr 1	Open (except Thu)
Apr 2-15	Open
Apr 16-May 27	Open (except Thu)
May 28-Jun 3	Open
Jun 4-Aug 31	Open (except Thu)
Sep 1-Oct 31	Open (except Wed & Thu)
Nov 1-Feb 29 92	Closed

Advance bookings may be accepted
from parties during winter closed
period: enquiries welcome

Baldersdale is a fully modernised farm
house with excellent self-catering
facilities and a workroom. Set in 10
acres of grounds Baldersdale is fully
equipped for campers. Situated high
in the Pennines north of Barnard
Castle, Baldersdale makes an ideal
base for self-catering parties who
wish to exploit the many educational
and outdoor recreation
opportunities in the vicinity: water
sports, rock climbing, horse riding
etc. Access to Baldersdale from
major roads into the region is
excellent. An Outdoor Activity
Programme is available for all types
of group: provided with fully qualified
instructors all activities can be tailor
made to the requirements of each
party. Subject to availability. Indoors:
snooker and a large selection of
games and books are provided

Ⓞ🆂 91, 92 ⒼⓇ 931179 Ⓑⓐⓡ 35

Attractions: Mid-point of Pennine
Way long distance footpath. 🚶 🚴 🎣
2m. Riding 4m. Bowes Museum 11m.
🅰 Ⓛ

🚌 United 75/A from BR Darlington,
alight Cotherstone, 7m (☎ 0325
468771)

🚉 Darlington 27m

Next Youth Hostels: Langdon Beck
15m by Pennine Way. Keld 15m by
Pennine Way. Kirkby Stephen 15m by
path. Grinton 23m by path

Baldersdale Youth Hostel

Administrative Region: Northern

Page 34

1991 YHA Guide

D UFTON
40 BEDS

Youth Hostel, 'Redstones',
Dufton, Appleby,
Cumbria CA16 6DB
📞 Appleby (07683) 51236

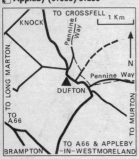

Overnight charge:
Young £3.80 Junior £4.70 Senior £5.90
📶 👤 🍴 🅿️ Evening meal 19.00 hrs. 🆂
Shop and 🅿️ in village open 7 days a
week Easter — Nov. 🕭 Sat. 🅿️ Cars
only; coaches — see warden. Pub in
village — no meals

Jan 1-3	Closed
Jan 4-Apr 1	Open
	(except Tue & Wed)
Apr 2-9	Open
Apr 10-May 22	Open (except Tue)
May 23-30	Open
May 31-Jun 30	Open (except Tue)
Jul 1-Aug 31	Open
Sep 1-Nov 16	Open (except Tue)
Nov 17-Jan 15 92	Closed
Jan 16-Feb 29	Open
	(except Tue & Wed)

Once a large private house in
pleasant 18th century village and
surrounded by fine scenery, on
Pennine Way. Secluded grounds to
the rear. South side of village green

🆗 91 🆖 688251 🚍 34, 35, 39

Attractions: Pennine Way. Cumbria
Cycle Way. Castles at Appleby
(private), Brougham and Brough.
Stone circles and prehistoric remains.
High Cup Nick. Cross Fell. Appleby
Horse Fair, June 5-12. Geology.
Settle-Carlisle Railway 3m

Cross-country ski-ing
This Hostel runs weekend courses in
cross country skiing for beginners
during February and March. Ski hire
is available when the Hostel is open.
Further details from warden

🚌 No Service

🚉 Appleby (not Sun, except May-
Sep) 3m; Penrith 13m

Next Youth Hostels: Langdon Beck
12m by Pennine Way. Kirkby Stephen
15m. Alston 22m by Pennine Way.
Ninebanks 20m. Carrock Fell 25m

D URHAM
40 BEDS

Youth Hostel,
Durham Sixth Form Centre,
The Sands, Providence Row,
Durham City DH1 1SG

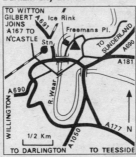

Overnight charge:
Young £3.50 Junior £4.40 Senior £5.50
🅰️ 📶 🅺 Camp beds. Small 🆂 Shops
and 🅿️ nearby. 🕭 Wed. 🅿️ Cars only

Jul 20-Aug 30 Open

Summer-only Hostel in school
building in famous cathedral and
university city. Near city centre,
opposite ice rink. Approach from
Milburngate Bridge and Freemans
Place — access from this direction
for pedestrians only

🆗 88 🆖 275429 🚍 39

Attractions: Castle and Cathedral
½m. Indoor swimming pool and ice
rink nearby. Riverside walks. Finchale
Abbey 4m. Beamish Museum. Dry
Ski Slope 12m. Gateshead Garden
Centre and Metro Centre 15m

🚌 Frequent from surrounding areas
(📞 091-384 3322)

🚉 Durham ½m

Next Youth Hostels: Newcastle
17m. Edmundbyers 21m. Acomb
30m. Osmotherley 37m. Saltburn
36m

Additional Information: Please do
not write to Hostel before 21 July,
advance bookings to YHA, D Floor,
Milburn House, Newcastle upon Tyne
NE1 1LF. 📞 091 221 2101

E DMUNDBYERS
40 BEDS

Youth Hostel, Low House,
Edmundbyers, Consett,
Co Durham DH8 9NL
📞 Edmundbyers (0207) 55651*

Overnight charge:
Young £3.10 Junior £4.00 Senior £5.10
📶 👤 🅰️ 1 🍴 🆖 🍴 Evening meal 18.30
hrs. Small 🆂 Shop and 🅿️ Edmundbyers

Jan 1-Feb 28	Closed
Mar 1-29	Open (except Sun)
Mar 30-Apr 6	Open
Apr 7-May 3	Open (except Sun)
May 4-10	Open
May 11-24	Open (except Sun)
May 25-31	Open
Jun 1-Jul 5	Open (except Sun)
Jul 6-Aug 31	Open
Sep 1-Oct 31	Open
Nov 1-Feb 29 92	Closed

Advance bookings may be accepted
from parties during winter closed
period: enquiries welcome

Old inn built in 1600 in an attractive
village on the edge of the moors and
the North Pennines AONB at the
junction of trackways from the Tyne
to Weardale and Allendale. 5m W of
Shotley Bridge, ½m from Derwent
Reservoir

🆗 87 🆖 017500 🚍 39

Attractions: 🅰️ club on Derwent
Reservoir 1m. Trout 🎣 1m. Country
Park 1m. Blanchland village 4m.
Beamish Museum 15m. Hadrian's Wall
17m. 🅰️ 🆄 Killhope Wheel and
Museum. Silksworth Dry Ski Slope
30m. 45m of railways walks

🚌 OK 869 Bishop Auckland -
Hexham (Tue only) (📞 0388
604581); otherwise Go-Ahead
Northern 719, 765 Durham -
Consett (pass close BR Durham),
alight Consett, 5m (📞 0207 504282)

🚉 Hexham 13m

Next Youth Hostels: Acomb 16m.
Newcastle 18m. Ninebanks 22m by
path

*Additional Information: Wardens
home telephone number (0207) 55681

LANGDON BECK

COMFORT IMPROVED

Youth Hostel, Langdon Beck, Forest-in-Teesdale, Barnard Castle, Co Durham DL12 0XN
Teesdale (0833) 22228

Overnight charge:
Young £4.00 Junior £5.10 Senior £6.30
🏥 🚿 1 🍴 ⚙ Evening meal 19.00 hrs.
S P Forest-in-Teesdale 1m. Shops Middleton-in-Teesdale 7m. ED Wed.
L

Jan 1-31	Closed
Feb 1-16	Open Fri & Sat
Feb 17-Mar 29	Open (except Sun & Mon)
Mar 30-Apr 12	Open
Apr 13-May 2	Open (except Sun)
May 3-9	Open
May 10-23	Open (except Sun)
May 24-30	Open
May 31-Jul 7	Open (except Sun)
Jul 8-Aug 31	Open
Sep 1-Oct 31	Open (except Sun)
Nov 1-30	Open Fri & Sat
Dec 1-27	Closed
Dec 28-Jan 4 92	Open
Jan 5-31	Closed

Advance bookings may be accepted from parties during winter closed period: enquiries welcome

Langdon Beck is a purpose built Hostel which has been extensively refurbished to provide an excellent standard of accommodation, whatever the time of year. Full central heating and carpeting, new furnishings and improved washroom facilities will all ensure a comfortable stay in this superb area. The Hostel lies on the Pennine Way in Upper Teesdale; an area of special interest to botanists, geologists and industrial archaeologists. Also an excellent location for skiing. 7m from Middleton-in-Teesdale on road to Alston. Subject to availability, outdoor activity breaks can be provided for all types of groups: instructors are fully qualified and activities can be tailor-made to the requirements of each party

OS 91, 92 GR 860304 Bart 35, 39

Attractions: Upper Teesdale Nature Reserve 2m. High Force 2m. Cauldron Snout 4m. Cow Green Reservoir 2m. Bowlees 🛈 4m. Skiing in winter. Killhope Wheel Museum 15m

🚌 United 75/A from BR Darlington, alight High Force (☎ 0325 468771)

🚆 Darlington 33m

Next Youth Hostels: Dufton 12m. Baldersdale 15m Pennine Way. Alston 15m. Keld 30m by path

Langdon Beck Youth Hostel

NINEBANKS

Youth Hostel, Orchard House, Mohope, Ninebanks, Hexham, Northumberland NE47 8DO
Haltwhistle (0434) 345288

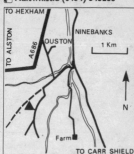

Overnight charge:
Young £2.60 Junior £3.50 Senior £4.40
🏥 2 🍴 Main Hostel — one coal fire.
🍴 🚿 S P and Shop Whitfield 5m.
ED Sat. P Daytime access by arrangement with warden

Jan 1-Feb 28	Closed
Mar 1-Oct 31	Open (except Thu)
Nov 1-Feb 29 92	Closed

During closed period advance bookings may be accepted from parties: enquiries welcome

Remote 200-years-old lead miner's cottage on road to Mohope Moor, with view of West Allendale. 1½m SW of Ninebanks village

OS 86, 87 GR 771513 Bart 39

Attractions: Peaceful Pennine valley in unspoilt country. Sparse traffic. Traces of old mine workings. Allendale town (trout fishing centre) 5m. Allen Banks (NT) and suspension bridge 8½m. Ridley House picnic area 9m. Vindolanda Roman fort 12m. Hadrian's Wall 13m. Heritage Centre: Allenheads 7m

🚌 Wright Bros BR Hexham — Alston, alight Ouston, 1m (☎ 0498 81200)

🚆 Haydon Bridge 11m

Next Youth Hostels: Alston 8m. Greenhead 16m. Once Brewed 16m (12m by fells). Acomb 18m. Edmundbyers 22m by path. Langdon Beck 21m

LAKE DISTRICT 3

The Lake District is the largest and one of the finest National Parks. The area offers attractions from breathtaking mountains and lakes, to picturesque villages and towns.

Thousands of people visit the Lake District each year. Many are attracted by activities such as walking, cycling, climbing and sailing. Others simply come to relax and enjoy the scenery. As well as physical activities, the Lake District offers attractions of cultural, historic and scientific interest. These include the homes of Wordsworth and Beatrix Potter, museums of Lake District industries such as bobbin mills and pencil making, and a number of forest and wildlife centres.

There are over thirty Hostels in the Lake District, many of which are linked together by walks. There is also plenty of scope for cyclists and, for the less energetic, most Hostels are accessible by car!

Useful Information

During Winter closed periods, early Spring and late Autumn, many Youth Hostels are available for exclusive use by parties booked in advance. For further details please contact the appropriate Hostel.

Bathing — Light footwear should be worn in streams, tarns and lakes, as severe injury from broken glass has been known.

Mountain Walking — In central Lake District, crossing the main ranges may entail long, hard going and navigation in bad weather. This should be borne in mind when planning a tour, as alternative routes can be long and expensive. Youth Hostels along the main valleys can be linked by low-level footpaths, or public transport when weather conditions are bad on the tops.

Weather Forecast — For daily local weather forecast telephone Windermere (09662) 5151.

Helpful Publications

Inter Hostel Walks in the Lake District —
*a comprehensive guide, particularly useful
to first time visitors to the Lakes* £1.30

Exploring Eskdale —
Eskdale Classroom Textbook £2.00

The Natural History of Silverdale and Arnside —
Arnside field study booklet £1.30

The above publications are available from YHA Northern Regional Office, D Floor, Milburn House, Dean Street, Newcastle upon Tyne NE1 1LF. Tel: 091 221 2101.

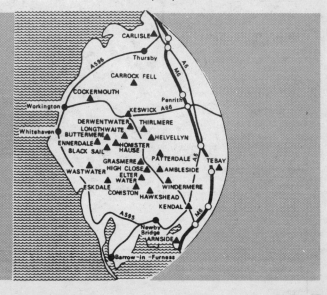

LAKE DISTRICT

3

AMBLESIDE

**Youth Hostel, Waterhead,
Ambleside, Cumbria LA22 0EU**
⌂ **Warden and bookings
Ambleside (05394) 32304**

Overnight charge:
Young £4.60 Junior £5.90 Senior £7.00
High Season Jul 1-Aug 31:
Young £5.50 Junior £7.00 Senior £8.30
🛉 🅰 🖼 ④ 🍴 Cafeteria facilities from
17.30 hrs. 🆂 Shop and 🅿🅾 Ambleside
1m. 🕑 Thu. 🅿 cars only; coaches in
public car park 200 yds

Jan 1-Feb 28	Open (except Wed)
Mar 1-Nov 2	Open
Nov 3-Dec 22	Open (except Wed)
Dec 23-28	Open
Dec 29-Feb 14 92 Closed	

Six Victorian town houses on shores
of Windermere, largest lake in
England, with panoramic view of
mountains, in Lake District National
Park. At Waterhead 1m S of
Ambleside village on the main A591
Windermere Road, 100 yds S of
steamer pier

🆂 Lake District Tourist 90 🅶🆁 377031
🅱🅰🆁🆃 34

Attractions: Lake bathing, 🛶 🅰
Good walks and viewpoints. Stock
Ghyll waterfall 1m. Roman fort site
½m. Bridge House (NT) 1m.
Brockhole National Park Centre 2m.
ℹ️ 🅻 ♿

🚌 CMS services from surrounding
areas (many pass close BR
Windermere) (⌂ 0539 733221)

🚉 Windermere 4m

Next Youth Hostels: Windermere
3m, Elterwater 3½m, High Close 4m,
Grasmere 5½m, Hawkshead 6m

Additional Information: To contact
resident members ⌂ Ambleside
(05394) 32486

Administrative Region: Northern

ARNSIDE

COMFORT IMPROVED

**Youth Hostel, Oakfield Lodge,
Redhills Road, Arnside,
Carnforth, Lancs LA5 0AT**
⌂ **Arnside (0524) 761781**

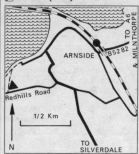

Overnight charge:
Young £4.60 Junior £5.90 Senior £7.00
🅰 🛉 🔍 ④ 🖼 🔥 Evening meal 19.00
hrs. 🆂 Shop and 🅿🅾 ½m. 🕑 Thu. 🎏 🅿
for cars and coaches

Jan 1-Mar 25	Open (except Sun)
Mar 26-Sep 22	Open
Sep 23-Dec 19	Open (except Sun)
Dec 20-28	Open
Dec 29-Feb 13 92	Closed
Feb 14-29	Open (except Sun)

Pleasant stone building, once a girls'
school, standing high above Kent
Estuary with views of Lakeland
mountains. Up hill from promenade,
then turn right on Redhills Road for
¼m. Footpath by Hostel down to
seashore

🆂 97 🅶🆁 452783 🅱🅰🆁🆃 34

Attractions: Marine biology,
geology, sea 🛶 canoeing. Leighton
Moss bird sanctuary 3m. Arnside
Knott nature trail 1m. Carnforth
Steam Town. Morecambe
illuminations (Sept/Oct). Limestone
scenery. Cumbrian Cycleway.
Lancashire Cycleway. Westmorland
Way. Furness Way. Tidal Bore. 🅻

🚌 CMS 552/3 from Kendal
(⌂ 0539 733221)

🚉 Arnside 1m

Next Youth Hostels: Hawkshead
(via rail to Grange) 18m. Ingleton
19m. Slaidburn 32m. Kendal 12m

Arnside Youth Hostel

Administrative Region: Northern

B LACK SAIL

18 BEDS

Youth Hostel, Black Sail Hut,
Ennerdale, Cleator,
Cumbria CA23 3AY

Overnight charge:
Young £3.10 Junior £4.00 Senior £5.10
Groups restricted to max 5 male and
5 female. △ ① ⌶ Evening meal 19.00
hrs — please try to book in advance.
Ⓢ UHT milk available, no bread. Shop
Wasdale Head 3m. **No access for cars**

Jan 1-Mar 14	Closed
Mar 15-Nov 2	Open (except Mon)
Nov 3-Feb 29 92	Closed

The most isolated and excitingly
situated Hostel in England. Former
shepherd's bothy at the head of
Ennerdale. Under Haystacks turn left
from foot of Scarth Gap Pass or
follow beck down from Windy Gap if
approaching over Sty Head. **No
access for cars**

Ⓞ Lake District Tourist 89, 90
Ⓖ 194124 Ⓑ 34

Attractions: Mountain walking and
🚶 on Pillar, Pillar Rock, Great Gable,
High Crag, High Stile, Red Pike
Range, Steeple, Scoat Fell and the
Haycock Ridge. River bathing. 🚲

🚌 CMS 79 Keswick — Seatoller,
thence 3½m (☎ 0900 603080) (For
BR connections see Keswick)

🚄 Whitehaven 19m

Next Youth Hostels: Honister 3m.
Buttermere 3½m. Ennerdale 4m.
Longthwaite 5m. Wastwater 7m.
Derwentwater 10m

Additional Information: Postal
service poor, bookings should be sent
well in advance. Do not send parcels
or telegrams

B UTTERMERE

71 BEDS

Youth Hostel, King George VI
Memorial Hostel, Buttermere,
Cockermouth, Cumbria CA13 9XA
☎ Buttermere (07687) 70245

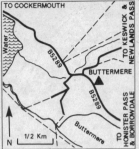

Overnight charge:
Young £4.00 Junior £5.10 Senior £6.30
🚻 🏠 △ ② ⌶ ⌶ Evening meal 19.00
hrs. Small Ⓢ Milk ¼m. Shop and Ⓟⓞ
Lorton 6½m. Ⓔ Sat. Ⓟ for cars and
coaches

Jan 1-Mar 21	Open (except Mon)
Mar 22-Sep 20	Open
Sep 21-Nov 2	Open (except Mon)
Nov 3-Dec 22	Closed
Dec 23-28	Open
Dec 29-Jan 5 92	Closed
Jan 6-Feb 29	Open (except Mon)

Built in Lakeland stone overlooking
Buttermere, with high fells behind.
⅓m S of Buttermere village on road
to Honister Pass and Borrowdale

Ⓞ Lake District Tourist 89, 90
Ⓖ 178168 Ⓑ 34

Attractions: Lake bathing. Rowing
boats on Buttermere and
Crummock. 🚶 🚲 Red Pike and High
Stile just across valley. Ⓛ

🚌 From Keswick (enquire for details
on ☎ 07687 73962) (For BR
connections see Keswick)

🚄 Workington 18m

Next Youth Hostels: Black Sail 3½m
by mountain path. Honister 4m.
Longthwaite 7m. Ennerdale 7½m by
path. Keswick 8½m. Cockermouth 10m.
Wastwater 11m by mountain path

Additional Information: To contact
resident members ☎ Buttermere
(07687) 70254

C ARLISLE

60 BEDS

Youth Hostel,
Etterby House, Etterby,
Carlisle CA3 9QS
☎ Carlisle (0228) 23934

Overnight charge:
Young £3.50 Junior £4.40 Senior £5.50
🚻 △ ① 🍴 Ⓢ Evening meal 19.00
hrs. Ⓢ Shop and Ⓟⓞ ¼m. Ⓟ for cars
and small coaches Ⓛ

Jan 1-Mar 30	Open (except Sun & Mon)
Mar 31-Apr 13	Open
Apr 14-May 21	Open (except Sun & Mon)
May 22-28	Open
May 29-Jun 30	Open (except Sun & Mon)
Jul 1-Aug 31	Open
Sep 1-Dec 21	Open (except Sun & Mon)
Dec 22-28	Open
Dec 29-Feb 29 92	Closed

On banks of River Eden, 1½m NW
from centre of historic city of
Carlisle. Good starting point for
exploring the Borders and Hadrian's
Wall. An ideal stepping stone when
travelling to and from Scotland. 1m
N of city on A7 turn W at Etterby
Street. After ¾m turn left at Etterby
Road, Hostel ¼m 1st house on left

Ⓞ 85 Ⓖ 386569 Ⓑ 38

Attractions: Excellent cycling area
(on Cumbrian Cycle Way). Castle.
Cathedral. Museums. Eden Valley.
Solway coast. Hadrian's Wall. Lanercost
Priory, Cumbrian Way. Sports
Centre, Dry Ski Slope. All weather
running track. Nature Reserve

🚌 CMS 62/A Town Hall — St Ann's
Hill, thence ¼m (☎ 0228 48484)

🚄 Carlisle 2m

Next Youth Hostels: Carrock Fell
17m. Greenhead 19m. Cockermouth
25m. Keswick 34m. Snoot (SYHA)
49m

C ARROCK FELL

16 BEDS

Youth Hostel, High Row Cottage, Haltcliffe, Hesket Newmarket, Wigton, Cumbria CA7 8JT
☎ Caldbeck (06998) 325

Overnight charge:
Young £3.50 Junior £4.40 Senior £5.50
🅰 🍴 🍽 Evening meal 19.00 hrs.
Small Ⓢ Shop and ⓅⓄ Hesket Newmarket 2¾m. 🅴🅳 Sat. Ⓟ for cars

Jan 1-Mar 14	Closed
Mar 15-May 26	Open (except Mon & Tue)
May 27-Aug 31	Open (except Mon)
Sep 1-Nov 2	Open (except Mon & Tue)
Nov 3-Feb 29 92	Closed

Converted farmhouse on the edge of Caldbeck Commons with superb aspect of Carrock Fell. 3m N of Mungrisdale at High Row. Turn right off Mungrisdale to Caldbeck Road. Hostel first house up track on left

🆗 Lake District Tourist 90 🅶🆁 358355
🅱🆁 38

Attractions: Centre for nothern fells in areas of great geological interest. River Caldew. Caldbeck. Bronze Age fort on Carrock Fell. Excellent cycling country, Cumbrian Way. Ⓛ

� No Service

🚌 Penrith 15m

Next Youth Hostels: Keswick 12m. Thirlmere 12m. Derwentwater 14m. Helvellyn 14m. Patterdale 14m. Carlisle 17m. Cockermouth 18m. Dufton 25m

C OCKERMOUTH

28 BEDS

Youth Hostel, Double Mills, Cockermouth, Cumbria CA13 0DS
☎ Cockermouth (0900) 822561

Overnight charge:
Young £3.50 Junior £4.40 Senior £5.50
🚻 🅰 ① 🍽 Evening meal 19.00 hrs.
Small Ⓢ Milk and potatoes ¼m. Shop and ⓅⓄ Cockermouth 10 mins. 🅴🅳 Thu. Limited Ⓟ — ask the Warden. Large cycle shed

Jan 1-Mar 31	Open (except Tue & Wed)
Apr 1-7	Open
Apr 8-May 26	Open (except Tue & Wed)
May 27-Aug 31	Open (except Wed)
Sep 1-Nov 2	Open (except Tue & Wed)
Nov 3-Dec 27	Closed
Dec 28-Jan 3 92	Open
Jan 4-Feb 29	Open (except Tue & Wed)

A 17th century watermill on south edge of the town where Wordsworth was born. From Main Street follow Station Street then Station Road. Keep left after war memorial then left into Fern Bank Road. Take track at end of Fern Bank. Hostel at bottom of track

🆗 Lake District Tourist 89 🅶🆁 118298
🅱🆁 34

Attractions: Wordsworth's house. Swimming pool and sports centre. Bassenthwaite Lake. Salmon and trout 🎣 Loweswater. Crummock Water. Ⓤ 2m. Good cycling country. Doll and Toy museum. Maryport Maritime museum 7m, river bathing

� Frequent from surrounding areas
(☎ 0900 603080)

🚌 Workington 8m

Next Youth Hostels: Buttermere 10m. Ennerdale 14m. Keswick 13m. Carrock Fell 18m. Carlisle 25m

C ONISTON (HOLLY HOW)

40 BEDS

Youth Hostel, Holly How, Far End, Coniston, Cumbria LA21 8DD
☎ Coniston (05394) 41323

Overnight charge:
Young £3.80 Junior £4.70 Senior £5.90
🅰 ② 🍽 🍴 Evening meal 19.00 hrs.
Small Ⓢ Milk, bread and potatoes ¼m. Shop and ⓅⓄ Coniston. Ⓟ limited — cars only; coaches in Coniston village ¼m

Jan 1-Mar 21	Open (except Sun)
Mar 22-Sep 20	Open
Sep 21-Nov 2	Open (except Sun)
Nov 3-Dec 20	Closed
Dec 21-28	Open
Dec 29-Jan 5 92	Closed
Jan 6-Feb 29	Open (except Sun)

Daytime access for groups in bad weather by arrangement with warden

Former guest house in its own beautiful grounds. Good wholesome home cooking with many vegetarian options. Just north of Coniston village, on Ambleside Road

🆗 Lake District Tourist 96, 97
🅶🆁 302980 🅱🆁 34

Attractions: Coniston Water for 🅰 'Gondola' steam yacht. Ruskin museum. Ruskin's home at Brantwood. Grizedale forest trails. Tilberthwaite Ghyll. Ⓤ River bathing. Cumbrian Way. Ⓛ

� CMS 505/516 from Ambleside
(☎ Kendal 73321). Connections to Windermere/Keswick from Ambleside

🚌 Windermere 11m; Ulverston 13m

Next Youth Hostels: Coniston Coppermines 1¼m by path. Elterwater 5m. Hawkshead 5m. Ambleside 6½m.

Additional Information: To contact resident members ☎ Coniston (05394) 41675

Coniston Coppermines

33 BEDS COMFORT IMPROVED

Youth Hostel,
Coppermines House, Coniston,
Cumbria LA21 8HP
Coniston (05394) 41261

Overnight charge:
Young £3.50 Junior £4.40 Senior £5.50
Evening meal 19.00 hrs.
Small S Shop and P0 in village 1m. P
for cars and coaches in Coniston
village 1m

Jan 1-Feb 14	Closed
Feb 15-Mar 24	Open (except Wed & Thu)
Mar 25-Apr 7	Open (except Wed)
Apr 8-May 26	Open (except Wed & Thu)
May 27-Aug 31	Open (except Wed)

Sep 1-Nov 9	Open (except Wed & Thu)
Nov 10-Dec 20	Open Fri & Sat
Dec 21-27	Closed
Dec 28-Jan 5 92	Open
Jan 6-31	Closed

Advance bookings may be accepted
during winter closed period, at the
discretion of the warden

A simple Hostel in spectacular
surroundings at the head of
Coppermines Valley. Popular for its
homely food. Hostel is 1¼m from
Coniston. From village take minor
road between Black Bull Hotel and
Co-op, this continues as a track for
1m to Hostel

OS Lake District Tourist 96, 97
GR 289986 Bus 34

Attractions: on Coniston
Water 1½m. Coniston Old Man. Tarn
Hows 3m. Ruskin's Museum 1¼m.
Ruskin's home at Brantwood 3m.
Theatre in the Forest, Grizedale 3m.
Forest trails. Stream bathing. L

CMS 505/516 from Ambleside
(Kendal 73321). Connections to
Windermere/Keswick from
Ambleside

Windermere 12m; Ulverston 14m

Next Youth Hostels: Coniston
(Holly How) 1½m by path. Elterwater
6m by path. Hawkshead 6m. Eskdale
10m by mountain path

Coniston Coppermines Youth Hostel

Administrative Region: Northern

3

LAKE DISTRICT

DERWENTWATER

Youth Hostel, Barrow House, Borrowdale, Keswick, Cumbria CA12 5UR
☎ (07687) 77246

Converted mansion with a beautiful 'Adam Room', overlooking Derwentwater 2m south of Keswick on road to Grange. The extensive grounds contain a 100ft waterfall, and are the home of the red squirrel. Meals at Derwentwater are healthy and substantial

OS Lake District Tourist 89, 90
GR 268200 Bart 34

Attractions: Lake swimming, canoeing, 🚣 boating. Waterbus round lake. 🎦 Watendlath (Herries country), Lingholme Gardens, Surprise View. Lodore Falls. Ashness Bridge. L Skiddaw, Scafell, Borrowdale Fells plus excellent low level walking with superb views

🚌 CMS 79 Keswick — Seatoller (☎ 0900 603080) (For BR connections see Keswick)

🚉 Penrith 20m; Windermere 24m

Next Youth Hostels: Keswick 2m. Longthwaite 5m. Thirlmere 5m. Grasmere 11m by path. Carrock Fell 14m

Overnight charge:
Young £4.60 Junior £5.90 Senior £7.00
🛏 🏠 4 🍴 🔲 Evening meal 19.00 hrs.
S Shop and PO Keswick 2m. 🔲 Wed.
P for cars and coaches

Jan 1-Mar 21	Open (except Sun)
Mar 22-Sep 20	Open
Sep 21-Nov 2	Open (except Sun)
Nov 3-Dec 27	Closed
Dec 28-Jan 3 92	Open
Jan 4-mid Mar	Open (except Sun)

Derwentwater Youth Hostel

ELTERWATER

Youth Hostel, Elterwater, Ambleside, Cumbria LA22 9HX
☎ Langdale (09667) 245

Overnight charge:
Young £3.80 Junior £4.70 Senior £5.90
🏠 1 🍴 🔲 Evening meal 19.00 hrs. S
Shop Elterwater. PO Chapel Stile 1m.
🔲 Sat. P for cars and coaches in village

Jan 1-Feb 14	Closed
Feb 15-Mar 21	Open (except Mon)
Mar 22-Sep 20	Open
Sep 21-Dec 20	Open (except Mon)
Dec 21-27	Closed
Dec 28-Jan 3 92	Open
Jan 4-mid Feb	Closed

Originally farm building in picturesque village in Great Langdale valley

OS Lake District Tourist 90 GR 327046
Bart 34

Attractions: Climbing on Langdale Pikes, Pike o' Blisco, Crinkle Crags, Bowfell. Waterfalls: Dungeon Ghyll, Colwith Force, Tilberthwaite Falls, Skelwith Force, Tarn Hows, Cumbria Way

🚌 CMS 516 from Ambleside (connections from BR Windermere) (☎ 0539 73321)

🚉 Windermere 9m

Next Youth Hostels: High Close 1m. Ambleside 3½m. Grasmere 4m. Coniston (Holly How) 5m. Hawkshead 7m. Windermere 8m. Longthwaite 10½m (via mountain path)

ENNERDALE (GILLERTHWAITE)

24 BEDS

Youth Hostel, Cat Crag,
Ennerdale, Cleator,
Cumbria CA23 3AX
📞 Lamplugh (0946) 861237

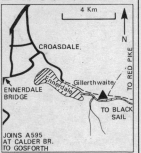

Overnight charge:
Young £3.50 Junior £4.40 Senior £5.50
🄰 ② 🄌 🄀 Evening meal 19.00 hrs.
Small 🅂 Shop and 🄿🄾 Ennerdale 6m

Jan 1-Mar 14   Closed
Mar 15-Nov 2   Open (except Thu)
Nov 3-Feb 29 92 Closed

Two converted forestry cottages in a
peaceful valley. 1¼m E of Ennerdale
Water. No access for cars — car park
2½m at end of forest road

🄾🅂 Lake District Tourist 89 🄶🅁 142141
🄱🄰🅁🄻 34

Attractions: Smithy Beck forestry
trail. Red Pike, High Stile and High
Crag Ridges. Hayock Steeple and
Pillar massif. Botany. Walking.
Prehistoric sites. River Lisa footpath

🚌 From Keswick (enquire for details
on 📞 07687 73962); otherwise CMS
17 from Whitehaven, alight Kirkland,
7m or CMS 79 from Keswick, alight
Seatoller, 7m by path (📞 0946 63222)
(For BR connections see Keswick)

🚆 Whitehaven 15m

Next Youth Hostels: Buttermere
3m by mountain path (via Red Pike),
7m by mountain path via Scarth Gap
(18m by road). Black Sail 4m.
Wastwater 8m by mountain path
(22m by road). Cockermouth 14m

ESKDALE

54 BEDS

Youth Hostel,
Boot, Holmrook,
Cumbria CA19 1TH
📞 Eskdale (09403) 219

Overnight charge:
Young £4.00 Junior £5.10 Senior £6.30
🄌 🄰 ② 🄌 🄀 Evening meal 19.00 hrs.
🅂 (UHT milk, no bread available).
Shop Eskdale Green 4m. 🄴🄳 Sat. Small
🄿🄾 Boot 1½m. 🄴🄳 Wed & Sat. 🄲 with
daytime access suitable for functions;
details from warden. 🄐 subject to
classroom usage. 🄿 for cars and
minibuses only; coaches Dalesgarth
Station 1½m

Jan 1-Feb 14   Closed
Feb 15-Mar 21   Open
                (except Sun & Mon)
Mar 22-Apr 6   Open
Apr 7-May 25   Open (except Sun)
May 26-Jun 1   Open
Jun 2-30   Open (except Sun)
Jul 1-Aug 31   Open
Sep 1-Dec 20   Open
                (except Sun & Mon)
Dec 21-27   Closed
Dec 28-Jan 4 92 Open
Jan 5-mid Feb   Closed

Purpose-built Hostel in extensive
open grounds in one of Lakeland's
quietest unspoilt valleys. ¼m up dale
from Woolpack Inn (now open in
winter) 1½m E of Boot

🄾🅂 Lake District Tourist 89, 90
🄶🅁 195010 🄱🄰🅁🄻 34

Attractions: Ravenglass and Eskdale
narrow gauge railway 1½m. Scafell
Pike. Harter Fell. Hardknott Roman
fort. Boot mill museum. 🄻 Outdoor
activities can be provided — details
from warden

🚌 No service

🚆 Eskdale (Ravenglass & Eskdale
Rly), 1½m; Ravenglass (not Sun) 10m;
Drigg (not Sun) 10m

Next Youth Hostels: Wastwater 7m.
Black Sail 10m. Coniston Coppermines
10m. All by mountain path

GRASMERE (BUTHARLYP HOW)

105 BEDS

Youth Hostel, Butharlyp How,
Grasmere, Ambleside,
Cumbria LA22 9QG
📞 Grasmere (09665) 316

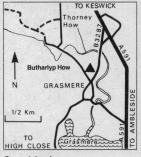

Overnight charge:
Young £4.40 Junior £5.40 Senior £6.60
High Season Jul 1-Aug 31:
Young £4.60 Junior £5.90 Senior £7.00
🄌 🄰 ④ 🄌 🄀 Evening meal 19.00 hrs.
Small 🅂 🄴🄳 Thu. 🄿 for cars only;
coaches ¼m village

Jan 1-Feb 14   Closed
Feb 15-Nov 2   Open
Nov 3-Dec 27   Closed
Dec 28-Feb 29 92 Open

Victorian house built in Lakeland
stone. Its large grounds are
particularly lovely when the azaleas
and rhododendrons are in bloom. N
of Grasmere village, follow road to
Easedale for 150 yds, turn right (or E)
down drive

🄾🅂 Lake District Tourist 90 🄶🅁 336077
🄱🄰🅁🄻 34

Attractions: Wordsworth museum
(Dove Cottage). Wordsworth's
grave. Popular tourist village. 🄐 🄵
canoeing, 🄹 geology. 🄻

🚌 CMS 555-7 Lancaster - Keswick,
alight Grasmere, ¼m (all pass close
BR Windermere) (📞 0539 73321)

🚆 Windermere 8½m

Next Youth Hostels: Grasmere
(Thorney How) ¾m. High Close 2m.
Elterwater 3m. Ambleside 5½m.
Thirlmere 7½m. Helvellyn 8m by
mountain path. Longthwaite 8½m by
mountain path. Coniston (Holly
How) 8¾m. Patterdale 9m by path

Administrative Region: Northern

Administrative Region: Northern

Administrative Region: Northern

GRASMERE (THORNEY HOW)
46 BEDS · COMFORT IMPROVED

Youth Hostel, Thorney How, Grasmere, Ambleside, Cumbria LA22 9QW
☎ Grasmere (09665) 591

Overnight charge:
Young £4.00 Junior £5.10 Senior £6.30
👫 🏚 1 🍽 🍴 Evening meal 19.00 hrs.
Small S Shop and PO Grasmere 1m.
ED Thu. P for cars and minibuses only

Jan 1-Mar 21	Open (except Tue)
Mar 22-Sep 20	Open
Sep 21-Dec 20	Open (except Tue)
Dec 21-28	Open
Dec 29-mid Feb 92	Closed

An old Lakeland farmhouse, first opened as a Youth Hostel in 1932, it is 1 mile from the village centre. Take Easedale road from village for ⅜m. Turn right at road junction (Hostel sign) then turn left after 400 metres

OS Lake District Tourist 90 GR 331084 Bart 34

Attractions: Ascent of Helvellyn. Walks to Helm Crag, Sour Milk Gill, Easedale Tarn, Wordsworth Museum and grave. Within easy distance of many beauty spots. Coast to Coast Walk. L

🚌 As for Grasmere (Butharlyp How)
🚆 Windermere 9m

Next Youth Hostels: Grasmere (Butharlyp How) ¾m. High Close 2½m. Elterwater 4m. Ambleside 6m. Thirlmere 7m. Helvellyn 8m by mountain path. Patterdale 9m by path. Longthwaite 9m (via Coast to Coast Path)

HAWKSHEAD
116 BEDS · COMFORT IMPROVED

Youth Hostel, Esthwaite Lodge, Hawkshead, Ambleside, Cumbria LA22 0QD
☎ Hawkshead (09666) 293*

Overnight charge:
Young £4.60 Junior £5.90 Senior £7.00
👫 🏚 room rates 🏚 🔲 4 🍽 🍴
Evening meal from 18.30 hrs. S Shop and PO Hawkshead, 1m. No ED FS P

Jan 1-Feb 14	Closed
Feb 15-Mar 21	Open (except Sun)
Mar 22-Nov 2	Open
Nov 3-Dec 27	Closed
Dec 28-Jan 3 92	Open
Jan 4-Feb 29	Open (except Sun)

Handsome Regency mansion and courtyard development in spacious grounds overlooking Esthwaite Water, once home of novelist Francis Brett Young. An ideal location for families. 1m S of Hawkshead on Newby Bridge Road. From ferry turn left at Near Sawrey, follow Esthwaite Water. Outdoor games at Hostel

OS Lake District Tourist 96, 97 GR 354966 Bart 34

Attractions: Hawkshead village, boyhood home of Wordsworth, Beatrix Potter museum at Near Sawrey. Beatrix Potter Gallery 1m. Wildlife and forestry museums in Grizedale. Theatre in the Forest, Tarn Hows. Latterbarrow. Claife Heights. Silurian Way. 🚴 Excellent cycling area. 🚲 🏚 1m. Orienteering and cycle trails in Grizedale Forest

🚌 CMS 505 from Ambleside (connections from BR Windermere), alight Hawkshead, 1m (☎ 0539 73321)
🚆 Windermere 7m (by vehicle ferry)

Next Youth Hostels: Coniston (Holly How) 5m. Ambleside 5½m. Coniston Coppermines 6m. Elterwater 7m. High Close 8m. Windermere 9m by ferry. Grasmere 11m

*Telephone Number
During 1991 the number may change to Hawkshead (05394) 36293

HELVELLYN
64 BEDS

Youth Hostel, Greenside, Glenridding, Penrith, Cumbria CA11 0QR
☎ Glenridding (07684) 82269

Overnight charge:
Young £3.80 Junior £4.70 Senior £5.90
👫 🏚 2 🍽 🍴 Evening meal 19.00 hrs.
S (UHT milk). Shop and PO (fresh milk) 1½m. ED Wed. P for cars and minibuses only; coaches in Glenridding 1½m

Jan 1-3	Open
Jan 4-Mar 21	Open (except Mon & Tue)
Mar 22-Sep 20	Open
Sep 21-Nov 2	Open (except Mon & Tue)
Nov 3-Dec 27	Closed
Dec 28-Jan 3 92	Open
Jan 4-Feb 29	Open (except Mon & Tue)

Over 900ft above sea level, the former home of the manager of the now disused lead mines. 1½m up Greenside Road from Glenridding village

OS Lake District Tourist 90 GR 366173 Bart 34

Attractions: Ullswater Lake. Helvellyn. Aira Force Waterfall (3m). 🪨 geology, U Activity courses including ski-ing, canoeing, 🏹 multi-activity and other winter skills. Also multi-activity adventure weeks for school parties and groups, details from warden

🚌 From Keswick, Windermere, alight Glenridding, 1½m. (☎ 07687 73962)
🚆 Penrith 14m; Windermere 15m

Next Youth Hostels: Patterdale 2½m. Thirlmere 4m by mountain path. Grasmere 8m by mountain path. Keswick 10m by mountain path. Ambleside 12m. Carrock Fell 14m. Windermere 14m

Additional Information: To contact resident members ☎ Glenridding (07684) 82488

HIGH CLOSE (LANGDALE)

96 BEDS

Youth Hostel, High Close,
Loughrigg, Ambleside,
Cumbria LA22 9HJ
Langdale (09667) 313

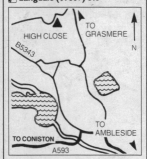

Overnight charge:
Young £4.00 Junior £5.10 Senior £6.30
[symbols] 2 [symbols] Evening meal 18.30 hrs.
S Shop Elterwater 1m, Sat. Shop and PO Grasmere 2m, Thu. RS P for cars only; coaches in Elterwater village 1m, cannot reach Hostel

Jan 1-Mar 21	Open (except Sun)
Mar 22-Sep 20	Open
Sep 21-Nov 9	Open (except Sun)
Nov 10-Dec 20	Closed
Dec 21-28	Open
Dec 29-Jan 5 92	Closed
Jan 6-31	Open Fri & Sat

Advance booking may be accepted during Jan 92 midweek, at the discretion of the warden

Rambling old house in extensive National Trust Grounds, with views over the Brathay Valley to Windermere and of the Langdale Fells. On summit of road over Red Bank leading from Grasmere to Elterwater and Langdale

OS Lake District Tourist 90 GR 338052 Bart 34

Attractions: Hostel grounds. Great Langdale Valley and Pikes. Lake bathing 1m. Rydal Mount (Wordsworth) 2m. Loughrigg Terrace footpath and viewpoint ½m. Windermere 4m. Pool table, table tennis and garden games at Hostel. L

CMS 516 from Ambleside (connections from BR Windermere), alight ¾m SE of Elterwater, thence ¾m; otherwise any of the services to Grasmere Hostels, alight Grasmere, thence 1¾m (0539 73321)

Windermere 10m

Next Youth Hostels: Elterwater 1m. Grasmere 2m. Ambleside 4m. Hawkshead 8m

Additional Information: To contact resident members, Langdale (09667) 212

Administrative Region: Northern

HONISTER HAUSE

30 BEDS

Youth Hostel, Honister Hause,
Seatoller, Keswick,
Cumbria CA12 5XN
Borrowdale (07687) 77267

Overnight charge:
Young £3.50 Junior £4.40 Senior £5.50
[symbols] 1 [symbols] Evening meal 19.00 hrs.
Small S Milk 1¼m. Shops including bread, potatoes, Keswick 9m. Wed. PO Stonethwaite 2½m. Thu. P for cars and coaches adjacent to Hostel

Jan 1-Mar 14	Closed
Mar 15-24	Open (except Wed & Thu)
Mar 25-Apr 7	Open
Apr 8-May 26	Open (except Wed & Thu)
May 27-Jun 2	Open
Jun 3-30	Open (except Wed & Thu)
Jul 1-Aug 31	Open
Sep 1-Nov 2	Open (except Wed & Thu)
Nov 3-Dec 17	Open Weekends
Dec 18-Feb 29 92	Closed

Purpose-built Hostel situated at summit of Honister Pass; comfortable base for the walker and climber

OS Lake District Tourist 89, 90 GR 224135 Bart 34

Attractions: Great Gable, Fleetwith Pike and Haystacks. Ridge walking. F Slate quarries. Sunsets. Mountain flowers. L

CMS 79 Keswick — Seatoller, thence 1½m (0900 603080) (For BR connections see Keswick)

Workington 23m

Next Youth Hostels: Black Sail 3m by mountain path. Longthwaite 2m by path. Buttermere 4m. Wastwater 8m by mountain path. Cockermouth 13m

Administrative Region: Northern

KENDAL

50 BEDS

Youth Hostel,
Highgate, Kendal,
Cumbria LA9 4HE
(0539) 724066

Overnight charge:
Young £4.40 Junior £5.40 Senior £6.60
[symbols] 1 [symbols] Evening meal 19.00 hrs.
S Shop and PO 200 yds. P Pay & display car park (for cars only). Entrance to car park 10 yards before Hostel, at Brewery Arts Centre

Jan 1-Feb 14	Closed
Feb 15-Mar 25	Open (except Mon)
Mar 26-Sep 22	Open
Sep 23-Nov 11	Open (except Mon)
Nov 12-Dec 27	Closed
Dec 28-Feb 29 92	Open (except Mon) (but Open Dec 30)

Groups wishing to use the Hostel on days when it is normally closed please contact the warden in advance

Former Georgian Town House with much character offering a high standard of residential accommodation

OS Lake District Tourist 97 GR 515924 Bart 31, 34
(old Hostel on Milnthorpe Road now closed)

Attractions: Brewery Arts centre, theatre, films, workshops, jazz, folk, photographic gallery, for details each month s.a.e. to warden. Museum of Lakeland Life and Industry. Abbot Hall. Leisure Centre. Scout Scar. Dales Way. Westmorland Way. Access to secluded Kentmere and Longsledale Valleys. L

Frequent from surrounding areas (0539 733221)

Kendal ¾m; Oxenholme 1¾m

Next Youth Hostels: Windermere 11m. Arnside 12m. Tebay 11m. Ingleton 17m

Administrative Region: Northern

KESWICK

91 BEDS · COMFORT IMPROVED YHA

**Youth Hostel, Station Road,
Keswick, Cumbria CA12 5LH**
⌂ Warden and bookings
Keswick (07687) 72484

Overnight charge:
Young £4.60 Junior £5.90 Senior £7.00
🏠🔥④📺🍴 Evening meal 19.00
hrs. Breakfast 08.00-09.00 hrs. Ⓢ
Shops and PO 2 mins. 🚌 Wed. P for
cars and coaches in town

Jan 1-Feb 28	Open (except Wed)
Mar 1-Nov 2	Open
Nov 3-Dec 22	Open (except Wed)
Dec 23-28	Open
Dec 29-Feb 15 92	Closed

Former hotel near centre of busy and
popular Lakeland resort at the
northern end of Derwentwater. On
River Greta, overlooking Fitzpark.
From County Hotel go down Station
Road. Turn left on to walkway by river

OS Lake District Tourist 89, 90
GR 267235 Bart 34

Attractions: Lake swimming,
boating, and launch trips. Mini golf.
Playground, tennis courts, putting in
park opp. Hostel. Museums.
Convenient for ascent of Skiddaw,
Blencathra and North Western fells.
Castle Rigg stone circle. Whinlatter
Forest Centre. Cumbria Way. 🚲 L

🚌 CMS 104 from Carlisle (past BR
Penrith) (☎ 0228 48484); 34/5 from
Whitehaven (pass BR Workington)
(☎ 0900 603080); 555/7 from
Lancaster (pass BR Windermere)
(☎ 0539 733221)

🚂 Penrith 16m

Next Youth Hostels:
Derwentwater 2m. Thirlmere 5m.
Longthwaite 7m. Buttermere 8½m.
Helvellyn 10m by mountain path.
Cockermouth 13m. Carrock Fell
12m. Grasmere 12m.

Additional Information: To contact
resident members ⌂ Keswick
(07687) 72485

LONGTHWAITE

94 BEDS

**Youth Hostel, Longthwaite,
Keswick, Cumbria CA12 5XE**
⌂ Warden and bookings
Borrowdale (07687) 77257

Overnight charge:
Young £3.80 Junior £4.70 Senior £5.90
🏠🔥④🍴 Evening meal 19.00
hrs. Ⓢ Shop Rosthwaite 1m. PO
Stonethwaite 1m. P for cars and
minibuses; coaches in Seatoller 1m

Jan 1-Feb 14	Closed
Feb 15-Mar 21	Open (except Tue)
Mar 22-Nov 2	Open
Nov 3-Dec 20	Open (except Tue)
Dec 21-27	Closed
Dec 28-Jan 4 92	Open
Jan 5-mid Feb	Closed

Purpose-built Hostel of Canadian red
cedar wood in extensive natural
riverside grounds within beautiful
Borrowdale Valley. On W bank of
River Derwent, ½m south of
Rosthwaite

OS Lake District Tourist 90 GR 254142
Bart 34

Attractions: Good centre for
mountain walking, particularly Scafell
Pike and Great Gable. Excellent low
level walking. Castle Crag.
Watendlath (Herries Country). River
bathing, canoeing, 🛶 🎣 Cumbria
Way

🚌 CMS 79 from Keswick
(☎ 0900 603080) (For BR
connections see Keswick)

🚂 Workington 25m; Penrith 26m

Next Youth Hostels: Honister 2m.
Derwentwater 5m. Black Sail 5m by
mountain path. Buttermere 7m

Additional Information: To contact
resident members ⌂ Borrowdale
(07687) 77618

PATTERDALE

84 BEDS · COMFORT IMPROVED YHA

**YH, Goldrill House, Patterdale,
Penrith, Cumbria CA11 0NW**
⌂ Warden and bookings
Glenridding (07684) 82394

Overnight charge:
Young £4.60 Junior £5.90 Senior £7.00
④🍴📺 Evening meal 19.00 hrs. Ⓢ
Shop and PO village ½m. P for cars
and minibuses only; coaches ½m

Jan 1-Feb 14	Closed
Feb 15-Mar 21	Open (except Thu)
Mar 22-Sep 20	Open
Sep 21-Dec 22	Open (except Thu)
Dec 23-28	Open
Dec 29-mid Feb 92	Closed

Purpose-built Hostel skilfully
designed to blend with the fine
scenery to the south of Ullswater.
½m S of Patterdale village, just off
A592 leading to Kirkstone Pass

OS Lake District Tourist 90 GR 399156
Bart 34

Attractions: Ullswater (1m) is least
spoilt of larger lakes. Canoeing, 🛶 Ⓤ
🎣 Many footpaths at high and low
level. Aira Force 4m. Helvellyn
(3113 ft). L

🚌 As for Helvellyn, but the services
pass the Hostel

🚂 Penrith 15m

Next Youth Hostels: Tebay 36m.
Helvellyn 2½m. Thirlmere 6¼m.
Grasmere 9m by path. Ambleside
10m. Windermere 11m. Carrock Fell
14m

Additional Information: To contact
resident members ⌂ (07684) 82441

TEBAY

46 BEDS

Youth Hostel,
The Old School, Tebay,
Penrith, Cumbria CA10 3TP
☎ Orton (05874) 286

Overnight charge:
Young £3.80 Junior £4.70 Senior £5.90
🏠 🍴 🛏 ♿ (inc twin bedded rooms)
📮 ② 🍴 Evening meal 19.00 hrs.
No members' kitchen. Tumble dryer for members' use. Small 🅂 Shop and 📮 200 yds. 🍴 Sat. 🅿 for cars and minibuses

Jan 1-Feb 7	Closed
Feb 8-Dec 1	Open (except Thu)
Dec 2-Feb 6 92	Closed
Feb 7-29	Open (except Thu)

Open on Thu or any other closed period for groups by arrangement with warden

Converted school at north end of Tebay village. This is a privately owned Hostel adopted by the YHA. This Hostel does **not** have a members' kitchen. Easy access from M6 (junction 38)

🆗 91 GR 618045 Bart 34

Attractions: Walking on the Howgill Fells. Good cycling country linking Lake District with Yorkshire Dales, coast to coast walk, table tennis, recreation area and tennis courts opposite Hostel. Dalesway 5m. 🎣 Game fishing on River Lune

🚌 From Kendal, Penrith (passes close BR Kendal & Penrith) (☎ 05874 241 or 0228 48484)

🚉 Kendal 11m; Kirkby Stephen (not Sun, except May-Sep) 11m; Oxenholme 13m

Next Youth Hostels: Kirkby Stephen 10m. Kendal 11m. Patterdale 36m. Ingleton 24m. Dufton 14m

---

THIRLMERE

33 BEDS

Youth Hostel, The Old School,
Stanah Cross, Keswick,
Cumbria CA12 4TQ
☎ Keswick (07687) 73224

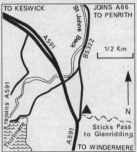

Overnight charge:
Young £2.60 Junior £3.50 Senior £4.40
🏠 ① Limited meals service — wholefood evening meal, packed lunch and continental breakfast, check availability with warden. 🅂 milk, bread and eggs. Shops Keswick 5½m. 🍴 Wed. 📮 Dale Head ½m. 🅿 for cars only

Jan 1-Mar 14	Closed
Mar 15-Jun 17	Open (except Mon & Tue)
Apr 1 (Mon)	Open Bank Hol
May 27 (Mon)	Open Bank Hol
Jun 18-Sep 30	Open (except Mon)
Oct 1-Nov 2	Open (except Mon & Tue)
Nov 3-Feb 29 92	Closed

Simple but cosy single storey wooden hut (former schoolhouse) 100yds N of A591/B5322 to St. John's in the vale, junction! Please note: this is one of the most basic Hostels in the Lake District. Facilities are very limited (no showers/bath for example) — but has a special character/atmosphere. It is ideal for individuals and small groups who prefer simple Hostels

🆗 Lake District Tourist 90 GR 318190 Bart 34

Attractions: Helvellyn range. 🎣 Castle Rigg stone circle. Choice of low level walking routes. Sticks Pass to Ullswater Valley Nature Trail. Raven Crag (viewpoint) 1m. Castle Crag fort 2m. River bathing ¼m. Large collection of board games

🚌 All services to the Grasmere Hostels, alight Stanah, 100 yds

🚉 Penrith 18m

Next Youth Hostels: Helvellyn 4m by mountain path. Keswick 5m. Derwentwater 6m. Longthwaite 6m by mountain path. Patterdale 6½m by mountain path. Grasmere 7m. Carrock Fell 12m

---

WASTWATER

50 BEDS

COMFORT IMPROVED

Youth Hostel, Wasdale Hall,
Wasdale, Seascale,
Cumbria CA20 1ET
☎ Wasdale (09406) 222

Overnight charge:
Young £4.00 Junior £5.10 Senior £6.30
♿ 🏠 🔍 ② 🛏 🍴 Evening meal 18.30 hrs. 🅂 Shop and 📮 Gosforth 5m. 🅿 for cars and coaches

Jan 1-Mar 21	Open (except Sun & Mon)
Mar 22-Sep 20	Open
Sep 21-Nov 2	Open (except Sun & Mon)
Nov 3-Dec 20	Closed
Dec 21-28	Open
Dec 29-Jan 7 92	Closed
Jan 8-Feb 29	Open (except Sun & Mon)

Groups wishing to use the Hostel on days when it is normally closed please contact warden in advance

'Wasdale Hall', built in 1829 and leased from the National Trust has recently been refurbished. It stands in its own extensive grounds on the lake shore at the Western end of the valley facing the dramatic Wastwater screes. If approaching via lakeside path at foot of screes, allow plenty of time, as going is very slow

🆗 Lake District Tourist 89 GR 145045 Bart 34

Attractions: 🎣 Scafell Pike, Scafell, Great Gable, Pillar, Red Pike and Kirk Fell. Good centre for experienced walkers. River and lake bathing. Viking Cross 5m Ⓛ

🚌 CMS 12 Whitehaven — Seascale (passes BR Seascale), alight Gosforth, 5m (☎ 0946 63222)

🚉 Seascale (not Sun) 9m; Irton Road (Ravenglass & Eskdale Rly) 5½m

Next Youth Hostels: Eskdale 7m. Black Sail 7m. Ennerdale 8m. Honister Hause 8m. Buttermere 11m. Coniston Coppermines 17m — all by mountain paths

---

Administrative Region: Northern | **Administrative Region: Northern** | **Administrative Region: Northern**

WINDERMERE

80 BEDS

Youth Hostel, High Cross,
Bridge Lane, Troutbeck,
Windermere, Cumbria LA23 1LA
☎ Windermere (09662) 3543

TO PATTERDALE
1/2 Km
N
TROUTBECK BRIDGE
A591
A592
TO KENDAL
A591
Stn
WINDERMERE
A592
JOINS A590   A5074

Overnight charge:
Young £3.80 Junior £4.70 Senior £5.90
Seasonal Prices Jul 1-Aug 31:
Young £4.00 Junior £5.10 Senior £6.30
🏠 may be available (ask warden) 🔥
2 ▦ 🍴 Evening meal 19.00 hrs.
Small S P for cars only; coaches 1m.
Shop & P.O. 1m

Jan 1-Feb 14	Closed
Feb 15-Nov 2	Open
Nov 3-Dec 27	Closed
Dec 28-mid Feb 92	Open

Large house in extensive grounds
with panoramic views of
Windermere Lake and mountains of
Southern Lakeland. Leave
Windermere-Ambleside road (A591)
1m N of Windermere at Troutbeck
Bridge. Hostel signposted ¾m up
Bridge Lane. (Avoid error of taking
A592 on leaving Windermere)

OS Lake District Tourist 90 GR 405013
Bart 34

Attractions: Brockhole National
Park Visitor Centre 1½m, indoor
swimming pool 1m. Windermere
Steamboat Museum 2m. Pony
trekking 1m. Cycle hire 2m.
Watersports & cruises on England's
largest lake 2m. Low level walks in
Troutbeck valley; high walks on quiet
eastern fells

🚌 Frequent from surrounding areas
(☎ 0539 733221)

🚇 Windermere 2m

Next Youth Hostels: Ambleside
3m. Hawkshead 9m by ferry.
Patterdale 11m. Kendal 11m

Additional Information: To contact
resident members ☎ (09662) 6147

Administrative Region: Northern

YORKSHIRE DALES

The Yorkshire Dales encompass the South and Central Pennines, an area of wild, heather-clad fells, green upland pastures and valleys cut by sparkling mountain streams. It includes the Yorkshire Dales National Park, the heart of which is Craven limestone. This is a rural area of great scenic beauty with spectacular features like Malham Cove, Kilnsey Crag, Gordale Scar and Gaping Ghyll.

The picturesque South Pennines Area of Outstanding Natural Beauty offers a different type of rural scenery. It is based predominantly on sand and gritstone, from which most of the towns and villages were built during the Industrial Revolution.

The Dales offer much scope for activities. Walking is the main recreation, whether gentle strolls, long distance inter-Hostel walks, or more challenging routes, such as the Three Peaks Walk.

Cycle routes have been set up in West Yorkshire and the Dales National Park passing close to many Hostels. There are also plenty of opportunities for caving, climbing, orienteering, water sports, horse riding and hang-gliding — all within easy reach of our Youth Hostels.

For those interested in history, the Dales offer stately homes, museums, ruined castles, industrial archaeology and traditional crafts.

Other interests can be satisfied with a visit to Brontë Country (stay at Haworth, Earby or Mankinholes). Or follow the paths walked by James Herriot through Wensleydale and Swaledale. You can also visit the picturesque village of Holmfirth which is featured in the popular television series 'Last of the Summer Wine'.

Useful Information

During Winter closed months, early Spring and late Autumn, many Youth Hostels are available for exclusive use by parties booked in advance. For further details please contact the appropriate Hostel.

Helpful Publications

Pennine Way Central Booking Service Information Pack —
including postage and packing £1.50
Herriot Way —
five day walking tour information pack .... please send A4 sae

The above publications are available from YHA Northern Regional Office, D Floor, Milburn House, Dean Street, Newcastle upon Tyne NE1 1LF. Tel: 091 221 2101.

AYSGARTH FALLS

64 BEDS

Youth Hostel,
Aysgarth, Leyburn,
North Yorkshire DL8 3SR
Aysgarth (0969) 663260

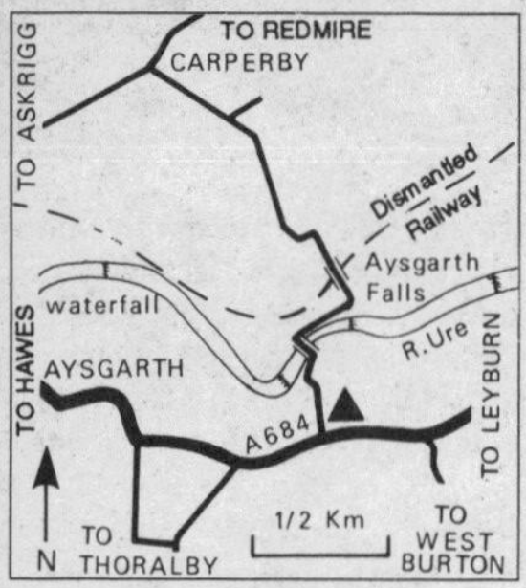

Overnight charge:
Young £3.80 Junior £4.70 Senior £5.90
C L 1 GSC
Evening meal 19.00 hrs. S PO Aysgarth. ECD Wed. P for cars and mini-buses only. Coaches at Motel at rear of Hostel

Jan 1-Feb 28	Closed
Mar 1-15	Open Fri & Sat
Mar 16-24	Closed
Mar 25-Sep 30	Open
Oct 1-31	Open (except Sun)
Nov 1-Dec 13	Open Fri & Sat
Dec 14-Jan 19 92	Closed
Jan 20-Feb 29	Open Fri & Sat

Large three storey building formerly a private school, on the main road through beautiful Wensleydale (Herriot Country) in Yorkshire Dales National Park. ½m E of Aysgarth on A684 to Leyburn at junction with road to Aysgarth Falls

OS 98 GR 012884 Bart 35

Attractions: Waterfalls at Aysgarth. Askrigg and Hawes. ¼m. Semerwater 9m. Earthworks on Addlebrough 6m. Roman Road, Bainbridge 5½m. Penhill (1685 ft) 4m. Carriage Museum by falls. Herriot Way. Car and mini-bus hire ¼m. Bolton Castle. Middleham Castle

United 26 from Richmond (infrequent) (connections from BR Darlington) (0325 468771); West Yorkshire Dales Bus (0423 566061)

Garsdale (not Sun, except May-Sep) 16m; Northallerton 24m; Skipton 28m

Next Youth Hostels: Grinton 8m. Hawes 10m. Kettlewell 14m (cyclists take care on Kidstones Hill)

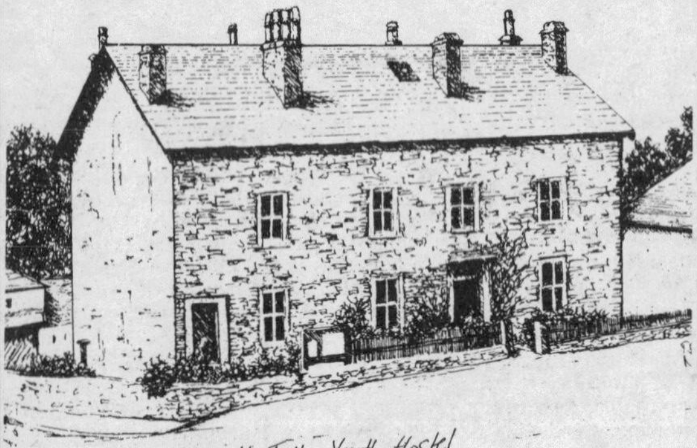

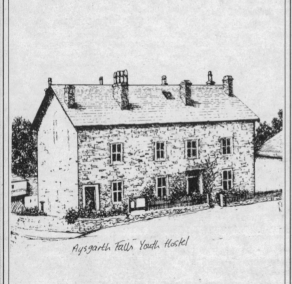

Aysgarth Falls Youth Hostel

Administrative Region: Northern

DENTDALE

40 BEDS

COMFORT IMPROVED

Youth Hostel,
Cowgill, Dent, Sedbergh,
Cumbria LA10 5RN
Dent (05875) 251

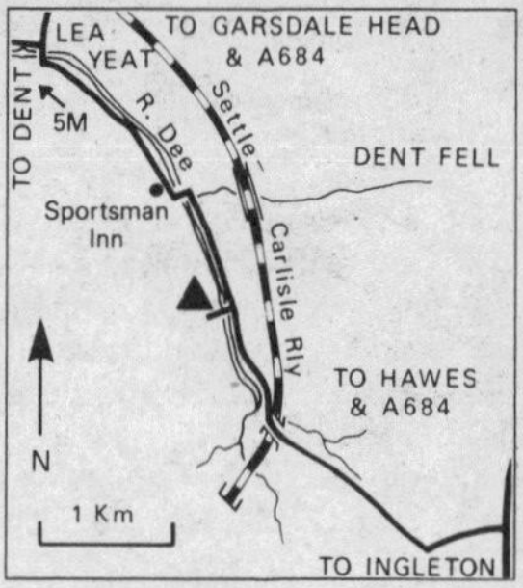

Overnight charge:
Young £3.50 Junior £4.40 Senior £5.50
1 GSC Evening meal 19.00 hrs. S PO Dent 6m. ECD Thu. P for cars and minibuses only. Coaches at viaduct. L

Jan 1-Feb 28	Closed
Mar 1-31	Open (except Wed & Thu)
Apr 1-Sep 30	Open (except Thu)
Oct 1-31	Open (except Wed & Thu)
Nov 1-Feb 29 92	Closed

Advance bookings may be accepted from groups during closed period: enquiries welcome

In a peaceful setting beside the River Dee, a former shooting lodge (listed building) in the Yorkshire Dales National Park. Marked on OS map as 'Deeside Ho'. On Dentdale road NE of Whernside, about 2m from junction with Hawes-Ingleton road, about 6m E of Dent. 7'6" width restriction at Cowgill; large vehicles approach via Newby Head

OS 98 GR 773850 Bart 34, 35

Attractions: Dent village. Whernside (2414 ft) 3m. Dales Way. Pennine Way 4m. Waterfalls. Arten Gill and Dent Head viaduct ½m. Introductory caving courses for groups arranged on request. Yorkshire Dales Cycleway.

As for Hawes, but alight Hawes, thence 8m

Dent (not Sun, except May-Sep) 2m; Giggleswick 17½m

Next Youth Hostels: Hawes 8m. Ingleton 11m. Stainforth 15m

Administrative Region: Northern

E ARBY
24 BEDS

Youth Hostel, Glen Cottage,
Birch Hall Lane, Earby, Colne,
Lancs BB8 6JX
☎ Burnley (0282) 842349

Overnight charge:
Young £3.10 Junior £4.00 Senior £5.10
⬚⬚⬚⬚⬚⬚ S Shops and ⬚ 1m.
⬚ Tue and Sat. P at centre of Earby
½m. Limited roadside parking for cars
and minibuses. Ask warden.

Jan 1-Mar 17	Closed
Mar 18-Nov 2	Open (except Mon) (but Open Bank Holiday Mondays)
Nov 3-Feb 29 92	Closed

Available for group and family
bookings during winter closed
period. Enquiries welcome to Hostel
or Northern Region Office.

The Katherine Bruce Glasier
Memorial Hostel. Cottage on NE
outskirts of town, about one mile
from Pennine Way, with picturesque
garden and waterfall, 300 yds past
Red Lion PH

OS 103 GR 915468 ⬚ 31, 32

Attractions: Pinhaw Beacon 2m.
Pendle Hill 8m. Castle and Museum
at Skipton 8m. Wycoller Country
Park. Yorkshire Dales Railway.
Embsay 9m. Pennine Way. Earby
Mining Museum (Sun and Thu).
Pendle Way

⬚ Various services from Burnley,
Skipton (passing close BR Colne &
Skipton), alight Earby, ½m
(☎ 0772 263333)

⬚ Colne 5m; Skipton 8m

Next Youth Hostels: Malham 15m.
(via Pennine Way). Linton 15m.
Haworth 17m (via Pennine Way).
Slaidburn 17m. Mankinholes 25m (via
Pennine Way)

E LLINGSTRING
18 BEDS

Youth Hostel, Lilac Cottage,
Ellingstring, Ripon,
North Yorkshire HG4 4PW
☎ (0677) 60216

Overnight charge:
Young £2.60 Junior £3.50 Senior £4.40
⬚⬚⬚⬚⬚ Small S Shops
Masham 6m. ⬚ East Witton 3m. P
for cars only. ⬚

Jan 1-Mar 21	Closed
Mar 22-Apr 6	Open
Apr 7-May 2	Closed
May 3-31	Open (except Wed & Thu)
Jun 1-Sep 7	Open
Sep 8-Oct 27	Open (except Wed & Thu)
Oct 28-Mar 26 92	Closed

Advance bookings may be accepted
from groups during winter closed
period: enquiries welcome

Special group rates during closed
periods — full details available from
Warden

Small cottage in isolated village just
outside the Yorkshire Dales National
Park, 4m NW of Masham,
Wensleydale

OS 99 GR 176835 ⬚ 35

Attractions: Jervaulx Abbey 2m.
Fountains Abbey 12m. East Witton
4m. Coverdale 5m. Druid's Temple
(folly). Ilton 3m. Middleham Castle
5m. Snape Castle 8m. ⬚⬚
Lightwater Valley Leisure Park 10m

⬚ United 159 (infrequent) from
Ripon to within 1m (☎ 0325
468771); otherwise postbus from
Ripon (☎ 0532 447470) or West
Yorkshire Dales Bus (☎ 0423 566061)

⬚ Thirsk 16m; Northallerton 17m

Next Youth Hostels: Grinton
Lodge 12m. Aysgarth 14m

Additional Information: Advance
bookings and enquiries to Mrs A.C.
Wright, Hollybreen, Ellingstring,
Ripon HG4 4PW

G RINTON LODGE
70 BEDS

Youth Hostel,
Grinton, Richmond,
North Yorkshire DL11 6HS
☎ Richmond (0748) 84206

Overnight charge:
Young £3.50 Junior £4.40 Senior £5.50
⬚⬚⬚⬚⬚⬚⬚ Evening meal
19.00 hrs. S ⬚ Grinton ¾m. ⬚⬚⬚

Jan 1-Mar 31	Open (except Sun & Mon)
Apr 1-Aug 31	Open
Sep 1-30	Open (except Sun)
Oct 1-Dec 28	Open (except Sun & Mon)
Dec 22, 23	Open
Dec 29-Feb 13 92	Closed
Feb 14-29	Open (except Sun & Mon)

Advance bookings may be accepted
from groups during winter closed
period: enquiries welcome

Built as shooting lodge, high on moors
above village; views of Swaledale and
Arkengarthdale in Yorkshire Dales
National Park. ¾m from Grinton due S
on Reeth-Leyburn road. Log fires

OS 98 GR 048975 ⬚ 35

Attractions: ⬚ Canoeing on River
Swale. Grazing available for ponies.
On Coast to Coast route. ⬚ Geology
(lead mines etc). Maiden Castle (pre-
historic earthworks) 1m. Reeth Folk
Museum 1½m. Richmond Castle 10m.
Tan Hill public house (highest in
England) 12m. ⬚ Herriot Way. Day
fishing permits for River Swale available,
contact warden. Yorkshire Dales
Cycleway. Swaledale Pony Trekking
Centre 1m (☎ 0748 84581). Barbecue
available — contact warden in advance

⬚ United 30 Richmond — Keld
(infrequent) (connections from BR
Darlington), alight Grinton, ¾m (☎
0325 468771); West Yorkshire Dales
Bus (☎ 0423 566061)

⬚ Kirkby Stephen (not Sun, except
May-Sep) 24m; Darlington 25m

Next Youth Hostels: Aysgarth 8m.
Keld 13m. Ellingstring 14m. Hawes
16m. Baldersdale 23m by path

4

YORKSHIRE DALES

Hawes

60 BEDS

COMFORT IMPROVED

Youth Hostel,
Lancaster Terrace, Hawes,
North Yorkshire DL8 3LQ
Hawes (0969) 667368

Overnight charge:
Young £4.00 Junior £5.10 Senior £6.30
[icons] [1] [icon] Evening meal 19.00
hrs. [S] Shops and [PO] nearby. [ED] Wed.
[P] for cars and coaches 300 yds. [L]

Jan 1-Feb 28	Closed
Mar 1-Mar 24	Open
	(except Tue & Wed)
Mar 25-Sep 22	Open
Sep 23-Dec 28	Open
	(except Tue & Wed)
Dec 24, 25	Open
Dec 29-Feb 13 92	Closed
Feb 14-29	Open
	(except Tue & Wed)

Advance bookings may be accepted
from groups during closed periods.
Enquiries welcome

Modern purpose-built Hostel in
Yorkshire Dales National Park.
Situated on a rise overlooking small
attractive market town and
Wensleydale beyond. Immediately W
of Hawes on Ingleton Road

[OS] 98 [GR] 867897 [Bus] 35

Attractions: Pennine Way and
Herriot Way. Hardraw Force (highest
single fall in England) 1m. Bainbridge
Roman fort 4m. Upper Dales folk
museum and ropemakers (visitors
welcome) in village. Buttertubs Pass
4m. Semerwater 5m. [i] Yorkshire
Dales Cycleway

[bus] United 26 from Richmond
(infrequent) (connections from BR
Darlington) (0325 468771); Mini
Bus service from BR Garsdale (May-
Sep) (0756 752748); West
Yorkshire Dales Bus (0423 566061).
Post Bus — Bedale - Hawes, Mon-Fri

[train] Garsdale (not Sun, except May-
Sep) 6m

Next Youth Hostels: Dentdale 8m.
Keld 9m. Aysgarth Falls 10m. Kirkby
Stephen 15m. Kettlewell 16m

Administrative Region: Northern

Haworth

90 BEDS

YH, Longlands Hall, Longlands
Drive, Lees Lane, Haworth,
Keighley, West Yorkshire BD22 8RT
Haworth (0535) 42234

Overnight charge:
Young £4.00 Junior £5.10 Senior £6.30
[icons] [3] [icon] Evening meal
18.30 hrs. [S] Shop and [PO] in village.
[ED] Tue. [P] for cars and coaches. [L]

Jan 1-27	Closed
Jan 28-Feb 28	Open (except Sun)
Mar 1-Oct 31	Open
Nov 1-16	Open (except Sun)
Nov 17-Jan 12 92	Closed
Jan 13-Feb 29	Open (except Sun)

Advance bookings may be accepted
from groups during closed periods.
Enquiries welcome

Built in 1884 for a local mill owner,
Victorian mansion set in substantial
grounds with interesting
architectural features in a
commanding position overlooking
the famous 'Bronte' village.
Renowned for its excellent
international cooking. 1m from
Haworth on Keighley road turn along
Longlands Drive

[OS] 104 [GR] 038378 [Bus] 32

Attractions: Guided walks for
groups. Bronte museum. Worth
Valley Steam Railway ½m. Pennine
Way. National Museum of
Photography, Bradford 8m. Cliffe
Castle Museum, Keighley 4m.
Saltaire Victorian village 10m.
Moorland walks. [U] [i]

[bus] Frequent from surrounding areas
(0535 603284)

[train] Keighley 4m; Haworth (Worth
Valley Rly) ½m

Next Youth Hostels: Mankinholes
12m (via Pennine Way 18m). Earby
(via Pennine Way 17m). York 45m

Administrative Region: Northern

Ingleton

74 BEDS

Youth Hostel, Greta Tower,
Ingleton, Carnforth,
Lancs LA6 3EG
Ingleton (05242) 41444

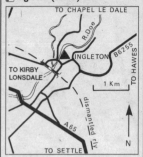

Overnight charge:
Young £3.50 Junior £4.40 Senior £5.50
[icons] [1] [icon] Evening meal 19.00 hrs.
[S] [PO] near. [ED] Thu. [P] in village beside
Community Centre. [L]

Jan 1-Feb 28	Open
	(except Mon & Tue)
Mar 1-30	Open (except Sun)
Apr 1-Aug 31	Open
Sep 1-Oct 31	Open (except Sun)
Nov 1-11	Open
	(except Mon & Tue)
Nov 12-Dec 27	Closed
Dec 28-Feb 29 92	Open
	(except Mon & Tue)
Dec 30, 31	Open

Enlarged cottage near centre of small
town (down lane between market
square and the swimming pool) on
edge of the Yorkshire Dales National
Park. A link Hostel between Dales
and Lakeland

[OS] 98 [GR] 695733 [Bus] 31, 32, 35

Attractions: Ingleborough (2373 ft)
4m. Glens and waterfalls 4m, circular
walk inc Thornton Force at 2m.
White Scar Caves 2½m. Whernside
(2424 ft) 6m. Open air heated public
swimming pool nearby (end May to
end Aug). North Lancs Cycleway 7m.
[i] Caving. [cycle] Yorkshire Dales
Cycleway. Children's playground
nearby

[bus] Ribble/Lancaster City 279, 280/1
from Lancaster (passes close BR
Lancaster & Bentham) (0772
263333)

[train] Bentham 3m; Clapham 4m

Next Youth Hostels: Stainforth
10m. Dentdale 11m. Slaidburn 18m

Administrative Region: Northern

1991 YHA Guide

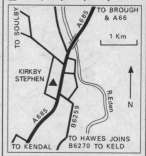

KELD

50 BEDS

Youth Hostel, Keld Lodge,
Upper Swaledale, Richmond,
North Yorkshire DL11 6LL
☎ Richmond (0748) 86259

Overnight charge:
Young £3.50 Junior £4.40 Senior £5.50
🏠 ♨ ② 🍴 Evening meal 19.00 hrs. Ⓢ
🅿🅞 Muker 3m. 🄴 Tue. Ⓛ

Jan 1-Feb 22	Closed
Feb 23-28	Open
	(except Mon & Tue)
Mar 1-Jun 30	Open (except Mon)
	(but Open Bank
	Holiday Mondays)
Jul 1-Aug 31	Open
Sep 1-Oct 31	Open (except Mon)
Nov 1-11	Open
	(except Mon & Tue)
Nov 12-Dec 27	Closed
Dec 28-Feb 29 92	Open
	(except Mon & Tue)
Dec 30, 31	Open

Former shooting lodge. Located ½m
from Pennine Way and at head of
Swaledale. Surrounded by moorland
and waterfalls. Situated W of Keld
village on B6270

ⓄⓈ 91, 92 ⒼⓇ 891009 🄱 35

Attractions: 🚶 In Yorkshire Dales
National Park. River Swale. Great
Shunner Fell (2349 ft). Pennine Way.
Coast to Coast footpath. Old Coffin
Road. Kisdon Force and other
waterfalls ½m. Buttertubs Pass 3m.
Tan Hill pub (highest in England) 5m.
Muker village 3m. Old lead mines.
Good area for wildflowers

🚌 United 30 from Richmond
(infrequent) (connections from BR
Darlington) (☎ 0325 468771); West
Yorkshire Dales Bus (☎ 0423 566061)

🚌 Kirkby Stephen (not Sun, except
May-Sep) 11m

Next Youth Hostels: Hawes 9m
(13m by Pennine Way). Kirkby
Stephen 10m. Grinton 13m.
Baldersdale 15m by Pennine Way.
Dentdale 16m. Aysgarth Falls 16m

Administrative Region: Northern

KETTLEWELL

48 BEDS

Youth Hostel, Whernside House,
Kettlewell, Skipton,
North Yorkshire BD23 5QU
☎ Kettlewell (075676) 232

Overnight charge:
Young £3.80 Junior £4.70 Senior £5.90
🏠 🗋 🍴 ④ 🍴 Evening meal 19.00 hrs.
Ⓢ 🅿🅞 50 yds. 🄴 Thu. Village hall
available for school groups by
arrangement. 🅿 in village. Leader
rooms. Special activity package
leaflet on request. Ⓛ

Jan 1-Feb 10	Closed
Feb 11-Mar 25	Open
	(except Sat & Sun)
Mar 26-Sep 30	Open
Oct 1-Dec 13	Open
	(except Sat & Sun)
Dec 14-Feb 9 92	Closed
Feb 10-29	Open
	(except Sat & Sun)

In centre of pretty Wharfedale village,
in Yorkshire Dales National Park.
Twinned with De Kleine Haar YH
Holland

ⓄⓈ 98 ⒼⓇ 970724 🄱 32, 35

Attractions: Dales Way. Great
Whernside (2310 ft). Buckden Pike
(2303 ft). Langstrothdale 5m. River
bathing. Ⓤ 🏊 Caving. 🎣 🚶

🚌 Keighley & District 71/2 from
Skipton (passes close BR Skipton),
alight Grassington 6m; also Dales Bus
(☎ 0535 603284)

🚉 Skipton 16m

Next Youth Hostels: Linton 8m.
Malham 10m by fell tracks (15m by
road). Aysgarth 14m (cyclists take
care on Kidstones Hill)

Administrative Region: Northern

KIRKBY STEPHEN

38 BEDS
COMFORT IMPROVED YHA

Youth Hostel, Fletcher Hill,
Market Street, Kirkby Stephen,
Cumbria CA17 4QQ
☎ Kirkby Stephen (07683) 71793

Overnight charge:
Young £3.80 Junior £4.70 Senior £5.90
🏠 🏠 room rate 🗋 ② 🍴 🅶🅢🅒 🍴
Evening meal 19.00 hrs. Ⓢ Shop and
🅿🅞 nearby. 🅿 Cars and coaches in
town. 🄴 Thu. Ⓛ

Jan 1-Feb 14	Closed
Feb 15-Mar 31	Open
	(except Tue & Wed)
Apr 1-Jun 30	Open (except Tue)
Jul 1-Aug 31	Open
Sep 1-30	Open (except Tue)
Oct 1-31	Open
	(except Tue & Wed)
Nov 1-Dec 16	Open Fri & Sat
Dec 17-Feb 13 91	Closed

Converted chapel in an interesting
market town, which is the focal point
of the upper Eden Valley. In centre of
town, S of market square. Easy
access from M6 (Junction 38)

ⓄⓈ 91 ⒼⓇ 774085 🄱 34, 35

Attractions: Nine Standards and
Wild Boar Fell. Coast to Coast Walk.
Eden Way. Cumbria Cycle Way. 🚣 in
Eden Valley. Howgill Fells 8m. Brough
Castle. Pendragon Castle.
Mallerstang Horseshoe. River
bathing. Within easy reach of
Yorkshire Dales and Lake District. 🄸
Settle-Carlisle railway

🚌 No service known

🚌 Kirkby Stephen (not Sun, except
May-Sep) 1½m

Next Youth Hostels: Tebay 10m.
Keld 10m. Baldersdale 15m by paths.
Dufton 15m. Hawes 15m. Dentdale
16m. Kendal 23m

🏠 Self-contained flat, sleeps up to 6.
No kitchen

Administrative Region: Northern

LINTON

(NR GRASSINGTON)

38 BEDS

Youth Hostel, The Old Rectory,
Linton-in-Craven, Skipton,
North Yorkshire BD23 5HH
☎ Grassington (0756) 752400

Overnight charge:
Young £4.00 Junior £5.10 Senior £6.30
🚻 🛏 2 🍴 GSC 🍳 Evening meal 19.00
🛆 S PO Grassington ⬛ Thu. P for
cars and minibuses only. Coaches ½m.
L

Jan 1-Feb 14	Closed
Feb 15-Mar 30	Open (except Sun & Mon)
Mar 31-Sep 30	Open (except Sun) (but Open Bank Holiday Sundays SC only)

Oct 1-Dec 21	Open (except Sun & Mon)
Dec 22-Feb 13 92	Closed
Feb 14-29	Open (except Sun & Mon)

17th century former rectory in one
of Wharfedale's most picturesque
and unspoilt villages. The Hostel has
recently been refurbished to provide,
amongst other things, smaller and
more comfortable dormitories,
improved washing facilities with
showers and better heating. Across
stream from village green

OS 98 GR 998627 Bart 32

Attractions: In Yorkshire Dales
National Park. On Dalesway and
Yorkshire Dales Cycleway. Pack
Horse Bridge. Linton Falls ½m (river
bathing). Ghaistrill's Strid 2m. Kilnsey
4m (Famous Crag. Trout farm/
aquarium, U). Stump Cross Caverns
5m. Grassington 1m (Folk museum.
National Park Information Centre).
Grass Wood Nature Reserve 3m. ⬛
◆

🚌 Keighley & District 71/2 from
Skipton (passes close BR Skipton)
(☎ 0756 795331); also Dales Bus
(☎ 0535 603284)

🚉 Skipton 8m

Next Youth Hostels: Kettlewell
8m. Malham 10m. Earby 15m

MALHAM

82 BEDS

John Dower Memorial Hostel,
Malham, Skipton,
North Yorkshire BD23 4DE
☎ Airton (07293) 321

Overnight charge:
Young £4.00 Junior £5.10 Senior £6.30
🚻 🛆 🍴 3 🍳 Evening meal 19.00
hrs. S PO in village (no Savings Bank
facilities). ⬛ Fri. P for cars and
minibuses only. Coaches in village. L
Coin-op Laundry

Jan 1-Feb 14	Closed
Feb 15-28	Open (except Sun & Mon)
Mar 1-18	Open (except Sun)
Mar 19-Sep 30	Open
Oct 1-Nov 11	Open (except Sun)
Nov 12-Dec 27	Closed
Dec 28-Feb 29 92	Open (except Sun & Mon)
Dec 29, 30	Open

A purpose built Youth Hostel in a
superb location close to the centre of
the picturesque village of Malham

OS 98 GR 901629 Bart 31, 32

Attractions: Malham Cove. Malham
Tarn. Janet's Foss 1m. Gordale Scar
2m. Kirby Malham church 1½m.
National Park Information Centre.
Pennine Way. 🛈 ◆ Caving. 🎣

🚌 Pennine 210 from Skipton (passes
close BR Skipton) (☎ 0756 749215);
West Yorkshire Dales Bus (☎ 0423
566061)

🚉 Gargrave 7m; Skipton 13m

Next Youth Hostels: Stainforth
8m. Kettlewell 10m. Linton 10m.
Earby 15m. Slaidburn 17m. Hawes
25m (via Pennine Way)

Linton Youth Hostel

Administrative Region: Northern

Administrative Region: Northern

MANKINHOLES HALL

Youth Hostel,
Mankinholes, Todmorden,
Lancs OL14 6HR
☎ Todmorden (0706) 812340

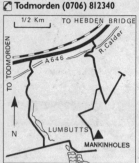

Overnight charge:
Young £3.50 Junior £4.40 Senior £5.50
👨‍👩 🏕 🚿 2 GSC 🍴 Evening meal 19.00
hrs. Table Licence for Beer and Wine
with evening meal. S Bread and milk
must be ordered in advance. Shop and
PO Todmorden. 🔌 Tue. P for cars and
minibuses only. Coaches 150 yds. L

Jan 1-Mar 24	Open (except Tue & Wed)
Mar 25-Sep 22	Open (except Wed)
Sep 23-Dec 16	Open (except Tue & Wed)
Dec 17-23	Closed
Dec 24-26	Open*
Dec 27-Feb 29 92	Closed

* Advance bookings only

Ancient manor house (listed building)
in a conservation village with typical
south Pennine architecture, half a mile
from Pennine Way and surrounded by
moorland. 2m ESE of Todmorden by
road. Calderdale way passes Hostel

OS 103 South Pennine Outdoor
Leisure Series GR 960235 🚲 31, 32

Attractions: Stoodley Pike 1m. U
Calderdale Way History trails.
Blackstone Edge 'Roman Road'.
Hollingworth Lake. Nature trails.
Amateur Astronomy centre, 🔭
Hebden Bridge 4m (Hardcastle
Craggs, Canal trips, Hang gliding
school, Clog factory, Automobile
Museum). Halifax 12m. (Piece Hall,
Shibden Hall, Folk Museum). Pennine
Way. 🛈

🚌 Yorkshire Rider T6 from
Todmorden (passes close BR
Todmorden) (☎ 0924 375555)

🚂 Todmorden 2m

Next Youth Hostels: Haworth 12m
(18m via Pennine Way). Crowden
24m (via Pennine Way). Earby 25m
(via Pennine Way)

SLAIDBURN

Youth Hostel, King's House,
Slaidburn, Clitheroe,
Lancs BB7 3ER
☎ Slaidburn (02006) 656

Overnight charge:
Young £2.60 Junior £3.50 Senior £4.40
🏕 2 🍴 GSC 🍴 Evening meal 19.00 hrs.
Small S PO closed Weds, Sat, Sun.
Shop open 7 days a week. P for cars
only, limited. L

Jan 1-Mar 8	Closed
Mar 9-May 31	Open (except Tue & Wed)
Jun 1-Aug 31	Open (except Sun)
Sep 1-Oct 28	Open (except Tue & Wed)
Oct 29-Feb 29 92	Closed

Once the 17th century 'Black Bull'
Inn, serves the Forest of Bowland
and is an important link between
Lakeland and the Yorkshire Dales.
Centre of Slaidburn village

OS 103 GR 711523 🚲 31, 32

Attractions: 300 square mile Area
of Outstanding Natural Beauty.
Pendle Hill ('home of witches') 10m.
Clitheroe Castle 9m. Sawley Abbey
7m. 15th century village church with
Norman Tower. Witches Way and
North Bowland Traverse long
distance walks. Lancashire Cycleway

🚌 Burnley & Pendle 110/1 from
Clitheroe (connections from BR
Blackburn) (☎ 0772 263333)

🚂 Long Preston 10m

Next Youth Hostels: Stainforth
15m. Ingleton 15m. Earby 17m.
Arnside 32m

YORKSHIRE DALES

4

50 BEDS

STAINFORTH

Youth Hostel, 'Taitlands', Stainforth, Settle, North Yorkshire BD24 9PA

Settle (07292) 3577

Overnight charge:
Young £3.80 Junior £4.70 Senior £5.90

Evening meal 19.00 hrs. Shop and PO in village. Wed (Settle), Tue (village). for cars and minibuses in grounds; coaches — ask warden. Classroom available

Jan 1-Feb 18	Closed
Feb 19-Mar 30	Open (except Sun & Mon)
Mar 31-Jun 30	Open (except Sun) (but Open Bank Holiday Sundays)
Jul 1-Aug 31	Open
Sep 1-Oct 31	Open (except Sun)
Nov 1-Dec 28	Open (except Sun & Mon)
Dec 22, 23	Open
Dec 29-Feb 13 92	Closed

An early Victorian listed building with fine staircase and plasterwork, much refurbished in recent years. Its extensive grounds include outdoor recreational space and grazing paddock. 2m north of Settle in the Yorkshire Dales National Park. ½m S of village on main Settle-Horton-in-Ribblesdale road. 3½m S of Pennine Way at Dale Head and 4m S of Pennine Way at Horton

OS 98 GR 821668 Marked at 'Taitlands' 31, 32

Attractions: Spectacular limestone area. Penyghent (2,273 ft) 4m. Packhorse Bridge and Stainforth Force 1m. Catrigg Force 1m. Victoria Cave 2m. Settle-Carlisle Railway. Settle 2m. (Folk museum.) Geology (faults, pavements, etc). Gaping Ghyll 7m. Pennine Way. Ribble Way and North Bowland Traverse long distance walks. Yorkshire Dales Cycleway. Caving and other activities available — details from wardens

Whaites Settle — Horton (07292 3235 or 3446) Also buses Skipton — Settle — Ingleton

Settle (not Sun, except May-Sep) 2½m; Giggleswick 3m

Next Youth Hostels: Malham 8m. Ingleton 10m. Kettlewell 12m. Dentdale 15m. Slaidburn 15m. Hawes 19m by Path

Stainforth Youth Hostel

Administrative Region: Northern

YORKSHIRE WOLDS, MOORS AND COAST

East Yorkshire contains three main types of landscape: the Wolds are primarily arable land, offering typical chalkland scenery with dry valleys and woods; the North York Moors (most of which are in the National Park) are the largest expanse of heather-covered moorland in the country; the coastal settlements built into the steep cliffs, from Saltburn to Scarborough, provide an excellent base for marine and coastal studies.

There are many long distance walks based on ancient tracks. Cyclists can enjoy many attractive by-roads and forest trails, as well as the challenge of steep roads in and out of the valleys and down to the sea. The moors lend themselves to other activities such as orienteering, rock climbing and water sports.

The area is steeped in history, from pre-historic burial mounds to the North York Moors Steam Railway. There are Roman roads, ruined castles and stone crosses marking routes between the many monasteries.

Other attractions in the area include many stately homes and, of course, the City of York. This city is a major tourist attraction, with its Minster, City Walls and many fine mediaeval buildings as well as the Jorvik Viking Centre.

Useful Information

During Winter closed months, early Spring and late Autumn, many Youth Hostels are available for exclusive use by parties booked in advance. For further details please contact the appropriate Hostel.

Helpful Publications

Cleveland Way Long Distance Footpath —
information sheet .... please send sae

The above publication is available from YHA Northern Regional Office, D Floor, Milburn House, Dean Street, Newcastle upon Tyne NE1 1LF. Tel: 091 221 2101.

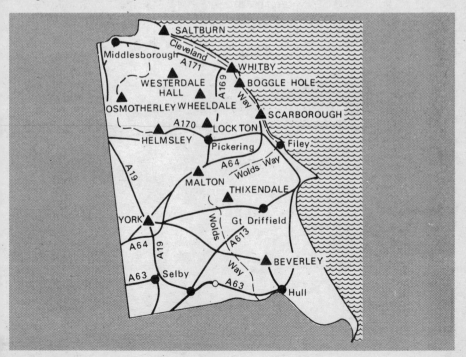

BEVERLEY FRIARY

34 BEDS

Youth Hostel, The Friary,
Friars' Lane, Beverley,
North Humberside HU17 0DF
📞 Hull (0482) 881751

Overnight charge:
Young £3.50 Junior £4.40 Senior £5.50
🏠 Ⓐ Ⓒ ① 🛏 ⓈⒼ Meals provided if
booked in advance. Ⓢ Shops and ⓅⓄ
nearby. ⒺⒹ Thu. Ⓟ cars and minibuses
only, coaches see warden. Ⓛ

Jan 1-Mar 14	Closed
Mar 15-May 31	Open (except Wed)
Jun 1-Aug 31	Open
Sep 1-Nov 2	Open (except Wed)
Nov 3-Feb 29 92	Closed

Group bookings may be accepted
during winter closed periods:
enquiries welcome

Restored medieval Dominican Friary
(listed building) mentioned in the
Canterbury Tales. ¼m SE of the town
centre and 100 yds NE of the Minster
on left side of Friars Lane off
Eastgate

ⓄⓈ 107 ⒼⓇ 038393 🗺 33

Attractions: The Minster. St Mary's
Church. North Bar. Swimming Baths.
National Museum of Army Transport.
Folk Festival. Skidby Mill 4m. Hull
10m. (Town Docks Museum.
Wilberforce House Museum. Ferens
Art Gallery. Old Town). 🦅 RSPB
Reserves at Hornsea Mere, Bempton
Cliffs and Blacktoft Sands. Wolds
Way. Hudson Way.

🚌 Frequent from surrounding areas
(📞 0482 881213)

🚆 Beverley ¼m

Next Youth Hostels: Thixendale
18m. Malton 28m. York 30m.
Scarborough 36m. Lincoln 47m.
Woody's Top 50m

BOGGLE HOLE

80 BEDS

Youth Hostel, Boggle Hole,
Mill Beck, Thorpe, Whitby,
North Yorkshire YO22 4UQ
📞 Whitby (0947) 880352

Overnight charge:
Young £4.00 Junior £5.10 Senior £6.30
🏠 Ⓐ Ⓒ Ⓠ 🛏 ④ 🍽 Evening meal
19.00 hrs. Ⓢ ⓅⓄ Fyling Thorpe and
Robin Hood's Bay. ⒺⒹ Wed. ⒻⓈ Ⓟ for
cars and coaches ¼m on road verge
near public car park. No parking on
beach road as this blocks road for
emergency access. Ⓛ

Jan 1-Feb 4	Closed
Feb 5-Mar 3	Open
	(except Sun & Mon)
Mar 4-Oct 26	Open
Oct 27-Dec 21	Open
	(except Sun & Mon)
Dec 22-Feb 29 92	Closed

An ideal centre for marine, coastal
and freshwater studies. Boggle Hole
also offers everything needed for
individual travellers, families and
groups

Field study facilities are
comprehensive and the Hostel
provides excellent residential
accommodation, day time access and
a full catering service

Former mill in a wooded ravine, with
the tides of Robin Hood's Bay coming
right up to its doorstep and the
North York Moors behind. 3m from
A171 Whitby-Scarborough.
Motorists use road signposted Boggle
Hole ¾m N of Flask Inn, 1½m S of
A171/B1416 junction. Walkers may
approach along beach if tide is out. If
tide in or coming in, use cliff path.
Cyclists may use beach, but not cliff
path. Walkers and cyclists may also
approach from Fyling Thorpe via
track from Farsyde Ho. Torch
essential on all routes after dark

ⓄⓈ North York Moors Tourist 94
ⒼⓇ 954040 🗺 36

Attractions: Robin Hood's Bay
village. Sea bathing. Cleveland Way.
Fossil hunting. Rock pools. Falling
Foss, moors. Eskdale and North York
Moors railways. 🌊 Sea 🏊 🅰
Archaeology

🚆 Tees & District 93A/B
Scarborough — Whitby (pass BR
Whitby & Scarborough), alight Robin
Hood's Bay, 1m (📞 0947 602146)

🚆 Whitby (not Sun, except May-Sep)
7m; Scarborough 15m

Next Youth Hostels: Whitby 7m.
Scarborough 13m. Wheeldale 15m
(13m by path)

Boggle Hole Youth Hostel

H ELMSLEY

40 BEDS

COMFORT IMPROVED YHA

**Youth Hostel,
Carlton Lane, Helmsley,
York YO6 5HB**
☎ Helmsley (0439) 70433

Overnight charge:
Young £3.80 Junior £4.70 Senior £5.90
[symbols] Evening meal 19.00 hrs.
⑤ Shops nearby. 🄴 Wed. [PO]
Helmsley (closed Sat afternoon)

Jan 1-Mar 4	Closed
Mar 5-25	Open
	(except Sun & Mon)
Mar 26-Apr 6	Open
Apr 7-30	Open (except Sun)
May 1-Aug 31	Open
Sep 1-Oct 31	Open (except Sun)
Nov 1-Dec 21	Open Fri & Sat
Dec 22-Jan 31 92	Closed
Feb 1-29	Open Fri & Sat

Purpose-built as a Hostel in North York Moors National Park near centre of small market town. ½m E of Helmsley Market Place at junction of Carlton Road and Carlton Lane.

[OS] North York Moors Tourist 100
[GR] 616840 [Bus] 36

Attractions: Start of Cleveland Way and Ebor Way. Helmsley Castle. Market Fri. Rievaulx Abbey and Terrace 2½m. [symbols] Ryedale Folk Museum 9m. North York Moors Railway 14m. Pickering Castle, Beck Isle Museum 14m

🚌 Scarborough & District 128 from Scarborough (passes close BR Scarborough) (☎ 0723 375463). Limited services from York (☎ 03476 237) and Thirsk: United

🚆 Thirsk 15m; Malton 16m; York 24m

Next Youth Hostels: Malton 17m. Lockton 19m. Wheeldale 21m over moors (31m by road). Osmotherley 15m (road), 20m Cleveland Way

---

L OCKTON

26 BEDS

**Youth Hostel, The Old School,
Lockton, Pickering,
North Yorkshire YO18 7PY**
☎ (Warden) Pickering (0751) 60376

Overnight charge:
Young £2.60 Junior £3.50 Senior £4.40
[symbols] ⑤ Shop and [PO] nearby. 🄴
Sat. [P] for cars and coaches in Hostel yard. Do not park in village square please

Jan 1-Mar 17	Open Fri & Sat
Mar 18-Oct 19	Open (except Sun)
	(but open Bank
	Holiday Sundays)
Oct 20-Feb 29 92	Closed

Available for group and family bookings during winter closed period: enquiries welcome

The former village school. In North York Moors National Park, on the edge of Newtondale and surrounded by forest and moorland. Village centre, next to church

[OS] North York Moors Tourist 94, 100
[GR] 844900 [Bus] 36

Attractions: Dalby Forest drive. Newtondale Gorge. Pickering Castle 5m. North Yorks Moors Steam Railway 2m. Forest trails. Flamingoland Zoo 9m

🚆 York City & District 92, 840 Whitby – Malton (passes close BR Whitby & Malton) (☎ 0904 624161)

🚌 Malton 14m; Levisham (North York Moors Rly & connecting with BR at Grosmont) 2m

Next Youth Hostels: Wheeldale 11m (8m by path). Malton 14m. Scarborough 19m (12m by path). Helmsley 19m

---

M ALTON

60 BEDS

**Youth Hostel, Derwent Bank,
York Road, Malton,
North Yorkshire YO17 0AX**
☎ Malton (0653) 692077

Overnight charge:
Young £3.50 Junior £4.40 Senior £5.50
[symbols] Evening meal 19.00 hrs. ⑤ [PO] Malton. 🄴 Thu.
[P] for cars and minibuses only.
Coaches ¾m

Jan 1-28	Closed
Jan 29-Mar 17	Open
	(except Sun & Mon)
Mar 18-Apr 30	Open (except Sun)
	Open Bank Hol Sun
May 1-Aug 31	Open
Sep 1-Nov 2	Open (except Sun)
Nov 3-Dec 23	Closed
Dec 24-26	Open*
Dec 27-Jan 27 92	Closed
Jan 28-Feb 29	Open
	(except Sun & Mon)

* Advance bookings only

Large Victorian house on bank of River Derwent, on edge of the Roman Settlement of Derventio and centrally placed for York, coast, moors and Wolds. Last house on left leaving Malton on York road, B1248

[OS] 100 [GR] 779711 [Bus] 33, 36

Attractions: Roman museum. Cattle market. Swimming Pool. Priory Church. Kirkham Priory 5m. Castle Howard 6m. Flamingoland Zoo and Funpark 5m. Pickering 8m. (Castle, Beck Isle Folk Museum. North York Moors Steam Railway. Pony Trekking). [symbols] at Hostel. Eden Camp Museum 2m. [i]

🚌 From surrounding areas
(☎ 0904 624161)

🚆 Malton ¾m

Next Youth Hostels: Thixendale 10m. Lockton 14m. Helmsley 17m. York 19m. Wheeldale 20m (via Stape). Scarborough 27m. Beverley 28m

Additional Information: To contact resident members ☎ (0653) 692664

5

YORKSHIRE WOLDS MOORS AND COAST

OSMOTHERLEY

Youth Hostel, Cote Ghyll, Osmotherley, Northallerton, North Yorkshire DL6 3AH
☎ (060983) 575

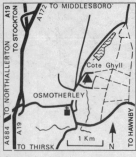

Overnight charge:
Young £3.80 Junior £4.70 Senior £5.90
🚿 🅰 C 📷 ▥ 2 🍴 Evening meal 19.00 hrs. S P0 in village. P for cars and coaches. ED Wed (all day). Pool table. C Daytime access by arrangement with warden. L

Jan 1-31	Closed
Feb 1-Mar 28	Open Fri & Sat
Mar 29-Sep 8	Open
Sep 9-24	Closed
Sep 25-Oct 27	Open
	(except Sun & Mon)
Oct 28-Dec 28	Closed
Dec 29-Jan 1 92	Open
Jan 2-Feb 6	Closed
Feb 7-28	Open Fri & Sat

Advance bookings may be accepted from parties of 20 or more during closed period: enquiries welcome

Situated within the North York Moors National Park the Hostel is an ideal residential centre for groups

Fully modernised the building has excellent facilities including a classroom. It is surrounded by woodland and only minutes from open hill country

The area is rich in flora and fauna, has great historic interest and is excellent for outdoor recreation

OS 100 (but village is on 99) Leisure Map North York Moors West
GR 461981 Bart 35, 36

Attractions: Coast to Coast footpath. Cleveland Way. Lyke Wake Walk. White Rose Walk. Mount Grace Priory 2m. Newton Dale steam railway. Sutton Bank, nature trail. U 4m

🚌 United 295 Stokesley — Northallerton, with connections from Middlesbrough (passes close BR Northallerton), alight Osmotherley Village Cross, ½m (☎ 0325 468771)

🚉 Northallerton 8m

Next Youth Hostels: Helmsley 15m (20m by Cleveland Way). Westerdale Hall 20m. Ellingstring 23m. Saltburn 25m (31m by path). Grinton 31m. York 33m

Additional Information: Answerphone Service when Hostel is closed

Osmotherley Youth Hostel

Administrative Region: Northern

SCARBOROUGH

Youth Hostel, The White House, Burniston Road, Scarborough, North Yorkshire YO13 0DA
☎ Scarborough (0723) 361176

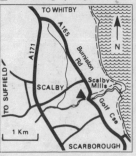

Overnight charge:
Young £3.50 Junior £4.40 Senior £5.50
🚿 🅰 ▥ 1 🍴 Evening meal 19.00 hrs. S ED Wed (not summer). P for cars and minibuses only. Coach park in town — warden will advise. L

Jan 1-Feb 28	Open Fri & Sat
Mar 1-27	Open
	(except Wed & Thu)
Mar 28-Apr 10	Open
Apr 11-May 23	Open (except Thu)
May 24-Jun 5	Open
Jun 6-30	Open (except Thu)
Jul 1-Sep 14	Open
Sep 15-Oct 31	Open
	(except Wed & Thu)
Nov 1-Dec 21	Open Fri & Sat
Dec 22-29	Closed
Dec 30-Jan 4 92	Open for New Year
Jan 5-Feb 29	Open Fri & Sat

Advance bookings may be accepted during winter closed periods: enquiries welcome

Ten minutes from the sea and 30 minutes from the moors, a converted watermill on the outskirts of the popular holiday resort. 2m N of town on sea road to Burniston, past Golf course, at bottom of hill. White building on river bank near bridge

OS North York Moors Tourist 101
GR 026907 Bart 36

Attractions: Cleveland Way. North York Moors National Park. Castle 1½m. Open air pool 1m. Hackness. Forge Valley 3m. Museum. Anne Bronte's grave. Fishing port. Forest drives and nature trails. Water ski-ing boats for hire. 🛈 🚲 U 🏊

🚌 Frequent from surrounding areas (☎ 0723 375463)

🚉 Scarborough 2m

Next Youth Hostels: Boggle Hole 13m. Lockton 19m (12m by path). Malton 27m. Thixendale 25m. Beverley 36m

Administrative Region: Northern

SALTBURN-BY-THE-SEA

72 BEDS

Youth Hostel, Riftswood Hall,
Victoria Road, Saltburn-by-the-Sea,
Cleveland TS12 1JD

📞 Guisborough (0287) 624389

Overnight charge:
Young £3.50 Junior £4.40 Senior £5.50
🛏 5 rooms available Ⓐ Ⓒ 🗐 ② ▼ 🅢🅢
🍽 Evening meal 19.00 hrs. Snack
meals available between 20.00-21.30
hrs. Ⓢ 🄿🄾 ½m. 🄴🄾 Tue. 🄵🅂 (including
urban studies room). 🄿 Pool and
table tennis. Ⓛ

Dec 28-Jan 2 91	Open
Jan 3-Feb 28	Closed
Mar 1-Apr 30	Open (except Sun)
Mar 31, Apr 7	Open
May 1-Aug 31	Open
Sep 1-Oct 31	Open (except Sun)
Nov 1-Dec 21	Open (except Sun & Mon)
Dec 22-28	Closed
Dec 29-Jan 1 92	Open
Jan 2-Feb 29	Closed

Advance bookings may be accepted
from parties during winter closed
period: enquiries welcome

The Hostel lies in extensive wooded
surroundings overlooking the
beautiful Riftswood valley. It has a
comprehensive range of Field Study
facilities including an Urban Study
Centre. Industrial visits to ICI and
British Steel, are popular with
Groups who use the Hostel. Nearby
is some of the finest coastal scenery
in Britain with low lying sandy
beaches backed by soaring cliffs

Along the coast are seaside resorts
and fishing villages, such as Staithes,
Runswick Bay and Redcar. From
Saltburn there is easy access into the
North York Moors National Park
which again is ideal for Study Groups

The Hostel has four family
dormitories (advance booking
essential), is comfortably furnished
and offers a full catering service

Location:
In Victoria Road, overlooking
Riftswood. From the Cleveland way:
stay on the path, and look for the
YHA sign. A stepped path by this sign
leads you into the Hostel grounds

🄾🅂 North York Moors Tourist 94
🄶🅁 662206 📟 36

Attractions: Cleveland Way 100
mtrs. Beach and seaside amusements
1m. Coastal scenery. Riftswood
Valley behind Hostel. North York
Moors National Park 5m. North York
Moors Steam Railway. 🚉 Saltburn

🚌 Frequent from surrounding areas
(📞 0642 210131)

🚆 Saltburn ½m

Next Youth Hostels: Westerdale
Hall 12m. Whitby 20m. Osmotherley
25m (31m by path)

THIXENDALE

18 BEDS

Youth Hostel, The Village Hall,
Thixendale, Malton,
North Yorkshire YO17 9TG

📞 Warden: Driffield (0377) 88238

Overnight charge:
Young £2.60 Junior £3.50 Senior £4.40
Ⓐ ① ▼ 🅢🅢 🅇 Small store and 🄿🄾 at
warden's house opposite (🄴🄾 🄿🄾 Sat).
Bread and milk if ordered in advance.
No smoking in hostel. 🄿 for cars and
coaches

Jan 1-Mar 22	Closed
Mar 23-Apr 6	Open
Apr 7-May 2	Closed
May 3-6	Open
May 7-23	Open Fri & Sat
May 24-Sep 28	Open (except Tue)
Sep 29-Feb 29 92	Closed

The old school in a quiet village on
the Wolds Way, near the foot of a
remarkable chalk dry valley

🄾🅂 100 🄶🅁 843610 📟 33

Attractions: Wharram Percy 'lost'
medieval village 2½m. Sledmere
House 6m. Castle Howard 16m.
North Wolds Family Walk. Wolds
Way. Ideal cycling country. The
Centenary Way Middle Distance
Walk. Burnby Hall Gardens 10m.
Millington Woods 7m. Ⓛ

🚌 East Yorks 135 from Driffield
(infrequent) (passing close BR
Driffield), alight Fridaythorpe, 3m
(📞 0377 42133)

🚆 Malton 10m

Next Youth Hostels: Malton 10m.
York 17m. Scarborough 25m.
Beverley 18m

Administrative Region: Northern

Administrative Region: Northern

W ESTERDALE HALL
54 BEDS

Youth Hostel, Westerdale Hall,
Westerdale, Whitby,
North Yorkshire YO21 2DU
☎ **Guisborough (0287) 660469**

Overnight charge:
Young £3.10 Junior £4.00 Senior £5.10
🚿 🔺 1 ▼ 🆑 ⓘⓞ Evening meal 19.30 hrs. No meals provided Mon night and Tue morning. Ⓢ ⓅⓄ village 300 yds. Day Ⓕⓢ by arrangement with Danby Lodge. Ⓟ

Jan 1-Mar 18	Closed
Mar 19-May 6	Open (except Mon) (but open Bank Holiday Monday)
May 7-13	Closed
May 14-Jul 7	Open (except Mon) (but open Bank Holiday Monday)
Jul 8-Aug 31	Open
Sep 1-21	Open (except Mon)
Sep 22-Oct 7	Closed
Oct 8-Nov 3	Open (except Sun & Mon)
Nov 4-Feb 29 92	Closed

Advance bookings may be accepted during winter closed periods: enquiries welcome

Turreted building, former shooting lodge, with spectacular views from all windows, in North York Moors National Park, 300 yds down lane by telephone kiosk.

Ⓞⓢ North York Moors Tourist 94
Ⓖⓡ 662059 ▦ 36

Attractions: Samaritan Way and Rosedale Circuit through Westerdale village. Coast to Coast footpath 2m. Lyke Wake Walk 2m. Ralph's Cross 2m. Cleveland Way 4m. Danby Lodge National Park Centre (day field study centre) 5m. Farndale Nature Reserve 7m. Hutton-le-Hole Folk Museum 12m.

🚌 No service

🚍 Castleton Moor (not Sun, except May-Sep) 3m

Next Youth Hostels: Saltburn 12m. Wheeldale 16m (footpath 14m). Whitby 18m. Helmsley 20m (17m over moor). Osmotherley 20m

Administrative Region: Northern

W HEELDALE
33 BEDS

Youth Hostel, Wheeldale Lodge,
Goathland, Whitby,
North Yorkshire YO22 5AP
☎ **Whitby (0947) 86350**

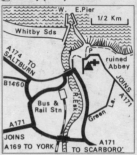

Overnight charge:
Young £2.60 Junior £3.50 Senior £4.40
🔺 1 ▼ 🆑 ⓘⓞ Evening meal 19.00 hrs. Ⓢ ⓅⓄ Goathland (closed Saturday afternoon). Ⓟ on roadside ¼m (above Hunt House). Access to hostel for mini-buses. Ⓛ

Jan 1-Feb 28	Closed
Mar 1-Nov 2	Open (except Wed)
Nov 3-Feb 29 92	Closed

Available for group bookings during winter closed periods. Enquiries to Hostel or Northern Regional Office.

Former shooting lodge surrounded by moorland in the heart of the North York Moors National Park. 2½m SW of Goathland ¼m beyond Hunt House. Cyclists approaching from Pickering or Wrelton proceed N through Stape and after 2m turn right down track alongside Roman road. After ¾m bear right down track to stepping stones and hostel. Look for signpost on crest of hill. Good map required. No access for motor cars within ½m of hostel. Torch advisable

Ⓞⓢ North York Moors Tourist 94, 100
Ⓖⓡ 813984 ▦ 36

Attractions: Well preserved section of Roman road ½m. Newtondale Gorge 3m. North York Moors Steam Railway 3m. Fen Bog 3m. Beck Hole 4m. Waterfalls. Coast to Coast Walk. Field studies programme available for schools and groups. Ⓕ (Wainstones). ☒

🚌 York City & District 92, 840 Malton – Whitby (passes close BR Malton & Whitby), alight near Goathland, 2m (☎ 0904 624161)

🚍 Grosmont (not Sun, except May-Sep) 6m; Goathland (North York Moors Rly & connecting with BR at Grosmont) 3m

Next Youth Hostels: (By path) Lockton 8m. Whitby 14m. Boggle Hole 13m. Westerdale 14m

Administrative Region: Northern

W HITBY
66 BEDS

Youth Hostel,
East Cliff, Whitby,
North Yorkshire YO22 4JT
☎ **Whitby (0947) 602878**

Overnight charge:
Young £3.50 Junior £4.40 Senior £5.50
🔺 ▼ 🆑 ⓘⓞ Ⓢ ⓅⓄ Whitby ½m. ⓔⓞ Wed. Ⓟ public nearby Ⓛ

Jan 1-Feb 28	Closed
Mar 1-21	Open Fri, Sat & Sun
Mar 22-Apr 6	Open
Apr 7-30	Open (except Sun)
May 1-Aug 31	Open
Sep 1-14	Open (except Sun)
Sep 15-Oct 31	Open (except Sun & Mon)
Nov 1-30	Open Fri, Sat & Sun
Dec 1-Jan 31 92	Closed
Feb 1-29	Open Fri, Sat & Sun

Advance bookings for parties may be accepted during winter closed period: enquiries welcome

Converted stable range near Abbey, on Cleveland Way and high above harbour of ancient fishing town on edge of North York Moors National Park. At top of 199 steps leading to Abbey. Cyclists from Scarborough direction are advised to come up by Green Lane at S end of town

Ⓞⓢ North York Moors Tourist 94
Ⓖⓡ 902111 ▦ 36

Attractions: Abbey and old St Mary's parish church adjacent to hostel. Beach, indoor swimming pool, seaside amusements. Boating. Cliff and coastal scenery Mulgrave Woods 2½m. North York Moors steam railway. Grosmont-Pickering 8m. Museum (Captain Cook) ¾m. Fossils. ☒ ⓘ

🚍 Frequent from surrounding areas (☎ 0947 602146)

🚍 Whitby (not Sun, except May-Sep) ½m

Next Youth Hostels: Boggle Hole 7m. Wheeldale 11m. Westerdale 18m. Saltburn 20m. Scarborough 20m

Administrative Region: Northern

Y ORK

Peter Rowntree Memorial Hostel, Haverford, Water End, Clifton, York YO3 6LT
☎ York (0904) 653147

TO THIRST
CLIFTON A19
B1363
WATER END
R.Ouse
Railway
yards York
Stn. The
Minster
A59
1224 A64
TO WETHERBY A19
A64
TO LEEDS TO SELBY
TO MALTON
N

Overnight charge:
Young £5.50 Junior £7.00 Senior £8.30
Supplementary charge Jun-Aug:
Senior £1.00

Ⓜ Ⓗ ⓌⒸ Ⓒ ▥ ④ Ⓢ Ⓒ Pre-booked meals and cafeteria facilities — 07.30-09.00, 17.30-20.00 hrs. Coin-op laundry. Ⓢ Ⓟ Clifton. ▣ Wed. Ⓟ for cars and coaches. Travel Ⓔ Ⓛ

Jan 1-6	Closed
Jan 7-Dec 7	Open
Dec 8-Jan 5 92	Closed
Jan 6-Feb 29	Open

Former home of Rowntree family with purpose built extensions just 20 minutes' walk from the centre of one of the most interesting and historic cities in Britain. Take main Thirsk road (A19) from City Centre and turn left at Clifton Green or follow riverside footpath from station.

Extensive building and refurbishment in recent years has provided a complete new wing, and improved washroom and shower facilities throughout the Hostel. All bedrooms have their own wash basin and individual bedlights. Most have only four beds. There is a large comfortable lounge in the new wing. The catering has been completely re arranged to provide cafeteria service. Groups booking in advance can still sit down together for traditional meals at a time which can be agreed with the Wardens.

ⓄⓈ 105 ⒼⓇ 589528 🏳 32, 33

Attractions: The ancient city of York is one of the main tourist attractions in the north of England. Modern archaeology has brought to light much of its past, notably in the crypt of York Minster and the Jorvik Museum. You can walk along the mediaeval City Walls and visit the magnificent Gothic Minster, now

happily restored after the fire of 1984. Old streets have been preserved, like the Shambles. There are many other historic buildings to visit — the Teasurer's House, St. Mary's Abbey, Clifford's Tower, Fairfax House, the Merchant Adventurers' Hall. York is also famous for its museums, notably the National Railway Museum, the Castle Museum and the City Art Gallery. In addition there is the Yorkshire Museum, the Friargate Wax Museum and the Regimental Museum of the 4/7th Royal Dragoon Guards and the Prince of Wales Own Regiment of Yorkshire. You can also take boat trips on the River Ouse. As a principal road and rail centre, York is a good place to start touring the rest of Yorkshire — the Dales, Wolds and North York Moors.

🚌 Frequent from surrounding areas
(☎ 0904 624161)

🚉 York 1m

Next Youth Hostels: Thixendale 17m. Malton 19m. Helmsley 25m. Beverley 30m. Osmotherley 33m. Haworth 45m

Additional Information: Reception Office open 07.00-23.30 hrs.

York Youth Hostel

Administrative Region: Northern

YORKSHIRE WOLDS MOORS AND COAST

5

6 PEAK DISTRICT

The Peak District has many outstanding features ranging from the show caves and caverns at Castleton to great houses like Chatsworth and Haddon Hall. It is an area steeped in history, but the biggest attraction is the magnificent scenery, a walker's paradise of limestone valleys and gorges, soaring gritstone edges and wild unspoilt moorland.

Walkers enjoy the choice of easy safe lowland rambles rarely far from a river such as the Dove, Derwent or Wye, to the first and one of the toughest sections of the 270 mile Pennine Way, rising up from Edale to the vast Plateau of Kinder Scout and Bleaklow.

For cyclists the lanes and roads linking beautiful towns and villages offer splendid routes between Youth Hostels. There are also easy rides along former railway routes, such as the famous Tissington Trail, High Peak Trail and Monsal Trail.

The number and variety of edges, of both gritstone and limestone, make the area a centre for rock climbing that attracts both novices and experts alike.

If you wish to spend an interesting or entertaining break with the family the variety of places to visit are numerous. The internationally famous pleasure park at Alton Towers and Gulliver's Kingdom at Matlock Bath thrill the children, whilst the unique cable cars at The Heights of Abraham give excitement to all ages. Learn about our industrial heritage at the Chatterley Whitfield Mining and Gladstone Pottery Museums at Stoke on Trent or the history of cotton production at Quarry Bank, Styal. Eyam reminds us of the sacrifice made by the villagers long ago to prevent the spread of the plague in 1665 and is famous for its Well Dressing, a tradition unique to this area and carried on by many villages at different times during the Summer.

Should you wish to take part in an organised activity many of our Youth Hostels run a variety of breaks designed to develop and improve personal skills varying from hang gliding to bat watching and caving to paper making. All the instructors are qualified in their particular field and, whilst safety is our first consideration, all activities are designed to be fun and are an excellent way of making new friends. A brochure

is available from National Office.

The Peak National Park was the first to be so designated and all building is controlled by the Planning Board ensuring the future well-being of the area. The contrast of scenery between the northern "Dark" and southern "White" Peak together with the western Staffordshire Moorlands make it a fascinating place to visit time and time again.

Families are especially welcome in our Hostels and most, especially the larger ones, offer small rooms that can be reserved in advance. These are, of course, extremely popular and should be booked as early as possible. There is usually plenty of accommodation available during school holidays but beds should be booked early in the Summer and Autumn school terms.

Discounts — have been negotiated on admission charges to various attractions in the Peak District.

Cycle Hire — Peak National Park operates a cycle hire scheme from 8 centres. Further information from Parsley Hay (029884) 493.

Inter-Hostel Walks — For details of routes contact: Inter-Hostel Walks, YHA Central Region, P.O. Box 11, Matlock, Derbyshire DE4 2XA.

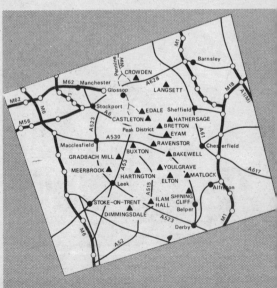

BAKEWELL 38 BEDS

**Youth Hostel,
Fly Hill, Bakewell,
Derbyshire DE4 1DN**
☎ Bakewell (0629) 812313

Overnight charge:
Young £3.50 Junior £4.40 Senior £5.50
🏠 🔺 1 💤 🍴 Evening meal 18.30 hrs.
🅂 🔒 Thu. 🅿🄾 Bakewell. 🅿 for cars
short term only. Long term and
coaches 300 yds

Jan 1-31	Closed
Feb 1-Mar 21	Open Fri & Sat
Mar 22-Nov 2	Open (except Thu)
Nov 3-Dec 21	Open Fri & Sat
Dec 22-Jan 30 92	Closed
Jan 31-Feb 29	Open Fri & Sat

When Hostel is closed bookings may
be accepted from parties; please
enquire

Small, purpose built Hostel close to
centre of market town famous for
pastry cake, in Peak District National
Park. Off North Church Street

🆗 119 Peak District Tourist
🆖 215685 🚆 29

Attractions: Monday Market. Parish
Church. Castle Hill earthwork.
Bakewell pudding shop. Well dressing
and carnival (July). Bakewell Show
(Aug). Old House Museum. Haddon
Hall 2m. Chatsworth House 4m.
Arbor Low stone circle 6m. Lathkill
Dale 3m. Alton Towers 40m. Heights
of Abraham and Cable Car, Matlock
Bath 12m. 🄸 in town. 🅻

🚌 Frequent from surrounding areas
(☎ 0332 292200)

🚉 Matlock 8m

Next Youth Hostels: Youlgrave
3½m. Ravenstor 7m. Elton 7m. Eyam
8m. Hartington 8m. Matlock 8m.
Hathersage 9m. Buxton 12m

BRETTON 18 BEDS

**Nr Eyam. Bookings c/o John &
Elaine Whittington, 7 New Bailey,
Crane Moor, nr. Sheffield S30 7AT**
☎ Sheffield (0742) 884541

Overnight charge:
Young £3.10 Junior £4.00 Senior £5.10
🔺 🏠 🔺 🚿 🆒 School parties, groups
and family accommodation midweek
by booking in advance. 🅇 — all food
must be brought. No 🅂 🄿🄾 Eyam
1¾m. 🅿 for cars and minibuses only;
coaches nearby ask booking
secretary. No resident warden

**Open every Saturday and Bank
Holiday Sundays with voluntary
Warden (except Xmas)**

Small purpose-built Hostel on 1250 ft
contour with breathtaking views
over Bretton Clough to the moors
and the edges of the Dark Peak
beyond. 1¾m NW of Eyam and is a
good centre for visiting many points
of interest in the Peak National Park

🆗 119 Peak District Tourist
🆖 200780 🚆 29

Attractions: Hostel situated high on
Eyam Edge on the boundary of the
Dark and White Peak. Bretton
Clough, scenic walks and 🌙 on Eyam
Edge. Gliding at Camphill 2m. Eyam
Church and plague monument 2m.
Chatsworth House 7m. 🅵 at Stoney
Middleton 3m. Frogatt and Stanage
edges 6m. 🚲 Monsal Head 7m and 🅄
Curbar Riding Stable 4m. 🅻

🚌 Various services from Sheffield,
Buxton & Chesterfield (passing close
BR Sheffield, Buxton & Chesterfield),
alight Foolow, 1m (☎ 0298 23098)

🚉 Gringleford 4m; Hathersage 4m

Next Youth Hostels: Eyam 1½m.
Hathersage 5m. Ravenstor 6m.
Bakewell 7m. Castleton 7m. Buxton
12m

BUXTON 65 BEDS

**Youth Hostel, Sherbrook Lodge,
Harpur Hill Road, Buxton,
Derbyshire SK17 9NB**
☎ Buxton (0298) 22287

Overnight charge:
Young £3.50 Junior £4.40 Senior £5.50
🏠 🔺 1 💤 🍴 Evening meal 19.00 hrs.
🅂 🄿🄾 Buxton. 🄴🄳 Wed. 🅿 for cars and
coaches

Jan 6-Feb 17	Closed
Feb 18-Nov 2	Open (except Sun)
Nov 5-Dec 14	Open (except Sun & Mon)
Dec 15-Feb 13 92	Closed
Feb 14-29	Open (except Sun)

Former home of wealthy quarry
owner, in woodland by spa town at
1,000 ft surrounded by Peak District
National Park. Accessible by public
transport from major cities. S side of
Buxton, ½m on Ashbourne Road
from Market Place (where Harpur
Hill Road meets Ashbourne Road).
Marked as Sherbrook Lodge on 🆗

🆗 119 Peak District Tourist
🆖 062722 🚆 28, 29

Attractions: Micrarium in town
centre. Poole's Cavern 1m. Goyt
Valley 4m. Pavilion gardens, indoor
swimming pool. The Crescent.
Solomon's Temple ½m. Opera House
(Festival in Jul/Aug). Museum and Art
Gallery. Well dressing and fair (Jul). 🄸
in town. 🅵 and walking areas nearby.
🚲 Parsley Hay 8m. 🅄 ½m and 4m

🚌 Frequent from surrounding areas.
Many different operators.
☎ 0298 23098

🚉 Buxton 1m

Next Youth Hostels: Gradbach 7m.
Ravenstor 7m. Castleton 9m.
Meerbrook 11m. Hartington 12m.
Bakewell 12m. Edale 13m

Administrative Region: Central   **Administrative Region: Central**   **Administrative Region: Central**

C ASTLETON

120 BEDS

Youth Hostel,
Castleton Hall, Castleton,
Sheffield S30 2WG
📞 Hope Valley (0433) 20235

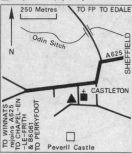

Overnight charge:
Young £3.50 Junior £4.40 Senior £5.50
🚻 🧺 🛏 🔍 quiet room, day room
available 📺 video ③ 🍴 Evening meal
18.30 hrs. ⓢ 🄿🄾 Castleton. 🄿

Jan 1-Feb 1	Closed
Feb 2-Dec 26	Open
Dec 27-Jan 31 92	Closed
Feb 1-29	Open

Dates partly from 1410, the rest from
1755, below Peveril Castle in Peak
District National Park. Hostel set in
village square

🅾🆂 110 Peak District Tourist, Outdoor
Leisure Map, Dark Peak
🄶🅁 150828 🄱🄼 29

Attractions: 🏰 11th century castle.
Old church. Good walking, 🅵 pot-
holing, geology area. 🅄 Famous Blue
John, Treak Cliff, Speedwell and Peak
Caverns. Winnats Pass. Mam Tor Hill
Fort. 🅹 near Hostel. Ancient Garland
Ceremony May 29. 🅛

🚌 South Yorks 272 from Sheffield
(passes BR Hope) (📞 0742 768688)
🚆 Hope 3m

Next Youth Hostels: Edale 4m.
Hathersage 6m. Ravenstor 8m. Eyam
8m. Buxton 9m. Gradbach 16m.
Hartington 18m

C ROWDEN-IN-LONGDENDALE

50 BEDS

Peak National Park Hostel,
Crowden, Hadfield,
Hyde, Cheshire SK14 7HZ
📞 Glossop (0457) 852135

Overnight charge:
Young £3.50 Junior £4.40 Senior £5.50
🚻 🧺 ① 🛏 🍴 Evening meal 19.30 hrs.
Small ⓢ Shop and 🄿🄾 Tintwistle 4m.
🍴 Tue. 🄿 for cars and coaches

Jan 1-Feb 28	Closed
Mar 1-Nov 3	Open (except Wed)
Nov 4-Dec 23	Closed
Dec 24-26	Open
Dec 27-Feb 29 92	Closed

Bookings for groups and parties may
be accepted when Hostel is closed —
please enquire

Row of Railwaymen's cottages on
Pennine Way in remote part of Long-
dendale, in Peak District National
Park. On N side of Manchester-
Barnsley Road, (A628). Marked
'Crowden' on map

🅾🆂 110 Peak District Tourist,
Outdoor Leisure Map, Dark Peak
🄶🅁 073993 🄱🄼 28, 29

Attractions: Pennine Way. Wain
Stones 2½m. 🅵 in Laddow Rocks and
Bleaklow. 🅹 at reservoirs 3m.
Melandra Castle Roman site 6m. 🏰
Dinting Steam Railway Centre 5m.
Glossop 6m. 🅛 Granada Studios Tour
(Manchester). Museum of Science &
Industry (Manchester). Macclesfield
Museums. Tameside Heritage Centre.
Camelot Theme Park 40m

🚌 National Express Sheffield -
Manchester service (📞 0742 754905)
🚆 Hadfield (not Sun) 5m

Next Youth Hostels: Langsett 10m.
Edale 15m. Mankinholes 24m via
Pennine Way

Additional Information: A National
Park Hostel, open to members of the
public, with accommodation available
to YHA members at YHA prices.
Make cheques payable to YHA

D IMMINGSDALE

26 BEDS

Youth Hostel, Little Ranger,
Dimmingsdale, Oakamoor,
Stoke-on-Trent, Staffs ST10 3AS
📞 Oakamoor (0538) 702304

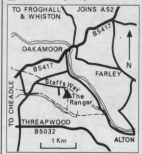

Overnight charge:
Young £3.10 Junior £4.00 Senior £5.10
🅰 ② 🛏 🅶🆂🅲 🄺 Small ⓢ Shop and 🄿🄾
Alton 2m, Oakamoor 1m. 🄿 for cars
only; coaches at Oakamoor (1m)

Jan 1-Mar 24	Open Fri & Sat
Mar 25-Oct 31	Open (except Sun)
	Open Bank Hol Sun
	Closed Bank Hol Mon
Nov 1-17	Closed
Nov 18-Dec 21	Open Fri & Sat
Dec 22-Jan 3 92	Closed
Jan 4-Feb 29	Open Fri & Sat

Purpose-built in secluded woods,
between River Churnet and
Dimmingsdale 5m outside Peak
District National Park. Marked on 🅾🆂
maps as the Ranger, 2m NW of Alton
village, 1m S of Oakamoor. From
Oakamoor take narrow road on
south bank of river. Fork right at end
of village. At top of hill (½m), turn left
and up cart track. When track forks
right keep straight across with wall
on left

🅾🆂 119, 128 🄶🅁 052436 🄱🄼 23, 24

Attractions: Alton Towers Leisure
Park 1½m. Dimmingsdale ponds ¼m.
Hawksmoor Bird Sanctuary 1m.
Croxton Abbey 3m. 🅄 6m. Steam
Railway Centre Cheddleton 6m. 🅛

🚌 Stoddard 18 from Uttoxeter
(passes close BR Uttoxeter), alight
Oakamoor, ¾m (📞 0538 752253)
🚆 Blythe Bridge 6m

Next Youth Hostels: Ilam 12m.
Meerbrook 14m. Gradbach 17m.
Hartington 18m. Copt Oak 37m.
Ironbridge 40m

EDALE

140 BEDS

Edale YH Activity Centre,
Rowland Cote, Nether Booth,
Edale, Sheffield S30 2ZH
☎ Hope Valley (0433) 670302

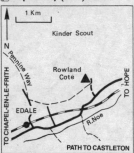

Overnight charge:
Young £4.60 Junior £5.90 Senior £7.00
🔲🅲🔲🔲🔲🔲 Evening meal
17.30-19.30 hrs. 🆂 🅿🄾 Edale 2m. 🔲
Wed. 🅿 for cars only; coaches at
bottom of drive

Jan 1-3	Closed
Jan 4-Dec 14	Open
Dec 15-Jan 3 92	Closed
Jan 4-Feb 29	Open

**Hostel open all day with hot and
cold drinks available**

Edale is one of YHA's Activity
Centres. Large former private house
in extensive grounds on hillside
below the edge of Kinder Scout
Plateau, in centre of Peak District
National Park 1m E of Edale village
marked 'Rowland Cote' on 🆗 110

🆗 110 Peak District Tourist,
Outdoor Leisure Map, Dark Peak
🄶🅁 139865 🖹 29

Hostel Attractions:
Multi Activity Leisure Breaks:
2, 4 and 7 nights for groups and
individuals could include caving,
climbing, canoeing, archery, mountain
biking, cross country skiing,
orienteering, gorge scrambles, BBQs,

discos. Enquiries: National Office 🄲
(0727) 55215. Reservations: National
Office 🄲 (0727) 45047. 🄻

Training & Leisure Weekend
Programme:
Caving, climbing, hillcraft, map &
compass. Enquiries: National Office
🄲 (0727) 55215. Reservations:
National Office 🄲 (0727) 45047

Personnel Development:
Courses for Business, Industry, Y.T.S.
TVEI tailored to your needs by our
Chief Instructor. Enquiries and
bookings direct to Centre 🄲 (0433)
670302

Conference & House Party Facilities:
In Spring, Autumn & Winter periods
at competitive prices. Our facilities
include licensed food service,
workrooms, lounges, white boards,
large games room with disco, space
for seminars, discussion groups.
Enquiries and bookings to Centre
🄲 (0433) 670302

Special Note:
Advance Booking is always essential.
During the Spring, Summer and
Autumn period only limited
accommodation is available to non-
activity bookings

Local Attractions: Castleton Show
Caves 6m, Ladybower Reservoir,
Kinder Scout

🚃 No service

🚌 Edale 1m

On **Friday Evenings Only** (16.00-
20.00 hrs) all trains are met at Edale
BR station to take you to the Hostel.
This service is free on presentation of
your YHA membership card or
booking receipt

Next Youth Hostels: Castleton 4m.
Eyam 11m. Hathersage 12m.
Ravenstor 12m. Buxton 13m.
Crowden 15m by moor

Additional Information: Fax
number: (0433) 670243. Telephone
number above is for manager and
enquiries. For residents 🄲 Hope
Valley (0433) 670225

ELTON

30 BEDS

Youth Hostel, Elton Old Hall,
Main Street, Elton,
Matlock, Derbyshire DE4 2BW
☎ Winster (062988) 394

Overnight charge:
Young £3.10 Junior £4.00 Senior £5.10
🔲🔲🔲🔲🔲🔲 but supper
cafeteria facilities available to 8.00
pm. Continental breakfast to order
on arrival. Small 🆂 Shop and 🅿🄾 in
village. 🅿 for cars in village; coaches
by prior arrangement

Jan 2-Mar 21	Closed
Mar 22-Nov 2	Open
Nov 3-Dec 26	Closed
Dec 27-Jan 1 92	Open
Jan 2-Feb 29	Closed

Party bookings in closed period by
prior arrangement

Stone built house in typical
Derbyshire lead mining village in Peak
District National Park. E end of Elton
village on main street

🆗 119 Peak District Tourist
🄶🅁 224608 🖹 24, 29

Attractions: Cratcliffe Tor and
Robin Hoods Stride 1m. Stanton
Moor stone circle 2½m. Arbor Low
stone circle 5m. High Peak Trail 2½m.
Tissington Trail 6m. Lathkill Dale 3m.
Hermit's Cave 1m. Haddon Hall 4m.
Chatsworth House 9m. Middleton
Top and Engine House 6m. Parsley
Hay 🚲 7m. 🄻

🚃 Hulleys 170 Chesterfield - Matlock
(passes close BR Chesterfield &
Matlock) (🄲 0298 23098)

🚌 Matlock 5m

Next Youth Hostels: Youlgreave
2½m. Bakewell 7m. Hartington 7½m.
Matlock 8m. Shining Cliff 10m.
Ravenstor 11m. Eyam 12m

Edale Youth Hostel & Activity Centre

Administrative Region: Central

Administrative Region: Central

Eyam

60 BEDS

Youth Hostel,
The Edge, Eyam,
Sheffield S30 1QP
☎ Hope Valley (0433) 30335

Overnight charge:
Young £3.80 Junior £4.70 Senior £5.90
▥ C ▥ 2 ▥ ▥ Evening meal 18.30
hrs. ⑤ ⑨ Shop and ⓟ in village. ⑤ ⓟ
for cars and coaches

Jan 1-13	Closed
Jan 14-Nov 2	Open (except Sun)
Nov 3-30	Open Fri & Sat
Dec 1-23	Closed
Dec 24-26	Closed
Dec 27-Jan 16 92	Closed
Jan 17-Feb 29	Open (except Sun)

Large Victorian house on the hill
above 'plague village', in Peak District
National Park. Turn N in village up
Hawkhill Road, bear right at junction,
Hostel on left, ½m from village

⑥ 119 Peak District Tourist
⑥ 219769 ▣ 29

Attractions: Mompesson's Well.
Lidgett graves. Riley graves. Caving
and ⑰ Plague cottages ¼m. Celtic
Cross ¼m. Bretton Clough scenic
walk 1½m. Well dressings in area (Jun
to Sep). Chatsworth House 6m.
Haddon Hall 8m. Curbar Riding
Stables 3m. Ⓛ

🚌 As for Bretton, but alight Eyam
🚋 Grindleford 3½m; Hathersage 4m

Next Youth Hostels: Bretton 1½m.
Hathersage 4m. Ravenstor 7m.
Castleton 8m. Bakewell 8m. Elton
12m. Buxton 16m.

Gradbach Mill

94 BEDS

Youth Hostel, Gradbach Mill,
Gradbach, Quarnford,
Buxton, Derbyshire SK17 0SU
☎ Wincle (0260) 227625

Overnight charge:
Young £4.40 Junior £5.40 Senior £6.60
▥ ▥ ▥ C 1 ▥ ▥ Evening meal
19.00 hrs. ⑤ ⑨ Hostel playing field.
Shop and ⓟ Flash (2½m). ▣ Wed
(Buxton). ⓟ for cars and coaches

Jan 2-Feb 17	Closed
Feb 18-Mar 28	Open (except Sun)
Mar 29-Nov 2	Open
Nov 3-Dec 21	Open (except Sun)
Dec 22-26	Closed
Dec 27-Jan 1 92	Open
Jan 2-Feb 13	Closed
Feb 14-29	Open (except Sun)

Flax mill and mill owner's house built
about 1785 in Peak District National
Park. On South side of River Dane.
Turn left at Manor Farm, off Flash to
Allgreave Road

⑥ 118 Peak District Tourist
⑥ 993661 ▣ 29

Attractions: Walks from the
Hostel. River bathing. ☒ ⑰ on
Roaches 2m. Ⓤ 2m. Buxton spa town
6m. Alton Towers 14m. Stoke
Potteries and Mining Museum 16m.
Styal Mill Museum 20m. Ⓛ

🚌 PMT X23 Sheffield — Hanley
(passes close BR Sheffield & Buxton),
alight Royal Cottage, 2½m
(☎ 0298 23098)
🚋 Buxton 7m; Macclesfield 9m

Next Youth Hostels: Meerbrook
5m. Buxton 6m. Hartington 12m.
Ravenstor 14m. Dimmingsdale 17m

Hartington Hall

120 BEDS

COMFORT IMPROVED

Youth Hostel, Hartington Hall,
Hartington, Buxton,
Derbyshire SK17 0AT
☎ Hartington (0298) 84223

Overnight charge:
Young £4.40 Junior £5.40 Senior £6.60
Main House
Young £5.50 Junior £7.00 Senior £8.30
Family Rooms (Barn)
▥ ▥ ▥ ▥ ⑨ C 3 ▥ ▥ Evening
meal 18.30 hrs. ⑤ ⓟ Hartington. ▣
Wed. ⑤ ⓟ for cars and coaches.
Coach hire available in village, ask
warden

Jan 2-Feb 15	Closed
Feb 16-Dec 23	Open
Dec 24-Feb 14 92	Closed
Feb 15-29	Open

Conference or group bookings may
be accepted when the Hostel is
closed — please ask the warden

Early 17th century manor, with room
where Bonnie Prince Charlie slept. A
stone barn adjacent to the main Hostel
building comprises 6 family rooms with
4 or 6 beds and en-suite facilities. Just
outside village at N end of Dovedale
in Peak District National Park, 2m W
of A515 Buxton-Ashbourne road.
Coach hire available in village — ask
warden or telephone 029884 211

⑥ 119 Peak District Tourist
⑥ 131603 ▣ 24, 29

Attractions: Paddock for ponies.
Dove and Manifold valleys. Cheese
factory and shop in village. Thor's
Cave. Pilsbury Castle 2½m. High Peak
and Tissington trails. 🚴 in village. Alton
Towers. Ⓛ The American Adventure
18m. Arbor Low Stone Circle 5m

🚌 Bowers 442 from BR Buxton; also
from other areas on Sun & Bank
Holidays only (☎ 0298 23098)
🚋 Buxton 12m; Matlock 13m

Next Youth Hostels: Youlgreave
6m. Bakewell 8m. Ilam 9m. Gradbach
12m. Meerbrook 12m. Ravenstor
12m. Buxton 12m. Matlock 13m.
Eyam 14m. Shining Cliff 18m

H ATHERSAGE

44 BEDS

Youth Hostel,
Castleton Road, Hathersage,
Sheffield S30 1AH
☏ Hope Valley (0433) 50493

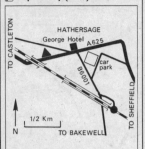

Overnight charge:
Young £3.80 Junior £4.70 Senior £5.90
🏠 ⚠ 1 🍴 🍽 Evening meal 19.00 hrs.
Shop and PO in village. P for cars and
coaches in village 300 yds

Jan 1-3	Closed
Jan 4-Feb 28	Open Fri & Sat
Mar 1-24	Closed
Mar 25-Nov 2	Open (except Sun)
Nov 3-Feb 29 92	Open Fri & Sat
Dec 20, 21	Closed

During closed period and when open
Fri & Sat only, bookings from parties
may be accepted when the Youth
Hostel is closed

Victorian Gothic building in village on
River Derwent in Peak District
National Park. 100 yds on right past
the George Hotel on road to
Castleton

OS 110 Peak District Tourist
GR 226814 🚶 29

Attractions: 'Little John' buried in
village churchyard. Jane Eyre
associations. Millstone Edge 2m.
Stanage Edge 3m. Outdoor
swimming pool. Abbeydale industrial
hamlet 6m. Gliding, Abney 4m.
Castleton Show caves 6m. 🚃 2m.
Carl Walk hill fort 3m. L

🚌 South Yorks 272 from Sheffield
(☏ 0742 768688)

🚂 Hathersage ½m

Next Youth Hostels: Eyam 4m.
Castleton 6m. Bakewell 9m.
Ravenstor 10m. Edale 12m. Buxton
15m. Hartington 19m

Administrative Region: Central

I LAM HALL

140 BEDS
COMFORT IMPROVED

Youth Hostel, Ilam Hall,
Ashbourne, Derbyshire DE6 2AZ
☏ Warden (033529) 212
☏ Members (033529) 379
Fax (033529) 350

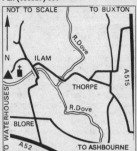

Overnight charge:
Young £4.40 Junior £5.40 Senior £6.60
Young £5.50 Junior £7.00 Senior £8.30
(New Rooms)
🏠 🏠 🅰 ©️ 4 🍴 🍽, with choice.
Evening meal 18.15-19.15 hrs. Beer
and wine available with Hostel meals.
S 🔊 Disco facility. Video. Quiet room.
No shop in village. PO Ashbourne
Market Place or Co-op. FS P for cars
and coaches in NT park at Hostel
(NT charge). Coach hire available in
village, ask warden or ☏ (033529) 204

Jan 1-Nov 3	Open
Nov 4-Dec 23	Closed
Dec 24-27	Closed
Dec 28-Jan 2 92	Closed
Jan 3-Feb 29	Open

Conferences or Group bookings may
be accepted during closed periods;
please contact the warden

Large country mansion built in Gothic
Revival style between 1820 and 1840,
above River Manifold in Peak District
National Park, Ilam village, Dovedale

OS 119 Peak District Tourist
GR 131506 🚶 24

**Attractions: Alton Towers Pleasure
Park** 10m. Church of St Bertram.
Country Park information centre and
Peak National Park Education Centre
in grounds. Dovedale and Manifold
Valley. Thor's Cave. Limestone geology.
Tissington Trail 3m. 🚃 Thorpe 1½m.
Waterhouses 3m, Ashbourne 5m.
Hang gliding courses. L

🚌 Infrequent from Ashbourne;
otherwise from Derby, Manchester
(passing close BR Derby & Macclesfield),
alight Ilam Cross Roads, 2½m (☏ 0332
292200). School bus to village daily
during term time

🚂 Matlock 14m; Derby 18m

Next Youth Hostels: Hartington
9m. Dimmingsdale 12m. Meerbrook
13m. Matlock 14m. Ravenstor 17m

Administrative Region: Central

L ANGSETT

32 BEDS

Nr Penistone. Bookings c/o John &
Elaine Whittington, 7 New Bailey,
Crane Moor, nr Sheffield S30 7AT
☏ Sheffield (0742) 884541

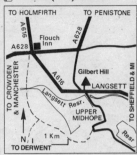

Overnight charge:
Young £3.10 Junior £4.00 Senior £5.10
🏠 🛏 School parties, groups and 🏠
midweek by booking in advance. 🔒
❌ — all food must be brought. No
S Shop and cafe in village, closed
Mon & Fri. PO Penistone 3m. 🍴 Wed.
P for cars and minibus only; coaches
nearby. No resident warden

**Open every Saturday and Bank
Holiday Sundays with voluntary
Warden (except Xmas)**

Purpose built Hostel (1967)
overlooking Langsett village and
reservoir, with wild moorland to
South West and gentler terrain to
North East

OS 110 Peak District Tourist
GR 211005 🚶 29

Attractions: Access to eastern side
of Bleaklow (2060 ft), Margery Hill
(1793 ft) 4m. Cut gate, ancient
packhorse route to Derwent
reservoirs. Hartcliffe Brow ¾m. 🚩 at
Wharncliff Rocks 5½m. Wortley Top
Forge 6m. Leisure centre at
Stocksbridge 4m. 🚃 3m. Penistone
cattle market Thu 3m. L

🚌 Yorkshire Traction 381/4 Circular
from Barnsley (pass close BR
Penistone & Barnsley) (☏ 0742
768688)

🚂 Penistone 3m

Next Youth Hostels: Crowden
10m. Hathersage 18m. Edale 20m.
Beverley Friary 62m. York 47m.
Mankinholes 35m

Administrative Region: Central

6

PEAK DISTRICT

Matlock

49 BEDS

**Youth Hostel & Training Centre,
40 Bank Road, Matlock,
Derbyshire DE4 3NF**
☎ Matlock (0629) 582983

Overnight charge:
Young £4.40 Junior £5.40 Senior £6.60
🛏🏠🛊🔺🚭🏨 Evening meal 19.00 hrs.
🅂 🔍 Shops and 🅿🅾 250 yds. 🔟 (local
shops) Thu. 🅿 for cars only; coaches
300 yds. 🅲 🅲 🅵 🅾 🅰 Vegetarian
meals available. Beer and wine
available with Hostel meals.
2 en-suite Tutor/Leader rooms

Jan 4-Dec 7	Open (except Sun) (but Open Bank Holiday Sundays)
Dec 8-Jan 2 92	Closed
Jan 3-Feb 29	Open (except Sun)

The former Smedleys hospital just
two minutes walk from the centre of
this attractive Peak District town. It
is reached by leaving Crown Square
up Bank Road approximately 200 yds
on the right hand side

Refurbishment in 1989 has resulted in
a well equipped Hostel with a
majority of smaller, tastefully
decorated bedrooms. The Common
Room enjoys panoramic views to the
south and there is a separate
Television Lounge

Matlock is a major gateway to the
Peak District being close to the M1
motorway as well as having a bus and
railway station. There is a regular
train service from Derby linking with
London, St Pancras

Matlock
Youth
Hostel

Apart from linking into the close
network of Hostels in the Peak
District the area around Matlock
offers a wide range of attractions and
activities. The dramatic scenery
provides a number of walks, there is
canoeing at Matlock Bath, and
numerous tourist attractions for all
the family including swimming,
cinema and magnificent country
houses

Adjoining the Hostel is the YHA
National Training Centre for use by
organisations or groups wishing to
take advantage of good facilities at
reasonable prices. There is a meeting
room suitable for about 20 persons
and two additional seminar rooms.
Basic Audio Visual aids are provided
and specialist equipment can be hired
on request. For further information
or leaflets please contact the Centre
Manager

🆗 119 Peak District Tourist White
Peak Outdoor Leisure Map
🅶🆁 300603 🚌 24, 29

Attractions: Spa town. Scenic walks
and 🚶 Matlock Bath 1m. Cable car
to Heights of Abraham. Peak District
lead mining museum. Old mineral
baths. Gullivers Kingdom. 🚶 High
Tor. Scenic gorge. River Derwent 400
yds canoeing (with own canoes), ⛵
boating. Riber Castle Zoo 1m.
Chatsworth House 4m. Haddon Hall
6m. National Tramway Museum 6m.
Awkwright's Cromford Mill 2m. High
Peak Trail 2m. Limestone Way.
Middleton Top Engine House. 🚲 3m.
National Stone Centre. Ⓛ Tales of
Robin Hood — Nottingham 25m,
Sherwood Forest Visitor Centre
(Major Oak) 25m. Midland Steam
Centre — Ripley. American
Adventure Theme Park 10m. Modern
swimming pool 200 yds. Alton
Towers 24m. Denby Pottery Visitors
Centre. Red House Stables &
Working Carriage Museum 2m

🚌 Frequent from surrounding areas
(☎ 0332 292200)

🚂 Matlock 400 yds

Next Youth Hostels: Bakewell 8m.
Elton 8m. Shining Cliff 8m.
Youlgreave 10m. Hartington 13m.
Eyam 14m. Ravenstor 14m

Meerbrook

26 BEDS

**Youth Hostel, Old School,
Meerbrook, Leek,
Staffs ST13 8SJ**
☎ Blackshaw (053834) 244

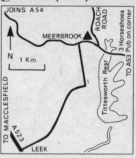

Overnight charge:
Young £3.10 Junior £4.00 Senior £5.10
🅰 🛏 ② 🚭 🆂🅲 🏨 Small 🅂 Shop and
🅿🅾 Leek 3m. 🔟 Thu. 🅿 for cars only;
coaches on outskirts of village

Jan 1-Mar 21	Open Fri & Sat
Mar 22-Nov 3	Open (except Mon)
Nov 4-Dec 23	Open Fri & Sat
Dec 24-28	Open
Dec 29-Feb 29 92	Open Fri & Sat

When open Fri & Sat only, bookings
may be accepted Sun or midweek;
please enquire

Converted school near the Roaches,
3m north of Leek, on edge of Peak
District National Park. Centre of
village

🆗 119 Peak District Tourist Map
🅶🆁 989608 🚌 29

Attractions: Visitors welcome at
Village Youth Club (Mon & Fri).
Roaches 1m. Ramshaw Rocks 2m.
Hen Cloud 1m. Red deer/Packhorse
roads and drove roads. Gawsworth
Hall 6m. Moreton Old Hall 7m. Hang
gliding school, Leek 2m. Staffordshire
moorlands. ⛵ 🚲 nature trail
Tittesworth Reservoir ¼m. Stoke
area pottery and mining museums.
Alton Towers Leisure Park 8m
(Water World, Superbowl, Dry Ski
Slope & Multi-Screen Cinema). Ⓛ
Tittesworth Reservoir & Adventure
Playground ¼m

🚌 PMT 465 BR Macclesfield — Leek
(Fri only); otherwise PMT X23
Sheffield — Hanley (passes close BR
Stoke-on-Trent & Buxton), alight
Blackshaw Moor, 2m (☎ 0298 23098)

🚂 Stoke-on-Trent 15m

Next Youth Hostels: Gradbach 5m.
Buxton 11m. Hartington 12m. Ilam
Hall 13m. Dimmimgsdale 14m.
Chester 42m

R AVENSTOR 72 BEDS

Youth Hostel, Ravenstor,
Millers Dale, Buxton,
Derbyshire SK17 8SS
☎ Tideswell (0298) 871826*

Overnight charge:
Young £4.00 Junior £5.10 Senior £6.30
🏠 👪 🚻 🍴 ① 📞 Evening meal 19.00
hrs. Beer and wine available with
Hostel meals. Ⓢ Ⓠ Ⓒ Ⓒ quiet room.
PO Tideswell 2m. ED Tue. P for cars
and coaches

Jan 2-Feb 7	Closed
Feb 8-Nov 30	Open (except Sun)
	Open Easter Sun
Dec 1-27	Closed
Dec 28-Jan 1 92	Open
Jan 2-30	Closed
Feb 1-29	Open (except Sun)

Mill owner's house in extensive
woodlands with views of Millers
Dale, in Peak District National Park.
1m from former Millers Dale station
on main Tideswell road or by steps
and footpath from junction of Millers
Dale and Tideswell Dale

OS 119 Peak District Tourist
GR 152732 ⛺ 29

Attractions: Orienteering in the
grounds. Treasure hunt, nature trails
and 📷 🎦 Monsal Trail. Tideswell
Church (Cathedral of the Peak). Old
lead mines. Limestone geology. 🦽
(from the Hostel if booked in
advance). Bakewell Monday Market
7m. Caverns at Buxton, 7m, and
Castleton, 8m. Peak Rail (steam) at
Buxton 7m. 🦽 Ⓛ

🚂 From Sheffield, Buxton
(☎ 0298 23098)
🚌 Buxton 8m

Next Youth Hostels: Eyam 7m.
Buxton 7m. Bakewell 7m. Castleton
8m. Hathersage 10m. Hartington
12m. Gradbach 14m

Additional Information:
Reception/enquiries open 9-12am
and 5-10pm, except Sun evening &
Mon morning. Members only ☎
(0298) 871204

S HINING CLIFF 26 BEDS

Youth Hostel, Shining Cliff Woods, nr
Ambergate, bookings c/o Mrs 1 Carlile,
Elton Youth Hostel, Main Street, Elton,
nr Matlock, Derbyshire DE4 2BW
☎ (062988) 394

Overnight charge:
Young £2.60 Junior £3.50 Senior £4.40
🏠 👪 🍴 Ⓢ Ⓢ School parties, groups
and family accommodation midweek
by booking in advance. ⊠ No Ⓢ
Shop and PO Ambergate. P for cars
½m; coaches only by prior
arrangement. No resident warden

**Open every Saturday and Bank
Holiday Sunday from Mar 23-Dec
14 with voluntary warden**

Isolated purpose built Youth Hostel
in secluded woodland in valley of
River Derwent. From Ambergate,
cross river by church. Cyclists up hill,
turn right into woods by third farm.
Walkers turn right by river, through
works yard and up path through
woods. From Wirksworth-Belper
road; turn left at Packhorse cross-
road, left into woods at first farm
and right at fork in woods. It is advisable
to bring a torch if arriving after dark

OS 119 Peak District Tourist
GR 335522 ⛺ 24

Attractions: Unspoilt woodlands.
📷 Crich tramway museum 2m.
Cromford Canal ½m. 🦽 Middleton
Top Engine house 4m. Cable cars at
Matlock Bath 7m. Ⓛ

🚂 Trent 123/4, 252 from Derby,
alighting ½m NW of Ambergate on
some, thence ¾m, or at Ambergate,
1m, on others (☎ 0332 292200)
🚌 Ambergate 1m (path), 2m (road)

Next Youth Hostels: Matlock 8m.
Elton 10m. Youlgreave 12½m.
Hartington 18m. Copt Oak 30m

Y OULGREAVE 46 BEDS

Youth Hostel, Fountain Square,
Youlgreave, Bakewell,
Derbyshire DE4 1UR
☎ Youlgreave (0629) 636518

Overnight charge:
Young £3.80 Junior £4.70 Senior £5.90
🏠 👪 Ⓒ ① 📞 Evening meal 19.00
hrs. Small Ⓢ Shop and PO in village. P
for cars in village (100 yds); coaches
by prior arrangement only

Jan 1-3	Closed
Jan 4-Mar 21	Open Fri & Sat
Mar 22-Nov 2	Open (except Sun)
Nov 3-Dec 21	Open Fri & Sat
Dec 22-26	Closed
Dec 27-Jan 1 92	Open
Jan 2-30	Closed
Jan 31-Feb 15	Open Fri & Sat
Feb 16-29	Open (except Sun)

During closed period, and when open
Fri & Sat only, bookings from parties
may be accepted when the Youth
Hostel is closed

19th century 'Co-op' store in small
village in Bradford Dale, close to
Lathkill Dale in Peak District
National Park. On main street
opposite the Fountain Well

OS Landranger 119 (1:50000). Tourist
— The Peak District (1:63360).
Outdoor Leisure 'The White Peak'
(1:25000). GR 210641 ⛺ 29

Attractions: Church Well dressing
in village (mid-Jun). Bradford Dale
(200 yds). Lathkill Dale 1m. Stanton
Moor stone circle 3m. Arbor Low
stone circle 3m. Haddon Hall 2m.
Robin Hood's Stride 2m. 🦽 Parsley
Hay 4m. Chatsworth House 4m. 📷
1m. On 3 unofficial Long Distance
Paths — White Peak Way, Limestone
Way and Limey Way. Ⓛ

🚂 Hulleys 170 Chesterfield —
Matlock (passes close BR
Chesterfield & Matlock), 171/8 from
Bakewell plus additional Sunday
services (☎ 0298 23098)
🚌 Matlock 11m

Next Youth Hostels: Elton 2½m.
Bakewell 3½m. Hartington 6m.
Matlock 10m

7 LINCOLNSHIRE

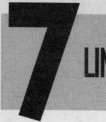

Visitors are surprised at the variety of Lincolnshire. Far from being flat, the county offers an enormous contrast from the bulbfields around Spalding through rolling farmland to the high Wolds of the North. The whole area is ideal cycling country with many quiet by-ways. Cyclists delight in exploring the many 'wool' churches, whilst market cafes, riverside pubs and the famous Lincolnshire pork butchers cater more than adequately for the demands of the inner man. Walkers come into their own on the Wolds with the Viking Way running from Oakham near Thurlby, through Lincoln and on past Woody's Top on the Wolds to the Humber Bridge; the World's longest single span suspension bridge. For a complete contrast try the Hereward Way from Bourne (Thurlby) via Peterborough (short bus link to Kings Lynn) then on across the Fens to Ely and Brandon on the edge of Thetford Forest. Far removed from the classic high level walks much of this one is actually at or below sea level!

The rich farmland has long given prosperity to the area. Besides the many fine churches the towns of Stamford, Boston and Lincoln are quite outstanding. Lincoln is dominated by its great medieval cathedral with the famous Lincoln Imp. In the steep surrounding streets there are many interesting shops and houses, ancient guildhalls and city gates. There is a Norman Castle and the Cathedral Library contains priceless manuscripts including an original of the Magna Carta.

In this uncrowded countryside there is something to see year round. Spring is spectacular with bulbs, Summer rich and green, and the Winter sees the arrival of flocks of wildfowl and waders along the coast and up the rivers to reserves such as Peakirk near Thurlby. Speed skating on the frozen fen drains provides a very different local spectacle.

Whether you are looking for a peaceful diversion off the main tourist trail, or a short interesting holiday Lincolnshire has much to offer.

The Youth Hostels are small, friendly, each with its own distinctive character and ideally spaced for touring by cycle or car. There are good links North and South to Beverley Friary and Kings Lynn Youth Hostels. Members discounts have been negotiated with various tourist attractions, and Lincoln Tourist Information on 0522 533151 will be pleased to update you on what's happening currently in the county, or even plan your tour for you.

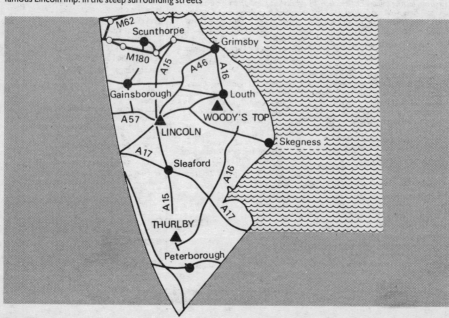

LINCOLN
60 BEDS

COMFORT IMPROVED YHA

Youth Hostel,
77 South Park,
Lincoln LN5 8ES

☎ Lincoln (0522) 522076

Overnight charge:
Young £4.60 Junior £5.90 Senior £7.00
🍴 🏠 ① 🏢 Set Hostel meal or a
wide selection of individual meals,
snacks and drinks available 5.00-8.00
pm. Ⓢ Shop and ℗ Lincoln. ⬛ Wed.
℗ for cars and coaches Ⓛ and group
information pack

Jan 2-5	Open
Jan 6-Feb 7	Closed
Feb 8-Mar 30	Open
	(except Sun & Mon)
Mar 31-Jun 30	Open (except Sun)
	Open Easter Sun
Jul 1-Aug 31	Open
Sep 1-Dec 14	Open (except Sun
	& Mon)
Dec 15-23	Closed
Dec 24-26	Open Xmas Party
Dec 27-Feb 13 92	Closed
Feb 14-29	Open
	(except Sun & Mon)

Groups may be accepted during
closed period at wardens discretion;
please enquire

Recently refurbished Victorian villa
opposite open parkland. Comfortable
small rooms, flexible meals service and
new purpose built study/meeting room.
Ideal base for groups or individual
tourists

⬛ 121 ⬛ 980700 ⬛ 30

Attractions: Roman remains.
Norman castle, Medieval cathedral.
Swimming pool and sports complex.
Marina. Museum of Lincolnshire Life.
City and County Museum. Viking
Way. Coast 30m. Roller skating rink.
⬛ ½m. Ⓛ National Cycle museum.
Usher Art Gallery Ⓛ. Magnificent
medieval buildings. On East of England
Heritage Route. 🛈 (0522) 512971

🚌 Frequent from surrounding areas
(☎ 0522 532424)

🚂 Lincoln 1m

Next Youth Hostels: Woody's Top
24m. Thurlby 36m. Matlock 53m.
York 74m. Beverley Friary 47m

THURLBY
36 BEDS

Youth Hostel, Capstone,
16 High Street, Thurlby, Bourne,
Lincolnshire PE10 0EE

☎ Bourne (0778) 425588

Overnight charge:
Young £3.80 Junior £4.70 Senior £5.90
🍴 🏠 ⬛ ⬛ 🌐 ⬛ ② Ⓢ Shop and ℗ 200
yds. ⬛ Wed (Bourne). ℗ cars only;
coaches by prior arrangement

Jan 1-2	Open
Jan 3-31	Closed
Feb 1-Mar 28	Open Fri & Sat
Mar 29-Oct 31	Open (except Thu)
Nov 1-Dec 23	Open Fri & Sat
Dec 29-Jan 2 92	Open

Open during period Jan 3-Mar 22 and
Nov 6-Dec 22 for parties booked in
advance

Originally a forge, with Georgian and
Victorian additions, in farming district
where the limestone uplands meet
the Fens. On left of the High Street
approaching village from East

⬛ 130 ⬛ 097168 ⬛ 25

Attractions: Fenland and Wildfowl
Trust land. Spalding Flower Festival
May. Forest walks. Rutland Water, ⬛
Ⓐ (dinghy hire), windsurfing. ⬛
tourist information centre in town,
nature trails. Historic town of
Stamford. Burghley House (open
Apr-Oct) and horse trials (Sep).
Nene Valley steam railway,
Peterborough 15m (ice rink, Ⓐ
tennis centre, rowing, cathedral).
Grimsthorpe Castle 3½m. Ⓛ available
for sae. Hereward Way. Viking Way.
Belvoir Castle 15m — YHA members
discount. 🛈 (0780) 55611. On East of
England Heritage Route

🚌 Delaine's service from
Peterborough (passes close BR
Peterborough) (☎ 0778 422866)

🚂 Peterborough 15m; Grantham
18m

Next Youth Hostels: Lincoln 36m.
Kings Lynn 36m. Copt Oak 45m.
Woody's Top 55m

WOODY'S TOP
24 BEDS

COMFORT IMPROVED YHA

Youth Hostel, Woody's Top,
Ruckland, near Louth

☎ Pay phone (0507) 533323
(No bookings to Hostel)*

*****Bookings and enquiries to:** Youth
Hostels Association, c/o P. Grant, 68
Pilleys Lane, Boston, Lincs. PE21 9RB
(NOT TO HOSTEL) ☎ Boston
(0205) 368651

Overnight charge:
Young £2.60 Junior £3.50 Senior £4.40
Ⓐ 🍴 Ⓐ Ⓛ ⬛ Wood stove 🌐 ⬛ No
Ⓢ Shop and ℗ 3m. ℗ for cars and
coaches

Open throughout the year by
booking. No resident Warden

Only party bookings accepted in
months of Jan, Feb, Nov and Dec.
Groups may book exclusive use of
the Hostel under the YHA's Rent-a-
Hostel scheme. Please send for details

Converted farm building on the
Greenwich Meridian, 6m due south
of market town of Louth. Hostel
ideal for self-wardening families,
groups, schools, youth groups with
leader. Accommodation is in six 4-
bedded rooms

⬛ 122 ⬛ 332786 ⬛ 30

Attractions: Adventure playground.
Viking Way 4m. Cadwell Park
International Race Circuit 4m.
Tennyson's birthplace, Somersby 5m.
Saltfleetby and Theddlethorpe
coastal nature reserves 15m.
Working windmill and craft market
Alford 16m. Mablethorpe seaside
town 16m. Wold market towns.
Snipe Dales Country Park 7m. ⬛ 🛈
Spilsby (0790) 52301

🚌 Lincolnshire Road Car 5, 51,
Grimsby/Cleethorpes 24 Grimsby —
Louth (both pass close BR Grimsby),
thence 6m (☎ 0522 532424)

🚂 Thorp Culvert (not Sun, except
May-Sep) 18m; Grimsby Town 22m;
Lincoln Central 25m

Next Youth Hostels: Lincoln 24m.
Thurlby 55m. Beverley Friary 50m

---

8 NORTH WALES

The Snowdonia National Park has the highest mountains in England and Wales, with steep passes and deep lakes. Although this is tough rock climbers' country, it has many hill and valley paths for ordinary walkers, and such attractions as narrow gauge railways, waterfalls and forest trails. The seaside Youth Hostels are close enough to the mountains to give pleasantly varied tours and there are exciting castles at Conwy, Caernarfon and Harlech. The slate quarrying industry has declined, leaving many sites and museums of interest to industrial archaeologists. Located beneath the extensive remains of the slate quarries at the foot of the Llanberis Pass, the Dinorwic Power Station is Europe's largest underground pumped storage electricity generating scheme.

In an area popular with cyclists, Bala Youth Hostel (Plas Rhiwaedog) lies close to Bala Lake (Llyn Tegid), a superb location for watersports and fishing. To the east, Cynwyd Youth Hostel gives access to the attractive Berwyn Hills and the nearby valley of the River Dee is particularly beautiful in late Autumn. Offa's Dyke long distance footpath starts on the north coast at Prestatyn and runs south towards Maeshafn and Llangollen Youth Hostels.

Further South, near North Wales' west coast are the Hostels of Kings (Dolgellau), and Llanbedr. The former, a country house, lies in the foothills of Cader Idris overlooking the Mawddach Estuary, the latter is a Victorian guest house just over one mile from the coast and still in the Snowdonia National Park.

Chester, a walled city with over 2000 years of history, is the principal gateway to North Wales for tourists. The Chester Youth Hostel is ideal both as a base for exploring the city and as a starting/finishing point for touring North Wales.

Useful Information

For advice and information covering all aspects of hostelling in North Wales contact YHA Regional Office, 1 Cathedral Road, Cardiff CF1 9HA. Tel: (0222) 396766 (Telephone Answering Machine outside normal office hours).

Discounts have been negotiated on admission charges to a number of attractions in the area and a list giving further details can be found under the Members Discounts section of this Guide.

During Winter closed months, early Spring and late Autumn many Youth Hostels are available for exclusive use by groups. Further details from the Regional Office at the above address or the warden concerned.

Helpful Publications

Available from the Regional Office at the above address. All prices include postage. Please make cheques/postal orders payable to YHA.

Youth Hostel leaflets/fact sheets	free for sae
Schools and Groups Information Pack	50p
Idwal Log	70p
Tourist Information Pack	60p

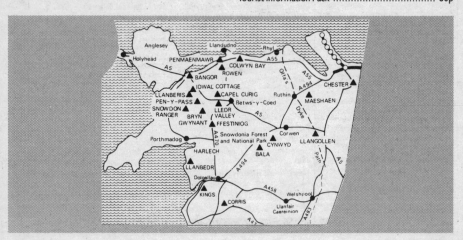

LLANGOLLEN YOUTH HOSTEL

STUDY & ACTIVITY CENTRE

Fully equipped, extensively refurbished 138 bed Centre offering study facilities and a wide range of Activities on site and within the beautiful surroundings of the Vale of Llangollen. For further details and for your FREE full colour brochure please contact:- The Centre Manager, YHA Study & Activity Centre, Tyndwr Hall, Tyndwr Road, Llangollen, Clwyd LL20 8AR. Tel: Llangollen (0978) 860330. (Answerphone service when the Centre is closed). Fax: Llangollen (0978) 861709

BALA YOUTH HOSTEL

A 60 bed Centre offering inclusive holidays designed to improve watersports techniques with a chance to gain RYA qualifications on the justly famous waters of Bala Lake. For further details please contact:- The Wardens, Bala Youth Hostel, Plas Rhiwaedog, Rhos-y-Gwaliau, Bala, Gwynedd LL23 7EU. Tel: Bala (0678) 520215 (Answerphone service when the Centre is closed)

OPEN DATES — WINTER 91/92

● HOSTELS OPEN
*except Sun 15 —— ALL HOSTELS CLOSED

HOSTEL	Mon	Tue	Wed	Thu	Fri	Sat	Sun	Mon	Tue	Wed	Thu	Fri	Sat	Sun*	Xmas	New Year	Mon	Tue	Wed	Thu	Fri	Sat	Sun	Mon	Tue	Wed	Thu	Fri	Sat	Sun
			NOV	91						DEC									JAN	92						FEB				
Bala					●	●																						●	●	
Bangor											●	●	●	●	●	●	●			●	●	●	●							
Bryn Gwynant										●	●	●	●	●	●		●	●		●	●	●	●	●						
Capel Curig			●	●	●	●	●																			●	●	●	●	●
Chester	●	●	●	●											●	●	●	●	●	●	●			●	●	●	●	●	●	●
Colwyn Bay																									●	●	●	●	●	●
Corris																														
Cynwyd																														
Ffestiniog									●			●	●	●	●	●	●	●		●	●	●	●							
Idwal Cottage	●			●	●	●	●																	●		●	●	●	●	●
Kings (Dolgellau)											●	●		●	●				●	●										
Llanbedr					●	●																						●	●	
Llanberis	●	●																						●	●			●	●	●
Llangollen	Group Bookings Only																													
Lledr Valley		●	●	●	●	●																			●	●	●	●	●	●
Maeshafn																														
Penmaenmawr																								●	●		●	●	●	●
Pen-y-pass		●	●	●	●	●																			●	●	●	●	●	
Rowen																														
Snowdon Ranger	●			●	●	●	●																	●		●	●	●	●	●

Administrative Region: Wales

NORTH WALES

8

8

BALA
60 BEDS

**Youth Hostel, Plas Rhiwaedog,
Rhos-y-Gwaliau, Bala,
Gwynedd LL23 7EU**
☎ Bala (0678) 520215

Overnight charge:
Young £3.80 Junior £4.70 Senior £5.90
🏠 A C 1 🛏 GSG 🍴 Evening meal
19.00 hrs. S PO Bala. 🍴 Wed/Sat.
Barbecue L P for cars — coaches
contact warden. 🅰 Hostel opens at
17.00 hrs

Jan 1-31	Open Fri & Sat
Feb 1-28	Closed
Mar 1-Apr 30	Open
	(except Sun & Mon)
	Open Easter W/E
May 1-Sep 30	Open
Oct 1-31	Open
	(except Sun & Mon)
Nov 1-30	Open Fri & Sat
Dec 1-Jan 31 92	Closed
Feb 1-29	Open Fri & Sat

Wales Tourist Board Approved
17th century manor house with
medieval wing, a mile from Bala Lake.
2m SE of Bala to hamlet of Rhos-y-
Gwaliau, over bridge and left along
farm road

OS 125 (NB 2nd edit series wrongly
locates YH). Bala Leisure Map
GR 947348 Bart 22, 27

Attractions: Watersports for groups
and individuals. Sailing — beginners
to RYA certificate standard. Canoeing
— lake and international standard
white-water. Windsurfing. Rubber
Rafting (subject to water conditions).
Cycling. Narrow gauge railway
along lake shore. U 🖭 Prehistoric
remains. Industrial archaeology. 🅸

🚌 Bws Gwynedd 94 Wrexham —
Barmouth (passes close BR Ruabon &
Barmouth), alight Bala, 2m
(☎ 0286 672556)

🚆 Ruabon 30m

Next Youth Hostels: Cynwyd 12m.
Ffestiniog 18m. Kings 20m.
Llangollen 22m. Llanbedr 35m by road

Additional Information: Members
☎ Bala (0678) 520655

BANGOR
86 BEDS
COMFORT yha IMPROVED

**Youth Hostel,
Tan y Bryn, Bangor,
Gwynedd LL57 1PZ**
☎ Bangor (0248) 353516

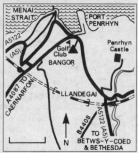

Overnight charge:
Young £4.00 Junior £5.10 Senior £6.30
🏠 A C 🔍 1 🛏 GSG 🍴 Evening meal
19.00 hrs. Laundry facilities available.
S Shop and PO Bangor ½m. P for cars
and coaches. Hostel opens at 17.00 hrs

Jan 1-Mar 26	Closed*
Mar 27-Sep 30	Open
Oct 1-31	Open
	(except Sun & Mon)
Nov 1-30	Closed
Dec 1-23	Open
	(except Tue & Wed)
Dec 24-Jan 6 92	Open Xmas/N Year
Jan 7-Feb 9	Open
	(except Tue & Wed)
Feb 10-Mar 2	Closed

*Closed for major refurbishment work

Wales Tourist Board Approved
The T E Fairclough Memorial Hostel.
Large house, just outside University
and Cathedral town, with spectacular
views over Snowdonia. On A5122
(A5) — look for gate on W, 50 yds
before sharp L bend entering Bangor.
From station proceed along High
Street onto A5122, Hostel on R 50
yds after sharp R bend leaving Bangor

OS 114, 115, Snowdon Leisure Map
GR 590722 Bart 27

Attractions: Bangor: Sports hall &
swimming pool, museums, Victorian
Pier — fully restored, Theatr
Gwynedd, Port Penrhyn. Penrhyn
Castle 2m. Plas Menai National
Watersports Centre 5m. Aber Falls
5m. Caernarfon Castle 12m.
Anglesey: Sea Zoo 5m, Newborough
Nature Reserve 7m. Beaumaris
Castle 5m. 🖭 🅸

🚌 Frequent from surrounding areas
(☎ 0286 672556)

🚆 Bangor 1½m

Next Youth Hostels: Idwal 9m.
Penmaenmawr 12m. Llanberis 11m.
Snowdon Ranger 17m

BRYN GWYNANT
70 BEDS

**Youth Hostel, Bryn Gwynant,
Nant Gwynant, Caernarfon,
Gwynedd LL55 4NP**
☎ Beddgelert (076686) 251

Overnight charge:
Young £4.00 Junior £5.10 Senior £6.30
🏠 A C 🖭 1 🛏 🍴 Evening meal
19.00 hrs. S FS Pool table. PO Nant
Gwynant 1m. 🍴 Sat. P for cars only;
coaches in layby (200 yds). Hostel
opens at 17.00 hrs

Jan 1-Feb 10	Closed
Feb 11-28	Open
Mar 1-25	Open
	(except Sun & Mon)
Mar 26-Sep 30	Open (except Sun)
Oct 1-31	Open (except Sun)
Nov 1-Dec 2	Closed
Dec 3-23	Open
	(except Sun & Mon)
Dec 24-Jan 4 92	Open Xmas/N Year
Jan 5-Feb 8	Open
	(except Sun & Mon)
Feb 9-Mar 1	Closed

Wales Tourist Board Approved
Stone built mansion with 40 acre
grounds overlooking lake in Snowdonia
National Park. In Gwynant Valley on S
side of Llyn Gwynant. 3½m from Pen-y-
Gwryd. 4m from Beddgelert on A498

OS 115, Snowdon Leisure Map
GR 641513 Bart 27

Attractions: 🅰 🖭 🎣 Watkin Path to
Snowdon summit. Waterfalls.
Cambrian Way footpath route.
Beddgelert — Gelert's Grave 4m.
Sygun Copper Mine 3m

🚌 Bws Gwynedd 97 from Porthmadog
(passes close BR & Ffestiniog Rly
Porthmadog); or 11 from Caernarfon,
note both alight Beddgelert, thence
4m; service 11 is extended to
Llanberis (passing the Hostel) Apr-
Oct only (☎ 0286 672556)

🚆 Betws-y-Coed (not Sun, except Jul/
Aug) 13m; Bangor 25m

Next Youth Hostels: Pen-y-Pass 4m.
Capel Curig 8m. Llanberis 8m via
Snowdon (11m by road). Snowdon
Ranger 9m. Lledr 9m by mountain

CAPEL CURIG

60 BEDS

COMFORT IMPROVED yha

Youth Hostel, Plas Curig, Capel Curig, Betws-y-Coed, Gwynedd LL24 0EL
☎ Capel Curig (06904) 225

Overnight charge:
Young £4.00 Junior £5.10 Senior £6.30
Seasonal Prices Jul 1-Aug 31:
Young £4.40 Junior £5.40 Senior £6.60
🏚 🔺 2 ▥ SC 🔲 Evening meal 19.00 hrs. S Pool table. L PO Capel Curig ¼m. P for cars only; coaches ask warden. Barbecue. Hostel opens at 17.00 hrs

Jan 1-Feb 12	Closed
Feb 13-28	Open
	(except Mon & Tue)
Mar 1-24	Open (except Sun)
Mar 25-Sep 30	Open
Oct 1-Nov 30	Open
	(except Mon & Tue)
Dec 1-Feb 12 92	Closed
Feb 13-29	Open
	(except Mon & Tue)

Wales Tourist Board Approved
Recently renovated former guest house in Snowdonia National Park. On A5 in Capel Curig village, with fine views of Moel Siabod, and the Llugwy Valley

OS 115, Conwy Valley Leisure Map GR 726579 Bart 27

Attractions: Mountain and low level walking. River swimming. Beginners' climbing. Plas-y-Brenin ½m — ski slope, climbing wall, canoeing and orienteering. Swallow Falls 3m. Sarn Helen and Miners' Bridge 4m. Gwydyr Forest waymarked routes

🚌 Bws Gwynedd 19, 95 from Llandudno, Llanrwst & Llanberis (pass BR Betws-y-Coed & Llandudno Junction) with connections from Bangor. All services run Apr-Oct only. (☎ 0286 672556)

🚂 Betws-y-Coed (not Sun, except Jul/Aug)

Next Youth Hostels: Lledr 5m by mountain. Pen-y-Pass 5½m. Idwal 6m. Bryn Gwynant 8m. Llanberis 12m

Administrative Region: Wales

CHESTER

COMFORT IMPROVED yha

120 BEDS

Youth Hostel, Hough Green House, 40 Hough Green, Chester CH4 8JD
☎ Chester (0244) 680056

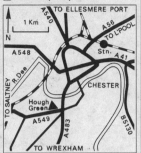

Overnight charge:
Young £4.60 Junior £5.90 Senior £7.00
🏚 🔺 ▥ 🔲 Full Cafeteria service. Laundry facilities available. S PO Chester. P for cars only. Official overnight coach park ¾m. Pool table. L Hostel opens at 15.00 hrs

Jan 1-31	Closed
Feb 1-Apr 30	See note*
May 1-Nov 30	Open
Dec 1-31	Closed
Jan 1-Feb 29 92	Open

*During this period extensive work will be carried out to refurbish the main building and greatly improve the facilities. Accommodation will be limited to about 30 beds in a separate building which has already been refurbished to a high standard. There will be no cooking facilities or meals provided. Advance booking is advisable

Large Victorian house in residential road one mile from centre of cathedral city. On SW side, 500 yds from Wrexham roundabout on right side of Saltney Road

OS 117 GR 397651 Bart 28

Attractions: Cathedral. Roman remains. 2m walk round Roman city walls. Town crier. Guided tours. Canals with narrow boats. Museums and Theatres. Boating on River Dee. Medieval 'Rows'. Zoo. Leisure centre 1m. 🚩 Large park nearby

🚌 Frequent from surrounding areas (☎ 0244 602666)

🚂 Chester 1½m

Next Youth Hostels: Maeshafn 16m. Llangollen 22m. Shrewsbury 40m. Colwyn Bay 41m

Chester Youth Hostel.

Administrative Region: Wales

8

NORTH WALES

COLWYN BAY

**Youth Hostel, Foxhill,
Nant-y-Glyn, Colwyn Bay,
Clwyd LL29 6AB**
☎ Colwyn Bay (0492) 530627

Overnight charge:
Young £3.50 Junior £4.40 Senior £5.50
Seasonal Prices Jul 1-Aug 31:
Young £3.80 Junior £4.70 Senior £5.90
🏠 C 🔥 ♿ 1 ▽ GSC 🍴 Evening meal
19.00 hrs. S no bread available 📮
Colwyn Bay 1½m. P for cars and
coaches, but access lane narrow.
Coaches 1½m. L Hostel opens at
17.00 hrs

Jan 1-Apr 30	Open (except Sun) Open Easter Sun
May 1-Aug 31	Open
Sep 1-Oct 31	Open (except Sun & Mon)
Nov 1-Feb 10 92	Closed
Feb 11-29	Open (except Sun & Mon)

Advance group bookings accepted at
warden's discretion during closed
periods

Wales Tourist Board Approved
Large house one mile inland from
popular seaside resort. 2m from
railway station in wooded Nant-y-
Glyn Valley. Turn off A55 exit
'Colwyn Bay' to join A547; at Park
Hotel on E outskirts of town turn up
Nant-y-Glyn road. Left by Nant-y-
Glyn Hall until Foxhill Youth Hostel
drive reached ¾m

OS 116 GR 847776 Bart 27

Attractions: Beach 1½m. Sea 🏊
Swimming. 🏋 Leisure centre 1½m.
Zoo. Riding stables 4m. Bryn Euryn
nature trail 2m. 🚲 locally. Conwy
Valley and Castle 4m. Little Orme
5m. Hill walking. Felan Isaf (working
mill) 6m. Watersports. 🎿 Artificial
ski-slope, Llandudno 8m

🚌 Frequent from surrounding areas
(☎ 0492 592111)

🚂 Colwyn Bay 2m

Next Youth Hostels: Rowen 12m.
Penmaenmawr 10m. Maeshafn 35m.
Chester 41m

Administrative Region: Wales

CORRIS

**Youth Hostel, Old School,
Old Road, Corris,
Machynlleth, Powys SY20 9QT**
☎ Corris (0654) 761686

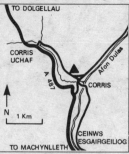

Overnight charge:
Young £2.60 Junior £3.50 Senior £4.40
♿ 🔥 ♿ 🔥 ▽ GSC 🍴 Small S Shop
and 📮 in village. 🍴 Wed/Sat, closed
Sun. P for cars 100 yds; coaches 300
yds. Hostel opens at 17.00 hrs

Jan 1-Feb 28	Closed
Mar 1-Oct 31	Open (except Tue)
Nov 1-Feb 29 92	Closed

Party bookings accepted at warden's
discretion during closed periods

Self-contained Family Annexe may be
available for sole-usage by small
parties (advance bookings only)

Slate built village school, typical of
area, near Cader Idris and Tal-y-llyn
Lake. In Corris on steep hill leading
to Corris Uchaf on east side of river

OS 124, Cader/Dyfi Forest Leisure
Map GR 753080 Bart 22

Attractions: Cader Idris (2927 ft)
5m. Tal-y-llyn Lake 3m. Centre of
Alternative Technology 2m. Narrow
gauge railway 7m. Forest trails. 🚣
River 🚣 Studies in geology and
geography. Corris railway museum
(out of season, advise in advance if
you wish to visit). Cambrian Way
footpath route. Dyfi Valley footpath
route

🚌 Bws Gwynedd 2, 34 Aberystwyth
- Caernarfon (passes BR Machynlleth
and BR Minffordd) (☎ 0286 672556)

🚂 Machynlleth 6m

Next Youth Hostels: Kings 15m
(10m via Cader Idris mountain).
Borth 19m. Bala 19m

🏠 Semi-detached house, sleeps 10 in
3 bedrooms plus 2 cots

Administrative Region: Wales

CYNWYD

**Youth Hostel,
The Old Mill, Cynwyd,
Corwen, Clwyd LL21 0LW**
☎ Corwen (0490) 2814

Overnight charge:
Young £2.60 Junior £3.50 Senior £4.40
♿ 🚲 ♿ 1 ▽ GSC 🍴 Small S 📮
Cynwyd. 🍴 Wed and Sat. P limited
at Hostel; public car park by 📮 200
yds; coaches — ask warden. L
Hostel opens at 17.00 hrs

Jan 1-Mar 28	Closed
Mar 29-Jun 30	Open (except Wed & Thu)
Jul 1-Aug 31	Open (except Thu)
Sep 1-30	Open (except Wed & Thu)
Oct 1-Feb 29 92	Closed

Party bookings accepted at warden's
discretion during closed periods.
Gwynedd Cottage Family Annexe may
be available for small parties (advance
bookings only)

Wales Tourist Board Approved
Former water mill on SE side of
village in Vale of Edeyrnion, on bank
of River Trystion at foot of Berwyn
Mountains. From Corwen direction
bear left before bridge and follow
roadway for 100 yds. From Bala turn
right before bridge then second right

OS 125 GR 057409 Bart 22, 27

Attractions: Mountain walking, high
Berwyn route. Good cycling country
with 'rough stuff' routes. Local
scenic walks. Waterfall ½m. Bathing
in river. 🚣 (permit)

🚌 Bws Gwynedd 94 Wrexham —
Barmouth (passes close BR Ruabon &
Barmouth) (☎ 0286 672556)

🚂 Ruabon 18m

Next Youth Hostels: Bala 12m.
Llangollen 12m. Maeshafn 18m

🏠 Cottage, sleeps 5 in 2 bedrooms
plus 1 cot

Administrative Region: Wales

F FESTINIOG

Youth Hostel, Caerblaidd, Llan Ffestiniog, near Blaenau Ffestiniog, Gwynedd LL41 4PH
☎ Ffestiniog (0766) 762765

Overnight charge:
Young £3.50 Junior £4.40 Senior £5.50
[symbols] Evening meal 19.00 hrs. [symbols] Ffestiniog ½m. [symbol] Thu. [P] for cars and minibuses only; coaches ¼m. Pool table. [L] Hostel opens at 17.00 hrs

Jan 1-Feb 13	Closed
Feb 14-Mar 31	Open (except Tue & Wed)
Apr 1-Aug 31	Open (except Sun)
Sep 1-Oct 31	Open (except Sun & Mon)
Nov 1-30	Closed
Dec 1-23	Open (except Tue, Wed & 15)
Dec 24-Jan 6 92	Open Xmas/N Year
Jan 7-Feb 9	Open (except Tue & Wed)
Feb 10-29	Closed

Wales Tourist Board Approved
Large house in Snowdonia National Park with magnificent views across the beautiful Vale of Ffestiniog. Situated on the N edge of the picturesque village of Llan Ffestiniog (not to be confused with the slate-mining village of Blaenau Ffestiniog)

[OS] 124, Harlech Leisure Map
[GR] 704427 [Bar] 22, 27

Attractions: Mountain walking on Moelwyns. Cycling. Dry ski slope. [symbol] Nature trail and waterfalls 1m. Narrow gauge railway. Llechwedd Quarry and Gloddfa Ganol Slate Mine. Cambrian Way footpath

[symbol] Bws Gwynedd 1, 2, 35 from BR & Ffestiniog Rly Blaenau Ffestiniog, Porthmadog and Machynlleth) (☎ 0286 672556)

[symbol] Blaenau Ffestiniog (Joint BR & Ffestioniog Rly) (no BR Sun service, except Jul/Aug) 3m

Next Youth Hostels: Lledr 10m. Bryn Gwynant 14m. Llanbedr 17½m. Bala 18m

---

H HARLECH

Youth Hostel, Pen-y-Garth, Harlech, Gwynedd LL46 2SW
☎ Harlech (0766) 780285

We regret that this Youth Hostel is no longer open

Llanbedr Youth Hostel is only 3½ miles south by road or rail from the town of Harlech

---

I IDWAL COTTAGE

Youth Hostel, Idwal Cottage, Nant Ffrancon, Bethesda, Bangor, Gwynedd LL57 3LZ
☎ Bethesda (0248) 600225

Overnight charge:
Young £3.50 Junior £4.40 Senior £5.50
Seasonal Prices Jul 1-Aug 31:
Young £3.80 Junior £4.70 Senior £5.90
[symbols] Evening meal 19.00 hrs. Barbecue. [symbols] Bethesda 5m. [symbol] Wed. [P] Public car park 20 yds for cars and space for coach. [L] Hostel opens at 17.00 hrs

Jan 1-Feb 10	Open (except Tue & Wed)
Feb 11-28	Closed
Mar 1-31	Open (except Tue & Wed)
Apr 1-Jun 30	Open (except Sun)
Jul 1-Aug 31	Open
Sep 1-Oct 31	Open (except Sun)
Nov 1-30	Open (except Tue & Wed)
Dec 1-Feb 12 92	Closed
Feb 13-29	Open (except Tue & Wed)

Wales Tourist Board Approved
Hostel by Lake Ogwen in Snowdonia National Park. Formerly a Quarry Manager's Cottage

[OS] 115, Snowdon Leisure Map
[GR] 648603 [Bar] 27

Attractions: Mountain walking and climbing. Devil's Kitchen ½m. Tryfan ½m. Glyders. Carnedds. Cambrian Way footpath route. Llyn Idwal bird sanctuary. [symbol] Penrhyn Castle 7m. Rhaedr Ogwen Waterfalls 200yd

[symbol] Bws Gwynedd 95 Bethesda — Llanrwst (Apr-Oct only) (passes BR Betws-y-Coed) (☎ 0286 672556); otherwise Bws Gwynedd 6/7 from Bangor (pass BR Bangor), alight Bethesda, 4m (☎ 0248 600207)

[symbol] Bangor 12m; Betws-y-Coed (not Sun, except Jul/Aug) 11m

Next Youth Hostels: Pen-y-Pass 5m by mountain route (10m by road). Capel Curig 6m. Llanberis, Glyder route 7m (road 12m). Bangor 9m. Lledr 12m

8

NORTH WALES

KINGS (DOLGELLAU)

56 BEDS

Youth Hostel,
Kings, Penmaenpool, Dolgellau,
Gwynedd LL40 1TB
📞 Dolgellau (0341) 422392

Overnight charge:
Young £3.50 Junior £4.40 Senior £5.50
🏠 🅰 🔥 1 📷 SC 🍴 Evening meal
19.00 hrs. S Shops and PO Dolgellau.
🍺 Wed. P small. Coaches contact
warden prior to visit. L Bonfire/
Barbecue site. Hostel grounds S.S.S.I.
Hostel opens at 17.00 hrs

Jan 1-31	Closed
Feb 1-28	Open Fri & Sat
Mar 1-31	Open
	(except Wed & Thu)
Apr 1-Jun 30	Open (except Sun) *
Jul 1-Aug 31	Open
Sep 1-Oct 31	Open (except Sun)
Nov 1-30	Closed
Dec 1-21	Open Fri & Sat
Dec 22-Jan 4 92	Open Xmas/N Year
Jan 5-Feb 1	Open Fri & Sat
Feb 2-29	Closed

Wales Tourist Board Approved
Country house set in wooded valley
in Snowdonia National Park, 4m
from Dolgellau. Follow main road for
Tywyn A493. Turn left at Abergwynant
bridge. Hostel is 1m along narrow
lane (not the old school).

OS 124, Cader Idris/Dovey Forest
Leisure Map GR 683161 🚌 22

Attractions: Cader Idris (2927 ft) 2m.
Beaches, Forest Trails (6m), Dry Ski
Slope (10m). Steam Railway. Rough
stuff cycling. 🚶 🌊 🚠 ⛵ Cambrian
Way footpath route

🚌 Bws Gwynedd 28 Dolgellau —
Tywyn (passes close BR Fairbourne),
alight 1½m W of Penmaenpool,
thence 1m (📞 0286 672556)

🚂 Morfa Mawddach 5m

Next Youth Hostels: Llanbedr 13m
by toll bridge (17m by road). Corris
15m. Bala 20m

*
Open B/H

LLANBEDR (HARLECH)

47 BEDS

Youth Hostel,
Plas Newydd, Llanbedr,
Gwynedd LL45 2LE
📞 Llanbedr (034123) 287

Overnight charge:
Young £3.50 Junior £4.40 Senior £5.50
🏠 🅰 1 📷 🍴 Evening meal 19.00 hrs.
S Shops and PO Llanbedr. 🍺 Wed. P
for cars and minibuses; coach
parking, ask warden. L Hostel opens
at 17.00 hrs

Jan 1-31	Closed
Feb 1-28	Open Fri & Sat
Mar 1-25	Open
	(except Sun & Mon)
Mar 26-Apr 6	Open
Apr 7-Jun 30	Open (except Sun) *
Jul 1-Aug 31	Open
Sep 1-Oct 31	Open (except Sun)
Nov 1-30	Open Fri & Sat
Dec 1-Jan 30 92	Closed
Jan 31-Feb 29	Open Fri & Sat

Party bookings accepted at warden's
discretion during closed periods

Wales Tourist Board Approved
Homely Victorian guest house in
centre of village 1½m from coast, in
Snowdonia National Park. E side of
main road, S of bridge over river

OS 124, Harlech Leisure Map
GR 585267 🚌 22

Attractions: Shell Island 2m. Farm
and nature trails 2m. River and sea
bathing. 🏛 Prehistoric sites. Harlech
Castle 3½m. Salem Chapel 2½m.
Roman steps 6m. Rhinogs 4m. Old
Clogau gold mines 8m. ⛵ Salmon
river. Excellent hill walking — access
to Rhinog mountains

🚌 Bws Gwynedd 38 from Barmouth
(📞 0286 672556)

🚂 Llanbedr ½m

Next Youth Hostels: Kings
Dolgellau 13m by toll bridge (17m by
road). Ffestiniog 17½m. Bala 37m

*
Open B/H

LLANBERIS

67 BEDS

Youth Hostel, Llwyn Celyn,
Llanberis, Caernarfon,
Gwynedd LL55 4SR
📞 Llanberis (0286) 870280

Overnight charge:
Young £4.00 Junior £5.10 Senior £6.30
🏠 🅰 🔥 1 📷 🍴 Evening meal 19.00
hrs. S PO Llanberis. 🍺 Wed. P for
cars and minibuses, coach parking ask
warden. No camping at hostel,
nearest site 3m. Pool table. L Hostel
opens at 17.00 hrs

Jan 1-Feb 10	Closed
Feb 11-Mar 31	Open
	(except Wed & Thu)
Apr 1-Sep 30	Open
Oct 1-Nov 30	Open
	(except Wed & Thu)
Dec 1-Feb 9 92	Closed
Feb 10-29	Open
	(except Wed & Thu)

Wales Tourist Board Approved
Large house on hillside above village
overlooking Llyn Padarn and Llyn
Peris in Snowdonia National Park. ½m
SW Llanberis. Take Capel Coch Road

OS 115, Snowdon Leisure Map
GR 574596 🚌 27

Attractions: 🚶 🅰 🚠 Excellent hill
walking, easiest ascent of Snowdon,
waymarked footpaths and trails. Lake
bathing from lagoons. Snowdon
Railway 1m. Llanberis Lake Railway 1m.
Dolbadarn Castle 1m. Caernarfon
Castle 8m. Padarn country park 1m.
Slate Quarry museum 1m. Dinorwig
Power Station 1m. Rock-climbing in
disused slate quarries 1m. Museum of
Wales and 🅸 on village by-pass

🚌 Bws Gwynedd 88, 98 from
Caernarfon (📞 0286 870880); 77
from Bangor (passes close BR Bangor)
(📞 0286 870484), on both alight
Llanberis, thence ½m

🚂 Bangor 11m

Next Youth Hostels: Snowdon
Ranger 4m by mountains (11m by
road). Pen-y-Pass 5½m. Idwal 7m by
mountains (12m by road). Bryn
Gwynant 8m via Snowdon (11m by
road). Capel Curig 12m

LLANGOLLEN

138 BEDS

YHA Study & Activity Centre,
Tyndwr Hall, Tyndwr Road,
Llangollen, Clwyd LL20 8AR
☎ (0978) 860330 Fax: (0978) 861709

Overnight charge:
Young £4.40 Junior £5.40 Senior £6.60
Ⓒ Ⓐ 4 📷 Ⓒ Hostel opens 13.00
hrs. 🍴 Cafeteria service. Laundry
facilities available. Ⓢ P0 Llangollen
1m. P for cars and coaches.
Licensed. Barbecue. Disco 🔌 Ⓛ

Jan 1-Mar 24 and **Nov 1-Mar 31 92**
During above periods Open for Group
Activity Holidays, Conferences,
Management Training, Study & School
Journey Parties and other group
bookings only
Mar 25-Oct 31 Open

Wales Tourist Board Approved
Extensively refurbished and re-
equipped Victorian half-timbered
manor house and coach house in 5½
acres of wooded grounds in the Vale
of Llangollen. Follow A5 from town
centre in Shrewsbury direction. Bear
right up Birch Hill. Keep to right at Y
junction in ½m. Hostel drive in ½m

Ⓞ 117 ⒼⓇ 232413 📷 23

Attractions: Offa's Dyke long
distance path. Woollen mill. Canal
museum and horse drawn barge
trips. Town trail. International
Eisteddfod. International and national
canoeing venue. Permanent Canoe
Slalom Course on River Dee. Plas
Newydd (Ladies of Llangollen)
Horseshoe falls, Pontcysyllte
aqueduct. Erddig Hall (NT). Chirk
Castle. (NT) Valle Crucis Abbey. Plas
Madoc leisure centre, Motor
museum, slate mine. 🅸 Steam
Railway. International Jazz Festival.
Castell Dinas Bran. Craft Centre,
Llangollen. Multi-Activity Holidays
for Groups and individuals — fully
inclusive residential packages for
weekend breaks and longer.
Activities available include Mountain
Biking, Archery, Climbing, Abseiling,
Rifle Shooting, Orienteering,
Canoeing, Hillwalking and Pony
Trekking

🚌 From Wrexham (passes close BR
Ruabon), alight Llangollen, 1½m
(☎ 0978 265327)

🚶 Chirk 5m; Ruabon 5m

Next Youth Hostels: Cynwyd 12m.
Maeshafn 16m. Chester 22m. Bala
22m. Shrewsbury 28m

Additional Information: Telephone
number is for Centre Manager and all
general enquiries. Answerphone
service when centre is closed.
☎ St Albans (0727) 45047 for all
Activity Holiday Booking enquiries

The Centre offers:

Study Facilities	Facilities for	Multi Activity Holidays
Y.T.S., T.V.E.I. &	Conferences, Meetings,	and 1 or 2 day 'Taster'
Personal Development	Club/Society A.G.M.'s	Holidays in wide range
Courses catered for	and Dinners	of activities

Facilities also available for Groups on Day-Usage basis at competitive
rates. Contact the Centre Manager for further details and for your free
copy of our full-colour brochure.

Llangollen Youth Hostel and Activity Centre.

Administrative Region: Wales

LLEDR VALLEY

(BETWS-Y-COED)   **68 BEDS**

Youth Hostel, Lledr House,
Pont-y-Pant, Dolwyddelan,
Gwynedd LL25 0DQ
☎ Dolwyddelan (06906) 202

8

Overnight charge:
Young £3.80 Junior £4.70 Senior £5.90
🏠 Ⓐ Ⓒ Ⓐ 2 Ⓣ 🍴 Evening meal
19.00 hrs. Ⓢ P0 Dolwyddelan 1½m.
ⒺⒹ Thu. Ⓕ🆂 P for cars and 1 coach. Ⓛ
Hostel opens at 17.00 hrs

Jan 1-Feb 11	Closed
Feb 12-28	Open
	(except Sun & Mon)
Mar 1-Apr 30	Open (except Sun)
	Open Easter Sun
May 1-Aug 30	Open
Sep 1-Oct 31	Open (except Sun)
Nov 1-30	Open
	(except Sun & Mon)
Dec 1-Feb 10 92	Closed
Feb 11-29	Open
	(except Sun & Mon)

Party bookings accepted at warden's
discretion during closed periods

Wales Tourist Board Approved
A cedar shingled former quarry
manager's house in wooded, steep-
sided valley in Snowdonia National
Park. On main Road A470 Betws-y-
Coed-Ffestiniog

Ⓞ 115, Conwy Valley Leisure Map
ⒼⓇ 749534 📷 27

Attractions: Valley walks. Gwydwr
Forest 2m — waymarked routes. Hill
walking — Moel Siabod. Traditional
rock-climbing — Moelwyns. Large
play area opposite hostel — river
bathing. 🚶 Ⓤ 3m. Sarn Helen ½m,
Dolwyddelan Castle 2m, Cethins
Bridge 2m, Betws-y-Coed 5m —
popular tourist centre. Llechwedd
and Glodfa Ganol slate mines 6m.
Superb centre for educational studies

🚌 No service

🚶 Pont-y-Pant (not Sun, except Jul/
Aug) ¾m

Next Youth Hostels: Capel Curig
5m by mountain. Bryn Gwynant 9m
by mountain. Ffestiniog 10m. Pen-y-
Pass 10m by mountain. Idwal 12m

Administrative Region: Wales

Maeshafn

31 BEDS — COMFORT IMPROVED

Youth Hostel, Holt Hostel, Maeshafn. Correspondence and enquiries to Wales Regional Office
Cardiff (0222) 396766

Overnight charge:
Young £3.50 Junior £4.40 Senior £5.50
Gwernymynydd 1½m, Mold 4m. Mold Thu. P for cars and minibuses. Hostel opens at 17.00 hrs

Jan 1-Mar 27	Closed
Mar 28-Apr 4	Open
Apr 5-Jun 30	Open Fri & Sat and May 5 & 26
Jul 1-Aug 31	Open
Sep 1-Oct 26	Open Fri & Sat
Oct 27-Feb 29 92	Closed

Party bookings for sole usage may be accepted during closed periods

Wales Tourist Board Approved
First purpose-built hostel in Britain designed by Clough Williams-Ellis. Situated high on shoulder of Moel Findeg in the Clwydian Hills, 4m SW Mold. From Mold — Ruthin road, A494(T), follow signposts to Maeshafn village. A narrow road leads E from village to hostel (½m)

OS 117 GR 208606 Bart 28

Attractions: Loggerheads Country Park and Alyn Valley — A.O.N.B. 2½m. Nature trail. Offa's Dyke long distance footpath 3m. Hill forts. Potholing. Theatr Clwyd 4½m. Flint Castle 10m

Crosville Wales Flint - Mold - Ruthin, with connections from and to Chester at Mold. Alight Maeshafn Road end, 1½m (0745 343721)

Buckley 8m; Flint 10m; Chester 16m

Next Youth Hostels: Llangollen 16m. Chester 16m. Cynwyd 18m. Colwyn Bay 35m

Additional Information: YHA Regional Office, 1 Cathedral Road, Cardiff. (0222) 231370. Advance booking recommended

Penmaenmawr

56 BEDS

Youth Hostel, Penmaenbach, Penmaenmawr, Gwynedd LL34 6UL
Penmaenmawr (0492) 623476

Overnight charge:
Young £3.50 Junior £4.40 Senior £5.50
Seasonal Prices Jul 1-Aug 31:
Young £3.80 Junior £4.70 Senior £5.90
(self contained) Evening meal 19.00 hrs. Penmaenmawr 1¾m. Wed. P for cars and coaches. Hostel opens at 17.00 hrs

Jan 1-31	Closed
Feb 1-Jun 30	Open Fri, Sat, Sun & Apr 1, May 6, 27
Jul 1-Aug 31	Open (except Wed)
Sep 1-Oct 27	Open Fri, Sat, Sun
Oct 28-Feb 9 91	Closed
Feb 10-29	Open (except Wed)

Party bookings accepted at warden's discretion during closed periods

Wales Tourist Board Approved
Wooden building in extensive grounds between mountains of Snowdonia and sea. Midway between Conwy and Penmaenmawr on coast side of railway ¼m W of tunnel under Penmaenbach. Ideally suited for use by disabled groups

OS 115, Conwy Valley Leisure Map GR 737780 Bart 27

Attractions: Conwy Castle and walled town 2½m. Sea bathing. Prehistoric sites. Sychnant Pass 2m. Aber Falls. Cambrian Way Footpath route. Penmaenmawr history trail. Colwyn Bay Mountain Zoo 10m. Druid Circle 2m. Plas Mawr — Elizabethan mansion. Conwy. Penrhyn Castle 10m

Bws Gwynedd X1, 5 Caernarfon — Llandudno (pass close BR Llandudno Junction & Conwy) (0492 592111)

Penmaenmawr 1¾m

Next Youth Hostels: Rowen 7m. Colwyn Bay 10m. Bangor 12m

Rowen

27 BEDS

Youth Hostel, Rhiw Farm, Rowen Correspondence and enquiries to Wales Regional Office
Cardiff (0222) 231370

Overnight charge:
Young £2.60 Junior £3.50 Senior £4.40
Small No bread or milk. Rowen 2m (0492267) 282. P limited at hostel (NB steep hill). Hostel opens at 17.00 hrs

Jan 1-Mar 27	Closed
Mar 28-Apr 4	Open
Apr 5-30	Closed
May 1-Aug 31	Open
Sep 1-Feb 29 92	Closed

Party bookings for sole usage may be accepted during Apr, Sep and Oct only

Wales Tourist Board Approved
Simple, remote Welsh hill farmhouse situated high above the unspoilt village of Rowen in the Conwy Valley. Access by very steep hill, unsuitable for some vehicles, following route of Roman road up to Tal-y-Fan and on to Aber village

OS 115, Conwy Valley Leisure Map GR 747721 Bart 27

Attractions: Roman road and camp. Prehistoric remains. Conwy 5m: castle, town walls, Telford's suspension bridge, Plas Mawr, boat trips. Aber Falls and Nature Trail 6m. Carneddau Tal-y-Fan (2000 ft). Cambrian Way footpath route. Bodnant Gardens 4m

Bws Gwynedd 19, 49 from Llandudno (pass close BR Llandudno Junction & Conwy) (0492 592111)

Tal-y-Cafn (not Sun, except Jul/Aug) 3m

Next Youth Hostels:
Penmaenmawr 7m. Colwyn Bay 12m. Bangor 12m by mountain. Idwal Cottage 12m by mountains

Additional Information: All bookings and correspondence to: YHA Regional Office, 1 Cathedral Road, Cardiff. (0222) 231370. Mark all correspondence "Rowen Enquiry". Advance booking recommended

P EN-Y-PASS

**Youth Hostel, Pen-y-Pass,
Nant Gwynant, Caernarfon,
Gwynedd LL55 4NY**
📞 **Warden Llanberis (0286) 870428**

Overnight charge:
Young £4.60 Junior £5.90 Senior £7.00
🚻 🅰 🔟 ©️ ♿ 🛏 SS 4 except on
the day following a hostel closed
night when the hostel opens at 17.00
hrs. 🍴 Evening meal 19.00 hrs. S
Shop and PO Nant Peris 3½m. ED Wed.
P public car park opposite hostel —
car parking permits available from
warden. L Boots for hire. Lecture
room with dark room facilities, small
library and other classroom
equipment

Jan 1-Feb 9	Open
	(except Sun & Mon)
Feb 10-28	Closed
Mar 1-25	Open
	(except Sun & Mon)
Mar 26-Oct 31	Open
Nov 1-30	Open
	(except Sun & Mon)
Dec 1-Feb 10 92	Closed
Feb 11-29	Open
	(except Sun & Mon)

Wales Tourist Board Approved
Formerly the Gorphwsfa Hotel, a
favourite with climbers earlier this
century, in heart of Snowdonia
National Park. At head of Llanberis
Pass, A4086. From Capel Curig turn
right at Pen-y-Gwryd

OS 115, Snowdon Leisure Map
Pathfinder 65/75. GR 647556 🚌 27

Attractions: Instruction for
mountain walking and 🎿 details from
warden. Miners and Pyg tracks to
Snowdon summit. Cambrian Way
footpath route

🚌 Bws Gwynedd 11, 19, 96 from
Llandudno, Llanberis & Caernarfon
(pass BR Betws-y-Coed & Conwy),
alight Pen-y-gwryd, 1½m. All services
run Apr-Oct only. Otherwise use
services to Llanberis, (see Llanberis
Hostel), thence 5m (📞 0286
672556)

🚂 Bangor 18m; Betws-y-Coed (not
Sun, except Jul/Aug) 12m

Next Youth Hostels: Bryn
Gwynant 4m. Capel Curig 5m, via
mountains (5½ miles by road). Idwal
Cottage 5m by mountains (10m by
road). Llanberis 5½m. Snowdon
Ranger 10m by Snowdon route

Additional Information: To contact
resident members 📞 (0286) 870501

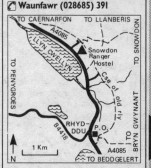

Pen-y-Pass Youth Hostel

S NOWDON RANGER

**Youth Hostel, Snowdon Ranger,
Rhyd Ddu, Caernarfon,
Gwynedd LL54 7YS**
📞 **Waunfawr (028685) 391**

[map showing TO CAERNARFON, TO LLANBERIS, LLYN CWELLYN, Snowdon Ranger Hostel, TO PENYGROES, RHYD DDU, P.O., Cae of old rly, BRYN GWYNANT, 1 Km, A4085, TO BEDDGELERT, TO SNOWDON]

Overnight charge:
Young £4.00 Junior £5.10 Senior £6.30
🚻 🅰 🔍 ©️ 🛏 SS Evening meal
19.00 hrs. S PO Rhyd Ddu 1½m ED
Thu. Caernarfon 8m. ED Thu. P for
cars and coaches. L Lake bathing
(from own beach). Hostel opens at
17.00 hrs

Jan 1-30	Closed
Jan 31-Mar 31	Open
	(except Tue & Wed)
Apr 1-Sep 30	Open
Oct 1-Nov 30	Open
	(except Tue & Wed)
Dec 1-Jan 29 92	Closed
Jan 30-Feb 29	Open
	(except Tue & Wed)

Wales Tourist Board Approved
Old inn named after former Snowdon
Mountain Guide. Situated by main
A4085 Caernarfon-Beddgelert road
on N side of Llyn Cwellyn. Marked
on map as "Snowdon Ranger"

OS 115, Snowdon Leisure Map
GR 565550 🚌 27

Attractions: Ranger path up
Snowdon. Ⓤ 4m, Gelerts Grave
Beddgelert 5m. Orienteering course
3m. Caernarfon Castle and Roman
fort 8m. Good mountain and valley
walking. Mountain craft and outdoor
pursuits courses for groups. Local
information packs — 35p stamps
please

🚌 Bws Gwynedd 11, 96 from
Caernarfon (connections from BR
Bangor) (📞 0286 672556)

🚂 Bangor 16m
Next Youth Hostels: Llanberis 4m
by mountain (11m by road). Bryn
Gwynant 9m (7m by path). Pen-y-
Pass 10m via Snowdon 3,500 ft 13m
by road, Idwal 12m over Glyders
3,000 ft and Snowdon, Llanbedr 24m

8

NORTH WALES

9 MID WALES

Mid Wales Mountains

For those who appreciate real peace and solitude, the **Elenith** area, which houses some of the 'Great Little Hostels of Wales' — Blaencaron, Bryn Poeth Uchaf, Dolgoch, Glascwm, Tyncornel, Ystumtuen — is the perfect choice.

The rolling hills and green river valleys are quite unspoilt; it is possible to walk all day and meet no-one but an occasional sheep farmer. In May, the only sounds to be heard are the rushing of streams, the baa-ing of lambs and the call of the cuckoo. There are many ruined and deserted farmhouses. Some valleys have been flooded to produce huge reservoirs, surrounded by forestry. Walkers need map-reading experience, as footpaths are not always easy to find. Pony-trekking is popular, especially in the countryside around Tregaron.

Mid Wales Coast

On the coast are several well-known holiday resorts, with sandy beaches and views of the hills behind.

Borth Youth Hostel situated on the sea front offers opportunities for individuals and/or groups to explore this relatively uncommercialised stretch of coastline.

Welsh/English Border

Knighton Youth Hostel on the other hand offers the magic of a quiet border town surrounded by hills and steeped in the history of Offa's Dyke long distance footpath.

Useful Information
Economy Packages

For details send sae to YHA Regional Office, 1 Cathedral Road, Cardiff CF1 9HA.

The Elenith Discount Package gives 7 nights for the price of 5 at any one or more of these Youth Hostels: Blaencaron, Bryn Poeth Uchaf, Dolgoch, Glascwm, Tyncornel, Ystumtuen — some of 'The Great Little Hostels of Wales'.

The Mid Wales Booking Bureau system which we operate will take the hassle out of booking tours. Elenith covers Blaencaron, Bryn Poeth Uchaf, Dolgoch, Glascwm, Tyncornel, Ystumtuen.

Send details of booking requirements, payments, and £1.75 fee to YHA Regional Office at the above address. Package Information free with booking fee. Credit Card payment accepted.

For Area Leaflets and Youth Hostel fact sheets send sae to Regional Office.

Helpful Publications

Available for sale from the Regional Office at the above address. All prices include postage. Please make cheques/postal orders payable to YHA.

Elenith —
walkers guide to Tywi and Elan Valley areas 50p
Offa's Dyke Strip Maps —
complete set of 9 .... £3.00
Inter-Hostel Routes —
Bryn Poeth Uchaf — Dolgoch — Tyncornel — Blaencaron ... 40p

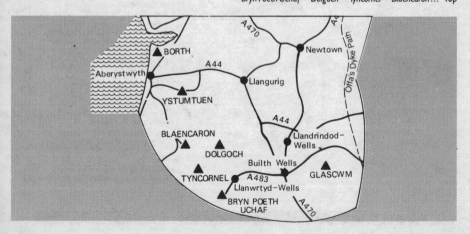

B LAENCARON

16 BEDS COMFORT IMPROVED YHA

Youth Hostel,
Blaencaron, Tregaron,
Dyfed SY25 6HL
☎ Tregaron (0974) 298441

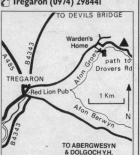

Overnight charge:
Young £2.60 Junior £3.50 Senior £4.40
👥🅰①🅰🍳🆖❌ Shop and 🅿
Tregaron 3m. 🔄 Thu. No 🆂 All food must be brought. 🅿 nearby

Jan 1-Feb 28	Open to advance group bookings
Mar 1-Oct 31	Open
Nov 1-Dec 31	Open to advance group bookings

Wales Tourist Board Approved
Small village school in remote, depopulated valley to west of Cambrian mountains. 3m ENE of Tregaron in the Afon Groes Valley. From Y Llew Goch (Red Lion) Inn, Tregaron, on road N, take first right (200 yds) to telephone box (2m). From here turn right, warden's house ½m, hostel 1m. Mobile store every two weeks (Wed). Bread van at warden house Fridays 9.30 am

🆗 146, 147 🆖 713608 🏷 17

Attractions: Walks in unspoilt Elenith. Drovers' road up valley. Bog of Tregaron, 4m. Llanddewi Brefi church 5½m. Teifi Falls 11m. Cradog Falls 9m. 🔲🔲🆄 Cambrian Way Footpath Route. Swimming bath available during school holidays at Tregaron. Booking Bureau — see Mid Wales heading page 84

🚌 Crosville Wales 515, 562 Aberystwyth — Lampeter (pass BR Aberystwyth), alight Tregaron, thence 2m (☎ 0970 617951)

🚂 Aberystwyth 20m; Devil's Bridge (Vale of Rheidol Rly – seasonal) 17m

Next Youth Hostels: Dolgoch 12m (9m by mountains). Tyncornel 14m (8m by mountains). Ystumtuen 21m. Borth 29m

---

B ORTH

60 BEDS

Youth Hostel, Morlais,
Borth, Dyfed SY24 5JS
☎ Borth (0970) 871498
Answerphone service

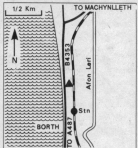

Overnight charge:
Young £4.00 Junior £5.10 Senior £6.30
🅰👥🍳②🍴🔄 Evening meal 19.00 hrs. 🆂🅿 Borth. 🔄 Wed. 🆖 Activities can be arranged. 🅿 for cars, coaches near-by. Hostel opens 17.00 hrs

Jan 1-31	Closed
Feb 1-28	Open Fri & Sat
Mar 1-24	Open (except Sun)
Mar 25-Sep 30	Open
Oct 1-31	Open (except Sun)
Nov 1-30	Open Fri & Sat
Dec 1-Jan 31 92	Closed
Feb 1-29	Open Fri & Sat

Wales Tourist Board Approved
Edwardian house on seafront overlooking Dyfi Estuary, with mountains behind. Between village and Ynyslas golf links

🆗 135 🆖 608907 🏷 22

Attractions: Safe bathing. Surf boards at hostel. 🅰 and 🆄 nearby. Natural history and 🔲 Dyfi Estuary 2½m. Prehistoric monuments. Drove roads. Industrial archaeology. Foel Goch 5m. East Rheidol Valley 6m. Plynlimon. Aberystwyth 8m. Sailing, canoeing, diving (details from warden). Courses: biology, ecology, natural history, geology, geography, art, drama, 🔲

🚌 Crosville Wales 512 from Aberystwyth (☎ 0970 617951)

🚂 Borth ¾m

Next Youth Hostels: Ystumtuen 18m. Corris 19m. Blaencaron 29m

---

B RYN POETH UCHAF

26 BEDS COMFORT IMPROVED YHA

Postal address: Youth Hostel,
Hafod-y-Pant, Cynghordy,
Llandovery, Dyfed SA20 0NB
☎ Cynghordy (05505) 235

Overnight charge:
Young £2.60 Junior £3.50 Senior £4.40
🅰👥🍳②🔄🆖❌ Shop and 🅿
Rhandirmwyn 2½m. Open 7 days. Cynghordy 2½m. 🔄 Sat. No 🆂 Bread and milk not provided. 🅿 for cars only at Hafod-y-Pant — small charge levied. No coach access

Jan 1-Feb 28	Open to advance group bookings
Mar 1-Oct 31	Open
Nov 1-Dec 31	Open to advance group bookings

Wales Tourist Board Approved
Old farmhouse and barn, isolated and lit solely by gas. It is situated high above the Tywi Valley with views over to the Brecon Beacons National Park. 2½m N of Cynghordy (Llanfair-ar-y-bryn on 🔄 17). Turn left off A483 at N of village. Right turn in ¾m to continue under viaduct alongside river. Follow metalled road, climb steep hill. Left turn at T-junction, then right (200 yds) and right again (600 yds) to warden's house, Hafod-y-Pant. From Tywi valley turn E at junction 1½m S of Rhandirmwyn. **Hostel ¾m walk** from warden's house by waymarked route. Sturdy footwear advised. Torch essential and access to Hafod-y-Pant strongly advised after dark

🆗 146, 147, 160 🆖 796439 🏷 17

Attractions: Walking in unspoilt Elenith, Twm Shon Catti's cave 4m. Lead mines. 🔲 Llyn Brianne reservoir 7m. 🆄🔲 Cambrian Way footpath route. Booking Bureau — see Mid Wales heading page 84

🚌 No Service

🚂 Cynghordy (not Sun, except May-Sep) 2¼m

Next Youth Hostels: Tyncornel 10m by mountains. Dolgoch 15m. Llanddeusant 16m

🛏 Sleeps 4 in 1 bedroom plus 1 cot

Administrative Region: Wales

Administrative Region: Wales

Administrative Region: Wales

Dolgoch

22 BEDS · yha COMFORT IMPROVED

Youth Hostel,
Dolgoch, Tregaron,
Dyfed SY25 6NR
📞 Tregaron (0974) 298680

Overnight charge:
Young £2.60 Junior £3.50 Senior £4.40
🔲2 🔺 ⛄ 🍴 ✖ Small 🅂 Bread not available. Shop Tregaron 9m. 🔲 Thu. 🅿 Abergwesyn 6m. 🅿 for cars only. Coaches Tregaron 9m

Jan 1–Feb 28	Open to advance group bookings
Mar 1–Oct 31	Open
Nov 1–Dec 31	Open to advance group bookings

Wales Tourist Board Approved
Remote farmhouse in the wild and lonely Tywi Valley in the Elenith, 9 miles from nearest shops. ¾m S of Abergwesyn-Tregaron mountain road in Tywi Valley at the Dyfed-Powys county boundary. If travelling W turn left along rough track immediately after crossing bridge. Cyclists must take care on very steep hills

ⓄⓈ 147 ⒼⓇ 806561 🗺 17

Attractions: 🦅 RSPB reserves at Dinas and Gwenffrwd. Llyn Brianne reservoir 2m. ⛺ Twm Shon Catti's Cave 11m. Drygarn Fawr 6m. Soar y Mynidd chapel 3m. Booking Bureau — see Mid Wales heading page 84

🚌 Crosville Wales 515, 562 Aberystwyth — Lampeter (pass BR Aberystwyth), alight Tregaron, 9m (📞 0970 617951). Post Bus available 6m. Contact post-office Abergwesyn for times

🚉 Llanwrtyd Wells (not Sun, except May-Sep) 10m

Next Youth Hostels: Tyncornel 5m by mountains. Blaencaron 12m (9m by mountains). Bryn Poeth Uchaf 15m

---

Glascwm

22 BEDS

Youth Hostel, The School,
Glascwm, Llandrindod Wells,
Powys LD1 5SE
📞 Hundred House (0982) 570415

Overnight charge:
Young £2.60 Junior £3.50 Senior £4.40
🔺 ⛄ 🔲2 🍴 ⛄ ✖ Small 🅂 Shop Hundred House 4m. 🔲 village. No milk. 🅿 nearby for cars and coaches

Jan 1–Feb 28	Open to advance group bookings
Mar 1–Oct 31	Open
Nov 1–Dec 31	Open to advance group bookings

Wales Tourist Board Approved
Old stone school building in hamlet which was once much larger, in Radnorshire Hills. 10m from Kington, 9m from Builth on road from Newchurch-Builth. In middle of village

ⓄⓈ 148 ⒼⓇ 158532 🗺 18

Attractions: St David's church. Radnor Forest. Giant's Grave and Mawn Pools. 🪨 Geology. Ⓤ 3m. Water-break-its-neck waterfall. Offa's Dyke long distance footpath 4m. Hergest Croft, Kington 10m. Booking Bureau — see Mid Wales heading page 84

🚌 Bus service to Builth Wells on Mondays only. Leave 9.45am return Glascwm 14.15hrs

🚉 Builth Road (not Sun, except May-Sep) 11m

Next Youth Hostels: Knighton 18m. Capel-y-ffin 20m. Ty'n-y-Caeau 25m

---

Tyncornel

18 BEDS · yha COMFORT IMPROVED

Youth Hostel, Tyncornel,
Post c/o Wales Regional Office,
1 Cathedral Road, Cardiff CF1 9HA
📞 (0222) 231370 — Office

Overnight charge:
Young £2.60 Junior £3.50 Senior £4.40
🔲2 🔺 ⛄ 🍴 ⛄ 🔲 Llanddewi-Brefi 7m. No 🅂 🅿 limited: coaches in layby 9m. 🅂 7m

Jan 1–Feb 28	Open to advance group bookings
Mar 1–Oct 31	Open
Nov 1–Dec 31	Open to advance group bookings

All bookings via Wales Regional Office 📞 (0222) 231370

Wales Tourist Board Approved
Isolated farmhouse in lonely valley in the Elenith. 7m E of Llanddewi-Brefi near head of Doethie valley. From Llanddewi-Brefi follow tarmac road SE up Brefi valley (not road SW to Farmers). Fork left at 4½m. At 6m, left downhill, over stream. Hostel 1m down valley (you will have crossed 2 cattle grids). From S via Rhandirmwyn and Doethie valley footpath (8m allow 3 hrs from ⒼⓇ 768480)

ⓄⓈ 146, 147 ⒼⓇ 751534 🗺 17

Attractions: Doethie valley. Llyn Brianne Reservoir 3m. Twm Shon Catti's Cave 6m. Soar-y-Mynydd chapel 2½m. 🪨 Cambrian Way Footpath Route. Booking Bureau — see Mid Wales heading page 84

🚌 Crosville Wales 515/16 Aberystwyth-Lampeter-Tregaron. All services at Llanddewi Brefi 7m. Save for last journey (Tue-Sun) at Tregaron 10m. Crosville/Davies Bros/Evans Aberystwyth-Tregaron at Llanddewi Brefi 7m, change at Lampeter (📞 0970 617951). Post Bus available 11m from East via mountains. Contact post-office Abergwesyn for times

🚉 Aberystwyth 28m

Next Youth Hostels: Dolgoch 5m by mountains. Bryn Poeth Uchaf 10m by mountains. Blaencaron 14m (8m by mountains)

Y STUMTUEN

24 BEDS

Youth Hostel, Glantuen,
Ystumtuen, Abersytwyth,
Dyfed SY23 3AE

☎ Ponterwyd (097085) 693

Overnight charge:
Young £2.60 Junior £3.50 Senior £4.40
🔺 🏠 ② 🍴 🔳 🔳 No 🆂 Small store at
warden's house. Shop and 🅿️
Ponterwyd 2m. 🅿️ for cars nearby.
Enquire with warden about coach
parking

Jan 1-Feb 28	Open to advance group bookings
Mar 1-Oct 31	Open
Nov 1-Dec 31	Open to advance group bookings

School in quiet old lead mining village
in the northern Elenith 13 miles from
Abèrystwyth. Approach by road
from A44, turn off up steep hill ¾m
W of Ponterwyd, signposted
Ystumtuen. Approach from Devil's
Bridge Ponterwyd (A4120) over
Parson's Bridge, unsuitable for cyclists
and dangerous after dark. Road from
village to A44 is very steep, cyclists
should take care

🆗 135, 147 🆖 735786 🔳 17

Attractions: Devil's Bridge and
waterfalls 1½m. Narrow gauge
railway 2m. George Borrow Hotel
2m. Plynlimon Fawr (2468 ft). Nant-
y-Moch reservoir 5m. Llywernog
silver and lead mines 2m. Rheidol
Power Station 4m. Trout 🎣 🐟
Cambrian Way footpath route.
Booking Bureau — see Mid Wales
heading page 84

🚌 Crosville Wales/Roberts 501 from
Aberystwyth (passes BR
Aberystwyth), alight 1m W of
Ponterwyd, thence 1½m
(☎ 0970 617951 & 611085)

🚃 Rhiwfron (Vale of Rheidol Rly —
seasonal) 2m; Aberystwyth 12m

Next Youth Hostels: Borth 18m.
Blaencaron 21m

Administrative Region: Wales

10 WEST WALES

The Pembrokeshire Coast National Park has breath-taking cliff scenery and a long distance footpath running round it. There are sandy beaches, small coves and fishing harbours. The climate is mild, because the surrounding sea is warmed by the Gulf Stream. Wild flowers, seals and sea birds are abundant, especially in the Spring. Visits may be made to the National Nature Reserve on Skomer Island.

Many ruined 13th century castles remain, as well as prehistoric relics and the 12th century Cathedral of St David's, hidden in a hollow beside the River Alun. In the North East are the Preseli Hills, rising to a height of 1760 feet and popular with walkers and pony trekkers.

Useful Information

The Booking Bureau will take most of the hassle out of booking tours. Along the Pembrokeshire Coast — covers Poppit Sands, Pwll Deri, Trevine, St David's, Broad Haven, Marloes Sands, Pentlepoir and Manorbier. Send details of booking requirements, payment, and £1.75 fee to YHA, Llaethdy, St David's, Haverfordwest, Dyfed SA62 6PR. Tel: (0437) 720345. To avoid disappointment allow 3 weeks booking in advance to St. David's Youth Hostel.

Self Catering Night — St David's Youth Hostel does not normally serve breakfast on the morning following the SC night indicated in the Youth Hostel details.

Helpful Publications

Available from the YHA Regional Office, 1 Cathedral Road, Cardiff CF1 9HA. All prices include postage. Please make cheques/postal orders payable to YHA.

Pembrokeshire Coast Path £2.00

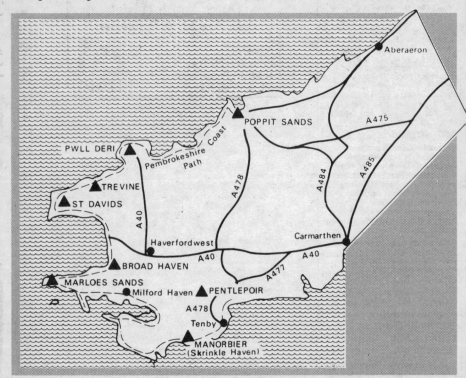

BROAD HAVEN
65 BEDS · COMFORT IMPROVED

Youth Hostel, Broad Haven,
Haverfordwest, Dyfed SA62 3JH
☎ Broad Haven (0437) 781688
Answerphone service

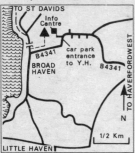

Overnight charge:
Young £4.00 Junior £5.10 Senior £6.30
Seasonal Prices Jul 1-Aug 31:
Young £4.40 Junior £5.40 Senior £6.60
🏠 C ⚿ ⚖ 2 ▦ Laundry facilities
available. 🍴 Evening meal served at
18.30 hrs. S Shop and ✉ ½m. No ⏰
FS P for cars and coaches. Hostel
open 17.00 hrs

Jan 1-Feb 18	Closed
Feb 19-23	Open
Feb 24-Mar 7	Closed
Mar 8-24	Open Fri & Sat
Mar 25-Apr 13	Open
Apr 15-Jun 23	Open (except Sun) but Open May 5, 26
Jun 24-Jul 20	Open
Jul 22-Aug 31	Open
Sep 2-7	Open
Sep 23-28	Open
Sep 30-Oct 31	Open (except Sun)

In closed periods warden may open
the Hostel to advance party
bookings of 15 or more

Wales Tourist Board Approved
Purpose built hostel and winner of 3
awards for its facilities for the
disabled. Close to beaches with
views of fine coastal headlands in the
National Park. At north end of village
adjacent to National Park car park
and between beach and B4341

OS 157 GR 863141 ▦ 11

Attractions: Fine beaches, coastal
scenery, U Sea ⛵ 🏄 Windsurfing,
UFO's, Skomer island. National Park
information centre next door.
Booking Bureau — see West Wales
heading, page 88

🚌 Edwards 311 from Haverfordwest
(passes close BR Haverfordwest)
(☎ 0437 890230)
🚉 Haverfordwest 7m

Next Youth Hostels: Marloes Sands
by coast path 13m, by road 8m. St
David's by coast path 25m, by road
15m. Pentlepoir 21m

MARLOES SANDS
36 BEDS

YH, Runwayskiln, Marloes,
Haverfordwest, Dyfed SA62 3BH
☎ (0646) 636667
Answerphone service

Overnight charge:
Young £3.10 Junior £4.00 Senior £5.10
🏠 ⛰ ⚿ 1 ▦ ⊠ Shop and ✉ 1m. ⏰
Tue. P for six cars at hostel. National
Trust car park 200 yds, 5pm-9am
free, 9am-5pm parking fee must be
paid. Coaches 200 yds or 1m.
Consult warden. S ⛰ only

Jan 1-Feb 28	Closed
Mar 1-16	Open Fri & Sat
Mar 22-Apr 13	Open
Apr 19-27	Open Fri & Sat
Apr 29-Jun 29	Open (except Sun)
Jul 1-Sep 28	Open
Oct 4-12	Open Fri & Sat
Oct 14-26	Open
Oct 28-Dec 31	Closed

In closed periods warden may be able
to open to advance bookings

Wales Tourist Board Approved
Range of farm buildings on National
Trust property, overlooking Marloes
Sands Bay in National Park. From
Haverfordwest take B4327 (Dale Rd)
for 11m. Turn right for Marloes. At
church turn left to Marloes Sands car
park. Hostel 200 yds down lane

OS 157 GR 778080 ▦ 11

Attractions: Large beach. Local
Naturalists Trust nature trail and
reserve 200 yds. Geology. Flowers
and plants. 🚢 Boats to Skomer
Island. Scuba Diving. Martins Haven
1½m. Canoeing and sailing. Puffins,
Razorbills, Choughs. Booking Bureau
— see West Wales heading, page 88

🚌 From Haverfordwest or Milford
Haven to Marloes (Infrequent),
thence 1m (☎ 0437 890230). Private
hire service (☎ 06465 662)
🚉 Milford Haven 11m;
Haverfordwest 14m

Next Youth Hostels: Broad Haven
12m (by coastal path), by road 8m.
St David's 22m. Pentlepoir 24m.
Manorbier by road 21m.

MANORBIER
68 BEDS · COMFORT IMPROVED

Youth Hostel,
Manorbier, Dyfed SA70 7TT
☎ (0834) 871803
Answerphone service

Overnight charge:
Young £4.00 Junior £5.10 Senior £6.30
Seasonal Prices Jul 1-Aug 31:
Young £4.40 Junior £5.40 Senior £6.60
🏠 ⛰ A C ⚿ ⚖ ▦ ⛰ 2 📞 S P
1m. Laundry facilities available. C P
for cars and coaches. Hostel open
17.00 hrs

Jan 1-Feb 18	Closed
Feb 19-23	Open
Feb 24-Mar 7	Closed
Mar 8-23	Open
Mar 25-Apr 6	Open (except Sun)
Apr 8-27	Open
May 13-18	Open
May 20-Jun 1	Open
Jun 3-29	Open (except Sun)
Jul 1-Aug 31	Open
Sep 2-Oct 31	Open (except Sun)

In closed periods warden may be able
to open family accommodation and to
advance party bookings of 15 or more

Wales Tourist Board Approved
Recently (1988) refurbished building,
modern and attractive with its lovely
sandy beach less than 200 yds away

OS 158 GR 081975

Attractions: Ideal location to discover
and explore the National Park. Tenby
popular seaside resort nearby. 2 beaches
within 5 minutes walk. A windsurfing
and surfing. 🚢 boat to Caldey Island.
🏄 Sea. ⚲ L Manorbier Castle
nearby. Pembrokeshire Coast booking
bureau see page 88

🚌 South Wales 358 Tenby —
Haverfordwest, alight Manorbier, 1m
(☎ 0792 475511)
🚉 Manorbier (not Sun, except May-
Sep) 2½m

Next Youth Hostels: Pentlepoir
13m. Broad Haven 28m by road.
Marloes Sands 21m

🏠 3 self-contained units, each with 2
bedrooms & cot. Facilities open 7
days a week

Administrative Region: Wales (×3)

N (CEI NEWYDD) **BARN 28 BEDS**
NEW QUAY SANDS

**YH, The Glyn, Church Street,
New Quay, Dyfed SA45 9NU**
New Quay (Dyfed) (0545) 560337
Answerphone service

10

WEST WALES

We regret that this
Youth Hostel is no
longer open.
Alternative coastal
Youth Hostels in West
or Mid Wales are listed
in this section, as well
as Borth in the Mid
Wales section.

The Association has reached an
agreement for 1991 for YHA
members with a Bunk House Barn
some 12m due south of New Quay
Sands near **Llandysul**.

**The Long Barn, Penrhiw Farm,
Capel Dewi, Llandysul, Dyfed
SA44 4PG**
Llandysul (0559) 363200

Overnight charge:
Young £2.60 Junior £3.50 Senior £4.40
SC dormitory style accommodation
A No S Based at working farm

Jul 19-Aug 31   Open

At other times group bookings may
be possible

Located on minor road between
Llandysul (B4476) and Capel Dewi
(B4459)

OS 146 GR 437417

Llandysul 2m

Carmarthen 15m

Next Youth Hostels: Poppit Sands
25m. Blaencaron 28m. Borth 38m

P **26 BEDS**
PENTLEPOIR

**Youth Hostel, The Old School,
Pentlepoir, Saundersfoot,
Dyfed SA69 9BJ**
Saundersfoot (0834) 812333

Overnight charge:
Young £3.50 Junior £4.40 Senior £5.50
Evening meal 19.00 hrs.
S Shop and PO nearby. Wed. P for
cars only. Coaches: Saundersfoot 1m.
Hostel opens 17.00 hrs

Jan 1-Feb 28   Closed
Mar 1-Jul 17   Open (except Thu)
Jul 18-Aug 31   Open
Sep 1-Oct 30   Open (except Thu)
Nov 1-Dec 31   Closed

In closed periods warden may be able
to open to advance party bookings
of 15 or more

Wales Tourist Board Approved
Old village school just inland from
Saundersfoot, in Pembrokeshire
Coast National Park. On A478, 1m S
of junction with A477

OS 158 GR 116060 Barn 11

Attractions: Pembrokeshire coast
long distance footpath 1m. Bathing
1m. Geology. Frequent regattas.
Local crafts. windsurfing, sea at
Saundersfoot. 1m. U 2m. Tenby
seaside resort for boating and snorkel
courses 4m. Caldy Island. Marros Sands
(remains of submerged forest). Ferry
to Rosslare from Pembroke Dock
10m. Booking Bureau — see West
Wales heading, page 88

Rapide Service London-Tenby
National Express stops at Kilgetty
1m. Local bus to Hostel. Silcox 351-
3, 361 from Tenby (0834 2189)

Saundersfoot ½m

Next Youth Hostels: Manorbier
13m. Broad Haven 21m. Marloes
Sands 24m. Poppit Sands 34m. St.
Davids 34m. Trevine 37m. Port
Eynon 63m

P **48 BEDS**
POPPIT SANDS

**Youth Hostel, 'Sea View',
Poppit, Cardigan,
Dyfed SA43 3LP**
Cardigan (0239) 612936

Overnight charge:
Young £3.50 Junior £4.40 Senior £5.50
Seasonal Prices Jul 1-Aug 31:
Young £3.80 Junior £4.70 Senior £5.90
Packed lunches to
order. S Village store open 7 days a
week. Laundry service at Hostel. PO
St Dogmaels 3m. P for cars only.
Coaches ¼m. 2 self contained units

Jan 1-6   Open
Jan 7-21   Closed*
Feb 1-Mar 23   Open Fri & Sat
Mar 24-Oct 31   Open
Nov 1-30   Open Fri & Sat
Dec 1-31   Open

*In closed periods warden may be
able to open to advance bookings by
phone or post

Wales Tourist Board Approved
A former inn in 5 acre grounds SSSI
reaching down to the sea and estuary
in Pembrokeshire Coast National
Park. 1m SE of Cemaes Head. From
St Dogmaels turn right for Poppit
(3m). Turn left at beach up hill along
'no through road'. Hostel second set
of buildings on right

OS 145 GR 144487 Barn 11, 17

Attractions: Fine sands. Rock pools.
Marine life. Geology. Canoe,
windsurf board hire. Boat and fishing
trips. Bird life. Cardigan Wildlife
Park. U Adjacent to Preselli
Hills. Coastal Path Booking Bureau
— see West Wales heading, page 88

Richards Bros 403/9 from
Cardigan to within ½m (Jul/Aug only),
but to St Dogmaels, 2m, at other
times. (0239 613756)

Fishguard Harbour 20m;
Carmarthen 26m

Next Youth Hostels: Pwll Deri 30m
on coast path. Blaencaron 44m.
Llanddeusant 42m. Port Eynon 50m.

2 self-contained units, each with 4
beds plus cot

P WLL DERI

Youth Hostel, Castell Mawr, Tref Asser, Goodwick, Dyfed SA64 0LR
☎ St Nicholas (03485) 233
Answerphone service

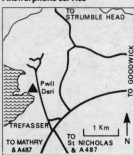

Overnight charge:
Young £3.10 Junior £4.00 Senior £5.10
Seasonal Prices Jul 1-Aug 31:
Young £3.50 Junior £4.40 Senior £5.50
Ⓐ 1 ⓉⓋ Ⓜ Evening meal 19.00 hrs. Ⓢ
Shop and Ⓟⓞ St Nicholas 2m. ⒺⒹ Wed.
Ⓟ for cars nearby. Coaches Fishguard
4½m

Jan 1-Feb 28	Closed
Mar 1-22	Open
	(except Sat & Sun)
Mar 25-Apr 12	Open
Apr 15-27	Open (except Sun)
Apr 29-May 11	Open
May 13-18	Open
May 20-31	Open
Jun 1-Jul 6	Open (except Sun)
Jul 8-Aug 31	Open
Sep 2-Oct 31	Open
	(except Sat & Sun)

In closed period warden may open for advance party bookings of 15 or more

Wales Tourist Board Approved
A former private house on 400ft cliffs overlooking Pwll Deri Bay in Pembrokeshire Coast National Park. 4½m W of Fishguard Harbour (Goodwick) and ¾m N of Tref Asser. Take Strumble Head road out of Goodwick, and follow first two Strumble Head signposts then follow Pwll Deri signposts. Approach from St David's-Fishguard road via St Nicholas

ⓄⓈ 157 ⒼⓇ 891387 🚶 11

Attractions: 🌅 Sunsets. Strumble Head. Bathing. Grey seals. 🌅 🚣 Geology. Hill fort behind hostel. Booking Bureau — see West Wales heading, page 88

🚌 Richards 410/11 Fishguard — Goodwick (☎0239 613756)
🚢 Fishguard Harbour 4½m

Next Youth Hostels: Trevine 10m (by path). St David's 19m. Poppit Sands 37m (by path)

Administrative Region: Wales

S T DAVID'S

Youth Hostel, Llaethdy, St David's, Haverfordwest, Dyfed SA62 6PR
☎ St David's (0437) 720345
Answerphone service

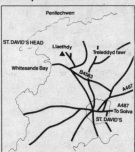

Overnight charge:
Young £3.50 Junior £4.40 Senior £5.50
Seasonal Prices Jul 1-Aug 31:
Young £3.80 Junior £4.70 Senior £5.90
🏠 Ⓐ 2 ⓉⓋ Ⓜ Evening meal 19.00 hrs.
Ⓢ Ⓒ night Thu — see West Wales heading. Ⓢ Shop and Ⓟⓞ St David's 2½m. ⒺⒹ Wed. Ⓟ for cars only. Coaches at Whitesands Bay 1m. Hostel opens at 17.00 hrs

Jan 1-Feb 28	Closed
Mar 1-27	Open (except Thu)
Mar 29-Apr 17	Open
Apr 19-May 22	Open (except Thu)
May 24-Jun 5	Open
Jun 7-Jul 3	Open (except Thu)
Jul 5-Aug 31	Open
Sep 1-Oct 31	Open (except Thu)
Nov 1-Dec 31	Closed

In closed period warden may be able to open to advance bookings

Wales Tourist Board Approved
White painted farmhouse with red doors under the summit of Carn Llidi in the National Park 2m NW of St David's

ⓄⓈ 157 ⒼⓇ 739276 🚶 11

Attractions: Bathing, beaches and surfing. Windsurfing. St David's Cathedral, Bishops Palace 2m. 🚣 Geology. Farm museum ¼m, 🚲 2m, sea 🚣 🎣 🐟 Ⓛ Oceanarium. Ramsey Island boat trips. Ⓤ Booking Bureau — see West Wales heading, page 88

🚌 Richards 340 from BR Haverfordwest or 411 from Fishguard, alight St David's on both, thence 2m (not Sun) ☎ (0437) 721428 or (0633) 820751
🚢 Fishguard Harbour 15m; Haverfordwest 18m

Next Youth Hostels: Trevine 12m. Pwll Deri 19m. Broad Haven 15m (25m by coast path). Marloes Sands 22m (36m by path)

🏚 Self-contained unit, sleeps 4 plus cot. Facilities open 7 days a week

Administrative Region: Wales

T REVINE

Youth Hostel, 11 Ffordd-yr-Afon, Trevine, Haverfordwest, Dyfed SA62 5AU
☎ Croesgoch (0348) 831414

Overnight charge:
Young £2.60 Junior £3.50 Senior £4.40
1 ⓉⓋ Ⓖⓢⓒ Ⓜ Shops & Ⓟⓞ in village. Ⓟ for cars nearby. Coaches St. David's 7m

Jan 1-Feb 28	Closed
Mar 2-21	Open
Mar 23-Apr 11	Open
Apr 13-May 2	Open (except Fri)
May 3-9	Open
May 11-23	Open (except Fri)
May 25-Jun 6	Open
Jun 8-Jul 4	Open (except Fri)
Jul 6-Aug 31	Open
Sep 2-Oct 31	Open (except Fri)
Nov 1-Dec 31	Closed

In closed period warden may be able to open to advance party bookings

Wales Tourist Board Approved
Former school in centre of village half a mile from the sea, in Pembrokeshire Coast National Park. Halfway between Fishguard and St David's. Leave A487 halfway between Croesgoch and Mathry at Trefin sign

ⓄⓈ 157 ⒼⓇ 840324 🚶 11

Attractions: Llanrian water wheel 1½m. Sea 🚣 trips 1m. Ⓐ 2m. Wool mill 2m. Porthgain village 2m. Geology. Marine biology. Wild flowers. Scolton Manor country park 11m. Booking Bureau — see West Wales heading, page 88

🚌 Richards 411 from Fishguard (passes close BR Fishguard Harbour) (connections from BR Haverfordwest on 412) (☎0437 721428)
🚢 Fishguard Harbour 12m; Haverfordwest 18m

Next Youth Hostels: Pwll Deri 8m on coast path. St David's 11m on coast path. Pentlepoir 37m

Administrative Region: Wales

10

W E S T   W A L E S

BRECON BEACONS AND SOUTH WALES

Brecon Beacons National Park

Parc Cenedlaethol Bannau Brycheiniog (as it is called in Welsh) takes its name from the shapely peaks at its centre, with Pen-y-Fan rising to 2907 ft. (886m). Old Red Sandstone rocks form a 'back-bone' of high ground — in four main mountain blocks — right across the Park from the English border, deeply cut by the broad and fertile valley of the Usk between Brecon and Abergavenny.

Confusingly, there are Black Mountains in the east and a Black Mountain in the west, beyond the Fforest Fawr range (once a royal hunting ground). Along the southern edge of the Park, narrow bands of Carboniferous Limestone and Millstone Grit produce dramatically different scenery, with remarkable cave systems and fine waterfalls. The total area is 519 square miles (1344 square kilometres).

A large part of the uplands are used for grazing sheep or cattle giving good access and fine views to walkers and pony trekkers.

There are several national nature reserves in the Park. For further details contact the National Park Office, Tel: (0874) 4437.

The Monmouthshire and Brecon Canal has recently been renovated and extended to 32 miles and is now used exclusively for pleasure cruising.

The Brecon mountain railway is also a favourite attraction for visitors.

Rhondda Valley — Llwynypia

Once the heart of industrial South Wales, the Rhondda Valley and surrounding area now offer the visitor beautiful scenery combined with the fascinating relics of an industrial heritage. Llwynypia Youth Hostel is set in seventy-five acres of woodland and is ideally situated for touring both the countryside and sites of local heritage.

The Gower Peninsula — Port Eynon

The Gower Peninsula is another of South Wales' areas of outstanding beauty with well renowned coastal splendours, sheer limestone cliffs, crescent shaped bays and breezy Worm's Head.

South Glamorgan — Cardiff

'City and Vale' — the county's motto reflects the contrasting nature of South Glamorgan.

Cardiff is the Capital City of Wales — see Cardiff Youth Hostel entry for further information.

The Vale of Glamorgan is mainly agricultural with many attractive villages and castles. The Heritage coastline 11 miles in length houses the 13th century St Donat Castle now the internationally renowned Atlantic College. Llantwit Major, an attractive small coastal town which has a 15th century church, was the site of a Christian settlement and is steeped in history.

Useful Information

The Brecon Beacons Booking Bureau will take most of the hassle out of booking tours.

Brecon Beacons — covers Capel-y-Ffin, Ty'n-y-Caeau, Llwyn-y-Celyn, Ystradfellte and Llanddeusant. Send details of booking requirements, payment and £1.75 fee to YHA Llwyn-y-Celyn, Libanus, Brecon, Powys LD3 8NH. Tel: (0874) 4261. Package information free with booking fee. Credit card payment accepted.

Self Catering Night — Capel-y-Ffin Youth Hostel does not normally serve breakfast on the morning following the Self Catering night indicated in the Hostel details.

Helpful Publications

Available for sale from YHA Regional Office, 1 Cathedral Road, Cardiff CF1 9HA. Prices include postage. Please make cheques/postal orders payable to YHA.

Offa's Dyke Strip Maps —
complete set of 9 @ £3.00

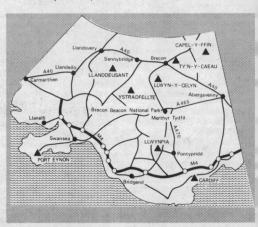

RIDING FROM CAPEL-Y-FFIN

Riding Courses & Trail Rides of 2, 4 & 6 Days

Day & Half Day Rides

11-18 Club
(For unaccompanied teenagers)

English or Western Riding

School Parties Welcome

Discount for Groups & YHA Members

Contact:
**Black Mountain Holidays,
The Youth Hostel,
Capel-y-ffin, Abergavenny,
Gwent NP7 7NP
Crucorney (0873) 890650**

*Approved by:
Pony Trekking & Riding Society of Wales
The Ponies Association (UK)*

CAPEL-Y-FFIN

**Youth Hostel, Capel-y-Ffin,
Abergavenny, Gwent NP7 7NP**
Crucorney (0873) 890650
Answerphone service

Jul 1-Aug 31	Open (SC Wed)
Sep 1-10	Open (except Wed)
Sep 20-Oct 31	Open (except Wed)
Nov 1-30	Open Fri & Sat (SC only)
Dec 1-Jan 31 92	Closed
Feb 1-28	Open Fri & Sat (SC only)

Wales Tourist Board Approved
King George VI Memorial Hostel. Farmhouse in 40 acre grounds on mountain side at 1400ft in Brecon Beacons National Park. In Black Mountains on lefthand side of road which runs from Llanthony to Hay. 1m northwards from Capel-y-ffin. 8m S of Hay-on-Wye. Marked 'The Castle' on maps

OS 161 Brecon Beacons (Eastern Area) Leisure Map GR 250328 Barl 13

Attractions: Offa's Dyke long distance footpath 1½m. Llanthony Priory 4m. Horse Riding Centre based at Hostel — separate brochure from warden. Forest walk. Fine high level ridge walking. Cambrian Way footpath route. Booking Bureau — see Brecon Beacons heading, page 92

National Welsh 39 Hereford — Brecon (passes close BR Hereford), alight Hay-on-Wye, 8m (0222 371331)

Abergavenny 16m.

Next Youth Hostels: Glascwm 20m. Ty'n-y-Caeau 23m via Hay

Overnight charge:
Young £3.50 Junior £4.40 Senior £5.50
Evening meal 19.30 hrs S and post box. Bread and milk to be ordered at least a week in advance. P for cars and minibuses at lay-by near hostel entrance. Coaches at Llanthony 5m or Hay-on-Wye 8m. Cycle shed at top of drive. Hostel opens 17.00 hrs

Jan 1-31	Closed
Feb 1-28	Open Fri & Sat (SC only)
Mar 1-16	Open (except Wed)
Mar 25-Apr 9	Open (SC Wed)
Apr 11-Jun 30	Open (except Wed)

Capel-y-ffin Youth Hostel

Administrative Region: Wales

BRECON BEACONS AND SOUTH WALES

CARDIFF

(CAERDYDD)

COMFORT IMPROVED

**Youth Hostel, 1 Wedal Road,
Roath Park, Cardiff CF2 5PG**
Cardiff (0222) 462303
Answerphone service

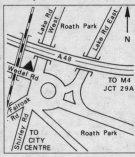

Overnight charge:
Young £4.60 Junior £5.90 Senior £7.00
Evening meal 18.30
hrs. Cafeteria service Jul-Aug only.
Laundry facilities available. Shop
¼m. PO ½m. ED Wed. P for cars only;
coaches nearby. Hostel opens 17.00
hrs. L

Jan 1-Feb 28	Open (except Sun & Mon)
Mar 1-Oct 31	Open
Nov 1-30	Open (except Sun & Mon)
Dec 1-31	Closed (try Llwynypia)

Wales Tourist Board Approved
Long red brick building on corner of
Wedal Road and Lake Road West,
near Roath Park Lake. 2m from the
city centre. It is readily accessible by
local bus services

OS 171 GR 185788 12

**Attractions: Capital City of
Wales.** Welsh Folk Museum:
Elizabethan Manor House, with
extensive gardens containing
centuries old Welsh cottages,
farmhouses, chapel, school and mill,
all furnished in their original style.
Bus 32 from City Centre

National Museum of Wales: Excellent
displays and exhibitions covering
Welsh history, the countryside, art
and science. City Centre

Cardiff Arcades: Historical City
Centre thoroughfares, linked with
interesting shops including Welsh
craft stores. Just the place to buy a
souvenir of Wales

Llandaff Cathedral and village:
Magnificent Medieval Cathedral and
historic village situated two miles
from City Centre. Bus no's 25 or 33

National Rugby Stadium — Cardiff
Arms Park. National Ice Skating Rink.
St David's Concert Hall. Theatres.
Cinemas etc

Penarth and Barry Island: Two
seaside resorts close to Cardiff.
Barry Island has a sandy beach and
funfair. Trains from Cathays, Cardiff
Central or Heath High/Low level

Open Top Bus Tours: Operates from
May-Sep from the City Centre and
provide an excellent way of visiting
many of the above sites

Further afield: The Mountains of the
Brecon Beacons National Park, fine
beaches and cliffs of the Glamorgan
Heritage Coast and other attractions
such as the Big Pit Mining Museum,
with its memorable underground
tour, are all easily reached from
Cardiff, as is the Wye Valley

National Welsh services, frequent
from surrounding areas. (0222
371331); Cardiff Bus 78/80/82 from
BR Cardiff Central stops outside
hostel (0222 396521)

Cardiff Central Bus Station

Next Youth Hostels: Llwynypia
18m. Chepstow 28m. Llwyn-y-Celyn
42m. Port Eynon 56m

Cardiff Youth Hostel

Administrative Region: Wales

BRECON BEACONS AND SOUTH WALES

L LANDDEUSANT

28 BEDS

Youth Hostel, The Old Red Lion,
Llanddeusant, Llangadog,
Dyfed SA19 6UL
☎ Gwynfe (05504) 634 and 619

TO MYDDFAI & LLANDOVERY — TO TRECASTLE — Cross Inn — TO TWYNLLANAN — 1/2 Km — N — LLANDDEUSANT

Overnight charge:
Young £2.60 Junior £3.50 Senior £4.40
▥ ▲ 2 ▥ ▼ ▧ ▨ No ⑤ No bread
and milk. ℙ Twyn-Llanan 1½m. ℙ for
cars only. Coaches Llangadog 6½m

Jan 1-Feb 28	Open to advance group bookings
Mar 1-Oct 31	Open
Nov 1-Dec 31	Open to advance group bookings

Wales Tourist Board Approved
Former inn adjacent to 14th century
church, in area where Welsh is the
first language, in Brecon Beacons
National Park. Best approach from
Trecastle-Llangadog mountain road

⑯ 160 Brecon Beacons (Western
Area) Leisure Map ⒼⓇ 776245
▥ 12, 17

Attractions: Pottery. Riding School
(☎ 05504 661). Fishing available Usk
reservoir. 🅙 Llandovery (☎ 0550
20693). Mountains and Lakes
including Llyn-y-fan Fach 4¼m and
Bannau Brycheiniog (2632ft) 5½m.
Prehistoric and Roman remains. Usk
reservoir 4m, Carreg Cennen castle
9m. National Park guided walks,
Cambrian Way Footpath Route. Ⓤ
🚕 Taxi — Llangagadog 0550 777706.
Booking Bureaux — see Brecon
Beacons heading, page 92 and Mid
Wales heading, page 84. Leaflet on
walks around Hostel from Hostel
20p and s.a.e.

🚐 No service

🚌 Llangadog (not Sun, except May-
Sep) 7m

Next Youth Hostels: Bryn Poeth
Uchaf 16m. Llwyn-y-Celyn 16m by
mountains. Ystradfellte 23m

L LWYN-Y-CELYN

(BRECON BEACONS) **46 BEDS**

Youth Hostel, Llwyn-y-Celyn,
Libanus, Brecon, Powys LD3 8NH
☎ Brecon (0874) 4261
Answerphone service

TO SENNYBRIDGE — A4215 — A470 — TO BRECON — Pen Milan — A470 — LLWYN-Y-CELYN — 1 Km — N — JOINS A4059 TO HIRWAUN — TO MERTHYR TYDFIL

Overnight charge:
Young £3.50 Junior £4.40 Senior £5.50
① ▲ ▼ ▧ ▥ ⑤ Evening meal. Shops
Brecon 6m. 🅔 (Brecon) Wed, (Merthyr)
Thu. ℙ for small vehicles. Coaches
layby on main road 200 yds. Hostel
opens 17.00 hrs

Jan 1-Feb 28	Closed
Mar 1-23	Open (except Sun)
Mar 25-Apr 13	Open
Apr 15-27	Open (except Sun)
Apr 29-May 11	Open
May 13-18	Open
May 20-Jun 1	Open
Jun 3-Aug 17	Open (except Sun)
Aug 19-31	Open
Sep 2-Oct 31	Open (except Sun)
Nov 1-Dec 31	Closed

In closed period warden may be able
to open for advance party bookings

Wales Tourist Board Approved
Traditional Welsh farmhouse in woodland high in Afon Tarell Valley in the heart
of the Brecon Beacons National Park.
Access over river Tarell by footbridge

⑯ 160 Brecon Beacons (Central
Area) Leisure Map ⒼⓇ 973225 ▥ 12

Attractions: Brecon Beacons, Pen-
y-Fan (2907ft) 3m. Fforest Fawr.
Brecon cathedral and town 6m.
Garwnant Forest Centre 8m. Mountain
centre 3m. Mountain railway, Dan yr
Ogof show caves. Summer walks led
by National Park staff. Brecon Jazz
Festival mid August. Ⓛ Group leader's
package available. Cambrian Way
Footpath route. Booking Bureau —
operates from this Hostel for Brecon
Beacons Hostels, page 92. 🎣 🛶 ▲
🚣 Ⓤ

🚐 Silverline Rail-Link 43 BR Merthyr
Tydfil — Brecon (☎ 0685 82406)

🚌 Merthyr Tydfil 11m; Abergavenny
28m

Next Youth Hostels: Ty'n-y-Caeau
9m. Ystradfellte 12m. Llandeusant
16m by mountains. Cardiff 42m

P ORT EYNON

(GOWER) **34 BEDS**

Youth Hostel, The Old Lifeboat
House, Port Eynon, Swansea,
West Glamorgan SA3 1NN
☎ Gower (0792) 390706

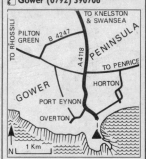

TO KNELSTON & SWANSEA — PILTON GREEN — B 4247 — TO RHOSSILI — A 4118 — PENINSULA — TO PENRICE — GOWER — HORTON — PORT EYNON — OVERTON — 1 Km — N

Overnight charge:
Young £3.50 Junior £4.40 Senior £5.50
Seasonal Prices Jul 1-Aug 31:
Young £3.80 Junior £4.70 Senior £5.90
▥ ▲ ▼ ▧ ▨ for small groups may
be available. ⑤ Shop and ℙ in village
¼m. No bread or milk delivered. ℙ
for cars and coaches ¼m. Hostel
opens 17.00 hrs

Jan 1-Mar 10	Closed
Mar 11-Jun 16	Open (except Mon)
Jun 17-Jul 1	Closed
Jul 2-Oct 11	Open (except Mon)
Nov 1-Dec 31	Closed

In closed period warden may be able
to open for advance party bookings

Wales Tourist Board Approved
Historic lifeboat house on beach in
Gower Area of Outstanding Natural
Beauty. ¼m SW of Port Eynon. Path
across beach from bus terminus

⑯ 159 ⒼⓇ 468848 ▥ 12

Attractions: Fine sands. Bathing
(check locally). Culver Hole ½m.
Geology. 🛶 Ⓤ nearby. Paviland Cave
2½m. Oxwich Castle 3m. Worms
Head, Rhossili 5m. Surfing 5m. Hang
gliding. Farm trail. 🚣 🚴 canoe and
sailboard equipment hire nearby. 🎣

🚌 South Wales 18/18B from Swansea
(passing close BR Swansea)
(☎ 0792 475511)

🚆 Swansea 16m

Next Youth Hostels: Ystradfellte
39m. Llwynypia 44m. Pentlepoir
63m. Cardiff 56m

L LWYNYPIA

**YHA, Glyncornel Centre, Llwynypia
Rhondda, Mid Glamorgan CF40 2JF**
☎ **Tonypandy (0443) 430859**
Answerphone service

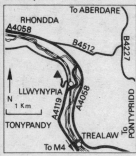

Overnight charge:
Young £4.00 Junior £5.10 Senior £6.30
▥Ⓐⓓⓒ🅛①🔟🆂🄲 Evening
meal 18.30 hrs. 🆂 Shop & 🄿 Ⓜ meals
Thu. 🅵🆂🄿 for cars, for coaches check
with warden. Hostel opens 17.00 hrs

Jan 1-Feb 17	Closed
Feb 18-23	Open
Mar 1-23	Open (except Sun)
Mar 25-Apr 13	Open
Apr 15-May 18	Open (except Sun)
May 20-Jun 1	Open
Jun 3-22	Open (except Sun)
Jun 24-Aug 31	Open
Sep 2-Oct 31	Open (except Sun)
Nov 1-30	Closed
Dec 1-28	Open (except Sun)

In closed periods warden may be able
to open to advance bookings

Wales Tourist Board Approved
Glyncornel Environmental Studies
Centre and Hostel. A former mine-
owner's house finely situated on
wooded hillside overlooking the
Rhondda Valley. In Llwynypia village.
Entrance on opposite side of road
from rail station. Follow signs for
Glyncornel Centre

🄾🅂 170 🄶🅁 993939 🄱🄼 12

Attractions: Extensive grounds.
Nature trails. Mountain walks.
Archery centre. Leisure centre at
Cwm Rhondda. Small museum in
hostel opened by request to warden.
🚗🅙 Museum. 🅛

🚆 Frequent from surrounding areas
(☎ 0222 371331)

🚉 Llwynypia ½m

Next Youth Hostels: Cardiff 18m.
Ystradfellte 19m. Chepstow 43m.
Port Eynon 44m

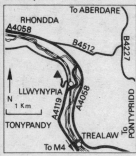

Llwynypia Youth Hostel —

T Y'N-Y-CAEAU

**YH, Ty'n-y-Caeau, Groesffordd,
Brecon, Powys LD3 7SW**
☎ **Llanfrynach (087 486) 270**
Answerphone service

Overnight charge:
Young £3.50 Junior £4.40 Senior £5.50
Seasonal Prices Jul 1-Aug 31:
Young £3.80 Junior £4.70 Senior £5.90
▥Ⓐ①🔟🆂🄲Ⓜ Evening meal 19.00
hrs. 🆂 🄿 Groesffordd ½m and Brecon.
Ⓜ Wed. 🄿 Coaches 1m please contact
warden in advance. 🅛 Hostel opens
17.00 hrs

Jan 1-Feb 16	Closed
Feb 17-23	Open
Feb 24-Mar 10	Closed
Mar 11-24	Open (except Sun)
Mar 25-Apr 13	Open
Apr 14-May 18	Open (except Sun)
May 20-Jun 1	Open
Jun 2	Closed
Jun 3-Aug 31	Open
Sep 1-Oct 31	Open (except Sun)
Nov 1-Dec 31	Closed

In closed periods **Feb & Nov** warden
may open to advance party bookings
of 15 or more

Wales Tourist Board Approved
Large country house in own grounds
on edge of National Park

🄾🅂 160 Brecon Beacons (Central
Area) Leisure Map 🄶🅁 073288 🄱🄼 17

Attractions: Brecon Beacons 8m.
Canal 1m. Cathedral. Jazz Festival
mid August. 🚲🅙🚣Ⓤ caving,
archaeology, steam railway. Booking
Bureau — see page 92

🚌 National Welsh 21 Newport —
Brecon (passes close BR Abergavenny),
alight Llanfrynach turn, 1m; 39 from
Hereford (passes close BR Hereford),
alight Llanddew turn, 1m; (☎ 0638
65100); Silverline Rail-Link 43, alight
Brecon, thence 1¾ by bridle-path
(☎ 0685 82406)

🚉 Merthyr Tydfil 20m; Abergavenny 19m

Next Youth Hostels: Llwyn-y-
Celyn 9m. Ystradfellte 21m.
Llanddeusant 23m. Capel-y-ffin 23m
(17m by mountains). Glascwm 25m

Y STRADFELLTE

28 BEDS · COMFORT yha IMPROVED

**Youth Hostel, Tai'r Heol,
Ystradfellte, Aberdare,
Mid-Glamorgan CF44 9JF**
☎ Glyn Neath (0639) 720301

TO SENNYBRIDGE

P.H.

Afon Mellte

YSTRADFELLTE

TAI'R HEOL

N

CAVE
PORTH-YR-OGOF · JOINS A4059

1/2 Km

TO GLYN NEATH

Overnight charge:
Young £3.10 Junior £4.00 Senior £5.10
🚻 ⚠ 🅰 🍴 🆑 ✖ Small 🆂 Bread and
milk not available. Garage shop 1m S
of hostel open 7 days a week. 🅿 Ystradfellte ½m. 🅿 for cars only.
Coaches Merthyr 9m

Jan 1-13	Closed
Jan 14-Feb 28	Open*
Mar 1-31	Open (except Thu)
Apr 1-24	Open
Apr 26-May 29	Open (except Thu)
May 30-Jun 5	Open
Jun 7-Jul 17	Open (except Thu)
Jul 18-Aug 31	Open
Sep 1-Oct 31	Open (except Thu)
Nov 1-Dec 14	Open*
Dec 15-31	Closed

*Open to group (10+) advance
bookings

Three cottages near Upper Neath
and Mellte rivers in Brecon Beacons
National Park. ½m S of village of
Ystradfellte on Pont Neath Vaughan
Road

🆗 160 Brecon Beacons (Central
Area) Leisure Map GR 925127 🚌 12

Attractions: Waterfall country.
Scwd Clyn Gwyn 2m. Scwd Isaf Clyn
Gwyn 2½m. Natural swimming pool
at Porth yr Ogof ¼m. Peaks of
Fforest Fawr. Cave systems. Booking
Bureaux — see Brecon Beacons
heading, page 92 and Mid Wales
heading, page 84

🚌 National Welsh 188 from
Aberdare (passes close BR
Aberdare), alight Penderyn, 3½m
(☎ 0222 371331)

🚉 Aberdare 10m

Next Youth Hostels: Llwyn-y-
Celyn 12m. Llwynpia 19m. Ty'n-y-
Caeau 21m. Llanddeusant 23m

BRECON BEACONS AND SOUTH WALES

12 WYE VALLEY AND FOREST OF DEAN

From the estuary of the River Severn, northwards almost to Hereford, the Wye Valley is an Area of Outstanding Natural Beauty. Wordsworth wrote a poem on the banks of the Wye a few miles above picturesque Tintern Abbey. The winding course of the river includes a well-known viewpoint from Symonds Yat Rock. Another viewpoint is at Wyndcliff, which is a Forest Nature Reserve. There are ruined castles at Chepstow and Goodrich.

Perhaps the best way to see this beautiful part of the country is by walking. Both the Wye Valley walk and the Offa's Dyke footpath offer attractive low level walking in this area.

The Forest of Dean is an area of wild woodland and forestry plantation with many waymarked trails. In Norman times, St Briavels Castle was the administrative centre of the forest.

Helpful Publications

Available for sale from YHA Regional Office, 1 Cathedral Road, Cardiff CF1 9HA. All prices include postage. Please make cheques/postal orders payable to YHA.

Offa's Dyke Strip Maps —
complete set of 9 .... £3.00

Map 1 —
Beachley and Severn Bridge to St Briavels (2 routes) 60p

Map 2 —
St Briavels and Monmouth to Symonds Yat,
Forest of Dean, Welsh Bicknor 60p

Waymarked Path Leaflets —
St Briavels — Mitcheldean etc 30p
Highmeadow Woods and Symonds Yat 30p

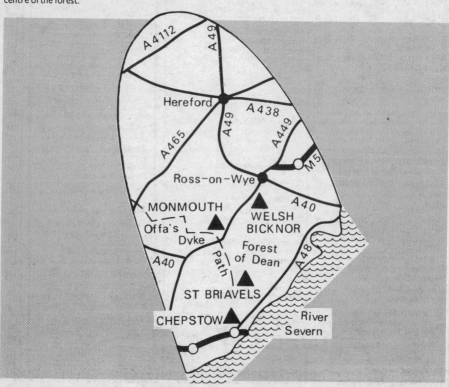

C HEPSTOW

70 BEDS

Youth Hostel, Mounton Road,
Chepstow, Gwent NP6 6AA
☎ Chepstow (0291) 622685
Answerphone service

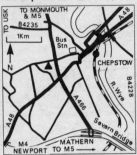

Overnight charge:
Young £4.00 Junior £5.10 Senior £6.30
🚻 Ⓒ ⬛ 🅿 1 🍴 Evening meal
18.30 hrs. Ⓒ able to seat 30+. ⓈⒼⓒ
Sun. 🅿 in town. 🅴🅳 Wed. 🅿 for cars
only. Coaches in layby opp hostel

Mar 1-23	Open (except Sun)
Mar 25-Apr 6	Open
Apr 8-Jun 29	Open (except Sun)
	Open May 5, 26
Jul 1-Aug 31	Open
Sep 1-Oct 31	Open (except Sun)

In closed periods Jan, Feb, Nov, Dec,
warden may be able to be open to
advance party bookings of 15 or more

Wales Tourist Board Approved
Large mansion, once the home of the
Sheriff of Monmouth (1778) with fine
views of the Bristol Channel. 1m W of
Chepstow on the Mounton Road. From
Severn Bridge (M4) take the Monmouth
road. After roundabout turn left on
Mounton Road at St Lawrence
hospital (Burns unit). Classroom
facilities available in the Hostel annexe

Ⓞ🅢 162, 172 Wye Valley & Forest of
Dean Leisure Map Ⓖ🅡 523934 🅱🅰🅡🅣 7, 13

Attractions: 🔍 Norman castle
ruins. Museum. Leisure centre/
swimming pool ¾m. Medieval town
walls. St Mary's church, Hocker Hill.
Start of Offa's Dyke long distance
footpath. Start of Wye Valley walk.
Tintern Abbey 4½m. 🚶 at Symonds
Yat 7m. Wintour's Leap 3½m. Wynd
Cliff 3m. Severn Bore. Geology.
Severn Bridge (open to walkers and
cyclists). 🅱 Bristol Zoo. Ⓛ

🚌 Frequent from surrounding areas
(☎ 0291 622947)
🚉 Chepstow 1m

Next Youth Hostels: St Briavels
11m. Monmouth 16m. Welsh Bicknor
23m. Slimbridge 24m. Bath 28m.
Cardiff 28m

M ONMOUTH

42 BEDS

Youth Hostel, Priory Street School,
Priory Street, Monmouth,
Gwent NP5 3NX
☎ Monmouth (0600) 5116

Overnight charge:
Young £3.10 Junior £4.00 Senior £5.10
🚻 ⬛ 🅿 1 🍴 Ⓖⓒ ⬛ Ⓢ Shops and 🅟🅞
nearby. 🅴🅳 Thu. 🅿 nearby. Coaches
near bus station. Hostel opens 17.00
hrs

Jan 1-Feb 28	Closed
Mar 1-Oct 31	Open
Nov 1-Dec 31	Closed

In closed periods warden is likely to
open to advance party bookings

Remains of late 15th century priory,
used as a school 1770 to 1970, near
centre of town, where River
Monnow flows adjacent to Priory
Street

Ⓞ🅢 162 Wye Valley and Forest of
Dean Leisure Map Ⓖ🅡 508130 🅱🅰🅡🅣 13

Attractions: Offa's Dyke long
distance footpath 2m. Town trail.
Leisure centre. Nelson collection in
Market Hall. Shire Hall. Castle
remains. Monnow Bridge. Wye Valley
Walk. Tintern Abbey 9m. 🚶 🚲
Geology. Forest of Dean trails 5m.
Heated swimming pool ½m. Ⓛ

🚌 Red & White 65/9 from Chepstow
(pass close BR Chepstow); 60, X49
from Newport (pass close BR
Newport) (☎ 0222 371331)

🚉 Hereford 16m; Chepstow 16m;
Abergavenny 17m

Next Youth Hostels: Welsh
Bicknor 8m. St Briavels 8m.
Chepstow 16m

S T BRIAVELS CASTLE

60 BEDS

Youth Hostel, The Castle,
St Briavels, Lydney,
Glos GL15 6RG
☎ Dean (0594) 530272

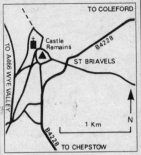

Overnight charge:
Young £4.00 Junior £5.10 Senior £6.30
Seasonal Prices Jul 1-Aug 31:
Young £4.40 Junior £5.40 Senior £6.60
⬛ 🅿 1 🍴 Ⓖⓒ 🍴 Evening meal 19.00
hrs. Breakfast 08.30 hrs. Medieval
Banquets £4.15. Ⓢ🅟🅞 and Shop in
village. 🅴🅳 Sat 🅿 for cars and coaches

Jan 1-Feb 17	Closed
Feb 18-Oct 31	Open
Nov 1-Dec 31	Closed

In closed periods warden may be able
to open to advance party bookings:
enquiries 10.00-12.00 hrs

Wales Tourist Board Approved
Norman Castle used by King John as
a hunting lodge, in centre of village at
700ft above sea level. In conservation
area on edge of Forest of Dean

Ⓞ🅢 162 Wye Valley and Forest of
Dean Leisure Map Ⓖ🅡 558045 🅱🅰🅡🅣 13

Attractions: 🔍 Offa's Dyke long
distance footpath. Moated castle and
village. Wye Valley Walk. Tintern
Abbey 5m. Clearwell Caves 3m.
Forest of Dean trails. Ⓤ 3m. Speech
House 8m. Swimming, Chepstow
10m, Monmouth 8m (heated pools).
Guided tours 35p. Heated dormitories
include prison, chapel, hanging room,
and King John's Banqueting Hall

🚌 Red & White 69 from Chepstow
(passes close BR Chepstow), alight
Bigsweir Bridge, 2m (☎ 0222
371331). Local services very
infrequent — ask warden

🚉 Lydney 7m

Next Youth Hostels: Monmouth
8m. Chepstow 11m. Welsh Bicknor
12m. Bath 38m

Additional Information: Reception
open 09.00-10.00, 17.00-22.30 hrs in
winter closed period

12

WYE VALLEY AND FOREST OF DEAN

WELSH BICKNOR

YH, Welsh Bicknor Rectory,
Welsh Bicknor, Ross-on-Wye,
Herefordshire HR9 6JJ
☎ Dean (0594) 60300

Jan 1-Mar 23	Closed
Mar 25-Aug 31	Open
Sep 2-Oct 31	Open (except Sun)
Nov 1-Dec 31	Closed

In closed periods warden may be able to open to advance party bookings of 15 or more

Wales Tourist Board Approved
Early Victorian rectory in 25 acre grounds on west bank of River Wye near Forest of Dean. From Goodrich village take lane from Castle entrance, signposted Courtfield and Welsh Bicknor. The hostel is 1¾m along this lane. Go up hill across cattle grid, start to descend. Ignore farm lane on right by large tree, keep right at next two forks. This is the drive to the hostel. Large building at hill bottom. Drive slowly and take special care on right-hand hairpin bend. Foot and cycle access also possible from Lydbrook via footbridge (old railway bridge) at factory

Ⓞ 162 Gloucester & Forest of Dean Area — Landranger ⒼⓇ 591177 Ⓞ 14 Wye Valley & Forest of Dean — Outdoor Leisure ⒷⓇ 13

Attractions: Self contained 'Laundry Cottage': a 14 bedded group or family cottage. Own river landing stage. Local canoe and mountain bike hire for day trips or longer, also climbing and caving — see warden for details. Wye Valley Walk. Cider press and church in hostel grounds. Goodrich Castle 2½m. Clearwell Caves 5m. Monmouth Castle 8m. Symonds Yat Rock, Butterfly Farm and Maze 5m. Forest of Dean trails. Roman iron workings. Dean heritage centre 10m.
ⓁⒹ𝑓 archaeology

🚌 AH Martin & Sons 61 Ross-on-Wye — Monmouth with connections from Hereford & Newport, alight Goodrich Village, 1½m (☎ 0873 821241). Various operators 35 from Ross-on-Wye, alight Lower Lydbrook 1m over footbridge. N.B. No Sunday buses

🚆 Lydney 12m; Gloucester 19m

Next Youth Hostels: Monmouth 8m. St Briavels 11m. Chepstow 23m

Additional Information:
Answerphone service

Overnight charge:
Young £3.80 Junior £4.70 Senior £5.90
Seasonal Prices Jul 1-Aug 31:
Young £4.00 Junior £5.10 Senior £6.30
🛉 🚿 ▲ ⚠ 🚪 1 🍴 ⒼⓈⒸ in Annexe 🍳
Evening meal 19.00 hrs. Includes 'Laundry Cottage' (14). Laundry facilities available. Ⓢ ⓅⓄ Goodrich, Lydbrook. 🎫 Sat. Ⓒ Ⓟ limited. Coaches on lay-by on B4228 across river from hostel ½m. Hostel opens 17.00 hrs

🏠 Self-contained cottage sleeps 10-14, 3 families or a group

Welsh Bicknor Youth Hostel

HEART OF ENGLAND

nland waterways pass near all the Hostels in the south of this area, the Grand Union Canal linking with the River Avon at Warwick. The waterways museums are well worth a visit. Although Milton Keynes, the new City, extends over several small towns and villages, much of the countryside is still pleasantly green and open.

The Malvern Hills are an Area of Outstanding Natural Beauty. The Malverns, dominated by the 1395 ft Worcestershire Beacon, inspired the composer, Sir Edward Elgar. Their 10 mile ridge is easy walking with splendid views.

The Shakespeare country around Stratford-upon-Avon attracts visitors from all over the world. Along the River Avon are the romantic castles of Warwick and Kenilworth, and the fertile Vale of Evesham, noted for its fruit blossom in spring. This is the heart of rural England. Both here and further north, cyclists can find quiet lanes and picturesque old villages.

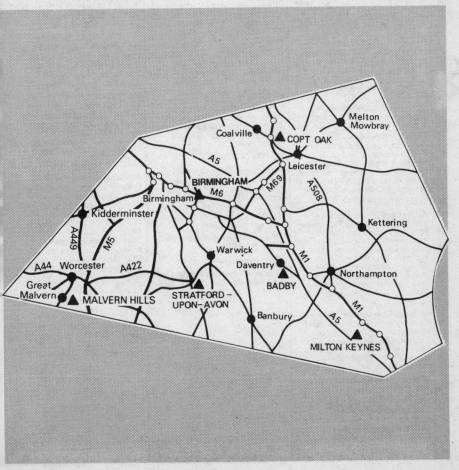

BADBY

Youth Hostel, Church Green,
Badby, Daventry,
Northants NN11 6AR
☎ Daventry (0327) 703883

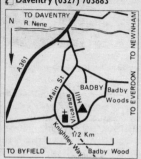

Overnight charge:
Young £2.60 Junior £3.50 Senior £4.40
🏠 🏦 ♨ 1 🍴 GSC Ⓢ Shop & PO in
village. ECO PO Wed. Haynes store Sat.
P see warden

Jan 1-3	Closed
Jan 4-Feb 23	Open Fri & Sat
Feb 24-Mar 28	Closed
Mar 29-Oct 31	Open (except Wed)
Nov 1-Dec 14	Open Fri & Sat
Dec 15-Jan 2 92	Closed
Jan 3-Feb 29	Open Fri & Sat

When hostel is closed or open Fri &
Sat only, bookings may be accepted
Sun or midweek, please enquire

Three late 17th century cottages in
one of the most beautiful villages in
Northamptonshire. 2m S of Daventry
on A361, turn left at sign 'Badby Village'.
Continue to Main Street and turn left
at Haynes store and up Vicarage Hill
to hostel at Church Green

OS 152 GR 561588 🚲 19

Attractions: Walks, nature trail in
Badby Woods. Knightly Way Fawsley
Park, church and lakes. Daventry
country park 3m. Grand Union Canal
at Braunston 5m. Althorpe House
9m. Three Rivers Ramble. Guilsborough
Grange Wildlife Park 13m. Holdenby
House, Northampton. Ⓛ at hostel
(bicycles suitable for day hire only).
🚲 Garden available for picnics and
barbeques

🚌 United Counties X64 Corby —
Coventry (unreliable service - YHA
opinion); 41 from Northampton
(both pass BR Northampton) (☎
0604 36681) Geoff Amos from BR
Rugby (☎ 0327 702181). On all,
alight Daventry, 2m

🚉 Long Buckby 6m; Northampton
12m; Rugby 12m;

Next Youth Hostels: Milton Keynes
21m. Stratford-upon-Avon 24m.
Charlbury 29m. Stow-on-the-Wold
34m. Birmingham 45m. Copt Oak 46m.

Administrative Region: Central

BIRMINGHAM

YH, Cambrian Halls, Brindley
Drive, off Cambridge Street,
Birmingham B1 2NB
☎ (021) 233 3044*

*Advance bookings prior to July 8th:
Stratford-upon-Avon Youth Hostel,
Hemmingford House, Alveston,
Stratford-upon-Avon, Warwickshire
CV37 7RG. ☎ (0789) 297093. Fax:
(0789) 205513

Summer Hostel: Open Jul 8-Sep 20
Single rooms with private facilities
and room keys, SC only. 🍴 GSC No Ⓢ
Shops nearby. P Cars on site

Jul 8-Sep 20	Open

Halls of residence close to all city
centre amenities. Located close to
Central Library, Paradise Circus and
Birmingham Repertory Theatre,
Broad Street

OS 139 GR 063870

Attractions: Shops, Cinemas,
Theatres, Restaurants, Wine Bars,
Museum and Art Gallery, Library,
City Hall, N.E.C., Athletics Stadium
and Events, Superprix City Centre
Motor Racing. International Travel
connections. YHA Shop

🚌 Frequent from surrounding areas
(☎021-200-2601)

🚉 Birmingham New Street ½m

Next Youth Hostels: Stratford
20m. Ironbridge 25m. Malvern 30m

Administrative Region: Central

COPT OAK

Youth Hostel,
Copt Oak, Markfield,
Leicester LE6 0QB
☎ Markfield (0530) 242661

Overnight charge:
Young £2.60 Junior £3.50 Senior £4.40
🏠 1 GSC 🚫 but supper snacks
available to 9.30pm. Small Ⓢ PO
Markfield 2m. P for cars and coaches

Jan 2-Mar 24	Open Fri & Sat
Mar 25-Nov 3	Open (except Mon)
Nov 4-Dec 15	Open Fri & Sat
Dec 16-Jan 2 92	Closed
Jan 3-Feb 29	Open Fri & Sat

Village school built in 1839 on the
edge of Charnwood Forest in good
walking and cycling country. One
minute drive from M1 (Junction 22),
10m NW of Leicester, 7m SW of
Loughborough and 4m East of
Coalville on B587 near Copt Oak Inn

OS 129 GR 482129 🚲 24

Attractions: Beacon Hill 2m.
Bradgate deer park 3m. Swithland
Woods 4m. Mount St Bernard Abbey
4m. Old John Folly 3m. Ulverscroft
Priory ruins 2m. Loughborough
Leisure Centre 5m. Bosworth
Battlefield (1485) 10m. Great Central
Steam Railway 5m. Bosworth Steam
Railway 9m. Canal boat trips. Ⓤ 1m.
🚲 🚲 There is no Public Transport
from Loughborough to Copt Oak

🚌 Midland Fox 117-9 Leicester —
Coalville, alight Flying Horse Pub, 1m
(☎ 0530 36517)

🚉 Leicester 10m

Next Youth Hostels: Shining Cliff
30m. Matlock 35m. Ilam 36m.
Dimmingsdale 37m. Thurlby 45m.
Badby 46m. Stratford 45m. Lincoln
50m

Administrative Region: Central

13

M ALVERN HILLS

59 BEDS

Youth Hostel, 'Hatherley',
18 Peachfield Road, Malvern Wells,
Malvern, Worcs WR14 4AP
☎ Malvern (0684) 569131

Members ☎ Malvern (0684) 573300

Overnight charge:
Young £3.80 Junior £4.70 Senior £5.90
🚿 🅰 🔍 ② 🛏 ◻ Evening meal 19.00
hrs. Snacks and late meals available
between 20.00hrs–22.00hrs. Ⓢ ℗⊙
Great Malvern. 🔲 Wed. 🅿

Jan 2-31	Closed
Feb 1-Mar 25	Open
	(except Tue & Wed)
Mar 26-Oct 31	Open
Nov 1-Dec 21	Open Fri & Sat
Dec 22-26	Closed
Dec 27-Jan 4 92	Open
Jan 5-31	Closed
Feb 1-29	Open
	(except Tue & Wed)

Bookings from groups may be
accepted, at times when the hostel is
normally closed, or only open Fri &
Sat. Please enquire

Large house in own grounds next to
common. Great Malvern is a Victorian
Spa town and the Malvern Hills an Area
of Outstanding Natural Beauty. 1½m
S of Great Malvern on the Great Malvern-
Malvern Wells road (A449). Turn opp
Railway Inn into Peachfield Road.
Hostel is 200 yds down road on right

ⓄⓈ 150 ⒼⓇ 774439 🛏 13, 18

Attractions: 10 mile ridge of hills
with extensive views and walks.
Priory, museum, theatre, cinema.
New Leisure Pool. 🎫 Great Malvern
1m. 🅰 🚣 Upton-on-Severn 7m.
Elgar's birthplace, Broadheath 8m.
Eastnor Castle 5m, Worcester
Cathedral & Museums 8m, Falconry
Centre, Newent 15m. 🅛 🚲 Ⓤ

🚌 Frequent from surrounding areas
(☎ 0345 212 555). Citibus 42 from
Great Malvern passes Hostel

🚉 Great Malvern 1½m

Next hostels: Cleeve Hill 23m.
Welsh Bicknor 28m. Ludlow 31m.
Stratford-upon-Avon 35m.

Administrative Region: Central

M ILTON KEYNES

38 BEDS

Youth Hostel, Manor Farm,
Vicarage Road, Bradwell,
Milton Keynes MK13 9AJ
☎ (0908) 310944

Overnight charge:
Young £3.80 Junior £4.70 Senior £5.90
🚿 🅰 ① 🛏 ◻ Ⓢ Ⓒ ⊙ Evening meal 19.00
hrs. Ⓢ Shop in village. 🔲 Wed. 🅿 for
cars only. Coaches in Vicarage Road

Jan 1-Feb 28	Closed
Mar 1-30	Open
	(except Sun & Mon)
Mar 31-Sep 28	Open (except Sun)
	Open Bank Hol Sun
Sep 29-Oct 31	Open
	(except Sun & Mon)
Nov 1-30	Open Fri & Sat
Dec 1-Feb 29 92	Closed

When hostel is closed bookings from
groups may be accepted Sun or
midweek, please enquire

18th century farmhouse in village of
Bradwell, 1m NW of central Milton
Keynes. The A422 Bedford to
Buckingham road (which also crosses
the A5) is known as Monks Way
(H3). Turn off this road just E of
railway line into Colley Hill, signposted
'Bradwell'. Proceed to mini-roundabout,
right into Loughton Road; after approx
¼m right into Vicarage Road. Hostel
at bottom of street in short cul-de-sac.
'Redway' system serves both cyclists
and walkers and signposts lead to
Bradwell and Youth Hostel

ⓄⓈ 152 ⒼⓇ 831395 🛏 14

Attractions: Bradwell Abbey, 5 mins
walk. Urban Studies Centre 4m.
Grand Union Canal with towpath
walks, and Waterways and Rural Life
Museums. Woburn Abbey and Park
approx 10m

🚌 Frequent from surrounding areas
(☎ 0908 668366)

🚉 Milton Keynes Central 1m
☎ (0908) 370883

Next Youth Hostels: Ivinghoe 19m
(bus ride and 9m walk). Badby 21m.
Oxford 35m. Cambridge 41m.
Stratford 40m.

Administrative Region: Central

S TRATFORD-UPON-AVON

154 BEDS

YH, Hemmingford House,
Alveston, Stratford-upon-Avon,
Warwickshire CV37 7RG
☎ (0789) 297093

Hostel open 07.30-10.00 hrs and
13.00-23.15 hrs

Overnight charge:
Young £4.60 Junior £5.90 Senior £7.00
🚿 🅰 Ⓒ 🔍 🛏 ⊙ Cafeteria facilities
from 17.00 hrs. Set meals for groups
as required. Ⓢ ℗⊙ and shop Tiddington
1m. 🅿 for cars and coaches

Jan 16-Dec 10	Open
Dec 11-Feb 29 92	Closed

Large house over 200 years old, in
village near busy tourist town on
River Avon, 2m from Stratford on
Wellesbourne road (B4086). Hostel
at Alveston-Loxley crossroads

ⓄⓈ 151 ⒼⓇ 231562 🛏 19

Attractions: Shakespeare
properties and theatre 2m. River
Avon. Stratford Canal. Boating.
Swimming baths. Charlecote Park
2m. Warwick Castle 8m. 🚲 at
hostel. 🎫 Motor Museum, Ragley
Hall, Alcester. 🚲 🅛 🅰

🚌 Midland Red South 18 Warwick –
Stratford-upon-Avon (passes close
BR Warwick, Stratford and
Leamington Spa) (☎ 0788 535555)

🚉 Stratford-upon-Avon (not Sun,
except May-Sep) 2½m

Next Youth Hostels: Stow-on-the-
Wold 20m. Badby 24m. Cleeve Hill
25m. Oxford 42m

Additional Information: Advance
Theatre Booking Service (Groups
12+) available at hostel. Hostel Fax:
(0789) 205513

**Package Breaks (Educational and/
or Leisure) for Groups of 12 or
more, tailored by professionals to
suit your needs and budgets.
Please enquire**

Administrative Region: Central

13

HEART OF ENGLAND

---

14 SHROPSHIRE AND THE WELSH BORDERS

T The Shropshire Hills are an Area of Outstanding Natural Beauty.

Ludlow is an old town on two rivers with many timber-framed houses. Walking the historic border country of the Shropshire Hill is not too strenuous, with plenty of castles and manor houses to visit. Wenlock Edge and the Wrekin are two good viewpoints.

Situated in a loop of the River Severn, the county town of Shrewsbury has interesting old houses and inns. Where the famous Iron Bridge spans the River Severn to the south east at Telford an open air museum complex now covers six square miles of fascinating industrial sites.

Useful Information

Party bookings may be accepted at Wardens' discretion during winter closed periods (except Clun Mill). Please enquire at relevant Youth Hostel.

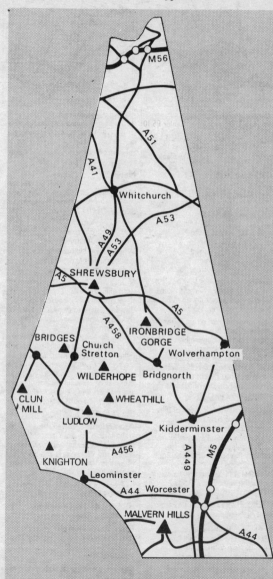

B RIDGES

34 BEDS

Youth Hostel,
Bridges, Ratlinghope,
Shrewsbury SY5 0SP
Linley (058861) 656

Overnight charge:
Young £3.10 Junior £4.00 Senior £5.10
No family rooms ⚹ 2 ⚹ ⚹ ⚹
Evening meal 19.00 hrs. Bread and
milk must be ordered in advance. PO
and Shop Wentnor 3m. Wed and
Sat. P for cars and minibuses only.
at warden's discretion

Jan 4-31	Closed
Feb 1-28	Open
	(except Tue & Wed)
Mar 1-28	Closed
Mar 29-Sep 8	Open (except Tue)
Sep 9-26	Closed
Sep 27-Oct 31	Open (except Tue)
Nov 1-Dec 22	Open
	(except Tue & Wed)
Dec 23-Jan 30 92	Closed
Jan 31-Feb 29	Open
	(except Tue & Wed)

The Hugh Gibbins Memorial hostel.
Old village school in beautiful
countryside, situated between the
Long Mynd and Stiperstones; in
Shropshire Hills Area of Outstanding
Natural Beauty. Ideal centre for
walking, cycling, observing wildlife
and getting away from it all. No video
games or TV! From Church Stretton,
take "The Burway" (steep and narrow
road), turn right at fork on top of
Long Mynd, then first left and first
right at bottom. 2 hours to walk.
Unsuitable for cars in winter. From
Shrewsbury, take road via Longden
and Pulverbatch (13m). Turn left at
sign for Horse Shoe Inn (100 yds)

OS 137 GR 394964 Bart 18

Attractions: Long Mynd 1m. Stiperstones 2m. Acton Scott Farm Museum
8m. Bishop's Castle 8m. Geology
3m. Quiet lanes for cycling. 5m

No service

Church Stretton 5m

Next Youth Hostels: Wilderhope
13m. Clun Mill 16m. Shrewsbury 14m.
Ludlow 18m. Ironbridge 24m

C LUN MILL

30 BEDS

Youth Hostel, The Mill,
Clun, near Craven Arms,
Shropshire SY7 8NY
(05884) 582

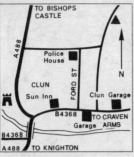

Overnight charge:
Young £3.10 Junior £4.00 Senior £5.10
⚹ ⚹ 1 ⚹ GSC ⚹ Members
kitchen. Shops in Clun. Wed. PO
Clun (closed Sat pm). P for cars and
minibuses. H&C and indoor wc. No
No drying room. No family room.
Hostel opens 17.00 hrs

Jan 1-Mar 14	Closed
Mar 15-Nov 16	Open
Nov 17-Feb 29 92	Closed

Former Watermill on outskirts of
small border town in Shropshire Hills
Area of Outstanding Natural Beauty.
From Clun High Street (B4368
Craven Arms Road), go via Ford
Street. At end of Ford Street, turn
right and immediately left. Hostel
250 yds on right

OS 137 GR 303812 Bart 18

Attractions: Welsh border country
with outstanding scenery. Norman
Castle. Traditional stone and timber
houses. Offa's Dyke path 3m. Quiet
lanes for cyclists. Stokesay Castle
10m.

Midland Red weekday service to
and from Ludlow (pass close BR
Ludlow), alight Clun 1m (0345
212515). Shrewsbury - Bishops Castle
(Minsterley Motors). **Phone warden
for details of local bus and rail
services**

Broome or Hopton (not Sun,
except May-Sep) both 7m; Craven
Arms 10m

Next Youth Hostels: Knighton 7m
(10m by Offa's Dyke). Bridges 16m.
Ludlow 18m. Wilderhope 20m.
Wheathill 24m. Glascwm 25m

I RONBRIDGE GORGE

68 BEDS

Youth Hostel,
Paradise, Coalbrookdale,
Telford, Shropshire TF8 7NR
Ironbridge (0952) 433281

Overnight charge:
Young £4.60 Junior £5.90 Senior £7.00
⚹ ⚹ ⚹ 2 ⚹ ⚹ ⚹ Evening meal
19.00 hrs. Shops and PO
Ironbridge. Wed. P Small car park
in Hostel grounds. Coaches ½m at
Museum of the River

Jan 2-31	Closed
Feb 1-Feb 28	Open (except Sun)
Mar 1-Oct 31	Open
Nov 1-Dec 28	Open (except Sun)
Dec 29-Feb 3 92	Closed
Feb 4-29	Open (except Sun)

The Ironbridge Gorge Hostel and
Walker Study Centre, built in 1859
by local ironmasters for literary, art
and scientific classes, and now part of
the Ironbridge Gorge Museum
complex. L. From the Ironbridge
follow the Wellington Road towards
the power station. After ½m turn
right at petrol station on road to
Wellington and Coalbrookdale
Hostel ½m on the right up the hill
opposite foundry

OS 127 GR 671043 Bart 18, 23

Attractions: World's first iron
bridge and Museum sites, most open
all year. River Severn. Nature Trail
from Ironbridge Toll House. Ice Rink
and Ski Slope in Telford. Acton Scott
Farm Museum 21m

Many services available from
Wellington B.R. and Telford town
centre. (0345 056785 for details)

Telford Central 5m; Wellington
Telford West 5m

Next Youth Hostels: Wilderhope
13m. Shrewsbury 14m. Wheathill
23m. Bridges 24m. Ludlow 26m

Additional Information: To contact
resident members ((0952) 433278

SHROPSHIRE AND THE WELSH BORDERS

14

K NIGHTON

54 BEDS

Youth Hostel, Old Primary School, West St., Knighton, Powys LD7 1EN
☎ Knighton (0547) 528807
Answerphone service

Overnight charge:
Young £3.50 Junior £4.40 Senior £5.50
🏠 🄰 ⚤ ⚤ 🄿 1 ▾ GSC Small S PO ¼m.
ED Sat. Heritage Centre classroom available next door. P for cars only; coaches nearby. Family annexe has 8 beds and 1 cot. ⊗ Hostel opens 17.00 hrs

Mar 1-Oct 31	Open (except Sun)
Bank Hol Sun	Open (ex Aug 25)
Bank Hol Mon	Closed

In self-contained family unit, facilities open 7 days a week

Wales Tourist Board Approved
Old school in quiet border town in Teme Valley surrounded by wooded hills, at halfway point on Offa's Dyke long distance footpath. 200 yds W of clock tower in centre of Knighton

OS 148, 137 GR 285725 🚌 18

Attractions: Offa's Dyke information and heritage centre next door. Good sections of Offa's Dyke near at hand. Glyndwrs Way. 🛶 in River Teme. Cycling in quiet Border lanes

🚌 Midland Red West 736-40 from Ludlow, alight Knighton, ½m (☎ 0345 056 785)

🚂 Knighton (not Sun, except May-Sep) ½m

Next Youth Hostels: Clun Mill 7m (10m by Offa's Dyke path and lanes). Ludlow 17m. Glascwm 18m

Additional Information: Children under five not accepted for safety reasons (except in family annexe)

🏠 Sleeps 7 plus 1 cot

Administrative Region: Central

L UDLOW

52 BEDS

Youth Hostel, Ludford Lodge, Ludford, Ludlow, Shropshire SY8 1PJ
☎ Ludlow (0584) 872472

Overnight charge:
Young £3.50 Junior £4.40 Senior £5.50
🄰 1 🚌 GSC 🄾 Evening meal 19.00 hrs. S Shops and PO in town. ED Thu. P in town; ask warden

Dec 30-Jan 6 91	Closed
Jan 7-31	Open (except Sun)
Feb 1-28	Closed
Mar 1-Nov 30	Open (except Sun)
Dec 1-Jan 5 92	Closed
Jan 6-Feb 1	Open (except Sun)
Feb 2-29	Closed

Large house facing the town across medieval Ludford Bridge; in good touring centre for Shropshire Hills and Welsh Marches. At bottom of Broad Street, cross Ludford Bridge; hostel on river bank

OS 137, 138 GR 513741 🚌 18

Attractions: 11th C castle. Half timbered buildings. Geological trail. Whitcliffe common by hostel. Mortimer Forest Trails ¼m. Quiet lanes for cyclists. Stokesay Castle 7m. Berrington Hall (NT) 8m. 🏅 L 🛶 🄰 ⚤ U Acton Scott Farm Museum 14m

🚌 Midland Red West X92, 292 Birmingham — Hereford to within ½m (☎ 0345 212555)

🚂 Ludlow ¼m

Next Youth Hostels: Wheathill 9m. Wilderhope 15m. Bridges 18m. Clun 18m. Ironbridge 26m. Shrewsbury 28m. Malvern 31m

Administrative Region: Central

S HREWSBURY

75 BEDS

YH, The Woodlands, Abbey Foregate, Shrewsbury SY2 6LZ
☎ (0743) 60179
Answerphone service

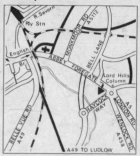

To contact resident members ☎ (0743) 56397. Hostel open 07.30-10.00 hrs and 17.00-23.00 hrs. Same day telephone bookings — will keep bed until 18.00 hrs

Overnight charge:
Young £4.00 Junior £5.10 Senior £6.30
🏠 🄰 ⚤ 🄾 Evening meal 19.00 hrs. S PO 5 mins. ED Thu. P for cars and coaches

Jan 1-31	Closed
Feb 1-28	Open Fri & Sat
Mar 1-Sep 15	Open
Sep 16-Oct 31	Open (except Sun)
Nov 1-Dec 21	Open Fri & Sat
Dec 22-30	Closed
Dec 31-Jan 2 92	Open
Jan 3-31	Closed

Victorian ironmaster's house in historic 14th century country town. Opposite Lord Hills Column, 10 mins walk from English Bridge (do not confuse with Welsh Bridge). Follow signs to Shirehall, then YHA signs

OS 126 GR 505120 🚌 23

Attractions: Castle. Abbey. 342 listed buildings. English and Welsh Bridges. Military museums. The Quarry riverside park 1m. 🛶 Ironbridge Gorge Museums 12m. Roman Viriconium 4m. Acton Scott farm museum 14m. The Wrekin 8m. 🏅 L. Swimming in town. Ice skating and dry ski slope in Telford 14m. Rare Poultry Collection 25m

🚌 Frequent from surrounding areas. No 8 or 26 bus from town centre to hostel. Bus station (☎ 0345 056 785)

🚂 Shrewsbury 1m

Next Youth Hostels: Bridges 14m. Ironbridge 14m. Wilderhope 18m. Clun 28m. Ludlow 28m. Llangollen 28m. Wheathill 30m

Administrative Region: Central

WHEATHILL

28 BEDS

Youth Hostel, Malthouse Farm,
Wheathill, Bridgnorth,
Shropshire WV16 6QT
☎ Burwarton (074633) 236

Overnight charge:
Young £2.60 Junior £3.50 Senior £4.40
Use of caravan by arrangement with
warden ⚠ 2 🍴 GSC ✕ Well stocked.
🅂 Helps if bread and milk ordered in
advance. Snack meals available. Shop
& PO Farlow 2m. 🕕 (Farlow) Thu. 🅿
for cars only; coaches ¾m

Jan 1–Jun 1	Open (except Mon)
	Open Bank Hol Mon
Jun 2–11	Closed
Jun 12–29	Open (except Mon)
Jun 30–Sep 14	Open
Sep 15–24	Closed
Sep 25–Dec 22	Open (except Mon)
Dec 23–28	Closed
Dec 29–31	Open
Jan 1–Feb 29 92	Open (except Mon)

Part of buildings of Malthouse Farm,
dating from 17th century, in
Shropshire Hills Area of Outstanding
Natural Beauty. In Clee Hills about
midway between Ludlow and
Bridgnorth, E of B4364. Take turning
at "Three Horseshoes", 2½m SW of
Burwarton; hostel 1m along road

OS 138 GR 613818 📖 18

Attractions: Work of farm. Lambing.
Calving. Haymaking. 🚲 in quiet lanes
and woods. Geology. Brown Clee Hill
1½m. Forest trail 2½m (leaflet available).
Titterstone Clee Hill 3m. Archaeological
sites on farm and in locality. Discount
for members. Upton Cresset Hall 9m.
Shropshire Way Long Distance Walk.
Shropshire Challenge Walk and
longer 93m Shropshire Ring Walk
🚌 Infrequent from Ludlow, alight
Three Horseshoes, 1m; otherwise
Midland Red West X92, 292 Hereford
— Birmingham (passes close BR
Ludlow & Kidderminster), alight
Hopton Bank, 5m (☎ 0345 056 785)
🚆 Ludlow 9m

Next Youth Hostels: Ludlow 9m.
Wilderhope 12m. Clun 24m. Bridges
23m. Ironbridge 23m. Shrewsbury 30m

Administrative Region: Central

WILDERHOPE MANOR

68 BEDS

Youth Hostel, The John Cadbury
Memorial Hostel, Easthope,
Much Wenlock, Shrop TF13 6EG
☎ Longville (06943) 363

Overnight charge:
Young £4.00 Junior £5.10 Senior £6.30
🅰 at warden's discretion — please
enquire. ⚠ 1 🍴 ✕ Evening meal
19.00 hrs. 🅂 PO Church Stretton or
Much Wenlock. 🅵🅂 🅿 for cars and
coaches. Coaches advised to drive up
from Longville.
**No Smoking Hostel due to
historic nature of building**

Jan 2–Feb 28	Open only for parties booked in advance
Mar 1–Oct 31	Open (except Sun) Open Bank Hol Sun Closed Bank Hol Mon
Nov 1–Feb 29 92	Open only for parties booked in advance

Externally unaltered 16th century
National Trust manor house on
Wenlock Edge in Shropshire Hills
Area of Outstanding Natural Beauty.
From Church Stretton turn right at
signpost in Longville. From Much
Wenlock turn left 100 yds after
railway bridge in Longville (signposted)

OS 137, 138 GR 544928 📖 18

Attractions: Geology. Caer
Caradoc 6m. Long Mynd 7m.
Ironbridge Gorge Museum 13m.
Acton Scott Farm Museum 9m. Much
Wenlock Priory and Guildhall 8m.
Carding Mill Valley 7m. Stokesay
Castle 11m. 🚲 Ů
🚌 No service
🚆 Church Stretton 8m

Next Youth Hostels: Wheathill
12m. Bridges 13m. Ironbridge 13m.
Ludlow 15m. Shrewsbury 18m

Administrative Region: Central

SHROPSHIRE AND THE WELSH BORDERS

14

15 COTSWOLDS

ocal yellow stone gives a mellow warmth to buildings in this area, which has some of the loveliest villages in Britain. Fine "wool" churches and manor houses remain from the days when sheep-rearing was a prosperous industry. The Cotswolds Area of Outstanding Natural Beauty covers about 660 square miles from near Bath to just south of Evesham. Its hills are gentle, rising to nearly 1,100 feet. For walkers, the Cotswold Way runs for 100 miles from Bath to Chipping Campden. It is an unofficial route, but signposted and waymarked. Several other walks may be enjoyed in this area. The Oxfordshire Way, The Ridgeway Long Distance Route, The Charlbury to Stow Inter-Hostel Routes and Ridgeway to Inglesham Route.

To the west is the River Severn. Wintering geese are attracted in thousands to the riverside marshes, where the Wildfowl and Wetlands Trust at Slimbridge has its grounds.

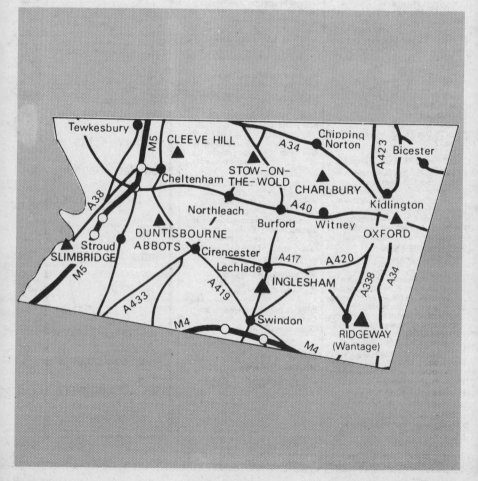

C HARLBURY
52 BEDS

Youth Hostel, The Laurels,
The Slade, Charlbury,
Oxford OX7 3SJ
☎ Charlbury (0608) 810202

Overnight charge:
Young £3.50 Junior £4.40 Senior £5.50
🏠🔺🔍①🎒🍴 Evening meal 18.00
hrs. Ⓢ Shops ½m. 🅴🅾 Thu. 🅿🅾
Charlbury. 🄵🅂 🅿 in layby 150 yds and
limited on site. **Absolutely no
parking in Ditchley Road**

Jan 1-10	Closed
Jan 11-31	Open Fri, Sat & Sun
Feb 1-Mar 31	Open (except Mon
Apr 1-Aug 31	Open & Tue)
Sep 1-Oct 31	Open (except Mon
Nov 1-Dec 23	Closed & Tue)
Dec 24-28	Open
Dec 29-Jan 9 92	Closed
Jan 10-31	Open Fri, Sat & Sun
Feb 1-29	Open (except Mon
	& Tue)

When Hostel is closed,
bookings may be accepted from
parties of 12 or more: please enquire

Cotswold Stone House, about 150
years old, and glove factory in
unspoilt village on River Evenlode.
Hostel and area ideal for families. N
of Charlbury. From town centre
follow road signposted Enstone. At
the B4022 crossroads go straight
across. Hostel is 50 yds on left

🅾🅂 164 🄶🅁 361198 🌃 14

Attractions: Cotswolds Area of
Outstanding Natural Beauty.
Blenheim Palace educational service
5m. Oxfordshire Museum. Woodstock
5m. North Leigh Roman Villa 3½m.
Manor Farm Museum educational
service Witney 7m. Cotswolds
Wildlife Park, Burford 10m. Oxfordshire
Way footpath. Walks through ancient
Wychwood Forest. Circular walking
routes available at Hostel. 🆇 Ⓛ 🆄

🚃 No service

🚌 Charlbury 1m

Next Youth Hostels: Stow-on-the-
Wold 12m. Oxford 15m. Inglesham
22m. Stratford-upon-Avon 31m.
Ridgeway 32m

C LEEVE HILL
66 BEDS

Youth Hostel, Rock House,
Cleeve Hill, Cheltenham,
Glos GL52 3PR
☎ Cheltenham (0242) 672065

TO WINCHCOMBE
1. PARKING AREAS
2. PUBLIC TOILETS
3. PHONE BOX
4. REDMONDS HOTEL
5. RISING SUN P.H.

Walkers
only
entrance

WOODMANCOTE

250 Meters

BISHOPS
CLEEVE

TO CHELTENHAM

Overnight charge:
Young £3.50 Junior £4.40 Senior £5.50
🏠🔺①🌃🍴 Evening meal 19.00 hrs.
Ⓢ 🅿🅾 Woodmancote 1m. 🅴🅾 (Bishops
Cleeve) Wed. 🅿 for cars and coaches
lay-by parking 200 yds. No access to
common or any local hotel car park

Jan 1-Feb 28	Closed
Mar 1-Oct 31	Open (except Mon)
	Open Bank Hol Mon
Nov 1-Feb 29 92	Closed

Wooden panelled Victorian golf-
clubhouse located on the very edge
of Cleeve Common in Cotswolds
Area of Outstanding Natural Beauty.
4m North of Cheltenham, just off
B4632. Path to Hostel, next to and
below "Redmond's" Hotel. Cyclists
must use track entering common
either 200 yards uphill opposite
telephone box, or 150 yards downhill
into Rising Sun Lane

🅾🅂 163 🄶🅁 983267 🌃 13, 14

Attractions: Cotswold Way.
Panoramic Views. Ideal walking
country across common. 🅵 ½m. Hill
fort 1½m. Sudeley Castle 3m. Belas
Knap Long Barrow 3m. Hailes Abbey
4m. Ⓤ golf, Cotswold villages. 🆇 Ⓛ
Gold Cup Race Meeting — March.
Music Festival — July. Literary
Festival — October. 🃏 available in
Cheltenham

🚃 Castleways from Cheltenham Bus
Stn (local bus from BR to
Cheltenham Bus Stn) (☎ 0242
602949)

🚌 Cheltenham Spa 5m

Next Youth Hostels: Duntisbourne
14m. Stow-on-the-Wold 16m.
Slimbridge 22m. Malvern Hills 23m.
Stratford 25m

D UNTISBOURNE ABBOTS
59 BEDS

Youth Hostel,
Duntisbourne Abbots, Cirencester,
Glos GL7 7JN
☎ Miserden (028582) 682

Overnight charge:
Young £3.50 Junior £4.40 Senior £5.50
🏠🔺①🌃🍴 Evening meal 19.00
hrs. Ⓢ 🅿🅾 Winstone 1m. Shops and 🅿🅾
Cirencester 5m. 🅴🅾 Thu. 🄵🅂 🅿 for
cars and one coach

Jan 1-2	Open
Jan 3-Feb 28	Closed
Mar 1-Oct 31	Open (except Sun)
	Open Bank Hol Sun
Nov 1-Feb 29 92	Closed

When Hostel is closed, bookings may
be accepted from parties, please
enquire

Rectory built about 1860 with 2 acre
grounds in hilly village in centre of
Cotswolds Area of Outstanding
Natural Beauty. 5m NW of
Cirencester, 1m off main Gloucester
road A417 dangerous for walkers and
cyclists. Alternative attractive route
from Cirencester via Daglingworth
and The Duntisbournes. Hostel 100
yds N of church

🅾🅂 163 🄶🅁 970080 🌃 13, 14

Attractions: Walking in Cotswold
Hills. Quiet lanes for cycling.
Cirencester Corinium Museum 5m.
Norman/Saxon churches in
Duntisbourne valley. Chedworth
Roman Villa 8m. Barnsley House,
Cirencester 8m. Cotswold Water
Park 8m. Crickley Hill Country Park
6m. Ⓛ 🆇 Ⓤ

🚃 No service

🚌 Kemble 10m; Gloucester 14½m;
Cheltenham Spa 14½m; Swindon 22m

Next Youth Hostels: Cleeve Hill
14m. Stow-on-the-Wold 20m.
Inglesham 20m. Slimbridge 23m

COTSWOLDS

15

INGLESHAM

30 BEDS

Youth Hostel, 'Littleholme',
Upper Inglesham, Highworth,
Swindon, Wilts SN6 7QY
☎ Faringdon (0367) 52546

Overnight charge:
Young £2.60 Junior £3.50 Senior £4.40
⚠ 👫 🍴 Meals available. ② S Shops
and PO Lechlade and Highworth. ☒
Thu (Lechlade) Wed (Highworth). P
nearby, not on restaurant forecourt;
please ask warden

Jan 1-Mar 28	Closed
Mar 29-Sep 29	Open (except Tue)
Sep 30-Mar 31 92	Closed

Stone-built cottage about 250 years
old in small Thames Valley farming
community. 2m S of Lechlade and 2m
N of Highworth on A361 next to
Inglesham Forge Restaurant. For
walkers, a bridle path from Hannington
Bridge (GR 174960) avoids main road
OS 163 GR 204964 🏃 14

Attractions: 🏊 and ⚓ 2m. 11th C
church 1m. River Thames at Lechlade
2m. Lechlade Gardens and Fuschia
centre. Highworth recreation centre
and swimming pool. 5 picturesque
Cotswold villages within 8 miles.
Cotswold Wildlife Park 9m. Badbury
Hill 5m. Whitehorse Hill, Uffington
7m. Buscot Park stately home 4m.
Swindon railway museum 9m. Filkins
Cotswold woollen weavers Museum
5m (refreshments available). Cotswold
countryside collection and mechanical
music museum, Northleach. Cirencester
Corinium Museum 13m. Chedworth
Roman Villa nr Cirencester. Cotswold
attractions L from warden send s.a.e.
Good area for cycling. L

🚌 Thamesdown 77 Swindon —
Cirencester (☎ 0793 523700);
Swanbrook 64 Swindon — Burford
(☎ 0242 574444). Both pass close
BR Swindon

🚉 Swindon 9m

Next Youth Hostels: Ridgeway
14m. Duntisbourne Abbots 20m.
Stow-on-the-Wold 22m. Charlbury
22m. Oxford 23m. Streatley 30m

Administrative Region: Central

THE RIDGEWAY

The Court Hill Ridgeway Centre,
Court Hill, Wantage,
Oxfordshire OX12 9NE
☎ Wantage (02357) 60253

COMFORT IMPROVED

To contact residents ☎ (02357)
68865

Overnight charge:
Young £4.40 Junior £5.40 Senior £6.60
7 × 4 berth cabins, with 🛏 and
private washing facilities. Ideal for
families and all on the ground floor.
Also available self-contained holiday
flat for members and non-members
of the YHA. Sleeps 5. Contact
Hostel for details.
**No Smoking Hostel due to fire
risk**

Overnight charge:
Young £3.80 Junior £4.70 Senior £5.90
Long loft and "A Room with a View"
all on first floor
⚠ 👫 🅰 ① 🍴 🍴 Evening meal 19.00
hrs. S Shops and PO Wantage 2m. P
ample for cars and coaches. Stabling
for horses/cycles. C and display area

Jan 1-31	Closed
Feb 1-28	Open Fri & Sat
Mar 1-May 31	Open (except Sun)
	Open Bank Hol Sun

Administrative Region: Central

Jun 1-Aug 31	Open
Sep 1-Oct 31	Open (except Sun)
Nov 1-Dec 14	Open Fri & Sat
Dec 15-Jan 30 92	Closed
Jan 31-Feb 29	Open Fri & Sat

When Hostel is closed, bookings
from parties may be accepted, please
enquire

This modern Hostel on the Ridgeway
has been beautifully reconstructed
from four interesting barns, now
sited on the Ridgeway footpath, with
exceptional panoramic views. The
grounds include a beechwood,
campsite, barbecue and picnic-site,
and the barns have been built around
a courtyard in traditional style. No
direct access from Ridgeway route
from west. Access only from A338
OS 174 GR 393851

Attractions: Midpoint of Ridgeway
Long Distance Route. Many walking
routes. U Lains Barn, a restored
tithe barn with capacity for 200. Ideal
for conferences etc. Vale and
Downland Museum in Wantage.
Home Farm, Charlton, Wantage.
Conservation and farm studies with
classroom. Uffington White Horse
5m. Kingston Lisle Stately Home 5m.
Littlecote Park 12m. Didcot Railway
and Steam Museum 12m. City of
Oxford 17m. Many sites of
archaeological interest nearby

🚌 Oxford Minibus 32/A, 36, X32;
Oxford 302 Oxford — Wantage,
thence 2m (☎ 0865 778849 or
711312)

🚉 Didcot Parkway 10m; Hungerford
12m. No bus connection from
Hungerford

Next Youth Hostels: Streatley
14m. Inglesham 14m. Oxford 17m

Court Hill Ridgeway Centre and Youth Hostel

Page 110

1991 YHA Guide

OXFORD

116 BEDS

Youth Hostel,
Jack Straw's Lane,
Oxford OX3 0DW
☎ Oxford (0865) 62997

Reception open 13.00 hrs

Overnight charge:
Young £4.00 Junior £5.10 Senior £6.30
Supplementary charge Jun-Aug:
Senior £1.00
⌂ ▨ ▨ Evening meal 18.00 hrs. ⑤
No bread available. ℗ Marston road
½m. ℗ for cars only; coaches — see
warden. No Smoking Hostel

Jan 1-6	Closed
Jan 7-Feb 28	Open (except Sun)
Mar 1-Oct 31	Open
Nov 1-30	Open (except Sun)
Dec 1-28	Closed
Dec 29-Feb 29 92	Open (except Sun)

Victorian mansion surrounded by
trees in conservation area of ancient
university city. Approximately 1¼m
along Marston Road from foot of
Headington Hill

ⓄⓈ 164 ⒼⓇ 533074 ▨ 14

Attractions: Colleges. Churches.
Museums. Cathedral. ▨ Swimming.
Start of Oxford Canal. Oxfordshire
Way. Blenheim Palace (birthplace of
Winston Churchill) 8m. Waddesdon
Manor 15m. ⓘ Cogges Farm Museum
10m. Brass rubbing Iffley Church 3m.
Bladon (Churchill's grave) 8m

▨ Frequent minibus from Job Centre
near ⓘ and Queen's College

▨ Oxford 2½m

Next Youth Hostels: Charlbury
15m. Ridgeway 17m. Streatley 19m.
Inglesham 23m. Stow-on-the-Wold
30m. Ivinghoe 35m. Milton Keynes
38m. Stratford 42m

Administrative Region: Central

SLIMBRIDGE

56 BEDS **COMFORT yha IMPROVED**

Youth Hostel,
Shepherd's Patch, Slimbridge,
Gloucester GL2 7BP
☎ Dursley (0453) 890275

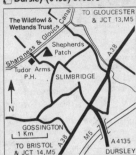

Overnight charge:
Young £4.60 Junior £5.90 Senior £7.00
⌂ ▨ Ⓒ ▨ ▨ Evening meal
19.00 hrs. ⑤ Shop and ℗ Slimbridge
1m. ▨ Wed. ⒻⓈ Special admission fee
to Wildfowl & Wetlands Trust for
Field Study groups, details from
Education Service, Wildfowl and
Wetlands Trust, Slimbridge, Glos
GL2 7BT. ℗ for cars and coaches

Jan 1-Mar 24	Open (except Sun)
Mar 25-Sep 30	Open
Oct 1-Nov 30	Open (except Sun)
Dec 1-23	Closed
Dec 24-28	Open
Dec 29-Jan 5 92	Closed
Jan 6-Feb 29	Open (except Sun)

Purpose-built, with its own ponds
and wildfowl collection by Sharpness
Canal and Peter Scott's Wildfowl and
Wetlands Trust. From A38 (Bristol-
Gloucester) take minor road through
Slimbridge, turn right at Tudor Arms

ⓄⓈ 162 ⒼⓇ 730043 ▨ 13

Attractions: Wintering birds and
permanent collection at Wildfowl
and Wetlands Trust (reduced
entry for members staying previous
night at Hostel). Frampton Court
gravel pits for ▨ Sharpness Docks
4m. Berkeley Castle 5m. Jenner
Museum, Berkeley 5m. Ⓛ ▨ Ⓤ
Severn Bore at Stonebench 10m.
National Waterways Museum,
Historic Docks, Gloucester
Cathedral, Gloucester 13m

▨ Badgerline 308 Bristol — Gloucester
City of Gloucester 91 Gloucester —
Dursley (passes close BR Gloucester)
(☎ 0452 27516). On both alight
Slimbridge Cross Roads, 1½m

▨ Stonehouse 7½m; Gloucester 14m

Next Youth Hostels: Cleeve Hill
22m. Duntisbourne Abbots 23m.
Chepstow 24m. Bristol 25m. Bath
30m. Malvern Hills 35m

Administrative Region: Central

STOW-ON-THE-WOLD

60 BEDS

Youth Hostel,
Stow-on-the-Wold, Cheltenham,
Glos GL54 1AF
☎ Stow-on-the-Wold (0451) 30497

Overnight charge:
Young £3.50 Junior £4.40 Senior £5.50
⌂ ▨ ▨ Evening meal 19.00 hrs. ⑤
Shops in village ℗ 2 mins. ▨ Wed. ℗
in square

Jan 1-31	Closed
Feb 1-28	Open Fri, Sat & Sun
Mar 1-Oct 31	Open
Nov 1-Dec 15	Open Fri, Sat & Sun
Dec 16-Jan 31 92	Closed
Feb 1-29	Open Fri, Sat & Sun

When Hostel is closed, bookings
from parties may be accepted, please
enquire

16th century building between White
Hart Hotel and Old Stock Hotel in
historic market square of hilltop
town in the Cotswolds. E side of
square

ⓄⓈ 163 ⒼⓇ 191258 ▨ 14

Attractions: St Edward's church.
Stocks. Cross. Cotswold Falconry
Centre 4m. Bourton-on-the-Water
tourist village 5m. Chastleton House
4½m. Folly Farm, Duckpool Valley
7m. Broadway Tower Country Park
8m. Rollright stones 9m. Cotswold
Rare Breeds Survival Farm Park 6m.
Wildlife Park, Burford 10m. Sudeley
Castle 12m. Chedworth Roman Villa
13m. Area of Outstanding Natural
Beauty. ▨ ⓘ Ⓛ

▨ Pulhams Cheltenham Spa —
Moreton-in-Marsh (passes close BR
Cheltenham Spa & Moreton-in-
Marsh) (☎ 0451 20369)

▨ Kingham 4m; Moreton-in-Marsh 4m

Next Youth Hostels: Charlbury
12m. Cleeve Hill 16m. Stratford 20m.
Duntisbourne Abbots 20m.
Inglesham 22m. Oxford 30m

Additional Information: To contact
members ☎ (0451) 30740

Administrative Region: Central

---

16 NORFOLK COAST AND BROADS

The northern coastline has many good beaches, with several seaside resorts. Away from these, on the sand-dunes and cliffs, are a large number of bird and nature reserves. King's Lynn has many historic buildings with Sandringham in easy reach. The whole of Norfolk is well known for its fine churches.

North east of the cathedral city of Norwich are the Broads, a series of connecting lakes and waterways. Watersports of all kinds can be enjoyed here and boats of all sizes are available for hire. Holiday-makers staying in this area can also visit the nearby coast. Cycling is a good way to get around in Norfolk, with quiet roads and no real hills.

The Peddars Way Long Distance Footpath, a fine stretch of Roman Road, forms a good cycling route across the country.

Useful Information

Party bookings for 10 or more will be accepted at all Youth Hostels at the resident warden's discretion when they are shown as closed during the winter months.

British Rail have an excellent Anglia Rover ticket available throughout the summer. This offers one week's unlimited travel on trains and rail link buses throughout East Anglia and Norfolk for a bargain price. We have a number of Go As You Please suggestions, cycle hire packages, and Special Interest breaks available from the Central Regional Office, PO Box 11, Matlock, Derbyshire. Tel: (0629) 825850.

For up to date information on tourist attractions and happenings throughout East Anglia and Norfolk, call the tourist board on (0473) 822922.

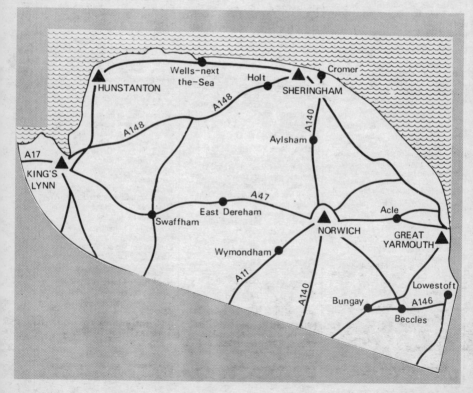

G REAT YARMOUTH

COMFORT IMPROVED · yha

Youth Hostel, 2 Sandown Road,
Great Yarmouth,
Norfolk NR30 1EY

📞 Great Yarmouth (0493) 843991

Overnight charge:
Young £4.00 Junior £5.10 Senior £6.30
Seasonal Prices Jul 1-Aug 31:
Young £4.60 Junior £5.90 Senior £7.00
👫 🛅 1 ⚡ ✉ Evening meal
19.00 hrs and snacks service. ⑤ Shop
50 yds. Shops in town. Ⓟ⒪ ½m. ⒠Ⓓ Thu.
Ⓟ on roadside by hostel

Jan 1-Feb 28	Closed
Mar 1-31	Open (except Sun & Mon)
Apr 1-Jun 30	Open (except Sun)
Jul 1-Aug 31	Open
Sep 1-Oct 31	Open (except Sun & Mon)
Nov 1-Feb 29 92	Closed

End house of large Victorian terrace
in quiet area close to beach. Recently
refurbished to give a very high level
of comfort, small family rooms and
flexible catering arrangements. Just
off North Drive, not far from centre
of town

Ⓞ§ 134 ⒼⓇ 529083 🛏 26

Attractions:
Resort Yarmouth:
Miles of safe, sandy beaches; 2 piers;
theatres and a wide variety of
entertainment. Ⓤ sea 🚣 ⛵ boat hire
and trips, ♨ all weather pleasure
pool and sports centre. Arts centre
and galleries. Caister Castle and Car
Collection 3m. Burgh Castle Roman
Fort, Yacht Station 5m. Fritton Lake
Country Park — windsurfing tuition
6m. Thrigby Hall Wildlife Gardens
6m. Pleasurewood Hills American
Theme Park 8m. Oulton Broad,
Watersports Centre 10m. Fishing
port and headquarters of the
offshore oil and gas industry

The "Other" Yarmouth:
Medieval town walls, restored historic
houses on the "Rows". Tolhouse
museum. Maritime museum. Dickensian
and Anna Sewell connections.
"Wilderness" areas of sand dune coast,
salt marsh, estuary and Breydon
Water. 📷 photography and 🧵 Weavers
Way and Waveney Way long distance
footpaths, Berney Arms Windmill
5m, Norfolk Broads. Halvergate
Marshes; a unique and attractive area
of secluded low lying pasture

🚌 Frequent from surrounding areas,
also local services (📞 0603 613613)

🚃 Yarmouth ¾m

Next Youth Hostels: Norwich 21m.
Sheringham 39m. Blaxhall 41m.
Brandon 55m

Great Yarmouth Youth Hostel

H UNSTANTON

COMFORT IMPROVED · yha

Youth Hostel,
15 Avenue Road, Hunstanton,
Norfolk PE36 5BW

📞 Hunstanton (0485) 532061

Overnight charge:
Young £4.00 Junior £5.10 Senior £6.30
Seasonal Prices Jul 1-Aug 31:
Young £4.60 Junior £5.90 Senior £7.00
👫 🛅 ⚡ C Ⓣ ⒼⓈⒸ ✉ Evening meal
19.00 hrs. ⑤ Shops and ⓅⓄ 200 yds.
⒠Ⓓ Thu. Ⓟ for cars by hostel on
roadside. Coaches in town.
Darkroom and classroom available if
booked in advance

Jan 2-31	Closed
Feb 1-11	Open Fri & Sat
Feb 12-23	Open (except Sun & Mon)
Feb 24-Mar 21	Open Fri & Sat
Mar 22-May 31	Open (except Sun) Open Bank Hol Sun
Jun 1-Aug 31	Open
Sep 1-Oct 31	Open (except Sun & Mon)
Nov 1-30	Open Fri & Sat
Dec 1-22	Closed
Dec 23-27	Open Xmas Party

Detached Victorian Carrstone house
in seaside resort on the Wash. In
centre of town off Sandringham
Road, near bus station (off A149)

Ⓞ§ 132 ⒼⓇ 674406 🛏 25, 26

Attractions: Sealife Centre. Leisure
Centre. Park Farm. Local bird
reserves. Windsurfing. Long distance
walks. Good cycling area. Hosts of
attractions to suit all ages, all year
round. Send sae for information pack
and activity calendar

🚌 Eastern Counties 401, 411 from
King's Lynn (passes close BR King's
Lynn) (📞 0553 772343) also Rail-
Link service — see BR timetable,
table 26A

🚃 King's Lynn 16m

Next Youth Hostels: King's Lynn
16m. Sheringham 38m. Norwich
40m. Brandon 40m

16

K ING'S LYNN

36 BEDS

Youth Hostel, Thoresby College,
College Lane, King's Lynn,
Norfolk PE30 1JB
📞 King's Lynn (0553) 772461

Overnight charge:
Young £3.80 Junior £4.70 Senior £5.90
🏠♿Ⓒ👥🏧GSC🍴 Meals service
throughout the evening. Ⓢ Shop 100
yds. PO ½m. ⓔⓓ Wed. Ⓟ on quayside
by hostel

Jan 1-Feb 7	Closed
Feb 8-16	Open
Feb 17-Mar 31	Open Fri & Sat
Apr 1-Jun 30	Open (except Tue)
Jul 1-Aug 31	Open
Sep 1-Oct 31	Open (except Tue & Wed)
Nov 1-30	Open Fri & Sat
Dec 1-27	Closed
Dec 28-Jan 2 92	Open

Hostel may be able to open to
parties and families booked in
advance when normally open Fri &
Sat only, please enquire

Part of an old chantry college built in
1500 on quayside in historic town and
port on River Ouse. Interesting internal
exposed timber framework. In centre
of town near St Margaret's Church,
College Lane is opposite Town Hall

NO SMOKING ANYWHERE IN
THE BUILDING DUE TO FIRE RISK

ⓄⓈ 132 ⒼⓇ 616199 ☐ 25, 26

Attractions: Many historic buildings,
Museums. Tue, Fri and Sat markets.
Castle Rising 4m. Sandringham 7m.
🚶 The Peter Scott Wash Coast Path
Walk. Nationally renowned Arts
Festival in late July. Tours of Caithness
Crystal works Ⓛ Video and literature
for group organisers — contact ⓘ
Tourist Information on (0553) 763044

🚌 Frequent services from
surrounding areas (📞 0553 772343)

🚉 King's Lynn ¾m

Next Youth Hostels: Hunstanton
16m. Ely 24m. Brandon 25m.
Norwich 44m. Cambridge 44m.
Sheringham 45m. Thurlby 35m.

Administrative Region: Central

N ORWICH

71 BEDS
COMFORT IMPROVED

Youth Hostel,
112 Turner Road,
Norwich NR2 4HB
📞 Norwich (0603) 627647

Overnight charge:
Young £4.40 Junior £5.40 Senior £6.60
Leaders rooms with separate
washing facilities and separate coach
drivers room available. 👥♿ⒸⒸ
♿♿②🛏 Set Hostel meals
available for groups and individuals
booked in advance (18.00-19.00 hrs).
Cafeteria available throughout
evening. Ⓢ½m. ④ Jul & Aug. PO ½m.
ⓔⓓ Thu. ⒸⓅ for cars and coaches.
GCSE and Primary study packages
available

Jan 3-12	Closed
Jan 13-Mar 14	Open (except Fri & Sat)
Mar 15-Aug 31	Open
Sep 1-Nov 30	Open (except Fri & Sat)
Dec 1-Jan 11 92	Closed
Jan 12-Feb 29	Open (except Fri & Sat)

Large house near River Wensum on
outskirts of cathedral city. In heart of
East Anglia and within easy reach of
Norfolk Broads. From city centre
follow St Benedict Street and
Dereham Road (A1074) westwards to
Turner Road (opp Earl of Leicester
public house)

ⓄⓈ 134 ⒼⓇ 213095 ☐ 26

Attractions: Norman and RC
cathedral and castle (and museum).
Colmans Mustard shop. Theatres and
folk museums. River trips. Elm Hill
cobbled medieval street. Guildhall,
350 pubs, 33 churches. Norfolk
Broads for boating, windmills and 🚌
7m. ♿Ⓛ Beeston Hall — YHA
members discount. ♿ⓘ (0603) 666071

🚌 Frequent from surrounding areas
(📞 0603 761212)

🚉 Norwich 2m

Next Youth Hostels: Great
Yarmouth 21m. Sheringham 25m.
Brandon 37m.

Administrative Region: Central

S HERINGHAM

101 BEDS
COMFORT IMPROVED

Youth Hostel,
1 Cremer's Drift, Sheringham,
Norfolk NR26 8HX
📞 Sheringham (0263) 823215

Overnight charge:
Young £4.40 Junior £5.40 Senior £6.60
Seasonal Prices Jul 1-Aug 31:
Young £4.60 Junior £5.90 Senior £7.00
👥♿Ⓐ②🛏 Cafeteria service.
Ⓢ Shop and PO 5 mins. ⓔⓓ Wed. ⒻⓈⓅ
for cars only. Coaches 250 yds.
Hostel open from 13.00 hrs Mar 24-
Aug 31

Jan 1-Mar 24	Closed
Mar 25-Aug 31	Open
Sep 1-Nov 30	Open (except Sun)
Dec 1-31	Closed

Spacious modernised building with 22
family dorms, field study rooms and
excellent facilities. Off the A149 coast
road behind St. Joseph's R.C. church.
Sheringham is a family resort around
an original fishing village with many
local tourist attractions

ⓄⓈ 133 ⒼⓇ 159428 ☐ 26

Attractions: Sea bathing ¼m.
Sheringham Woods 1m. Pretty
Corner 1m. Weyborne via cliff path
3m. Roman Camp (NT) 1½m. North
Norfolk steam railway ¼m runs 7m
along coast and inland to Holt giving
access to beaches and National Trust
properties. Fare reductions to YHA
members. Sheringham Park & Hall
1m. Felbrigg Hall 4m. Blickling Hall
15m. Mannington Hall and Countryside
Centre 7m. Shire Horse Centre ½m. 🚌
Blakeney Point 10m. Cley Marshes
6m. Binocular hire. Forest walks. ♿ⓘ
(0263) 824329 Ⓛ Military Museum
"The Muckleburgh Collection" at
Weybourne 3m

🚌 Eastern Counties 758/9, 761 from
Norwich (📞 0603 613613). Sanders
Coaches Sheringham — Norwich
(📞 0263 713261)

🚉 Sheringham ¼m

Next Youth Hostels: Norwich
25m. Hunstanton 38m. Great
Yarmouth 39m. King's Lynn 45m

Administrative Region: Central

EAST ANGLIA

The Suffolk coast and heaths are officially designated as an Area of Outstanding Natural Beauty with several nationally important nature reserves for bird-watchers and botanists.

To the south in Essex, the seaside resorts are busier and there are more large towns. Peaceful villages and pastoral scenery can still be found along the lanes and byways, and particularly by the river estuaries. Explore Constable Country near Colchester to find the lovely views made famous by the painter.

To the north is Thetford Forest and the vast sandy heaths and warrens of the Breckland on the Suffolk and Norfolk border. Much of Suffolk is gently rolling farming land. Ancient timbered buildings and fine flint-built churches remain from the days when the wool trade prospered. The countryside is varied enough to make cycling one of the main attractions as no area is too strenuous.

Useful Information

Party bookings for 10 or more will be accepted at all Youth Hostels at the resident warden's discretion when they are shown as closed during the winter months.

British Rail have an excellent Anglia Rover ticket available throughout the summer. This offers one week's unlimited travel on trains and rail link buses throughout East Anglia and Norfolk for a bargain price. We have a number of Go As You Please suggestions, cycle hire packages, and Special Interest breaks available from the Central Regional Office, PO Box 11, Matlock, Derbyshire. Tel: (0629) 825850.

For up to date information on tourist attractions and happenings throughout East Anglia and Norfolk, call the tourist board on (0473) 822922.

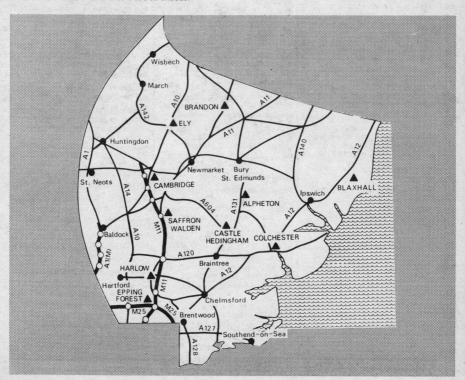

ALPHETON

Youth Hostel, Monks Croft,
Bury Road, Alpheton, Sudbury,
Suffolk CO10 9BP
📞 Cockfield Green (0284) 828297

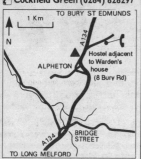

Overnight charge:
Young £2.60 Junior £3.50 Senior £4.40
🏠 🅰 ✕ 1 🅶 🆂 Shop Long Melford
3m. 📮 Bridge Street 1½m. 🔲 Long
Melford and Sudbury Wed. 🅿 in lay-
by 250 yds south of Hostel. Resident
owner requests No Smoking in this
Hostel

Mar 28-Oct 31   Open (except Tue)

Former farm building, with open
views, near Suffolk wool towns. On
A134 in village centre, 4m north of
Long Melford

🆗 155 🅶🆁 882511 🅱🅰🆁 21

Attractions: Long Melford Hall and
15th C church 3m. Ickworth House
14m. Lavenham Guildhall 4m. Bury St
Edmunds (medieval buildings) 9½m.
Kentwell Hall 3m with re-enactments
of Tudor life in June and July. Children's
Riding School 4m. Ⓛ available for
sae. 🖪 ☑ Ⓤ

🚌 From Sudbury (passing close BR
Sudbury), alight Long Melford, 3m.
Various operators, (📞 Suffolk CC
public transport dept. 0473 230000)

🚆 Sudbury 8m; Bury St Edmunds
12m

Next Youth Hostels: Colchester
20m. Brandon 25m. Castle
Hedingham 11m. Blaxhall 35m.
Cambridge 35m. Saffron Walden
30m

BLAXHALL

YH, Heath Walk, Blaxhall,
Woodbridge, Suffolk IP12 2EA
📞 Snape (0728) 88206 (warden)
📮 Snape (0728) 888946 (members)

Overnight charge:
Young £3.50 Junior £4.40 Senior £5.50
🏠 🅰 2 🔲 🖾 Evening meal 19.00 hrs.
Cot and high chair available. Childrens
play area. Choice of menu on all
meals. 🆂 Shop and 📮 250 yds. 🔲 Sat
and Tue all day. 🆁🆂 🅿 for cars and
coaches. Study packs available for
school groups. Games equipment

Jan 1-Feb 7	Closed
Feb 8-Mar 28	Open Fri, Sat & Sun
Mar 29-Jun 30	Open (except Sun) Open Bank Hol Sun
Jul 1-Aug 31	Open
Sep 1-Oct 31	Open (except Sun & Mon)
Nov 1-Dec 15	Open Fri, Sat & Sun
Dec 24-26	Open
Dec 27-Feb 6 92	Closed
Feb 7-29	Open Fri, Sat & Sun

Group bookings may be accepted
mid-week when Hostel normally only
open at weekends

Old school near Suffolk Heritage
Coast and Heathland Area of
Outstanding Natural Beauty. In
centre of Blaxhall village, 5m E of
Wickham Market 2m SE of A12

🆗 156 🅶🆁 369570 🅱🅰🆁 21

Attractions: Aldeburgh Festival
(Snape Maltings) 6m. Coastal and
heathland bird reserves. Minsmere
12m. Havergate Island 7m. Blaxhall
Heath ½m. Concert Hall and river walks
1½m. Sutton Hoo 8m. ☑ Ⓛ Send sae
for cycle routes Ⓛ 🛈 (0394) 282126

🚌 Eastern Counties 80/1, X80
Ipswich — Aldeburgh (pass close BR
Saxmundham), alight ½m SW of
Stratford St Andrew, 2m (📞 0473
253734)

🚆 Wickham Market 3m;
Saxmundham 5m

Next Youth Hostels: Colchester
32m. Norwich 39m. Great Yarmouth
41m. Alpheton 35m. Brandon 39m

BRANDON

Youth Hostel, Heath House,
off Warren Close, Bury Road,
Brandon, Suffolk IP27 0BU
📞 Thetford (0842) 812075

Overnight charge:
Young £4.00 Junior £5.10 Senior £6.30
🏠 🅰 🔲 🖾 Evening meal 19.00 hrs —
children's menu available. 🆂 Shop and
📮 200 yds. 🔲 Wed. 🅿 cars in grounds.
Coaches - see warden. 🅶 Cot available.
Barbecue facilities in Hostel grounds
(bookable to groups in advance). Large
play area with games available

Jan 11-Feb 7	Open Fri & Sat
Feb 8-17	Open
Feb 18-Mar 30	Open Fri & Sat
Apr 1-May 31	Open (except Sun)
Jun 1-Aug 31	Open
Sep 1-Oct 30	Open (except Sun & Mon)
Nov 1-30	Open Fri & Sat
Dec 1-28	Closed
Dec 29-Jan 2 92	Open N Year Party

Group bookings may be accepted
mid week at wardens discretion

Detached house in old riverside town
adjacent to Thetford Chase, largest
forested area in England and once the
centre of the Flint-Knapping industry.
Adjacent to Community Centre and
Public Library on private road off
B1106 from town centre towards
Bury St Edmunds

🆗 144 🅶🆁 786864 🅱🅰🆁 21

Attractions: Brandon Country Park
½m. Forest trails, Grimes Graves
3½m. Peddars Way. Icknield Way. ☑
(binocular hire). Aircraft spotting
from RAF Lakenheath and Mildenhall.
🖪 Ⓛ Coach/Boat hire available locally.
Ⓤ Hereward Way. 🖪 🅰 Kilverstone
Wildlife Park. Wayfaring and orienteering course ½m. 🛈 (0787) 248207

🚌 National Express 096, 098, 099,
call warden for local times

🚆 Brandon ¾m

Next Youth Hostels: Ely 16m. King's
Lynn 25m. Alpheton 25m. Cambridge
36m. Norwich 37m. Colchester 50m.
Thurlby 59m. Hunstanton 40m

CAMBRIDGE

**Youth Hostel,
97 Tenison Road,
Cambridge CB1 2DN**
☎ Cambridge (0223) 354601

Overnight charge:
Young £5.50 Junior £7.00 Senior £8.30
Supplementary charge Jun-Aug:
Senior £1.00

🏠🚻♿Ⓒ🏠⊙🍴🗄🚲 ⓩ4 🛏 ⊠ Full
cafeteria service. PO ¼m. ⓔ Thu. Ⓟ
limited roadside around Hostel.
Coaches — coach park 4m.

Jan 1-Dec 31   Open

The Hostel is one of our busiest
international meeting places.
Conveniently situated by the railway
station — follow station signs if
arriving by road

You can book in at almost any time
of day and there is a display to help
you plan your sightseeing. You can
even hire a bike next door to the
Hostel to help you get around
"Cambridge style"

Accommodation is mainly in smaller
4, 5, 6, or 7 bedded dormitories.
These have increased Cambridge's
popularity with families and groups.
The Bridges restaurant is open for
tea/coffee on arrival in the afternoon.
An evening meal or snack can be
enjoyed in the company of new friends,
the restaurant being open between
the hours of 17.30 and 20.00. Most
tastes are catered for, with specially
prepared home cooked meals.

There are special facilities for groups
and Cambridge's unique position as a
regional and academic centre makes
it ideal for residential or day
conferences and meetings

ⓄⓈ 154 ⒼⓇ 460575 🛏 20

Attractions: A cosmopolitan city
with a lazy river, green fields and
cows grazing just a stone's throw
from the ancient colleges

Cambridge has a wealth of old
buildings, museums, art galleries
extending from the classical
Fitzwilliam to collections of modern
art and holographics. Take a punt on
the river, walk along the "backs" to
Grantchester or cycle out to the
surrounding villages

Cambridge is easily reached from
London (20 trains a day — 65
minutes) and is a great touring
centre. Send for free leaflet of days
out

Theatre and cinemas. Sports centre.
Swimming pools (open and indoor).
Student pubs and cafes. King's
College Chapel and Choir. Concerts.
Cricket. Wildlife on the fens.
Duxford Imperial Air Museum 10m.
Ely Cathedral and Stained Glass
Museum 17m. Wimpole Hall and
Farm Park 8m. Anglesey Abbey and
gardens 4m. Shuttleworth Air and
Motor Collection 19m. National
Horseracing Museum, Newmarket
16m

🚌 Frequent from surrounding areas
(☎ 0223 423554)

🚆 Cambridge ½m (☎ 0223 31999)

Next Youth Hostels: Saffron
Walden 15m. Ely 17m. Castle
Hedingham 29m. Harlow 32m.
Brandon 36m. King's Lynn 44m.
Milton Keynes 44m. Ivinghoe 46m

Cambridge Youth Hostel

Administrative Region: Central

C ASTLE HEDINGHAM

50 BEDS

Youth Hostel, 7 Falcon Square,
Castle Hedingham,
Halstead, Essex CO9 3BU
☎ Hedingham (0787) 60799

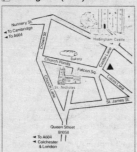

Overnight charge:
Young £4.00 Junior £5.10 Senior £6.30
Evening meal 19.00 hrs. nearby. on roadside around Hostel

Jan 1-Feb 17	Closed
Feb 18-Mar 28	Open (except Fri, Sat & Sun)
Mar 29-Jun 30	Open (except Sun) Open Bank Hol Sun
Jul 1-Aug 31	Open
Sep 1-Oct 31	Open (except Sun)
Nov 1-Dec 22	Closed
Dec 23-27	Open Xmas Party
Dec 28-Feb 16 92	Closed
Feb 17-29	Open (except Fri, Sat & Sun)

16th C lath and plaster building in attractive village of half-timbered houses dominated by Norman Castle. Centre of village at junction of Castle Lane with Luce's Lane (parallel to St James Street near church)

OS 155 GR 786355 Bart 16, 21

Attractions: Castle keep ½m. Church with original Norman doors. Little Maplestead 'round' church 3m. Railway museum 2m. Finchingfield 'model' village 10m. Educational packages available. ☎ (0376) 550066. Renowned cycle shop adjacent to Hostel. Excellent cycling on quiet lanes

Hedingham Omnibuses 6, 89/A from Braintree (pass close BR Braintree) ☎ 0787 60621)

Braintree 8m

Next Youth Hostels: Alpheton 11m. Colchester 18m. Saffron Walden 20m. Cambridge 29m. Brandon 35m. London 57m

---

C OLCHESTER

61 BEDS

Youth Hostel, East Bay House,
18 East Bay, Colchester,
Essex CO1 2UE
☎ Colchester (0206) 867982

Overnight charge:
Young £3.80 Junior £4.70 Senior £5.90
Evening meal 19.00 hrs. Snacks available. Shop and 2 mins. Thu. for cars only; coaches — see warden. Hostel open from 13.00 hrs during Jul & Aug

Jan 1-Feb 4	Closed
Feb 5-28	Open (except Sun & Mon)
Mar 1-Aug 31	Open
Sep 1-30	Open (except Sun)
Oct 1-Nov 9	Open (except Sun & Mon)
Nov 10-Feb 10 92	Closed
Feb 11-29	Open (except Sun & Mon)

Group bookings accepted when the Hostel would otherwise be closed at warden's discretion

Large Georgian house in England's oldest recorded Roman town. E end of town on river bank opp Colchester Mill Hotel, ⅓m E from Castle and bus park near junction of roads from Ipswich and Clacton

OS 168 GR 006252 Bart 16

Attractions: Castle Museum. Roman wall. Saxon church. Bourne Mill (NT). The Hythe (port). Stanway Zoo 2m. Dedham Vale and Constable country 8m. Clacton seaside resort 13m. ☎ (0206) 46379. Fingringhoe Nature Reserve 5m. Schools information pack. Out of season special interest breaks

Frequent local services (☎ 0206 571451)

Hythe (not Sun, except May-Sep) ½m; St Botolph's (not Sun, except Jul/Aug) ¼m; Colchester 1½m

Next Youth Hostels: Castle Hedingham 18m. Alpheton 20m. Blaxhall 32m. Saffron Walden 39m

---

E LY

36 BEDS

YH, Ely Sixth Form Centre,
St Audrey's, Downham Road,
Ely, Cambs CB6 1AD
☎ Ely (0353) 667423*

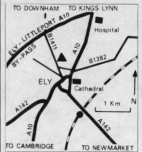

Overnight charge:
Young £3.50 Junior £4.40 Senior £5.50
Temporary Hostel. Limited cooking facilities. Small Shop and ½m. Tue. for cars and coaches

May 24-Aug 27 Open

Summer-only Hostel close to cathedral in area still known as the Isle of Ely, although the surrounding Fens have been drained. In College Campus in Downham Road on approach road from Cambridge (A10)

OS 143 GR 538908 Bart 20

Attractions: 11th C cathedral with stained glass museum. Monastic buildings. 15th C Bishops Palace. 17th-19th C Chantry. St Mary's Church (Norman). Vicarage where Oliver Cromwell lived, now Cromwell Heritage Centre. Wicken Fen (NT) 7m. Streatham steam engine 4m. River bathing. Riverside Walk. Park Museum, Brass Rubbing Centre, Old Maltings (Ely public hall). Weekly market. Hereward Way. ☎ (0353) 662062

Frequent from surrounding areas (☎ 0353 662445)

Ely ½m

Next Youth Hostels: Brandon 16m. Cambridge 17m. King's Lynn 24m. Thurlby 40m

Additional Information: *During open period only. Advance bookings prior to May 24 to Cambridge Youth Hostel, 97 Tenison Road, Cambridge CB1 2DN. ☎ (0223) 354601

E PPING FOREST

40 BEDS

Youth Hostel, Wellington Hall,
High Beach, Loughton,
Essex IG10 4AG
☎ (081) 508 5161

Overnight charge:
Young £3.50 Junior £4.40 Senior £5.50
🅰🄷🄰🄰🅇 🎲 🅂 🕾 🄶🅂🄲
🄿🄾 Loughton 2m. 🄿 for cars only.
Not open until 19.00 hrs Fri except
by prior arrangement

Jan 1-Mar 31	Open Fri & Sat*
Apr 1-Oct 31	Open
Nov 1-Dec 31	Open Fri & Sat*

* The Hostel is also open mid-week
Nov-Mar to groups who book in
advance

Fresh air, birdsong and forest walks
just 15km from central London. Enjoy
traditional hostel atmosphere with
small dorms suitable for families at
out of town prices. Walk freely or
relax in 6,000 acres of woodland
which was formerly a Royal hunting
forest. Single storey brick building
4m S of Epping town at High Beach,
W from King's Oak Hotel. Hostel is
first building on left down Wellington
Hill. From Loughton station (Central
Line) proceed N along Station Road,
Forest Road, Earls Path, cross A104
at Robin Hood Inn, fork right for
King's Oak Hotel

🄾🅂 167, 177 🄶🅁 408983 🕮 15, 16

Attractions: Forest walks.
Connaught Water 2m. 🅄 ½m.
Waltham Abbey (Norman) 3m. High
Beach Conservation Centre ½m. 🄰

🚌 County Bus 250 BR Waltham Cross
— Loughton Tube Station, alight
Volunteer Inn, ¾m (☎ 0279 26349)

🚇 Loughton (Underground) 2m;
Chingford (BR) 3½m

Next Youth Hostels: Harlow 11m.
Hampstead Heath (London) 13m.
Colchester (for Harwich) 35m.
Canterbury, Jordans and Windsor all
accessible via M25; 1m from Hostel
(junction 26, follow signs for Loughton,
then turn right at Volunteer Inn)

H ARLOW PARK

23 BEDS

Youth Hostel, Corner House,
Netteswell Cross, Harlow,
Essex CM20 2QD
☎ Harlow (0279) 21702

Overnight charge:
Young £3.50 Junior £4.40 Senior £5.50
🄷🄰 🎲 🅂 🄶🅂🄲 🅇 Small 🅂 Shop and 🄿🄾
1m. 🄿 25 yds

Jul 1-Aug 31   Open (except Sun)

At other times open for bookings
made in advance

Cottage of character in centre of
hamlet Netteswell Cross,
surrounded by public parkland on
edge of Harlow New Town. Junction
of School Lane and Park Lane, N of
swimming baths. Convenient starting
point for a tour of East Anglia. Five
minutes from main line railway
station and close to M11 and
Stansted airport

🄾🅂 167 🄶🅁 450109 🕮 15, 16

Attractions: Harlow Park for
swimming with aquachute, sports
centre, music, skating, playhouse,
mini zoo, ski slope. 🄰 and 🕾 on
River Stort. Three Forests Way.
Attractive Essex villages.
Windsurfing. Cycling museum

🚌 Frequent from surrounding areas
(☎ 0279 26349)

🚇 Harlow Town ½m

Next Youth Hostels: Epping Forest
11m. Saffron Walden 17m. St Albans
18m. London 24m. Cambridge 32m.
Colchester 40m

S AFFRON WALDEN

38 BEDS

Youth Hostel, 1 Myddylton Place,
Saffron Walden,
Essex CB10 1BB
☎ Saffron Walden (0799) 23117

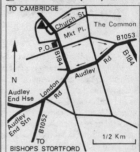

Overnight charge:
Young £3.50 Junior £4.40 Senior £5.50
🄷🄰 🎲 🅂 🄶🅂🄲 🕾 Evening meal 19.00
hrs. 🅂 Shop and 🄿🄾 nearby. 🄴🄾 Thu. 🄿
Free car park nearby

Jan 1-31	Closed
Feb 1-28	Open Fri & Sat*
Mar 1-28	Open
	(except Wed & Thu)
Mar 29-Jun 30	Open (except Thu)
Jul 1-Aug 31	Open
Sep 1-Oct 31	Open
	(except Wed & Thu)
Nov 1-30	Open Fri & Sat*
Dec 1-Jan 31 92	Closed
Feb 1-29	Open Fri & Sat*

* Outside opening dates party
bookings may be accepted at the
discretion of the warden

The oldest building (15th century) in
large Essex village which once
specialised in the growing of saffron
crocuses. At lower end of High Street,
on N side of town, W of church on
road to Cambridge, (B184)

🄾🅂 154 🄶🅁 535386 🕮 15, 20

Attractions: Sun Inn (NT). Old
houses with pargetting. Turf maze.
Audley End and Park 1m. Fine
perpendicular church. Leisure centre
1½m, museum. 🄻 Mole Hall Wildlife
Park 6m. Linton Zoo 7m. Stansted
Mountfichet Castle, Audley End
miniature railway, Bridge End
gardens, Benington Lordship 14m —
YHA members discount

🚌 From surrounding areas (many
operators) (☎ Essex CC public
transport dept. 0245 352232). Link
with BR Audley End by Hedingham/
Viceroy 59 (☎ 0787 606261 or 0799
22311)

🚇 Audley End 2½m

Next Youth Hostels: Cambridge
15m. Harlow 17m. Castle Hedingham
20m. Epping Forest 29m. London
41m. Milton Keynes 62m

18 CHILTERN HILLS AND THAMES VALLEY

Autumn among the Chiltern beechwoods is particularly lovely, but this is a favourite area for walkers, cyclists and other visitors at almost any season. There are many miles of well-marked footpaths and bridleways which are easy to follow. The Ridgeway long distance route starts at Ivinghoe Beacon and follows the line of the chalk uplands through the Chilterns Area of Outstanding Natural Beauty south-west to the Thames at Streatley. Further westwards, the path continues on the wide and ancient Ridgeway across the North Wessex Downs.

The River Thames attracts visitors to dozens of waterside beauty spots from Royal Windsor westwards. Recreations range from dinghy sailing to feeding the ducks.

Useful Information

Party bookings for 10 or more will be accepted at all Youth Hostels (except Streatley-on-Thames) at resident Warden's discretion when they are shown as closed during the winter months.

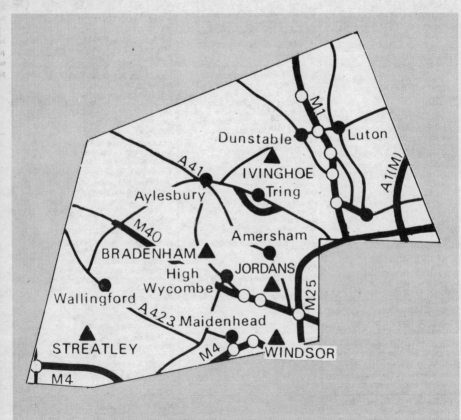

BRADENHAM

18 BEDS — COMFORT IMPROVED

The Village Hall, Bradenham, High Wycombe, Bucks ☎ Naphill (024024) 2929
Will change in 1991 to 0494-56-2929.
Bookings to G. Lee, 54a Brixham Crescent, Ruislip Manor, Middx HA4 8TX.
☎ (0895) 673168 Fax: (0895) 673188

Overnight charge:
Young £3.10 Junior £4.00 Senior £5.10

⚠ 🚿 🏠 🍴 ✕ Ⓢ 🔒 GSC 🅿 on roadside

Open Fri (19.30 hrs) and Sat (17.00 hrs) all year except **Dec 27 & 28**
Also open every night (17.00 hrs)
Mar 23-Apr 6, May 5, 25-31, Jul 6-Aug 31
Dec 20-Jan 3 available for pre-booked groups

Available on all other nights for pre-booked groups, families and schools at 7 days' notice

Old school on edge of large green in Chiltern village dominated by Manor House. At E end of village opp church. Turn off West Wycombe-Princes Risborough road A4010 at Red Lion

OS 165 GR 828972 Bart 14, 15

Attractions: Ridgeway long distance route 2¼m. Chiltern beech woods 1m. Fine church opposite Hostel. West Wycombe Park and village 2½m. View from Church Hill. Hell Fire Caves (R Styx). Hughenden Manor (Home of Disraeli) 1½m. Buckinghamshire Railway Centre

🚍 Beeline X14/15, 321-4 High Wycombe — Princes Risborough (pass close BR High Wycombe & Princes Risborough), alight Bradenham, ¼m on some, Walter's Ash, 1m on others (☎ 0494 20941)

🚃 Saunderton (not Sun) 1¼; High Wycombe 4½m

Next Youth Hostels: Jordans 12m. Ivinghoe 17m. Windsor 18m. Streatley 21m. Oxford 24m. London 32m

🏠 Hostel available for family groups at off-peak periods

Administrative Region: Central

IVINGHOE

67 BEDS

Youth Hostel, The Old Brewery House, Ivinghoe, Leighton Buzzard, Beds LU7 9EP
☎ Cheddington (0296) 668251

Overnight charge:
Young £3.50 Junior £4.40 Senior £5.50

🚿 ⚠ 🏠 🍴 ✕ Evening meal 18.30 hrs. Ⓢ 🅿 in village. 🔌 Wed. 🅿 for cars and coaches

Jan 1-31	Closed
Feb 1-28	Open Fri & Sat
Mar 1-28	Open (except Sun & Mon)
Mar 28-Sep 30	Open (except Sun) Open Bank Hol Sun
Oct 1-31	Open (except Sun & Mon)
Nov 1-Dec 14	Open Fri & Sat
Dec 15-28	Closed
Dec 29-Jan 1 92	Open
Jan 2-31	Closed
Feb 1-29	Open Fri & Sat

When Hostel is open Fri & Sat only, bookings may be accepted from parties, please enquire

Georgian mansion, once home of local brewer, next to village church in Chilterns Area of Outstanding Natural Beauty, 6m W of Dunstable

OS 165 GR 945161 Bart 15

Attractions: Start of Ridgeway long distance route 1m. Ivinghoe Beacon (NT). Pitstone Windmill. Dunstable Downs (gliding). Whipsnade Zoo 4m. Ashridge Park 3m. Aldbury village 3m. 🚤 on Tring Reservoirs 2m. Grand Union Canal 1m. Mentmore Park 4m. Ⓛ College Lake Nature Reserve 2m

🚍 Luton & District 61 Aylesbury — Luton (passes close BR Aylesbury & Luton) (☎ 0296 84919 or 0582 28899)

🚃 Tring 3m

Next Youth Hostels: 14m & 9m walk and bus ride to Milton Keynes and Jordans Hostels respectively. Milton Keynes 19m. Bradenham 17m. Jordans 19m. Oxford 35m. Windsor 30m. Streatley 30m

Administrative Region: Central

JORDANS

26 BEDS — COMFORT IMPROVED

Youth Hostel, Welders Lane, Jordans, Beaconsfield, Bucks HP9 2SN
☎ Chalfont St Giles (02407) 3135

Overnight charge:
Young £3.10 Junior £4.00 Senior £5.10

⚠ 🚿 🏠 🍴 ① 🍴 GSC ✕ Ⓢ 🅿 ½m. 🔌
Jordans village Wed and Sat (12.30).
Ⓛ 🅿 for cars and minibuses only.
Coaches by arrangement

Jan 1-31	Closed
Feb 1-28	Open Fri & Sat*
Mar 1-31	Open (except Wed & Thu)
Apr 1-Jun 6	Open (except Thu)
Jun 7-20	Closed
Jun 21-Sep 5	Open (except Thu)
Sep 6-21	Closed
Sep 22-Oct 31	Open (except Wed & Thu)
Nov 1-30	Open Fri & Sat*
Dec 1-23	Advance parties only
Dec 24-28	Closed
Dec 29-Jan 31 92	Closed
Feb 1-29	Open Fri & Sat*

* Also open midweek for parties booked in advance

Wooden buildings fully carpeted and heated in 2 acre woodlands in Chiltern village closely associated with early Quakerism (William Penn is buried nearby). Past Friends' Meeting House up Welders Lane signposted to Chalfont St Peter from Jordans Lane. 1m SE of Seer Green, 1½m W of Chalfont St Peter

OS 175, 176 GR 975910 Bart 9, 15

Attractions: Jordans Village, Meeting House, Mayflower Barn ½m, Good walking area. Beaconsfield Model Village 3m, Milton's Cottage, Chalfont St Giles 2m, Burnham Beeches 5m, Chiltern Open Air Museum & Courage Shire Horse Farm 4m

🚍 London Country NW 305/325 High Wycombe — Uxbridge, alight Seer Green, ¾m (☎ Bucks CC: 0296 382000)

🚃 Seer Green ¾m

Next Youth Hostels: Bradenham 12m. Windsor 13m. Bus ride and 9m walk to Ivinghoe Hostel. Ivinghoe 19m. London 20m. Streatley 31m. Oxford 36m

Administrative Region: Central

CHILTERN HILLS AND THAMES VALLEY

18

STREATLEY-ON-THAMES

56 BEDS

Youth Hostel, Hill House,
Reading Road, Streatley,
Reading, Berks RG8 9JJ
☎ Goring-on-Thames (0491) 872278

Overnight charge:
Young £3.50 Junior £4.40 Senior £5.50
🛏 ⚠ ① 🍴 GSC ❌ Evening meal
19.00 hrs. 🅂 P̄Ō Goring ½m. Ⓒ
Daytime use for groups. Payphone.
Sep leaders room. Baby equipment
available. P̄ Limited in grounds.
Coach parking — see warden.
Hostel opens 17.00 hrs

Jan 1-Feb 28	Open Fri & Sat
Mar 1-Sep 30	Open (except Sun)
	Open Bank Hol Sun
Oct 1-31	Open
	(except Sun & Mon)
Nov 1-30	Open Fri & Sat
Dec 1-31	Closed
Jan 1-Feb 29 92	Open Fri & Sat

**Advance bookings for groups of
10 or more accepted at the
warden's discretion, when Hostel
would otherwise be closed**

Homely victorian family house in the
beautiful village of Streatley-on-
Thames. On A329 Reading-Oxford
road 50mtrs south of The Bull pub
OS 174 GR 591806 Bart 8

Attractions: Ridgeway long distance
path. Thames towpath and walks.
Famous cheese shop. 🚂 day tickets.
Basildon House (NT) 2m. Child Beale
Wildlife Trust 2m. Mapledurham
working watermill 7m. Didcot Steam
Railway Centre 8m. City of Oxford
18m. Ⓛ 🚲 (0491) 35351 ext 3810
Wallingford. Ⓤ ✉

🚌 Oxford/Beeline 5 Reading —
Oxford (☎ 0734 581358)

🚊 Goring & Streatley 1m

Next Youth Hostels: Wantage 14m.
Oxford 19m. Bradenham 21m.
Overton 24m. Windsor 25m.
Inglesham 30m. Charlbury 30m

Administrative Region: Central

WINDSOR

80 BEDS COMFORT IMPROVED

Youth Hostel, Edgeworth House,
Mill Lane, Windsor,
Berks SL4 5JE
☎ Windsor (0753) 861710

Overnight charge:
Young £4.40 Junior £5.40 Senior £6.60
Supplementary charge Jun-Aug:
Senior £1.00
⚠ Laundrette 🛏 ④ 🍴 GSC ❌ Evening
meal 19.00 hrs. Licensed to serve
beer and wine with meals. 🅂 Shop
and P̄Ō Windsor. ED Wed. P̄ for cars
and minibuses only, coaches 5 mins
walk. **Hostel opens 13.00 hrs**

Jan 1-Feb 28	Closed
Mar 1-Dec 22	Open
Dec 23-Feb 29 92	Closed

Queen Anne residence in old village
of Clewer, a mile from centre of
historic Windsor on River Thames.
From town centre Eton or Windsor
take riverside via Barry Avenue,
Stovell Road, Clewer Court Road
and turn left into Mill Lane. From
Maidenhead or Windsor, road users
follow A308 to international YH sign
OS 175, 176 GR 955770 Bart 9

Attractions: Windsor Castle, State
Apartments and St George's Chapel.
Eton College and museum. Royalty
and Empire Exhibition. Windsor
Safari Park. Savill Gardens and
Windsor Great Park 7m. Magna
Carta and J.F. Kennedy Memorials
4m. Boat trips on the Thames.
Thorpe Park 8m. Dinton Pastures
Country Park 14m. Theatre Royal
Windsor. Leisure pool ½m. Heathrow
Airport 9m. 🚲 (0753) 854800. Ⓛ

🚌 Frequent from surrounding areas
(☎ 0734 581358)

🚊 Windsor & Eton Central ¾m;
Windsor & Eton Riverside 1m

Next Youth Hostels: Jordans 13m.
Bradenham 18m. London 23m.
Streatley 25m. Tanners Hatch 30m

Administrative Region: Central

London has something for everyone — shopping, from the fashionable Knightsbridge stores to the street market in Petticoat Lane; over 40 theatres, catering for all tastes; concert halls; disco dancing; folk music in pubs; and art galleries and museums, nearly all of which are free. There are plenty of green open spaces too, from formal squares to the fields, lakes and woodlands of Hampstead Heath.

The sights of London are world famous: Big Ben and the Houses of Parliament, the Tower, Buckingham Palace, Trafalgar Square, St Paul's . . . A few days in London are stimulating and exciting at any time of year. There are 8 Youth Hostels to choose from, each different in character. With over 900 beds available there's usually plenty of space, but Easter and Summer are very busy and beds should be booked well in advance to avoid disappointment. Bookings received at a Youth Hostel already fully booked, will automatically be transferred to another London Youth Hostel, unless members specifically request otherwise. Temporary accommodation at Wood Green, N22 will be available at Easter and during the Summer and White Hart Lane will also be open in the Summer (for advance bookings, contact Hampstead Heath Youth Hostel).

Members may book in up to 23.30 hrs: Youth Hostels close at midnight. With prior arrangement members may leave from 06.30 hrs onwards to catch early aircraft and trains.

Daytime access at all Youth Hostels.

L (general or individual Youth Hostels).

For further information contact London Office, YHA, 8 St Stephen's Hill, St Albans, Herts AL1 2DY. Tel: St Albans (0727) 55215.

CURRENCY EXCHANGE
service is available during Hostel opening hours at the following Hostels:
CARTER LANE, EARL'S COURT, HAMPSTEAD HEATH, HOLLAND HOUSE and OXFORD STREET

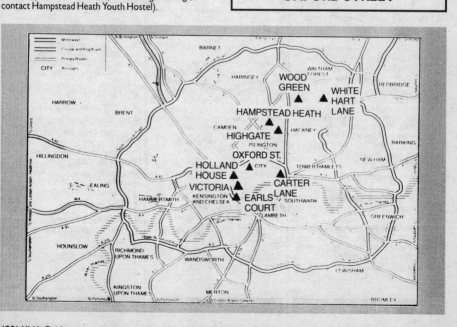

C ARTER LANE

196 BEDS

Youth Hostel,
36 Carter Lane,
London EC4V 5AD
📞 071-236 4965

Overnight charge:
Young £11.00 Junior £13.00 Senior £15.00
Supplementary charge from Aug 1:
Young £1.00 Junior £1.00 Senior £1.00
🏠 🍴 No member's kitchen. Cafeteria
facilities. 7.30am-9.30am, 11.30am-
10.30pm set meals for groups and
packed lunches are available. 🅿 400
yds. 🅿 available but expensive. It is
not advisable to attempt to bring
large vehicles into Carter Lane.
Coach park on South Bank opp
National Theatre 15 mins walk. Set
down point on S side of St Paul's.
Foreign exchange available at
competitive rates

Aug 1-Dec 31 Open

**Carter Lane is closed until Aug 91
for major refit. Contact London
Regional Office for further
information**

Victorian building, until 1968 the
home and school for choirboys of
St Paul's Cathedral

OS 176, 177 GR 319811 Bart 9

Attractions: In centre of City of
London. St Paul's Cathedral. Barbican
Arts Centre. Mansion House. Fleet
Street. Tower of London. River
Thames. HMS Belfast. Museum of
London. St Katherine's Dock.
Mermaid Theatre and Gallery. L

🚃 Frequent LT services
(📞 071-222 1234)
🚇 Underground: St Paul's ¼m

🚇 Direct train from Gatwick to
Blackfriars every hour. Blackfriars ¼m;
Cannon Street ½m (not weekends)
½m; Liverpool Street 1m

Next Youth Hostels: Oxford Street
2m. Earl's Court 5m. Holland House
5m. Hampstead Heath 6m. Highgate
5m. Kemsing 25m. Harlow 25m

Additional Information: Reception
office open 07.00-10.00 and 11.30-
23.30 hrs daily.

Administrative Region: London

E ARL'S COURT

131 BEDS *COMFORT yha IMPROVED*

Youth Hostel, 38 Bolton Gardens,
London SW5 0AQ
📞 071-373 7083 Telex: 913190
Fax: 071-835 2034

Overnight charge:
Young £9.00 Junior £11.00 Senior £12.00
Supplementary charge from June:
Young £1.00 Junior £1.00 Senior £1.00
🏠 🍴 Cafeteria facilities 7.00-9.00 hrs,
17.00-20.00 hrs daily. S 🅿 Earl's
Court Road. 🅿 very difficult. Foreign
exchange available at competitive
rates

Jan 1-Dec 31 Open

Old town house in residential street
close to busy area of small shops and
restaurants of many nationalities.
From Earl's Court Underground,
Earl's Court Road exit, turn right.
Take 5th turning on left marked
Bolton Gardens. From Gloucester
Road Underground turn right along
Gloucester Road, 200 yds to
Hereford Square, turn right to
Bolton Gardens

OS 176 GR 258783 Bart 9

Attractions: Direct access from
London Heathrow airport by
underground (Piccadilly Line to Earl's
Court). Principal museums within 15
mins walk. All London parks,
theatres, concert halls, art galleries
and historic buildings in easy reach by
bus or underground. L

🚃 Frequent LT services
(📞 071-222 1234)
🚇 Underground: Earl's Court/
Olympia ¼m

🚇 Kensington Olympia 1m

Next Youth Hostels: Holland
House 1m. Carter Lane 5m.
Hampstead Heath 5m. Oxford Street
5m. Highgate 6m. Tanners Hatch
23m. Crockham Hill 24m. Kemsing
26m

Additional Information: Reception
office open 7.00-24.00 hrs

Administrative Region: London

H AMPSTEAD HEATH

220 BEDS *COMFORT yha IMPROVED*

Youth Hostel, 4 Wellgarth Road,
London NW11 7HR
📞 081-458 9054/7196 Telex: 914774
Fax: 081-209 0546

Overnight charge:
Young £9.00 Junior £11.00 Senior £12.00
Supplementary charge from June:
Young £1.00 Junior £1.00 Senior £1.00
🏠 🍴 Cafeteria facilities 07.30-9.30,
17.30-20.00 hrs. S Shops and 🅿
Finchley Road. 🅿 in Hostel car park
only. Coaches ½m. Foreign exchange
available at competitive rates.
Limited C — contact Hostel for
details

Jan 1-Dec 31 Open

Former college for nursery nurses, in
an area of conserved architectural
and natural beauty. From Golders
Green Underground turn left along
North End Road. In ¼m turn left into
Wellgarth Road

OS 176 GR 258973 Bart 9

Attractions: 🔍 📷 Hampstead
Garden Suburb architecture.
Hampstead Heath. Hampstead
Village. Attractive garden. Easy
access to Central London. L

🚃 Frequent LT services
(📞 071-222 1234)

🚇 Underground: Golders Green ¼m

🚇 Hampstead Heath 1½m

Next Youth Hostels: Highgate 2m.
Carter Lane 6m. Holland House 5m.
Earl's Court 6m. Oxford Street 7m.
Ivinghoe 35m

Additional Information: Reception
area open 07.00-23.00 hrs daily

Administrative Region: London

HIGHGATE VILLAGE

74 BEDS

Youth Hostel,
84 Highgate West Hill,
London N6 6LU
☎ 081-340 1831 Fax: 081-341 0376

Overnight charge:
Young £7.00 Junior £8.00 Senior £9.50
Supplementary charge from June:
Young £1.00 Junior £1.00 Senior £1.00
⚠ 4 🍴 Breakfast only provided.
Small S Shops and PO Highgate
village. P roadside nearby. Heating
added

Jan 1-Dec 31   Open

Georgian house in a 'London village'
very near to the fields and woods of
Hampstead Heath, a 30 minute
journey from Central London. From
Archway Underground left up
Highgate Hill to Highgate village, left
at South Grove, Hostel 400 yds. Best
access via South Grove

OS 176 GR 281871 Bart 9, 15

Attractions: Kenwood House (art
collection). Dick Whittington's stone.
Highgate village architecture. Keats'
house. Highgate cemetery (tomb of
Karl Marx). Panoramic view of
London from Parliament Hill. 🚌 on
Hampstead Heath. 🚶 on Highgate
Ponds. L

🚌 Frequent LT services
☎ 071-222 1234)

🚇 Underground: Archway

🚆 Upper Holloway (not Sun, except
May-Sep) 1m

Next Youth Hostels: Hampstead
Heath 2m. Carter Lane 5m. Holland
House 6m. Earls Court 7m

HOLLAND HOUSE

186 BEDS

King George VI Memorial YH,
Holland House, Holland Walk,
Kensington, London W8 7QU
☎ 071-937 0748 Fax: 071-376 0667
Telex: 927535

Overnight charge:
Young £10.00 Junior £12.00 Senior £14.00
Supplementary charge from June:
Young £1.00 Junior £1.00 Senior £1.00
⚠ 🍴 Cafeteria open 7.15-9.15 hrs,
17.00-20.00 hrs. Dorms closed 10.00-
13.30 hrs. S Shops and PO Kensington
High Street. Cars and coaches NCP
Warwick Road 15 mins walk drop off/
pick up Phillimore Gardens but no
parking at that point. Foreign exchange
available at competitive rates

Jan 1-Dec 31   Open

Modern Hostel incorporating part of
Jacobean mansion, set in park with
woodland, lawns and playing fields.
From High Street Kensington
Underground (Circle and District
Lines) turn left on High Street, 2nd
right up Campden Hill Road, 3rd left
along Duchess of Bedford's Walk,
past junction with Upper Phillimore
Gardens, on to Holland Walk and
passageway into Hostel. From
Holland Park Underground (Central
Line) turn left along Holland Park
Ave, 2nd right up Holland Walk and
passageway into Hostel. Park is
closed at dusk; access then by
Phillimore Gardens only

OS 176 GR 248796 Bart 9, 15

Attractions: Commonwealth
Institute ¼m. Albert Hall and
museums (Science, Natural History,
Geology) 1m. Kensington Gardens
½m. Easy access to central London. L

🚌 Frequent LT services
☎ 071-222 1234)

🚇 Underground: Holland Park ¼m;
High Street Kensington ¼m

🚇 Kensington Olympia ½m

Next Youth Hostels: Earls Court
1m. Carter Lane 5m. Hampstead
Heath 5m. Oxford Street 5m.
Highgate 6m. Windsor 23m

OXFORD STREET

87 BEDS

COMFORT IMPROVED

Youth Hostel, 14-18 Noel Street,
London W1 1PD ☎ 071-734 1618
Fax: 071-734 1657

Overnight charge:
Young £11.00 Junior £13.00 Senior £15.00
Supplementary charge from June:
Young £1.00 Junior £1.00 Senior £1.00
Top three floors of modern building
with lift. Small rooms up to 4
persons. Open 24 hrs (night
security). Reception open 07.00-
23.00 hrs. Continental breakfast and
drinks. Vending machine only. No P
Foreign exchange

Jan 1-Dec 31   Open

🚇 Underground: To Oxford Circus
from Kings Cross, Euston, Paddington,
Charing Cross, Victoria

Next Youth Hostels: Carter Lane
2m. Earl's Court 5m. Holland House
5m. Hampstead Heath 7m

WHITE HART LANE

170 BEDS

Youth Hostel, All Saints Hall of
Residence, White Hart Lane,
London N17 ☎ 081-885 3234

Overnight charge:
Young £10.00 Junior £10.00 Senior £10.00
140 single rooms + 30 double rooms
(all with wash basins) 🍴 laundry
facilities 🧺

mid Jul-Aug 31   Open

During closed period
☎ 081-458 9054 (Hampstead)

WOOD GREEN

190 BEDS

Youth Hostel, Wood Green Halls
of Residence, Brabant Road,
London N22 ☎ 081-881 4432

Overnight charge:
Young £10.00 Junior £10.00 Senior £10.00
Single rooms 🍴 P (limited enclosed
parking for cars)

Easter and mid Jul-mid Sep   Open

During closed period
☎ 081-458 9054 (Hampstead)

20 NORTH DOWNS WAY AND WEALD

Surrey Hills

The Surrey Hills Area of Outstanding Natural Beauty lies just south of London's "stockbroker belt". Here are found such landmarks as Box Hill and Leith Hill. Much of the countryside around Hindhead is owned by the National Trust, including the deep-wooded combe "The Devil's Punchbowl".

North Downs

The North Downs Way, having started south at Winchester, passes through this area. The route coincides with "The Pilgrim's Way" for much of its route. Mainly along chalk ridgeway it gives superb views southwards over the Weald of Kent and Sussex. This area comprises rich farmland with medieval villages and weather-boarded cottages. The route finishes in Canterbury; this historic city offers not only a beautiful cathedral, but also Roman remains and interesting buildings.

This area is particularly popular because of its proximity to London. As well as walking and sightseeing, other outdoor activities can be enjoyed such as mountain biking, horse riding, cycling and even skiing on the dry ski slopes.

Useful Information

For general advice and information (including Area and Hostel leaflets) about hostelling in this region, contact: South England Regional Office, Rolfes House, 60 Milford Street, Salisbury, Wiltshire SP1 2BP.

Winter closed Hostels

The new Southern Region Booking Service offers the opportunity to book in advance when the Hostel is closed during the winter. See individual Hostel entries for further details.

Parties of 10 or more wishing to stay during the winter closed period, with meals provided, should contact the individual Hostel as many wardens are happy to open for a booking made in advance.

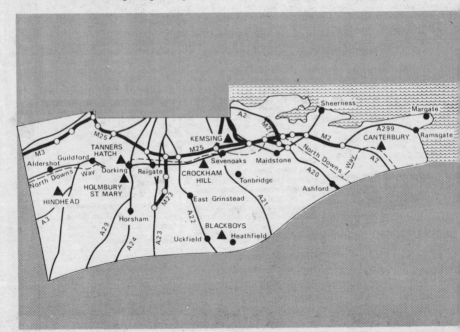

B LACKBOYS

Youth Hostel, Blackboys, Uckfield,
East Sussex TN22 5HU
☎ (0825) 890607
During Winter Closed Period:
☎ (0722) 337494

Overnight charge:
Young £3.10 Junior £4.00 Senior £5.10
△ ⚿ ① ▽ ⑤⑤ ⊠ Small ⑤ ℗
Blackboys. ℗ limited

Jan 1-Mar 28   Rent-a-Hostel*
Mar 29-Sep 30   Open
                 (except Mon & Tue)
Oct 1-Feb 29 92   Rent-a-Hostel*

During the Winter Closed Period, the
Southern Region Booking Service
will be pleased to help with bookings
and enquiries: Rolfes House, 60
Milford St, Salisbury, Wilts SP1 2BP
(☎ 0722 337494)

* Rent-a-Hostel: Hostel is available
during this period for the exclusive
use of groups booked in advance

Wooden cabin in tranquil setting
surrounded by woodland. From Cross-
in-Hand take left fork at Crown Inn,
then second right. From Uckfield take
Heatherfield Road, in 4m turn left
down Gun Road, cross stream, Hostel
in wood on right next to farmhouse.
From Lewes Road fork left at
Blackboys Inn and keep straight on

⑤ 199 ⑤⑤ 521215 ▭ 10

Attractions: 🏛 around Hostel.
Sheffield Park gardens (NT). Bluebell
railway at Horsted Keynes 5m. Church
of St Thomas a Becket. Framfield 2m.
Uckfield leisure centre 4m

🚃 Southdown 728 Eastbourne —
Uckfield (pass close BR Uckfield &
Rose BR Eastbourne), alight
Blackboys, ½m (☎ 0323 27354)

🚉 Buxted 2½m; Lewes 11m

Next Youth Hostels: Alfriston 17m.
Telscombe 17m. Brighton 18m.
Eastbourne 19m. Crockham Hill
22m. Hastings 24m. Truleigh Hill
34m. Kemsing 31m. Arundel 38m

C ANTERBURY

Youth Hostel, "Ellerslie",
54 New Dover Road,
Canterbury, Kent CT1 3DT
☎ Canterbury (0227) 462911

Overnight charge:
Young £4.60 Junior £5.90 Senior £7.00
⚿ △ ② ▽ ⊠ Evening meal 19.00 hrs.
Some baby equipment available on
request. Washing machine, tumble
dryer. ⑤ Shops and ℗ Canterbury. ⊞
Thu. ℗ limited. Hostel opens 13.00 hrs

Jan 1-Feb 7   Closed
Feb 8-28   Open (except Sun)
Mar 1-Oct 31   Open
Nov 1-10   Open (except Sun)
Nov 11-13   Closed
Nov 14-Dec 28   Open (except Sun)
Dec 29-Jan 31 92 Closed
Feb 1-29   Open (except Sun)

When closed, try Dover

Victorian villa in principal cathedral
city of England. Close to Kent Downs
Area of Outstanding Natural Beauty.
On main new Dover Road A2 about
½m SE of Canterbury bus station

⑤ 179 ⑤⑤ 157570 ▭ 10

Attractions: Cathedral, West Gate
Museum (military), Poor Priests'
Hospital (Heritage Museum), St.
Alphege Church (Canterbury centre),
Roman Mosaic Museum, City Guided
Tours, Theatre, Pilgrim's Way, North
Downs Way, East Kent Country Tour
3m ⊍ 🏛 Howletts Zoo Park 4m,
'Brambles' English Wildlife Park 5m,
Chilham Village and Castle 6m, Mount
Ephraim Japanese Gardens 6m, Stod-
marsh Bird Sanctuary 7m, Ramsgate
Motor Museum 12m, Romney Hythe
and Dymchurch Steam Railway 16m, △
Seaside Resorts (6m-10m), windsurfing
🚣 Eurotunnel Exhibition Centre 15m Ⓛ

🚌 Bus: Frequent from surrounding
area (☎ 0227 766151). Bus numbers
from town centre: 15, 16 & 17

🚉 Canterbury East ¾m; Canterbury
West 1¼m (BR: ☎ 0227 454411)

Next Youth Hostels: Dover 15m.
Hastings 40m. Kemsing 42m. London
(Earl's Court) 60m

C ROCKHAM HILL

YH, Crockham Hill House,
Crockham Hill, Edenbridge,
Kent TN8 6RB
☎ Edenbridge (0732) 866322

Overnight charge:
Young £3.50 Junior £4.40 Senior £5.50
⚿ △ ⚿ ① ▽ Limited ⑤⑤ ⊠ Evening
meal 19.00 hrs. Small ⑤ Shops and ℗
in village. ⊞ Wed. ℗ limited

Jan 1-Mar 25   Open Fri & Sat
Mar 26-Sep 30   Open (except Mon)
Oct 1-Dec 7   Open Fri & Sat
Dec 8-31   Closed
                 (try Kemsing)
Jan 1-Feb 29 92   Open Fri & Sat

Late Victorian house with fine views,
in 2 acre grounds on Greensand
Ridge in Kent Downs Area of
Outstanding Natural Beauty

⑤ 187 ⑤⑤ 441504 ▭ 6, 9 10

Attractions: Chartwell (home of
Winston Churchill) 1½m. Quebec
House (James Wolfe) 2½m. Haxted
Mill watermill museum 3½m. Bough
Beech Reservoir bird sanctuary 4m.
Hever Castle 5m. Penhurst Place 7m.
Ⓛ

🚌 No service

🚉 Edenbridge 2m; Edenbridge Town
(not Sun, except May-Sep) 3m;
Oxted 3m; Hurst Green 3m

Next Youth Hostels: Kemsing 13m.
Tanner's Hatch 21m. Blackboys 22m.
London (Earl's Court) 24m.
Holmbury 28m

HINDHEAD

16 BEDS

YH, Highcoombe Bottom, Bowlhead Green, Godalming, Surrey GU7 6NS
☎ Hindhead (042860) 4285
During Winter Closed Period:
☎ (0722) 337494

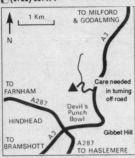

Overnight charge:
Young £2.60 Junior £3.50 Senior £4.40
🅰🅰 1 📶 GSC 🅇 Small 🆂 No bread or milk supplied. Shop and 📮 Hindhead 1m. 🕰 Sat. 🅿 for cars ½m by A3. Drive to Hostel is unsuitable for vehicles

Jan 1-Mar 28	Rent-a-Hostel*
Mar 29-Sep 30	Open (except Mon & Tue)
Oct 1-Dec 31	Open Fri & Sat
Jan 1-Feb 29 92	Rent-a-Hostel*

During the Winter Closed Period, the Southern Region Booking Service will be pleased to help with bookings and enquiries: Rolfes House, 60 Milford St, Salisbury, Wilts SP1 2BP (☎ 0722 337494)

* Rent-a-Hostel: Hostel is available during this period for the exclusive use of groups booked in advance

Traditional style Hostel converted from 3 National Trust cottages in AONB 1½m N of Hindhead along A3. Short stone pillar marked 'Highcombe'. Fork right just before Highcombe Farm's gate. Farmhouse is unable to give directions. Then take track through gate by Spring. Hostel on left over narrow bridge. Torch needed. Alternatively 2m along track from Thursley.

OS 186 GR 892368 Bus 5, 8, 9

Attractions: Pilgrim's Way 8m

🚌 Alder Valley 219, 268, 519/23 Aldershot — Haslemere (pass close BR Haslemere); 267, 274 from Guildford (pass close BR Godalming & Farnham). Alight in Hindhead areas: ½m to 1m according to stops (☎ 042873 5757)

🚆 Haslemere 2½m by path, 4½m by road

Next Youth Hostels: Holmbury St Mary 20m. Arundel 25m. Portsmouth 29m. Winchester 30m

---

HOLMBURY ST MARY

56 BEDS

Youth Hostel, Radnor Lane, Holmbury St Mary, Dorking, Surrey RH5 6NW
☎ Dorking (0306) 730777

Overnight charge:
Young £4.00 Junior £5.10 Senior £6.30
🚹🚺 🅰 1 📶 🅇 Evening meal 19.00 hrs. Cafeteria facilities 🆂 📮 1m. 🕰 Dorking Wed, Holmbury St Mary Wed and Sat. 🅿

Jan 1-Feb 9	Open Fri & Sat
Feb 10-Jun 30	Open (except Sun) Open Bank Hol Sun
Jul 1-Aug 31	Open
Sep 1-Nov 9	Open (except Sun)
Nov 10-30	Open Fri & Sat
Dec 1-29	Closed
Dec 30-Jan 4 92	Open (except Sun)
Jan 5-Feb 15	Open Fri & Sat
Feb 16-29	Open (except Sun)

When closed, bookings may be accepted from parties: please enquire

Purpose-built Hostel in large grounds in Surrey hills. ¼m up lane on W side of B2126, 2m S of Abinger Hammer, 1m N of Holmbury St Mary

OS 187 GR 104450 Bus 6, 9

Attractions: In Surrey Hills AONB. Common room & outdoor games. D of E camping. Many picturesque villages, Hatchlands (NT), Clandon Park (NT) & Polesden Lacey (NT) all 6m. Greensand Way and Downs Link paths pass nearby. Permanent Orienteering Course. Mountain Bike hire & guided weekends. Archery, Canoeing & Caving sessions can also be arranged. Send s.a.e. for Surrey guide

🚌 Tillingbourne 22 Guildford - Dorking (ask for Woodhouse Farm, as many drivers do not know the Hostel) (☎ 0483 276880)

🚆 Gomshall 3m; Dorking 6m

Next Youth Hostels: Tanners Hatch 6m. Windsor 27m. Crockham Hill 28m. Truleigh Hill 33m. London (Earl's Court) 30m. Arundel 31m. Hindhead 20m

---

KEMSING

58 BEDS

Youth Hostel, Cleves, Pilgrim's Way, Kemsing, Sevenoaks, Kent TN15 6LT
☎ Sevenoaks (0732) 61341

Overnight charge:
Young £4.00 Junior £5.10 Senior £6.30
🚹🚺 🅰 🅐 2 📶 🅇 Evening meal 19.00 hrs. 🆂 Shops and 📮 Kemsing. 🕰 Wed. 🅒 (capacity 30). 🅿 limited — access via Church Lane. Coaches in village, back of Wheatsheaf pub

Jan 1-31	Open (except Sun & Mon)
Feb 1-Feb 28	Closed
Mar 1-Apr 30	Open (except Sun)
May 1-Aug 31	Open
Sep 1-Nov 30	Open (except Sun & Mon)
Dec 1-Jan 31 92	Open Fri & Sat
Feb 1-29	Closed

When Hostel is closed, bookings may be accepted from parties: please enquire

Standing at the foot of the North Downs and on the Pilgrims' Way, this imposing building with its large grounds was once a 19th century vicarage. No vehicle access from the Pilgrims' Way

OS 188 GR 555588 Bus 9, 10

Attractions: On Pilgrims' Way and North Downs Way. Historic village and church. Lullingstone Castle and Roman Villa 4m. Knole House and Park 4m. Kemsing Down nature reserve. Greensand Ridge 1½m. Chartwell (home of Winston Churchill) 10m. Deciduous woodlands around Hostel. Ideal field study area for geology, history and geography. 👟 🅛

🚌 Kentish Bus 25/6 from Sevenoaks (pass close BR Kemsing), alight Kemsing 📮, 250 yds. (☎ 0474 321300)

🚆 Kemsing (not Sun) 2m; Otford 2m

Next Youth Hostels: Crockham Hill 13m. London 26m. Blackboys 31m. Canterbury 42m

---

Administrative Region: South

20

TANNERS HATCH

Youth Hostel, Polesden Lacey, Dorking, Surrey RH5 6BE
☎ Bookham (0372) 52528
(Warden's cottage)

Overnight charge:
Young £3.10 Junior £4.00 Senior £5.10
Ⓐ (limited numbers) ② ▼ ⊠ ⊠ Small
Ⓢ Order milk in advance (not always available), collect from warden's cottage. Shops Dorking. Ranmore Road 2½m. 🕒 Wed. Ⓟ Ranmore Common

Jan 1-Feb 4	Open (except Tue & Wed)
Feb 5-7	Closed

Feb 8-Mar 27	Open (except Tue & Wed)
Mar 28-Sep 30	Open (except Tue)
Oct 1-Dec 23	Open (except Tue & Wed)
Dec 24-26	Closed
Dec 27-Jan 2 92	Open
Jan 3-Feb 29	Open (except Tue & Wed)

A unique traditional hosteling experience in these isolated cottages situated in woods on a 1000 acre estate in Surrey Hills Area of Outstanding Natural Beauty. On N edge of Ranmore Common Woods and S edge Polesden Lacey estate. It should be noted that conditions at the Hostel are very spartan; no electricity or telephone. Tracks leading to the Hostel are muddy and without lights. It is therefore essential that members are properly attired and bring their own torch

Approach by path only 2m S of Great Bookham. 1¾m due W of Box Hill Station, 1m NW of Ranmore Church. a) From Box Hill Station take road towards Great Bookham and after 1¾m bear left through Polesden Lacey gate along drive towards main House. After 300 yds, drop down on the left side of bridge to reach cross track. Continue along this until reaching Hostel. b) From Dorking along Ranmore Common to small pond on left, then middle track opposite by house with YHA arrow. Follow track to Hostel. Both routes marked with YHA arrows. Warden at Prospect Lodge ½m W of Hostel

ⓄⓈ 187 ⒼⓇ 140515 🚌 6, 9

Attractions: North Downs Way. Pilgrims Way 1m. Box Hill 2m. Polesden Lacey (NT house open weekends). Nature trail around Hostel. Brass rubbing at 5 churches (equipment at Hostel). Orienteering on Ranmore Common. Ⓤ nearby. Tours and talks by farmer and gamekeeper (see warden). Ⓛ Orienteering in Norbury Park. Conservation work available and local Nature Reserve

🚌 London Country SW 514, 714 Kingston — Horsham, alight West Humble, 2¼m (☎ 081-668 7261)

🚇 Boxhill & Westhumble 1¾m; Dorking West 2½m (by paths); Bookham 3½m

Next Youth Hostels: Holmbury St Mary 6m. Crockham Hill 21m. London 23m. Hindhead 25m

Additional Information: During winter it may be necessary to collect key from warden's cottage. Telephone before 08.00 or 16.00-16.30 hrs

Tanners Hatch Youth Hostel

Administrative Region: South

NORTH DOWNS WAY AND WEALD

20

21 SOUTH COAST

The mild, sunny seaside resorts such as Brighton and Eastbourne attract both weekend visitors and those staying for longer holidays. To the east, near Dover and Hastings, the coastline is fairly flat, but further west, towards Brighton, it is backed by the hills of the South Downs. The hills reach as far as Beachy Head, with a spectacular range of chalk cliffs — the 'Seven Sisters'. The South Downs Way, for walkers, cyclists and horse riders, begins here. It follows the Sussex Downs Area of Outstanding Natural Beauty into Hampshire, and Youth Hostels such as Truleigh Hill mark the way.

Sussex and Kent offer many picturesque villages, old churches and leafy lanes, such as Alfriston and Telscombe. Romney Marsh, once the haunt of smugglers and pirates, stretches for 17 miles. Largely reclaimed, it is rich land for sheep pasture and tulip growing.

In addition to the countryside and coast, this area offers historical places of interest, such as Hastings and Arundel, a range of activities, and it is an ideal place to stay just before or after crossing the Channel.

Useful Information

For general advice and information (including Area and Hostel leaflets) about hostelling in this region, contact: South England Regional Office, Rolfes House, 60 Milford Street, Salisbury, Wiltshire SP1 2BP.

Also available: "The South Downs Way" leaflet, price 75p including postage. Please make cheques/postal orders payable to YHA.

Winter closed Hostels

The new Southern Region Booking Service offers the opportunity to book in advance when the Hostel is closed during the winter. See individual Hostel entries for further details.

Parties of 10 or more wishing to stay during the winter closed period, with meals provided, should contact the individual Hostel as many wardens are happy to open for a booking made in advance.

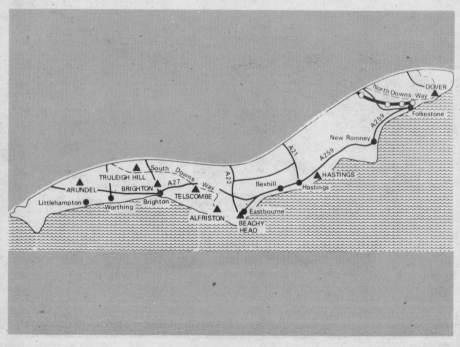

A LFRISTON

60 BEDS

COMFORT IMPROVED yha

Youth Hostel, Frog Firle, Alfriston, Polegate, East Sussex BN26 5TT
☎ Alfriston (0323) 870423

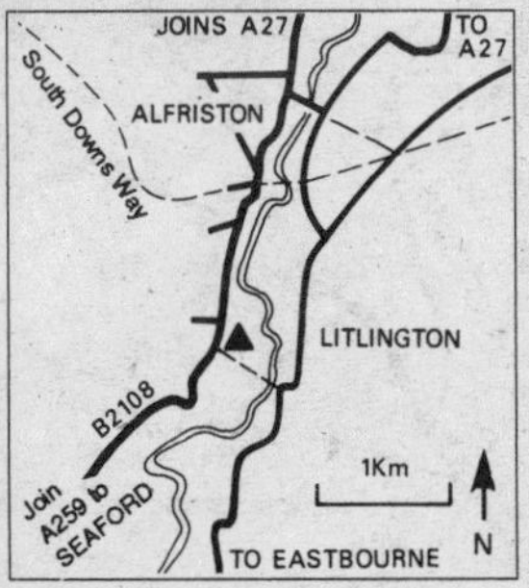

Overnight charge:
Young £4.40 Junior £5.40 Senior £6.60 C 2 Evening meal 18.30 hrs. S Shops and PO Alfriston. ECD Wed. P Coaches by arrangement through warden

Jan 1-31	Closed
Feb 1-Jun 30	Open (except Sun) Open Bank Hol Sun
Jul 1-Aug 31	Open
Sep 1-Nov 10	Open (except Sun)
Nov 11-14	Closed
Nov 15-Dec 14	Open Fri & Sat
Dec 23-28	Open for Xmas
Dec 29-Jan 31 92	Closed

When closed, try Eastbourne

Frog Firle is a spacious country house, partly dating from 1530 and recently refurbished, close to "show place" village in Sussex Downs Area of Outstanding Natural Beauty. 1m S of Alfriston E side of Alfriston-Seaford Road. Exceat Bridge approach, proceed to Litlington, take footpath 15 yds N of Plough and Harrow

OS 199 GR 518019 Bart 6

Attractions: South Downs Way 1m. Vanguard Way 1m. Weald Way 4m. Seven Sisters Country Park and Cuckmere Haven 3m. Firle Beacon 5m. High and Over 1m Seaford Head Nature Reserve 3m. Friston Forest Trail 2m. Wilmington Long Man 3m. Drusillas Zoo Park 2m. Michelham Priory 7m. Sheep Centre 7m. licences. Explorers Bus Tickets

Southdown 726 Eastbourne — Brighton (passes close BR Seaford & Polegate) (☎ 0323 27354)

Seaford 3m; Berwick 3m

Next Youth Hostels: Eastbourne 8m (7m by footpath). Telscombe 11m. Blackboys 17m. Brighton 18m. Hastings 24m

Administrative Region: South

A RUNDEL

75 BEDS

Youth Hostel, Warningcamp, Arundel, West Sussex BN18 9QY
☎ Arundel (0903) 882204

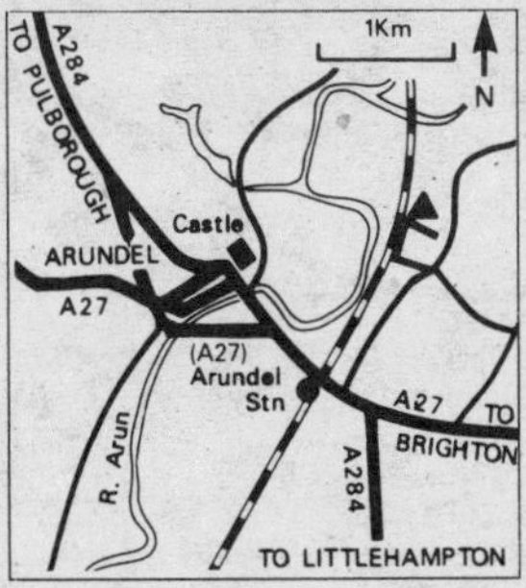

Overnight charge:
Young £3.50 Junior £4.40 Senior £5.50 2 GSC Evening meal 19.00 hrs. Snack service 20.00-21.30 hrs. S Shops and PO Arundel 1½m. ECD Wed. P limited for cars and mini-buses

Jan 1-Mar 25	Open (except Sun & Mon)
Mar 26-Sep 30	Open
Oct 1-Nov 10	Open (except Sun)
Nov 15-30	Open Fri & Sat
Dec 1-29	Closed
Dec 30-Feb 29 92	Open (except Sun)

Georgian building 1½m outside ancient town dominated by castle and close to Sussex Downs. From Arundel, take Worthing road, turn left immediately after station, then first left opp Warningcamp turning. First right, then right again

OS 197 GR 032074 Bart 6

Attractions: South Downs Way 4m. Castle 1½m. Cathedral and church 2m. River Arun ¼m. Wildfowl Reserve 1¼m. Museums. Fishbourne Roman Palace 12m. Beach 4m. Open air swimming pool 1½m. Bignor Roman Villa 7m. Amberley Chalk Pit Museum of Industrial History 6m. Chichester Festival Theatre 11m. Weald and Downland Open Air Museum 8m. Tangmere Military Aviation Museum 8m. Museum of Mechanical Music 10m. Goodwood House 9m. Parham House and Gardens 9m.* West Dean Gardens 14m* *discount to YHA members on production of a valid card

Southdown 212, 230/1 from Worthing, alight BR Arundel, thence 1m (☎ 0903 37661)

Arundel 1m

Next Youth Hostels: Truleigh Hill 16m. Brighton 20m. Portsmouth 26m. Blackboys 38m. Hindhead 25m. Holmbury St Mary 31m

Administrative Region: South

B RIGHTON

80 BEDS

COMFORT IMPROVED yha

Youth Hostel, Patcham Place, London Road, Brighton BN1 8YD
☎ Brighton (0273) 556196

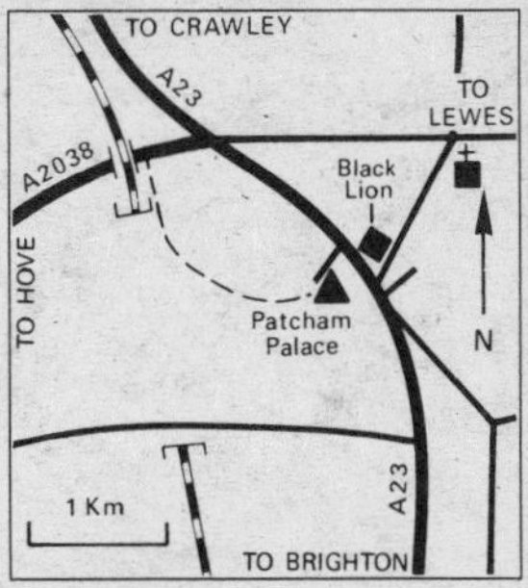

Overnight charge:
Young £4.60 Junior £5.90 Senior £7.00 4 Evening meal 18.00 to 20.00 hrs. Cafeteria facilities 13.00-22.00 hrs. Hostel opens 13.00 hrs. S Shops in village. ECD Wed. Incoming member telephone calls, Brighton (0273) 509897

Jan 1-31	Closed
Feb 1-Dec 22	Open
Dec 23-26	Closed
Dec 27-Jan 1 92	Open
Jan 2-31	Closed
Feb 1-29	Open

If full, try Truleigh Hill

Patcham Place, originally built by Baron de la Warr in 1588, eventually came into the possession of Squire John Paine who improved and altered the house considerably. In 1764 he added the spendid Queen Anne front. On W side of main London Road, opp Black Lion Pub 4m N of Brighton

OS 198 GR 300088 Bart 6

Attractions: South Downs Way 3½m. Doom painting in church, Devil's Dyke 3½m for views of Sussex Weald. Royal Pavilion. Regency architecture

Brighton & Hove 773 Brighton — Gatwick Airport (passes close BR Preston Park & passes BR Gatwick Airport) (☎ 0273 206666)

Preston Park 2m; Brighton 3½m

Next Youth Hostels: Truleigh Hill 6m. Telscombe 10m. Blackboys 18m. Alfriston 18m. Arundel 20m. Eastbourne 25m

Administrative Region: South

D OVER

135 BEDS

Youth Hostel, Charlton House,
306 London Road, Dover,
Kent CT17 0SY
☎ Dover (0304) 201314

Overnight charge:
Young £4.60 Junior £5.90 Senior £7.00
🅰 👪 4 Jul & Aug 🍴 Limited 🆖 🍴
Evening meal 19.00 hrs. 🆂 Shop and
PO nearby. 🔲 Wed

Jan 1-Dec 23	Open
Dec 24-27	Closed
Dec 28-31	Open
Jan 1-Feb 29 92	Open

The historic town of Dover has two
buildings for Hostel accommodation.
Dover central, a 69 bed Hostel and
an additional 66 bed building. Both
have recently been refurbished. The
main Hostel is on W side of old A2
Dover to London road ½m N of
Town Hall

OS 179 GR 311421 🔲 10

Attractions: North Downs Way.
12th C Dover Castle. Pharos
lighthouse (Roman). Seafront
swimming pool and sports complex.
Famous White Cliffs. Town Hall.
Interesting pubs. Romney, Hythe and
Dymchurch miniature railway 12m.
Near Kent Downs Area of
Outstanding Natural Beauty. 🔱 L
Channel Tunnel Exhibition,
Folkestone 7m. Dover is a good base
for day trips to London and France

🚌 Frequent from surrounding areas
(☎ 0304 240024)

🚉 Dover Priory 1m; Dover Western
Docks 1½m

Next Youth Hostels: Canterbury
14m. Hastings 38m. London 75m

E ASTBOURNE

40 BEDS

↓ TO BEACHY HEAD ↓

Youth Hostel,
East Dean Road, Eastbourne,
East Sussex BN20 8ES
☎ Eastbourne (0323) 21081

Overnight charge:
Young £3.50 Junior £4.40 Senior £5.50
🅰 🎓 1 📺 Limited 🆖 🍴 Evening
meal 19.00 hrs. 🆂 Shop and PO ½m
downhill just past traffic lights. 🔲
Wed. 🅿 for cars and coaches

Jan 1-Mar 25	Open Fri & Sat
Mar 26-Jun 30	Open (except Sun)
	Open Bank Hol Sun
Jul 1-Aug 31	Open
Sep 1-Oct 31	Open
	(except Mon & Tue)
Nov 1-Dec 1	Open Fri & Sat
Dec 2-26	Closed try Alfriston
Dec 27-Feb 29 92	Open Fri & Sat

When Hostel is closed, bookings may
be accepted from parties: please
enquire

Former golf clubhouse on South
Downs 450ft above sea level with
views across Eastbourne and
Pevensey Bay. From Eastbourne
station turn right and follow A259
(marked Seaford/Brighton) 1½m to
Hostel on right. Approaching from
the west, Hostel is on left of A259,
¼m down steep hill into Eastbourne,
2m from Beachy Head cliff

OS 199 GR 588990 🔲 6

Attractions: Start of South Downs
Way. Beachy Head white cliffs and
lighthouse. Popular "sun-trap" resort
1½m. Birling Gap 4m. Lullington
Heath nature reserve 4m. Seven
Sisters Country Park 6m. 🚶

🚌 Southdown 712 Eastbourne —
Brighton (passes close BR
Eastbourne & Newhaven Town)
(☎ 0323 27354)

🚉 Eastbourne 1½m

Next Youth Hostels: Alfriston 8m.
Telscombe 17m. Blackboys 19m.
Hastings 20m. Brighton 25m

H ASTINGS

64 BEDS

Youth Hostel, Guestling Hall,
Rye Road, Guestling, Hastings,
East Sussex TN35 4LP
☎ Hastings (0424) 812373

Overnight charge:
Young £3.50 Junior £4.40 Senior £5.50
👪 🅰 🎓 2 no daytime shelter 📺 🆖
🍴 Evening meal 19.00 hrs. 🆂 PO
Next PO 1½m towards Hastings. 🔲
Hastings Wed. 🅿 limited, for cars
and minibuses

Jan 1-31	Closed
Feb 1-Mar 25	Open Fri & Sat
Mar 26-Jun 30	Open (except Mon)
Jul 1-Aug 31	Open
Sep 1-Oct 31	Open (except Mon)
Nov 1-Dec 21	Open Fri & Sat
Dec 22-26	Closed
Dec 27-Jan 2 92	Open
Jan 3-Feb 29	Closed

When closed try Eastbourne or
Dover

Alternatively, when closed bookings
may be accepted at this Hostel from
groups: please enquire

Large house on high ground with
views across the Channel, 3 miles NE
of historic cinque port and popular
seaside resort. On W side of main
Hastings-Rye Road (A259). N of
White Hart, Guestling Hill. Raised
kerb at Hostel drive entrance,
cyclists take care

OS 199 GR 848133 🔲 6

Attractions: Hastings Castle and
harbour. Speedboat trips from pier.
Sea 🌊 Folk museum. Battle Abbey
(site of Battle of Hastings) 7m.
Picturesque village and bird sanctuary,
Rye 8m, Fire Hills, Fairlight 1½m

🚌 Hastings Buses/East Kent 11/12
Hastings — Rye (passes BR Hastings
& Rye) (☎ 0843 581333)

🚉 Three Oaks 1½m by footpath, 2½m
by road; Ore 2½m

Next Youth Hostels: Eastbourne
20m. Alfriston 24m. Blackboys 24m.
Dover 38m. Canterbury 40m

TELSCOMBE

28 BEDS · COMFORT IMPROVED

Youth Hostel, Bank Cottages,
Telscombe, Lewes,
East Sussex BN7 3HZ

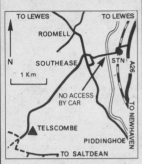

**All bookings and enquiries to
Brighton Youth Hostel** ☎ (0273)
556196

Overnight charge:
Young £3.50 Junior £4.40 Senior £5.50
🔲🔺🔺🔲🔲🔲 S Shop and PO
Peacehaven 2½m. 🔲 Wed. No P at
Hostel or in village. Incoming
member telephone ☎ (0273) 301357

Jan 1-Mar 28	Rent-a-Hostel*
Mar 29-Jun 30	Open (except Thu)
Jul 1-Aug 31	Open
Sep 1-Oct 12	Open (except Thu)
Oct 13-Feb 29 92	Rent-a-Hostel*

*Rent-a-Hostel: Hostel is available
during this period for the exclusive
use of groups booked in advance

Three 200-year-old cottages made
into one, in small unspoilt village 2
miles from coast in Sussex Downs
Area of Outstanding Natural Beauty.
S end of Telscombe village, 2m from
Lewes-Rodmell/Newhaven-Rodmell
road

OS 198 GR 405033 🔲 6

Attractions: South Downs Way 2m.
Norman church next to Hostel.
Rodmel church 2½m. Saltdean beach
2m. 🔲 on Downs. Seven Sisters
Country Park 11m

🚌 Brighton & Hove 14A/B from
Brighton (passes close BR Brighton),
alight Heathy Brow, ¾m
(☎ 0273 206666)

🚉 Southease 2½m; Lewes 6½m;
Brighton 7m

Next Youth Hostels: Brighton 10m.
Alfriston 11m. Eastbourne 17m.
Blackboys 17m. Truleigh Hill 21m

Administrative Region: South

TRULEIGH HILL

Youth Hostel, Tottington Barn,
Truleigh Hill, Shoreham-by-Sea,
West Sussex BN43 5FB
☎ Steyning (0903) 813419

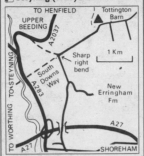

Overnight charge:
Young £4.00 Junior £5.10 Senior £6.30
🔲🔲🔲🔲🔲🔲 S 🔲 Evening meal
19.00 hrs. Snack service 20.00-22.00
hrs. Breakfast 8.00-9.00 hrs.
Separate diner for self-cookers. S
Shop and PO Shoreham 4m. 🔲 Wed.
Shop Beeding 2m. 🔲 Tue. P for cars
and coaches

Jan 1-Feb 7	Closed
Feb 8-Mar 18	Open (except Sun & Mon)
Mar 19-Aug 31	Open
Sep 1-Nov 10	Open (except Sun)
Nov 11-14	Closed
Nov 15-Dec 21	Open Fri & Sat
Dec 22-23	Closed
Dec 24-28	Open for Xmas
Dec 29-Feb 1 92	Closed

When closed, bookings may be
accepted from parties: please
enquire

Unusual modern building on old barn
site in 4½ acres grounds. On South
Downs Way, 600 ft above sea level
4m N of Shoreham, in Sussex Downs
Area of Outstanding Natural Beauty

Ideal base for family/group holidays.
No large dorms, several bookable
family rooms, large playing field.
Minibreak packages. Group and
Family Resource Packs available —
send sae. Good centre for adult
education/syndicate work groups,
geographical, historical, art, urban
and social studies. C

Vehicular approach: from A283 take
Upper Shoreham Road at Red Lion/
Amsterdam roundabout, 1m to
signpost on Erringham Road for only
route to Hostel via Mill Hill 3¼m

Cyclists and walkers: use South
Downs Way E or W. Various
connecting bridleways from
Southwick, Upper Beeding,
Edburton, Fulking, Devil's Dyke

OS 198 GR 220105 🔲 6

Attractions: Long distance footpath
and bridleway. Devil's Dyke (hang-
gliding) 2m. Chanctonbury 6m and
Cissbury Rings 5m Iron Age Hillforts.
Downslink 2m. Circular Walk.
Bramber Castle 2½m. Farm Tours
(Groups 8+) 2½m. 🔲 wildflowers
Fulking Escarpment (NT) 1m.
Southwick Hill (NT) 1m. Woods Mill
Nature Reserve 3m. Hollygate
Cactus Garden and West Wolves
Riding Centre, Ashington 5m. Sea 🔲
🔲 Marlipins Museum, beaches
Shoreham and Lancing 4m.
Domesday villages and churches,
river walks 1-5m. Steyning town trail
and conservation area guide, museum
5m. Swimming and leisure centres
Hove and Worthing 6m

🚌 Brighton & Hove 20/A from BR
Shoreham-by-Sea, alight ½m S of
Upper Beeding, thence 1½m by
bridlepath (☎ 0273 206666)

🚉 Shoreham-by-Sea 4m

Next Youth Hostels: Brighton 6m.
Arundel 16m. Telscombe 21m.
Blackboys 24m. Holmbury St Mary
33m

*Truleigh Hill
Youth Hostel*

Administrative Region: South

22 NEW FOREST AND ISLE OF WIGHT

New Forest

Lying between the River Avon and Southampton Water, the New Forest covers about 140 square miles of forest and heath. It is particularly attractive in June when the wild ponies have their foals. There are red, fallow and roe deer, and several areas are set aside as nature reserves. Stay at YHA Burley or Cranborne.

The Isle of Wight

The Isle of Wight is known for its seaside resorts, leafy chines and cliff paths. It also has a good network of paths for exploring the uncrowded chalk hills, forests and farmlands. Seven long-distance trails are marked. Pretty villages nestle in the interior and among buildings open to the public are Carisbrooke Castle and Osbourne House, Queen Victoria's country retreat.

The West Coast offers many outdoor pursuits, such as walking, horse riding and hang-gliding, while in the East, you'll find the more traditional seaside resorts. Visit YHA Totland Bay, Sandown and Whitwell.

Frequent Ferry Services: Portsmouth to Ryde
Southampton to Cowes
Lymington to Yarmouth

Hampshire

Hampshire offers many places of interest, including Winchester, the capital of historic Wessex; Portsmouth, a gateway with much naval interest; and Southampton, again on the water. Further North, the pretty village of Overton is situated between Salisbury Plain and the Berkshire Downs, rich in prehistoric sites.

Useful Information

For general advice and information (including Area and Hostel leaflets) about hostelling in this region, contact: South England Regional Office, Rolfes House, 60 Milford Street, Salisbury, Wiltshire SP1 2BP.

There's an excellent free guide for teachers available from the Isle of Wight Teachers' Centre, Upper St James Street, Newport, Isle of Wight. Send self-addressed envelope to cover 1lb weight.

Winter closed Hostels

The new Southern Region Booking Service offers the opportunity to book in advance when the Hostel is closed during the winter. See individual Hostel entries for further details.

Parties of 10 or more wishing to stay during the winter closed period, with meals provided, should contact the individual Hostel as many wardens are happy to open for a booking made in advance.

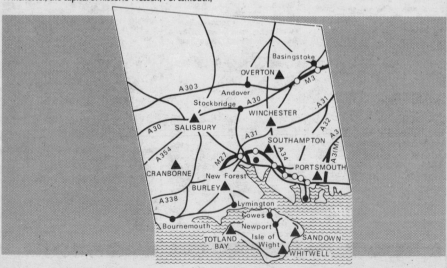

Burley

Youth Hostel, Cottesmore House, Cott Lane, Burley, Ringwood, Hants BH24 4BB
☎ Burley (04253) 3233

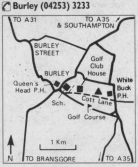

Overnight charge:
Young £4.00 Junior £5.10 Senior £6.30
🏠 🍴 △ bring own stoves 🄰 ① 🄿
Evening meal 19.00 hrs. 🆂 Shops and
🄿🄾 ½m. 🄴🄾 (🄿🄾) Sat. 🄿 limited for cars
and minibuses. Coaches at village end
of Cott Lane. **Hostel opens 17.00 hrs**

Jan 1-31	Closed*
Feb 1-Jun 30	Open (except Sun)
	Open Bank Hol Sun
Jul 1-Aug 31	Open
Sep 1-Nov 3	Open (except Sun)
Nov 4-8	Closed*
Nov 9-30	Open (except Sun)
Dec 1-22	Closed*
Dec 23-29	Open for Xmas
Dec 30-Jan 31 92	Closed try Totland
	Bay or Salisbury
Feb 1-29	Open (except Sun)

*Try Southampton

Victorian house with 1½ acres of grounds just outside village in open heathland of New Forest. From village centre take Brockenhurst Road uphill, then fork left past golf club sign on forest track, keeping right for ½m to Hostel. From Lyndhurst on A35 turn right on to Burley Road to village centre. From Holmsley on A35 take turning to Burley, eventually turning right at Durmast Cross Road to White Buck Inn (signposted) and enter track left of Inn

🄾🅂 195 and New Forest Tourist 🄶🅁 220028 🄱🄰🅁 5

Attractions: New Forest ponies. 🅄 🐴 🚴 (Ringwood). Forest walks. New Forest owl sanctuary 3m. Bolderwood Arboretum 4m. Knightwood Oak reptiliary, deer sanctuary 4m. Rufus Stone 7m. Bucklers Hard naval shipyard and Beaulieu motor museum 14m. Bournemouth Ice Rink. Ringwood market town. Butterfly Farm 10m. Lyndhurst: guided walks 🄵 (042128) 2269. 🄻

🚌 Wilts & Dorset X1 Poole — Southampton (passes BR Branksome, Lyndhurst Road & Southampton), alight Durmast Corner, ¼m; 105, 116 from Christchurch, alight Burley, ½m (☎ 0202 673555)

🚂 Sway 5½m; New Milton 6m

Next Youth Hostels: Cranborne 15m. Southampton 16m. Totland Bay 17m. Salisbury 21m. Winchester 23m. Swanage 29m

---

Cranborne

YH, 2 Crane Street, Cranborne, Wimborne, Dorset BH21 5QD
☎ Cranborne (07254) 285
During Winter Closed Period:
☎ (0722) 337494

Overnight charge:
Young £3.50 Junior £4.40 Senior £5.50
🏠 🍴 △ ① 🄿 🄶🅂🄲 🍴 Evening meal
19.00 hrs. 🆂 Shop and 🄿🄾 in village.
🄴🄾 Wed. 🄿 for cars and coaches 50
yds. DoE camping by arrangement.
Groups welcome. Barbecue. **Hostel opens 17.00 hrs**

Jan 1-Mar 26	Closed
Mar 27-Sep 30	Open (except Mon)
Oct 1-Feb 29 92	Closed

When closed, try Burley or Salisbury

During the Winter Closed Period, the Southern Region Booking Service will be pleased to help with bookings and enquiries: Rolfes House, 60 Milford St, Salisbury, Wilts SP1 2BP (☎ 0722 337494)

Large house in sheltered valley among the chalk downs just off Salisbury Plain, Cranborne Chase and New Forest. In centre of village opp fire station

🄾🅂 195 🄶🅁 056132 🄱🄰🅁 4, 5

Attractions: Poole Harbour 12m. Ackling Dyke Roman Road 3m. Bockerly Ditch 4m. Rockbourne Roman villa and museum 5m. Ox drove (Ridgeway). Win Greet NT 9m. Badbury Rings 10m. Knowlton Circles 3m. Heavy Horse Centre 3m. Nature Reserve Martin Down 5m. Cranborne Gardens (YHA discount). Moors Valley Park 6m. 🐴 🚴 2m. 🅄 4m. Medieval Jousting at Breamore House. 🄵 (0202) 841025. 🄻

🚌 Maybury 47 Fordingbridge - Cranborne (connects from close BR Salisbury) (☎ 07254 444 or 0722 336855 for connections)

🚂 Salisbury 15m

Next Youth Hostels: Burley 15m. Salisbury 15m. Swanage 30m. Lulworth Cove 32m. Litton Cheney 40m. Street 40m

---

Burley Youth Hostel

NEW FOREST AND ISLE OF WIGHT

22

Overton
26 BEDS

Youth Hostel, Red Lion Lane, Overton,
Basingstoke, Hants RG25 3HH
☎ (0256) 770516
During Winter Closed Period:
☎ (0722) 337494

Overnight charge:
Young £2.60 Junior £3.50 Senior £4.40
[A] [△] [1] [⊤] [SC] [⊠] Small [S] [PO] Shops
and take-away meals in village. [P]
Winchester Street opposite Post
Office. Payphone. **Hostel opens
17.00 hrs**

Jan 1-Mar 25	Rent-a-Hostel*
Mar 26-Sep 30	Open
Oct 1-Feb 29 92	Rent-a-Hostel*

During the Winter Closed Period, the
Southern Region Booking Service
will be pleased to help with bookings
and enquiries: Rolfes House, 60
Milford St, Salisbury, Wilts SP1 2BP
(☎ 0722 337494)

*Rent-a-Hostel: Hostel is available
during this period for the exclusive
use of groups booked in advance

One time Victorian village school,
close by the North Wessex Downs
Area of Outstanding Natural Beauty.
Turn S at Red Lion at W end of
village high street

[OS] 185 [GR] 513495 [Bart] 8

Attractions: Watership Down and
viewpoint 4m. Watercress Line
steam railway. Alresford 14m.
Basingstoke Icerink & Sports centre.
Wellington Country Park 14m.
Whitchurch Silk Mill. Highclere
Castle. Thruxton Motor Circuit 15m.
Finkley Down Farm Park 8m. [i]
(0962) 67871. [L]

🚍 Hampshire Bus 275/6 Basingstoke
— Andover (pass close BR
Basingstoke) (☎ 0256 464501)

🚆 Overton 1¼m

Next Youth Hostels: Winchester
14m. Streatley 24m. Southampton
25m. Salisbury 28m

Portsmouth
58 BEDS

Youth Hostel, Wymering Manor,
Old Wymering Lane, Cosham,
Portsmouth, Hants PO6 3NL
☎ Cosham (0705) 375661

Overnight charge:
Young £3.80 Junior £4.70 Senior £5.90
Seasonal Prices Jul 1-Aug 31:
Young £4.00 Junior £5.10 Senior £6.30
[A] [Ns] [1] [⊤] [SC] [iO] Evening meal 19.00
hrs. [S] Shop and [PO] ¼m. [ED] Wed. [P]
for cars on road side outside Hostel.
Hostel opens 17.00 hrs

Jan 1-Feb 15	Closed
Feb 16-Mar 15	Open
	(except Sun & Mon)
Mar 16-Jun 30	Open (except Sun)
	Open Bank Hol Sun
Jul 1-Aug 31	Open
Sep 1-Nov 10	Open
	(except Sun & Mon)
Nov 11-13	Closed
Nov 14-Dec 23	Open
	(except Sun & Mon)
Dec 24-30	Closed
Dec 31-Jan 4 92	Open
Jan 5-Feb 14	Closed
Feb 15-29	Open
	(except Sun & Mon)

Historic manor house with pre-
Elizabethan foundations, once owned
by Catherine Parr, on N outskirts of
busy seaport and naval dockyard.
From Cosham Post office proceed W
along Medina Road to church and
Old Wymering Lane

[OS] 196 [GR] 649055 [Bart] 5

Attractions: Historic flagships: HMS
Victory, Mary Rose, HMS Warrior. All
at HM Naval base 4m. RN Submarine
Museum Gosport. Charles Dickens'
birthplace 2½m. ✉ Farlington Marshes
2m. Continental ferries to: Cherbourg,
Le Havre, St Malo and Caen. Also
Channel Islands. Ferry terminal 2m, car
& passenger ferry to Isle of Wight 4½m

🚍 Frequent from surrounding areas
(☎ 0705 696911)

🚆 Cosham ½m

Next Youth Hostels: Sandown 10m
via ferry. Southampton 16m.
Winchester 25m. Arundel 26m

Salisbury
87 BEDS
COMFORT IMPROVED

Youth Hostel, Milford Hill House,
Milford Hill, Salisbury,
Wiltshire SP1 2QW
☎ Salisbury (0722) 327572

Overnight charge:
Young £4.40 Junior £5.40 Senior £6.60
[Nn] [A] [△] [O] [Ns] [Ns] [4] [⊤] [⊠] Laundry.
Evening meal service 17.30-20.30 hrs.
Vegetarian wholefood. Licensed to
serve beer and wine with meals.
(Evening meals for groups — please
book in advance.) [S] [PO] ¼m. [P]
Hostel opens 13.00 hrs

Jan 1-Dec 31	Open
Jan 1-Feb 29 92	Open

Listed building in two acres of
garden, secluded but only a few
minutes E from centre of cathedral
city. From bus station left into
Endless Street, cross Winchester
Street, left into Milford Street,
leading to Milford Hill. Motorists
avoid city centre & use ring road.
Travelling south on Churchill Way
East filter left for city centre service
traffic only and follow Youth Hostel
signs. Travelling from the south,
Hostel is signposted from A36
Southampton Road, near Henley's
garage. At railway station consult
map of city

[OS] 184 [GR] 149299 [Bart] 5, 8

Attractions: Cathedral. Museum.
Old Sarum 2m. Wilton House 4m.
Wilton Carpet Factory 4m. New
Forest 10m. 🏊 Swimming pool ½m.
🏛 Stonehenge 9m. Downland
walking, good cycling centre, on and
off road. [U] [i] (0722) 334956. [L]

🚍 Frequent from surrounding areas
(☎ 0722 336855)

🚆 Salisbury 1m

Next Youth Hostels: Cranborne
15m. Burley 21m. Southampton 23m.
Winchester 24m. Bath 39m. Bristol
53m

22

SOUTHAMPTON

Youth Hostel,
461 Winchester Road,
Bassett, Southampton SO1 7EH
☎ **Southampton (0703) 790895**

Overnight charge:
Young £3.50 Junior £4.40 Senior £5.50
Seasonal Prices Jul 1-Aug 31:
Young £3.80 Junior £4.70 Senior £5.90
🅰 🛈 ⬛ ◻ Evening meal 17.30-20.30
hrs (Groups of 10 or more 19.00 hrs).
Small 🆂 Shop and 🅿🅾 ½m. 🅴🅳 Wed. 🅿
for cars only. Coaches on road in
front of Hostel. Payphone. **Hostel
opens 17.00 hrs.**

Jan 1-3	Closed
Jan 4-31	Open (except Thu)
Feb 1-28	Closed (try Winchester)
Mar 1-Jun 30	Open (except Thu)
Jul 1-Aug 31	Open
Sep 1-Nov 10	Open (except Thu)
Nov 11-Dec 21	Open (except Wed & Thu)
Dec 22-27	Closed
Dec 28-Jan 31 92	Open (except Thu)
Feb 1-29	Closed

Pleasant Victorian house with
garden, close to the Civic Sports
Centre in northern suburb of historic
major port. 400 yds W of Bassett
roundabout

🆗 195 🄶🄽 415156 🄱🄼 5

Attractions: Int Boat Show Sep.
Eling Tide Mill 3m. Broadlands 5m.
New Forest 8m. National Motor
Museum 12m. Marwell Zoo 7m. Free
guided walks and museums. Sports
centre with dry ski slope ½m. 🛈 🄱
(0703) 221106

🚌 Southampton Citybus 45/7, Solent
Blue Line 54 from Southampton (all
pass close BR Southampton), alight
Bassett Roundabout, ¼m (☎ 0703
226235).

🚏 Swaythling 1½m; Southampton
2½m

Next Youth Hostels: Winchester
9m. Portsmouth 16m. Burley 16m.
Sandown (by Cowes ferry) 20m.
Salisbury 23m. Hindhead 39m

WINCHESTER

Youth Hostel, The City Mill,
1 Water Lane, Winchester,
Hants SO23 8EJ
☎ **Winchester (0962) 53723**

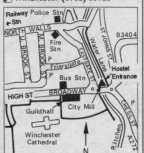

Overnight charge:
Young £4.00 Junior £5.10 Senior £6.30
🅰 🄽 ⬛ ◻ Evening meal 19.00 hrs.
Small 🆂 Shops and 🅿🅾 in town. 🅿
¼m. No smoking in Hostel. **Hostel
opens 17.00 hrs.**

Jan 1-2	Open
Jan 3-31	Closed*
Feb 1-Mar 28	Open (except Sun & Mon)
Mar 29-Sep 30	Open
Oct 1-Dec 14	Open (except Sun & Mon)
Dec 15-Jan 31 92	Closed*
Feb 1-29	Open (except Sun & Mon)

*When closed, try Southampton or
Salisbury

Charming 18th century watermill
(National Trust) straddling River
Itchen at east end of King Alfred's
capital. One of England's richest and
most ancient cathedral cities

🆗 185 🄶🄽 486293 🄱🄼 5, 8

Attractions: Cathedral. King
Alfred's statue. Bishops Palace.
Winchester College. Castle Hall &
King Arthur's Round Table. Hospital
of St Cross 1m. West Gate. King's
Gate. River Itchen walks. Marwell
Zoo Park (endangered species) 6m.
Mid Hants Steam Railway 7m. 🄱
(0962) 67871. 🛈

🚌 Frequent from surrounding areas
(☎ 0962 52352)

🚏 Winchester 1m

Next Youth Hostels: Southampton
9m. Overton 14m. Burley 23m.
Salisbury 24m. Hindhead 30m

NEW FOREST AND ISLE OF WIGHT

22 ▶

SANDOWN
78 BEDS

Youth Hostel, The Firs, Fitzroy Street, Sandown, Isle of Wight PO36 8JH
☎ Isle of Wight (0983) 402651
During Winter Closed Period:
☎ (0722) 337494

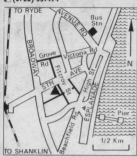

Overnight charge:
Young £3.80 Junior £4.70 Senior £5.90
Seasonal Prices Jul 1-Aug 31:
Young £4.40 Junior £5.40 Senior £6.60
🏠 🅰 1 🔌 GSC 🍴 Evening meal 19.00 hrs. 🆂 Shop and 🅿 in town. 🍴 Wed.
🅿 400 yds. Cars and coaches

Jan 1-Mar 26	Closed (try Totland Bay)
Mar 27-Jun 30	Open (except Mon)
Jul 1-Aug 31	Open
Sep 1-Nov 30	Open (except Mon & Tue)
Dec 1-Feb 29 92	Closed

When closed, try Totland Bay or Portsmouth

During the Winter Closed Period, the Southern Region Booking Service will be pleased to help with bookings and enquiries: Rolfes House, 60 Milford St, Salisbury, Wilts SP1 2BP (☎ 0722 337494)

Large house in popular seaside resort on east side of island, close to sandy beaches and unspoilt countryside inland

🆗 196 GR 597843 Bart 5

Attractions: Downs. Sea bathing. Sandy beaches. Boat trips. Bembridge Maritime Museum 5m. Roman villa 1½m. Steam railway 8m. 🔋 🅻

🚂 Frequent from surrounding areas (☎ 0983 862224)

🚌 Sandown ½m (No cycles permitted on island trains)

Ferry Terminal: Ryde Pierhead (Sealink) 6m; East Cowes (Red Funnel) 12m

Next Youth Hostels: Whitwell 9m. Portsmouth 10m. Southampton (by Cowes ferry) 20m. Totland Bay 21m

Administrative Region: South

TOTLAND BAY (WEST WIGHT)
78 BEDS

Youth Hostel,
Hurst Hill, Totland Bay,
Isle of Wight PO39 0HD
☎ Isle of Wight (0983) 752165

Overnight charge:
Young £4.40 Junior £5.40 Senior £6.60
🏠 1×2, 3×4, 1×5, 2×6. Cot available. 🅰 🅼 1 🔌 GSC 🍴 Evening meal 19.00 hrs. 🆂 Shop and 🅿 500 yds. 🍴 Wed. 🅿 cars and minibuses in Hostel grounds (very steep ramp access), coaches in road, contact the warden

Jan 1-Feb 14	Open (except Sun & Mon)
Feb 15-Jun 30	Open (except Sun) Open Bank Hol Sun
Jul 1-Aug 31	Open
Sep 1-Nov 3	Open (except Sun)
Nov 4-Dec 22	Closed
Dec 23-29	Open for Xmas
Dec 30-Jan 5 92	Closed
Jan 6-Feb 29	Open (except Sun & Mon)

When closed, try Southampton

Former private home and hotel on west side of island, near clifftop walks and beaches. Hostel offers small room ideal for families. From roundabout by war memorial in Totland, fork left up Weston Road. Take second left, Hostel on left at top of short hill, opp church

🆗 196 GR 324865 (ignore former Hostel at GR 345862) Bart 5

Attractions: Alum Bay 1½m. Needles Rocks 2m. Freshwater Bay 2m. St Agnes thatched church 2m. Safe beaches for swimming nearby. 🌊 Cowes week in August. 🆄

🚌 Southern Vectis 7/A, 13, 17, 42 from Yarmouth; 1B/C from Ryde, alight Totland War Memorial, ¼m (☎ 0983 523831)

Ferry Terminal: Yarmouth (Sealink) 3m; West Cowes (Red Funnel) 15m

Next Youth Hostels: Burley 12m by Yarmouth-Lymington ferry. Whitwell 18m. Sandown 21m

Administrative Region: South

WHITWELL
32 BEDS

Youth Hostel, Whitwell, Ventnor, Isle of Wight PO38 2PP
☎ Isle of Wight (0983) 730473
During Winter Closed Period:
☎ (0722) 337494

Overnight charge:
Young £3.80 Junior £4.70 Senior £5.90
🅰 🅼 1 🍴 🍴 Evening meal 19.00 hrs. 🆂 Please order bread and milk in advance. Members' kitchen very small. Shop and 🅿 nearby. 🍴 Whitwell Tue, Ventnor Wed. 🅿 limited, for cars and minibuses. Coaches Ventnor 2½m

Jan 1-Mar 26	Closed
Mar 27-Jun 30	Open (except Fri)
Jul 1-Aug 31	Open
Sep 1-30	Open (except Thu & Fri)
Oct 1-Feb 29 92	Closed

When closed, try Totland Bay

During the Winter Closed Period, the Southern Region Booking Service will be pleased to help with bookings and enquiries: Rolfes House, 60 Milford St, Salisbury, Wilts SP1 2BP (☎ 0722 337494)

Whitwell is a pleasant village only 2m from St Catherine's Point, the most southerly part of the island. The Hostel is an old Victorian vicarage, built of local stone with a large garden

🆗 196 GR 521776 Bart 5

Attractions: Good walking, easy terrain and well marked paths. Blackgang Chine pleasure gardens 4m. Model village, Godshill 3m. Smuggling History Museum, Ventnor 2½m. St Catherine's Point Lighthouse 2m. Carisbrook Castle 8m. Osborne House 12m. Sea bathing 3m

🚌 Southern Vectis 16A/C Newport – Ryde (☎ 0983 852288). Bus timetables vary seasonally

🚌 Shanklin 8m

Ferry Terminal: Fishbourne (Sealink) 11m; Ryde Pierhead (Sealink) 12m; West Cowes (Red Funnel) 12m

Next Youth Hostels: Sandown 9m. Totland 18m. Southampton 18½m. Portsmouth 19m

Administrative Region: South

22

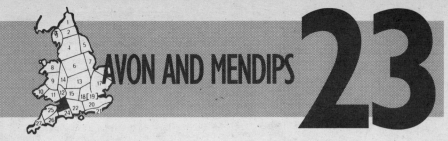

AVON AND MENDIPS 23

uch of the Mendip scenery is spectacular. Cheddar Gorge has cliffs of 450ft. Its caves, some of which are open to the public, are famous for their stalactites and stalagmites. Another amazing sight is the Great Cave at Wookey Hole, with its deep underground river. The Mendip Hills are also an Area of Outstanding Natural Beauty, rising at Black Down to 1,068ft.

Glastonbury, near Street, is the ancient Isle of Avalon, to which the first Christian missionaries came soon after the Crucifixion. Nearby is the tiny cathedral city of Wells, almost unchanged since the Middle Ages. Two other interesting cities are Bristol, a seaport with two cathedrals as well as Brunel's Clifton Suspension Bridge, and Bath Spa, the ancient Roman city with the only hot springs in Britain. The Roman Bath has an Abbey Church and a host of elegant 18th century buildings, including the Royal Crescent, Assembly Rooms and Pump Rooms.

Useful Information

For general advice and information (including Area and Hostel leaflets) about hostelling in this region, contact: South England Regional Office, Rolfes House, 60 Milford Street, Salisbury, Wiltshire SP1 2BP.

Winter closed Hostels

The new Southern Region Booking Service offers the opportunity to book in advance when the Hostel is closed during the winter. See individual Hostel entries for further details.

Parties of 10 or more wishing to stay during the winter closed period, with meals provided, should contact the individual Hostel as many wardens are happy to open for a booking made in advance.

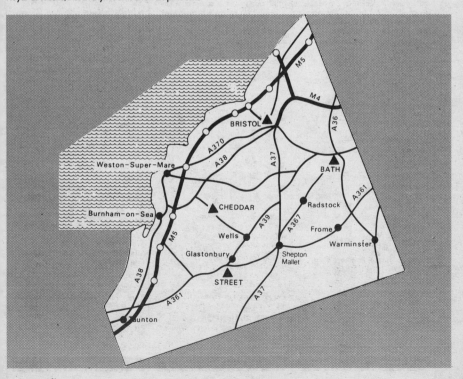

BRISTOL

COMFORT IMPROVED

INTERNATIONAL YHA CENTRE
Hayman House, 64 Prince Street,
Bristol BS1 4HU
☎ **(0272) 221659**

NOT TO SCALE

Overnight charge:
Young £7.40 Junior £8.90 Senior £10.80
🏠🅰🍴📺 FS C 🍴 Cafeteria open
during day. Payphone. Laundry,
common room, 🔍 P0 200 yds P at
National car park nearby in Prince
Street. Meter P outside centre

Accommodation is provided in a
variety of rooms, many with toilet
and shower facilities en suite and
mostly sleeping between 2-6 people
per room. Additional facilities include
a lift, laundry room, multi-purpose
teaching rooms and a public
cafeteria. There is also an associated
Countryside Information Bureau as
well as the City's Tourist Information
Centre

Jan 1-Dec 31   Open
Jan 1-Feb 29 92 Open

The Bristol International YHA Centre
offers excellent opportunities for a
whole range of educational and
leisure activities ranging from urban
and environmental studies to drama
workshops, sporting activities,
training courses and public events.
Our resident Environmental
Education Development Officer can
assist with developing course
programmes for all age groups from
primary through to tertiary level
with either purely curricular
objectives in urban/environmental
studies, ecology, history, art, drama,
etc, or more leisure-centred
activities. Your group will be
stimulated by their stay in this lively
centre with its unique facilities and
attractive waterfront surroundings

Situated in an impressive refurbished
warehouse on the quayside in
Bristol's historic harbour set in the
heart of the city, the study centre is
the first of a new generation of YHA
Urban Study Centres, bringing new
youth opportunities to the city. This
purpose-built centre was opened in
July 1989 and is equipped to a high
standard, designed to provide guests
with an imaginative and
comprehensive insight into city life.
The building enjoys extensive views
overlooking the harbour and
provides easy access to the many
cultural and leisure facilities in this
fascinating city. L

OS 172 GR 586725 🛏 7

Attractions: Exploratory — Hands
On Science Exhibition ¾m. Industrial
Museum, 5 mins walk. Maritime
Museum, 5 mins walk. SS Great
Britain, 10 mins walk. Arnolfini Art
Gallery, next door. Bristol Cathedral,
5 mins walk. St Mary Redcliffe
Church ¾m. City Museum ½m. Cabot
Tower ½m. Zoo 2½m. Suspension
Bridge/Downs/Camera Obscura
2½m. Ashton Park 2½m. City Farm
1m. Nature Garden Avon Wildlife
Trust 1m. Urban Wildlife Exhibition,
Weston-super-Mare 26m. Bath 15m,
Roman Baths, American Museum,
Costume Museum, Abbey. Dyrham
Park — house and gardens (National
Trust). Blaise Hamlet & Castle.
Willsbridge Mill. Dry Ski Slope/Horse
Riding 15m. 🅵 (0272) 260767

🚌 Frequent from surrounding areas
(☎ 0272 297979 or 553231)

🚇 Bristol Temple Meads ½m

Next Youth Hostels: Bath 14m.
Chepstow 15m. Cheddar 20m.
Slimbridge 25m

Bristol International YHA Centre

AVON AND MENDIPS

23

Administrative Region: South

BATH
112 BEDS

Youth Hostel,
Bathwick Hill,
Bath BA2 6JZ
☎ Bath (0225) 465674

NOT TO SCALE

Overnight charge:
Young £4.40 Junior £5.40 Senior £6.60
Seasonal Prices Jul 1-Aug 31:
Young £4.60 Junior £5.90 Senior £7.00
🅰 🔲 🔍 **laundry room. Hostel open all day.** 🍴 🔲 🔲 Evening meal 18.45 hrs for parties — please book in advance. Cafeteria facilities 17.00-19.30. Payphone available. 🆂 🅿 ½m. 🅿 for cars and coaches on Bathwick Hill. **Hostel open all day**

Jan 1-Dec 31   Open
Jan 1-Feb 29 92   Open

It is advisable to check in advance on availability of beds and to arrive early if not booked

Handsome Italian-style mansion with views of historic city and surrounding hills. ¾m E of city centre, follow signs for University/American museum. ½m up Bathwick Hill from roundabout in Pulteney Road by St Mary's church

🆂 172 🅖🆁 766644 🄱 7

Attractions: Spa town. Georgian architecture. Roman Baths. Many museums. Guildhall market and banqueting room. Abbey church of St Peter and St Paul. Royal Photo Society HQ. Bath Arts Festival late May and early Jun. Boat hire on river. Canalside walks. 🛈 (0225) 462831 🄻

🚌 Badgerline 18 from bus station, adjacent BR Bath Spa (☎ 0225 464446)
🚄 Bath Spa 1¼m

Next Youth Hostels: Bristol 14m. Cheddar 27m. Slimbridge 30m. Street 33m. Duntisbourne Abbots 35m. Salisbury 39m. Chepstow 28m

Administrative Region: South

CHEDDAR
54 BEDS

Youth Hostel,
Hillfield, Cheddar,
Somerset BS27 3HN
☎ Cheddar (0934) 742494

Overnight charge:
Young £3.50 Junior £4.40 Senior £5.50
🔲 🅰 🔲 🔲 🔲 🔲 Evening meal 18.30 hrs. Payphone service. 🆂 🅿 ¼m. 🅿 Sat (remainder staggered). 🅿 for cars only. Coaches nearby. **Hostel opens 17.00 hrs**

Jan 1-31   Closed try Bristol
Feb 1-Mar 28   Open
                 (except Sun & Mon)
Mar 29-Jun 30   Open (except Sun)
                 Open Bank Hol Sun
Jul 1-Aug 31   Open
Sep 1-Oct 31   Open
                 (except Sun & Mon)
Nov 1-Dec 21   Open Fri & Sat
Dec 23-30   Open for Xmas
Dec 31-Jan 31 92 Closed try Bristol
Feb 1-29   Open
                 (except Sun & Mon)

Modernised Victorian house in Mendip village close to famous Gorge and caves. On SW side of village off The Hayes. Hillfield is small road running alongside Cheddar Junior School, almost opp the Fire Station

🆂 182 🅖🆁 455534 🄱 7

Attractions: 400ft deep Cheddar Gorge and caves (inc. museum) 1m. Nature trails at Long Wood and Black Rock 2m. Ebbor Gorge 6m. Mendip Way footpath 1m. Swimming pool ½m. 13th century church ½m. 14th century market cross ½m. Wells Cathedral 8m. 🎣 at Cheddar reservoir 1m and Chew Valley reservoir 6m. Wookey Hole caves 6m. Organised caving. 🆄 🛈 (0749) 72552 🚶 (Wedmore). 🄻

🚌 Badgerline 126, 826 Weston-super-Mare — Wells (passes close BR Weston Milton & Weston-super-Mare) (☎ 0934 621201)
🚄 Weston Milton 10m; Weston-super-Mare 11m

Next Youth Hostels: Street 17m. Bristol 20m. Bath 27m. Crowcombe 31m. Holford 31m

Administrative Region: South

STREET
40 BEDS

COMFORT IMPROVED YHA

Youth Hostel, The Chalet, Ivythorn Hill, Street, Somerset BA16 0TZ
☎ Street (0458) 42961
During Winter Closed Period:
☎ (0722) 337494

Overnight charge:
Young £3.50 Junior £4.40 Senior £5.50
🔲 🅰 🅰 🔲 🆂 🅿 Store 2m. 🔲 Wed. 🅿 nearby. **Hostel opens 17.00 hrs**

Jan 1-Mar 26   Closed
Mar 27-Oct 31   Open (except Sun)
Nov 1-Feb 29 92 Rent-a-Hostel*

When closed try Crowcombe or Bristol

During Winter periods, the Southern Region Booking Service will be pleased to help with bookings and enquiries: Rolfes House, 60 Milford St, Salisbury, Wilts SP1 2BP (☎ 0722 337494)

*Rent-a-Hostel: from 1 Nov 91 Hostel is available during this period for groups' exclusive use

Swiss-style chalet on hill with views of Glastonbury Tor, Sedgemoor and Mendip Hills. From Street take Somerton Road B3151 south for 2m. Turn right at crossroads, signposted Bridgwater. Hostel 500 yds on right. From Somerton take B3151 for 4m north. Turn left at crossroads at top of Compton Dundon Hill signposted Bridgwater. Hostel 500 yds on right

🆂 182 🅖🆁 480345 🄱 4, 7

Attractions: Easy cycling country. Glastonbury Tor and ruined abbey 3½m. Museum of Somerset rural life. Wells Cathedral and Vicar's Close (oldest complete street in Europe) 8m. Swimming pool 2m. Wookey Hole cave 9m. Shoe museum in town. 🚶 Street and Glastonbury. 🄻 🛈 (0749) 72552

🚌 Badgerline/Southern National 376 Bristol — Yeovil (passes BR Bristol Temple Meads), alight S end of Leigh Road, thence 1m (☎ 0272 297979 or 0823 272033)
🚄 Castle Cary 11m; Bridgwater 13m

Next Youth Hostels: Cheddar 17m. Crowcombe Heathfield 24m. Holford 25m. Bristol 30m. Bath 33m

Administrative Region: South

AVON AND MENDIPS

23 ▶

24 DORSET COAST

Much of Dorset is designated as an Area of Outstanding Natural Beauty. The coastline is of great interest to geologists and fossil hunters. As well as unusual cliff formations, there is the unique Chesil Beach, a long line of shingle — sheltering a swannery with hundreds of birds. A section of the South West Peninsula Coast Path runs from Poole Harbour round to Lyme Regis. The seaside resorts on the way each have their own character.

Thomas Hardy described the towns and villages of Dorset in his novels, with the names thinly disguised. Inland are chalk downs, quiet villages, miles of lanes and fine old manor houses and churches. Famous prehistoric camps include the huge Maiden Castle near Dorchester.

This area is particularly popular for the diversity of nature and geology it provides.

Useful Information

For general advice and information (including Area and Hostel leaflets) about hostelling in this region, contact: South England Regional Office, Rolfes House, 60 Milford Street, Salisbury, Wiltshire SP1 2BP.

Winter closed Hostels

The new Southern Region Booking Service offers the opportunity to book in advance when the Hostel is closed during the winter. See individual Hostel entries for further details.

Parties of 10 or more wishing to stay during the winter closed period, with meals provided, should contact the individual Hostel as many wardens are happy to open for a booking made in advance.

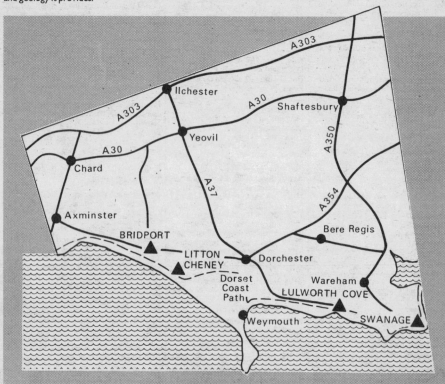

B RIDPORT

68 BEDS

Youth Hostel, West Rivers House,
West Allington, Bridport,
Dorset DT6 5BW
☎ Bridport (0308) 22655*

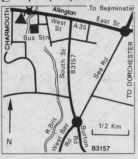

*Answerphone service in daytime

Overnight charge:
Young £3.80 Junior £4.70 Senior £5.90
🏠 🔥 C 1 🍴 GSC 🍽 Evening meal
19.00 hrs. Cot and high chair
available. Nine family rooms. S Shop
50 yds. PO ½m. ED Thu. Enquire of
warden for study facilities. P for cars
and coaches. **Hostel opens 17.00
hrs**

Jan 1-31	Closed
Feb 1-Mar 28	Open
	(except Wed & Thu)
Mar 29-Oct 31	Open
Nov 1-Dec 22	Open
	(except Wed & Thu)
Dec 23-29	Open for Xmas
Dec 30-Jan 31 92	Closed
Feb 1-29	Open
	(except Wed & Thu)

When closed try Exeter

Former flax warehouse and rope
works on edge of busy market town
surrounded by rolling hills and fine
coastal scenery. W side of town off
B3162. Overlooks recreation ground
adjoining bus station

OS 193 GR 461930 Barf 4

Attractions: Dorset coastal
footpath 1½m. Charmouth (7m)
fossils, esp Black Ven. Thomas Hardy
country, Maiden Castle (Iron Age Hill
Fort) Dorchester 15m. Lyme Regis
10m. Museum (including rope and net
making). 🛈 (0305) 67992. L

🚌 Southern National 31/X31
Weymouth — Taunton (pass close BR
Dorchester West & South & Taunton
and pass BR Axminster)
(☎ 0823 272033)

🚆 Axminster 11m; Dorchester South
or West, both 15m

Next Youth Hostels: Litton
Cheney 7m. Beer 20m. Street 32m.
Lulworth Cove 28m

L ITTON CHENEY

30 BEDS

Youth Hostel, Litton Cheney,
Dorchester, Dorset DT2 9AT
☎ Long Bredy (0308) 482340
During Winter Closed Period:
☎ (0722) 387494

Overnight charge:
Young £2.60 Junior £3.50 Senior £4.40
🏠 🔥 1 🍴 🍽 Evening meal 19.30 hrs.
Small S Bread cannot be supplied.
Shop and PO in village. ED Wed. P
limited. **Hostel opens 17.00 hrs**

Jan 1-Mar 28	Closed
Mar 29-Oct 31	Open (except Tue)
Nov 1-Feb 29 92	Closed

When closed try Swanage or Exeter

During the Winter Closed Period, the
Sothern Region Booking Service will
be pleased to help with bookings and
enquiries: Rolfes House, 60 Milford
St, Salisbury, Wilts SP1 2BP (☎ 0722
337494)

Dutch barn, once a cheese and milk
factory, in Area of Outstanding
Natural Beauty, at southern end of
village in the Bride Valley. Close to
White Horse Public House

OS 194 GR 548900 Barf 4

Attractions: Sea bathing 3m. Hardy
country. Abbotsbury Swannery 5m.
Chesil Beach 3m. 🔷 Geology.
Prehistoric sites. Maiden Castle,
Dorchester 10m. Valley of Stones
3½m. Weymouth 14m 🛈 (0305)
67992. L

🚌 As for Bridport, but alight
Whiteway, 1½m

🚆 Dorchester South or West, both
10m

Next Youth Hostels: Bridport 7m.
Lulworth Cove 25m. Beer 28m.
Swanage 33m. Street 37m.
Cranborne 40m

L ULWORTH COVE

36 BEDS

Youth Hostel, School Lane,
West Lulworth, Wareham,
Dorset BH20 5SA
☎ W Lulworth (092941) 564

Overnight charge:
Seasonal Prices Jul 1-Aug 31
Young £3.80 Junior £4.70 Senior £5.90
Young £4.40 Junior £5.40 Senior £6.60
🏠 🔥 1 🛏 GSC 🍽 Evening meal 19.00
hrs. S Shop 800 yds. PO Lulworth
Cove 1m. ED Wed. P for cars and
coaches. **Hostel opens 17.00 hrs**

Jan 1-31	Closed try Exeter
Feb 1-28	Open
	(except Sun & Mon)
Mar 1-Jun 30	Open (except Sun)
	Open Bank Hol Sun
Jul 1-Aug 31	Open
Sep 1-30	Open (except Sun)
Oct 1-Nov 2	Open
	(except Sun & Mon)
Nov 3-Feb 1 92	Closed try
	Swanage or Exeter
Feb 2-29	Open
	(except Sun & Mon)

Purpose built Hostel of cedar wood,
which has been recently refurbished,
is situated on South West Peninsula
Coast Path, in Dorset Area of
Outstanding Natural Beauty. 700 yds
E of B3070. Turn opposite inn into
School Lane

OS 194 GR 832806 Barf 4

Attractions: Coastal footpath ½m.
Lulworth Cove 1m. Durdle Door 2m.
Fossil Forest 1m. Unique rock
formations. Lulworth Castle 2m. Sea
bathing and boat trips. For range
walks opening times contact the
warden or phone Bindon Abbey
(0929) 462721 Ext 824. L 🛈 (0929) 422885

🚌 Garrison Cars 225 BR Wool -
Lulworth Cove (☎ 0929 462467)

🚆 Wool 5m

Next Youth Hostels: Swanage 17m.
Litton Cheney 25m. Bridport 30m.
Cranborne 32m. Burley 38m

DORSET COAST

24

SWANAGE

106 BEDS · COMFORT IMPROVED yha

**Youth Hostel,
Cluny, Cluny Crescent,
Swanage, Dorset BH19 2BS**
☎ Swanage (0929) 422113

NOT TO SCALE

Overnight charge:
Young £4.40 Junior £5.40 Senior £6.60
Seasonal Prices Jul 1-Aug 31:
Young £4.60 Junior £5.90 Senior £7.00
⚠ 👥 C 🔍 C 1 ▥ GSC 🍴 Evening
meal 18.30 hrs. S FS P for cars and
coaches. **Hostel opens 17.00 hrs**
(16.30 hrs in winter). Payphone

Jan 1-31	Closed try Salisbury
Feb 1-Nov 30	Open*
*Nov 6 & 7	Closed
Dec 1-27	Closed try Bridport
Dec 28-31	Open for New Year
Jan 1-4 92	Open
Jan 5-31	Closed try Salisbury
Feb 1-29	Open

Large house built on site of
monastery of Cluny order and
recently refurbished, in well-known
seaside resort of Isle of Purbeck.
Take Stafford Road from White Swan
Inn in High Street. (Walkers going
towards Weymouth should keep
close to the coast except for military
area near Tyneham, Worbarrow Bay
and Arishmel Gap)

OS 195 GR 030785 ▥ 4, 5

Attractions: Major unspoilt family
resort on the Isle of Purbeck. High
sunshine ratings, safe sandy beaches.
Spectacular coastal scenery along the
Dorset coastal footpath. 🎣 ⚠ ⬇ 📷
ℹ (0929) 422885. L

🚌 Wilts & Dorset 150 from
Bournemouth (passes BR Branksome);
142-4 from Poole (pass BR Wareham).
Alight Swanage bus station on all
services, thence ½m (☎ 0202 673555)

🚆 Wareham 10m

Next Youth Hostels: Lulworth Cove
17m. Burley 29m. Cranborne 30m.

Additional Information: Daytime
Answerphone service

Administrative Region: South

NORTH DEVON, EXMOOR AND THE QUANTOCKS

25

An easy section of the South West Peninsula coast path starts (and finishes) at Minehead. With the sea in view all the way, the route passes through Exmoor National Park and the North Devon Area of Outstanding Natural Beauty. This magnificent coastline has a number of well-known seaside resorts: including Minehead, Lynton and Ilfracombe. There are high cliffs (a good example can be seen near Hartland Hostel), jutting headlands, long sandy beaches and waterfalls.

Exmoor, with heather-covered moors and deep wooded combes, is mainly in Somerset. Pony trekking is popular and available near most Hostels, including Instow and Exford.

The Brendon Hills to the East are good walking country. Red deer and Exmoor wild ponies may be seen. "Lorna Doone" by R D Blackmore was set in this area.

The Quantock Hills, in Somerset, are designated an Area of Outstanding Natural Beauty with Kilve Beach known for its fossils. Visitors to this area can combine hillwalking with a seaside holiday.

Travel

The hidden, unspoilt corner of North Devon has now been made more easily accessible from the M5 by the opening of the new North Devon Link Road.

Useful Information

For general advice and information (including Area and Hostel leaflets) about hostelling in this region, contact: South England Regional Office, Rolfes House, 60 Milford Street, Salisbury, Wiltshire SP1 2BP.

Winter closed Hostels

The new Southern Region Booking Service offers the opportunity to book in advance when the Hostel is closed during the winter. See individual Hostel entries for further details.

Parties of 10 or more wishing to stay during the winter closed period, with meals provided, should contact the individual Hostel as many wardens are happy to open for a booking made in advance.

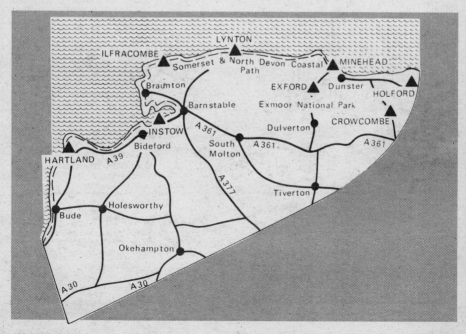

Youth Hostel, Denzel House,
Crowcombe Heathfield, Taunton,
Somerset TA4 4BT

☎ Lydeard St Lawrence (09847) 249

Overnight charge:
Young £3.50 Junior £4.40 Senior £5.50
🅼 🅰 ① ⊤ ⒼⓈⒸ ⓄⓁ Evening meal 19.00
hrs. Payphone service. Cot available.
🅵🆂 🆂 Shop and 🅿🅾 Lydeard St
Lawrence 1m. 🅿 for cars only. Coaches
100 yds. **Hostel opens 17.00 hrs**

Jan 1-31	Closed
Feb 1-Mar 28	Open
	(except Wed & Thu)
Mar 29-Aug 31	Open (except Fri)
	Open Bank Hol Fri
Sep 1-22	Closed
Sep 23-Oct 31	Open (except Fri)
Nov 1-26	Open
	(except Wed & Thu)
Nov 27-Jan 31 92	Closed
Feb 1-29	Open
	(except Wed & Thu)

When closed, try Exford or Exeter

Large house in beautiful grounds and
surrounded by woodlands, 2m from
village below Quantock Hills. Turn
SW off Taunton-Minehead road
opposite turning to Triscombe
(signposted Crowcombe station and
Lydeard St Lawrence; YH sign on
signpost). Do not take turning by
Flaxpool Garage signposted
Crowcombe Station and Crowcombe
Heathfield. Hostel second house on
right after crossing railway bridge,
1m NE of Lydeard St Lawrence

ⓄⓈ 181 ⒼⓇ 138339 ⒷⓐⓇⓛ 4, 7

Attractions: Large field for games.
Footpaths and nature trails on
Quantocks. North Somerset Coast
(Watchet 10m). Natural history (🦋
butterflies etc). Geology. Castle
Museum. Taunton 10m. Combe
Sydenham Country Park (Sir Francis
Drake) 6m. Cleeve Abbey 10m. West
Somerset Railway. Ⓛ 🅸 (0823)
274785

🚌 Southern National 28/C Taunton
— Minehead (passes BR Taunton),
alight Triscombe Cross, ¾m (☎ 0823
272033)

🚃 Taunton 10m; Crowcombe (West
Somerset Rly) ½m

Next Youth Hostels: Holford 7m
over Quantocks (walkers) 10m by
road. Minehead 16m. Exford 22m.
Lynton 40m. Ilfracombe 45m

Crowcombe Heathfield Youth Hostel

Youth Hostel, Elmscott, Hartland,
Bideford, Devon EX39 6ES
☎ Hartland (0237) 441367
During Winter Closed Period:
☎ (0722) 337494

Overnight charge:
Young £2.60 Junior £3.50 Senior £4.40
🅰 ② ⒼⓈⒸ 🆇 No meals provided. 🆂 🅿🅾
and Shop Hartland 5m. 🅴🅳 Tue. 🅿 for
cars and minibuses only. Hostel opens
17.00 hrs

Jan 1-Mar 26	Closed
Mar 27-Jun 30	Open
	(except Wed & Thu)
Jul 1-Aug 31	Open
Sep 1-30	Open
	(except Wed & Thu)
Oct 1-Feb 29 92	Closed

When closed try Instow or Plymouth

During the Winter Closed Period, the
Southern Region Booking Service
will be pleased to help with bookings
and enquiries: Rolfes House, 60
Milford St, Salisbury, Wilts SP1 2BP
(☎ 0722 337494)

Converted village school and
schoolhouse with view of Lundy
Island, on Hartland Peninsula, an
Area of Outstanding Natural Beauty.
3m SW of Hartland village, by
footpath through St Leonards Valley.
Cyclists from Bideford via Hartland
(signposted near Anchor Inn). From
Bude/Kilkhampton (A39) first left
immediately beyond West Country
Inn

ⓄⓈ 190 ⒼⓇ 231217 ⒷⓐⓇⓛ 3

Attractions: Devon coastal
footpath ½m. Cliff scenery including
Hartland Quay (rock folding).
Nature reserve 1m, with waterfall —
Speke Mill Mouth. 🦋 🅰 🔺
Welcombe Mouth. Ⓛ 🅸 (02372)
77676 and 74591

🚃 Filer's 319 from Bideford with
connections from BR Barnstaple,
alight Hartland, 3½m (☎ 0271 63819)

🚃 Barnstaple 25m

Next Youth Hostels: Instow 19m.
Boscastle 27m. Tintagel 32m

E XFORD (EXMOOR)

50 BEDS

COMFORT yha IMPROVED

Youth Hostel, Exe Mead,
Exford, Minehead,
Somerset TA24 7PU
☎ Exford (064383) 288

Overnight charge:
Young £4.00 Junior £5.10 Senior £6.30
🏠🔥1🍳🍽 Evening meal 19.00 hrs.
🛒 Shop & 📮 200 yds. 🚪 Sat. 🅿 for
cars only. Coaches 200 yds. **Hostel
opens 17.00 hrs** (16.30 hrs in winter)

Jan 1-Mar 27	Closed*
Mar 28-Jun 30	Open (except Sun)
	Open Bank Hol Sun
Jul 1-Aug 31	Open
Sep 1-Oct 31	Open (except Sun)
Nov 1-Dec 21	Open
	(except Sun & Mon)
Dec 22-26	Closed
Dec 27-Jan 4 92	Open
Jan 5-Feb 1	Closed try Exeter
Feb 2-29	Open
	(except Sun & Mon)

*Closed for major building works, try
Lynton during Feb and Mar

Recently refurbished Victorian house
by River Exe in centre of village

os 181 GR 853383 🗺 3

Attractions: Group and family
centre for exploring Exmoor
National Park. Moorland and
riverside walks. Dunkery Beacon 4m.
Doone Valley 6m. Winsford 5m. Tarr
Steps 6m. Landacre Bridge 2m.
Culbone Church 7m. Two Moors
Way (long distance footpath) 2m.
Wild red deer. Wimbleball Lake.
Combe Sydenham Country Park
14m. Several inter-Hostel walking
routes available — ideal for families.
🛈 (0398) 23665. L

🚌 Southern National 39, Scarlet
Coaches from Minehead, alight
Porlock, 7m (☎ 0823 272033 or
0643 4204)

🚋 Taunton 28m; Minehead (West
Somerset Rly) 13m

Next Youth Hostels: Minehead
13m by road. 10m across the moor
(walkers). Lynton 15m. Crowcombe
Heathfield 22m

Administrative Region: South

H OLFORD

38 BEDS

Youth Hostel, Sevenacres, Holford,
Bridgwater, Somerset TA5 1SQ
☎ Holford (027874) 224
During Winter Closed Period:
☎ (0722) 337494

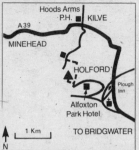

Overnight charge:
Young £3.50 Junior £4.40 Senior £5.50
🏠🔥1🔺🍳🍽 Evening meal 19.00
hrs. Vegetarian choice available. 🛒
Shop and 📮 Holford & Kilve. 🅿 for
cars only; no access for coaches.
Track to Hostel is not surfaced.

Hostel opens 17.00 hrs

Jan 1-Mar 26	Closed try
	Crowcombe/Lynton
Mar 27-Jun 30	Open (except Sun)
	Open Bank Hol Sun
Jul 1-Aug 31	Open
Sep 1-Oct 31	Open
	(except Sun & Mon)
Nov 1-Dec 31	Closed try
	Crowcombe/Exford
Dec 31-Feb 29 92	Closed

During Winter periods, the Southern
Region Booking Service will be pleased
to help with bookings and enquiries:
Rolfes House, 60 Milford St, Salisbury,
Wilts SP1 2BP (☎ 0722 337494)

This characteristic Hostel is situated
in a wooded area of the Quantock
Hills with red deer and birds. From
Kilve, take Pardlestone Lane opp.
Hood Arms (1m). From Holford,
take road via Alfoxton Park Hotel
(1½m), keep right after passing hotel

os 181 GR 145416 🗺 7

Attractions: Inter-Hostel walking
routes over Quantocks. Ideal for
families. Riding stables nearby — special
rates for YHA members. Coleridge
Cottage 3m. U 🏊 🚲 🛈 (0823) 274785.
Fossils at Kilve Beach. L

🚌 Southern National 15 from
Bridgwater (passing close BR
Bridgwater), alight Nether Stowey,
3½m (☎ 0823 272033)

🚋 Bridgwater 13m

Next Youth Hostels: Crowcombe
Heathfield 7m over Quantocks
(walkers), 10m by road. Minehead
14m. Exford 23m. Street 25m

Administrative Region: South

I LFRACOMBE

50 BEDS

Youth Hostel, Ashmour House,
1 Hillsborough Terrace,
Ilfracombe, Devon EX34 9NR
☎ Ilfracombe (0271) 865337

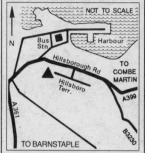

Overnight charge:
Young £4.00 Junior £5.10 Senior £6.30
🏠🔥🏊1🍳🍽 Evening meal 19.30 hrs.
🛒 Shop 300 yds. 📮 250 yds. 🚪 Thu.
🅿 limited — ask warden; coaches
½m. Hostel opens 17.00 hrs

Jan 1-Mar 26	Closed
Mar 27-Jun 30	Open (except Sun)
	Open Bank Hol Sun
Jul 1-Aug 31	Open
Sep 1-28	Open (except Sun)
Sep 29-Feb 29 92	Closed

Parties of 10 or more wishing to stay
when Hostel is normally closed,
please contact warden. Full central
heating installed for winter groups

End house of a fine Georgian terrace
overlooking picturesque harbour and
Bristol Channel, above the Ilfracombe
to Combe Martin Road

os 180 GR 524476 🗺 3

Attractions: Coastal, woodland, old
railway and valley footpaths. Guided
walks programme from Apr-Sep. 🚣
boat trips. Freshwater 🚣 — Slade
reservoir 1m. Summer Steam-Boat
trips to Lundy Island, Wales &
Channel coastline. Coves, Rock
Pools, Tunnel to beach. Woolacombe
sandy beach (surfing, bathing) 4m. U
1m. Indoor heated swimming pool
½m. Approach golf ½m. Golf Club
1m. Chambercombe Manor 1m.
Museum. Working Farm 4m. Exmoor
Bird Gardens 10m. Braunton Burrows
Nature Reserve 10m. Watermouth
Castle 2m. N. Devon Leisure Centre
10m. 🔺🚲🛈 (0271) 63001

🚌 Red Bus 6, 62 & 306 from
Barnstaple passing close BR
Barnstaple) (☎ 0271 45444)

🚋 Barnstaple 13m

Next Youth Hostels: Lynton 18m.
Instow 18m. Exford 25m

Administrative Region: South

INSTOW
60 BEDS COMFORT IMPROVED yha

Youth Hostel, Worlington House,
New Road, Instow,
Bideford, Devon EX39 4LW
Instow (0271) 860394

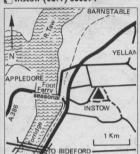

Overnight charge:
Young £4.00 Junior £5.10 Senior £6.30
⚤ ♿ 2 ♨ 🅲🅳 GSC 🅴 Evening meal
19.00 hrs. 🆂 Shop and 🅿🅾 Instow ⅓m.
🅴🅳 Barnstaple and Bideford Wed. 🅵🆂
🅿 limited. Cars only. Coaches and
additional car parking 150 yds. Hostel
opens 17.00 hrs

Jan 1-31	Closed
Feb 1-28	Open
	(except Thu & Fri)
Mar 1-Jun 30	Open (except Fri)
	Open Good Fri
Jul 1-Aug 31	Open
Sep 1-Oct 31	Open (except Fri)
Nov 1-30	Open
	(except Thu & Fri)
Dec 1-22	Closed
Dec 23-29	Open for Xmas
Dec 30-Feb 15 92	Closed
Feb 16-29	Open (except Fri)

When closed try Exford or Exeter

Late Victorian country house with
fine views across Torridge Estuary,
about ⅓m from beach. Turn off main
Barnstaple-Bideford road at signpost,
Hostel ½m. Hostel at top of hill

🆗🆂 180 🄶🅁 482303 Bart 3

Attractions: Beach and sand dunes
nearby. Craft centre, Bideford 3m.
Devon Coastal Footpath. Ⓤ Surfing
at Westward Ho, 4½m. Also
submerged forest and pebble ridge.
🔶🅰♿🆂🅻 (0271) 47177

🚌 Red Bus 1, 2, B from Barnstaple
(passing BR Barnstaple), alight
Instow, ⅓m (0271 45444)

🚃 Barnstaple 6m

Next Youth Hostels: Ilfracombe
18m. Elmscott 19m. Lynton 25m.
Exford 27m. Exeter 46m

LYNTON (DEVON)
38 BEDS COMFORT IMPROVED yha

Youth Hostel,
Lynbridge, Lynton,
Devon EX35 6AZ
Lynton (0598) 53237

Overnight charge:
Young £3.80 Junior £4.70 Senior £5.90
Seasonal Prices Jul 1-Aug 31:
Young £4.40 Junior £5.40 Senior £6.60
⚤ ♿ 1 🅲🅳 🅴 Evening meal 19.00
hrs. Vegetarian and Vegan choice. 🆂
Shop and 🅿🅾 Lynton 1m. 🅴🅳 Sat.
Public telephone 250 metres. Cot &
highchair available. 🅿 limited for cars
and minibuses, coaches ⅓m (Lynton),
alight at Ye Olde Cottage Inn.
Hostel opens 17.00 hrs

Jan 1-31	Closed
Feb 1-28	Open
	(except Sun & Mon)
Mar 1-Jun 30	Open (except Mon)
	Open Easter Mon
Jul 1-Aug 31	Open
Sep 1-Oct 31	Open
	(except Mon & Tue)
Nov 1-Dec 27	Closed
Dec 28-Jan 4 92	Open for New Year
Jan 5-Feb 14	Closed

When closed, try Exford or Exeter

Homely Victorian house in steep
wooded gorge of West Lyn River,
where Exmoor meets the sea at
Lynmouth Bay. By car: Approach by
Lynway opposite Ye Olde Cottage Inn
on B3234 between top of Lynmouth
Hill and Barbrook. On foot: From
Lynton take steps opposite St Mary's
Church, down to Queen Street, then
up Sinai Hill for 100 metres. Then turn
left on to Lynway following YH signs

🆗🆂 180 🄶🅁 720487 Bart 3

Attractions: In Exmoor National
Park. Cliff, moor, woodland and
riverside walks including several
inter-Hostel walking routes. Ideal for
families. Sea bathing. Cliff Railway. Ⓤ
🔶🅰♿🅸 (0598) 52225. 🅻

🚌 Red Bus 310 from Barnstaple (passes
close BR Barnstaple) (0271 45444)

🚃 Barnstaple 20m

Next Youth Hostels: Exford 15m.
Ilfracombe 18m. Minehead 21m

MINEHEAD
53 BEDS

Youth Hostel, Alcombe Combe,
Minehead, Somerset TA24 6EW
Minehead (0643) 702595
During Winter Closed Period:
(0722) 337494

Overnight charge:
Young £3.50 Junior £4.40 Senior £5.50
♿ 1 🆃 GSC 🅴 Evening meal 18.30 hrs.
Payphone. 🆂 Shop and 🅿🅾 Alcombe
1m. 🅴🅳 Wed. 🅿 limited, cars only:
coaches at West Somerset School
with prior permission. **Hostel opens
17.00 hrs**

Jan 1-Mar 21	Closed try Lynton
Mar 22-Jun 30	Open (except Sun)
	Open Bank Hol Sun
Jul 1-Aug 31	Open
Sep 1-Oct 31	Open
	(except Sun & Mon)
Nov 1-Dec 31	Closed try Exford
	or Exeter
Jan 1-Feb 29 92	Closed try Exford
	or Exeter

During Winter periods Southern
Region Booking Service will be pleased
to help with bookings and enquiries:
Rolfes House, 60 Milford St, Salisbury,
Wilts SP1 2BP (0722 337494)

In a secluded position up a wooded
combe on edge of Exmoor, 2m from
sea. Turn off Bridgwater-Minehead
road into Brook Street or Church
Street, Alcombe. Continue on Manor
Road, past Britannia Inn. Hostel is ⅓m
on the left, beyond gate posts at
entrance to private road. Difficult to
find after dark

🆗🆂 181 🄶🅁 973442 Bart 3

Attractions: Moorland and forest
walks. Inter-Hostel walking routes.
Coastal footpath. Dunster Castle
(NT) 2m. West Somerset railway. Ⓤ
🔶🅰🅸 (0643) 702624. 🅻

🚌 As for Crowcombe Heathfield, but
alight Alcombe, ⅓m

🚃 Taunton 25m; Minehead or
Dunster (both West Somerset Rly)
both 2m

Next Youth Hostels: Exford 13m
by road, 10m across moors (walkers).
Holford 14m. Crowcombe 16m

Administrative Region: South | **Administrative Region: South** | **Administrative Region: South**

25

The mild climate makes this a popular holiday area. Walkers following the South West Peninsula Way will find spectacular cliffs, wide estuaries, bustling resorts and remote bays (Salcombe, Maypool and Beer), as well as the historic towns of Exeter and Plymouth. Inland, there are the winding Devon lanes around Dartington, lined in Spring with a multitude of wild flowers. Villages of thatched cottages nestle in the valleys, tempting you to pause awhile and treat yourself to a real cream tea!

Dartmoor, the vast major wilderness in Southern England, is founded on solid granite. Surmounting many of the hilltops are the tors, curiously shaped as a result of thousands of years' exposure to the weather. Bellever and Steps Bridge offer the opportunity to visit the prehistoric remains on the moor — hut circles, burial mounds and standing stones — all evidence that Dartmoor was the home of man from very early times. Many beauty spots are easily accessible and are convenient for picnics.

Travel

Brittany Ferries. Plymouth-Roscoff, Plymouth-Santander (Spain). Details from Brittany Ferries, Millbay Docks, Plymouth. Tel: (0752) 21321.

Useful Information

For general advice and information (including Area and Hostel leaflets) about hostelling in this region, contact: South England Regional Office, Rolfes House, 60 Milford Street, Salisbury, Wiltshire SP1 2BP.

South West Way Coastal Footpath information is available from: Mr E Wallis, "Windlestraw", Penquit, Ermington, Devon PL21 0LU.

Winter closed Hostels

The new Southern Region Booking Service offers the opportunity to book in advance when the Hostel is closed during the winter. See individual Hostel entries for further details.

Parties of 10 or more wishing to stay during the winter closed period, with meals provided, should contact the individual Hostel as many wardens are happy to open for a booking made in advance.

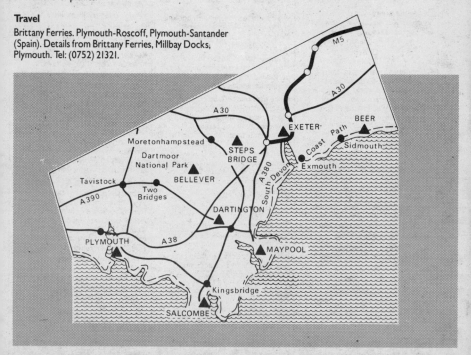

BEER

38 BEDS

Youth Hostel, Bovey Combe, Townsend, Beer, Seaton, Devon EX12 3LL
Seaton (0297) 20296
During Winter Closed Period:
(0722) 337494

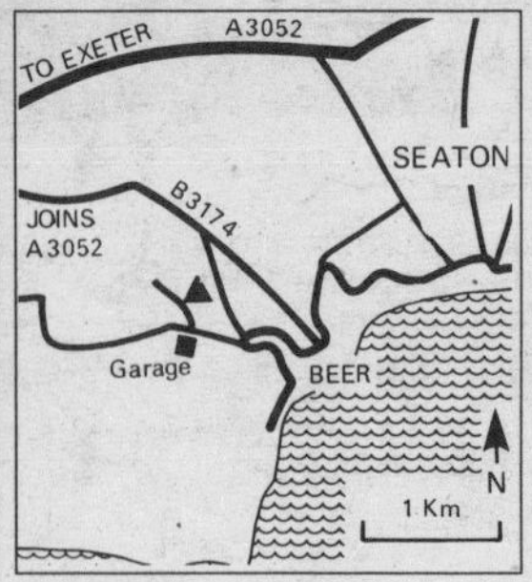

Overnight charge:
Young £3.50 Junior £4.40 Senior £5.50 Evening meal 19.00 hrs. Shop and PO Beer ½m. ECD Thu. P limited, cars only; coaches 200 yds. Hostel opens 17.00 hrs

Jan 1-Mar 26	Closed
Mar 27-Jun 30	Open (except Fri)
Jul 1-Aug 31	Open
Sep 1-Oct 31	Open (except Fri)
Nov 1-Feb 29 92	Closed

When closed try Bridport or Exeter

During the Winter Closed Period, the Southern Region Booking Service will be pleased to help with bookings and enquiries: Rolfes House, 60 Milford St, Salisbury, Wilts SP1 2BP (0722 337494)

A large house standing in landscaped grounds on hillside to the west of a picturesque 'old world' fishing village. Large safe play area. ½m NW of village of Beer at Townsend down lane opp garage

OS 192 GR 223896 Bart 4

Attractions: village. Swimming. Axe estuary 2m. Model railway exhibition. Devon Coastal footpath. Farway country park (rare breeds, U) 6m. 12th C pub at Axmouth 3m. Narrow Gauge tramway, Seaton-Colyton 1m. (Trips arranged round Beer caves Roman mining remains, geology, bats). Diving school and windsurfing hire at Seaton. Pleasure Gardens. i (0395) 516441

Axe Valley from Seaton with connections from BR Axminster (029780 338)

Axminster 7m

Next Youth Hostels: Bridport 20m. Exeter 24m. Litton Cheney 28m. Steps Bridge 32m

Administrative Region: South

BELLEVER

36 BEDS

COMFORT IMPROVED yha

Youth Hostel, Bellever, Postbridge, Yelverton, Devon PL20 6TU
Tavistock (0822) 88227
During Winter Closed Period:
(0722) 337494

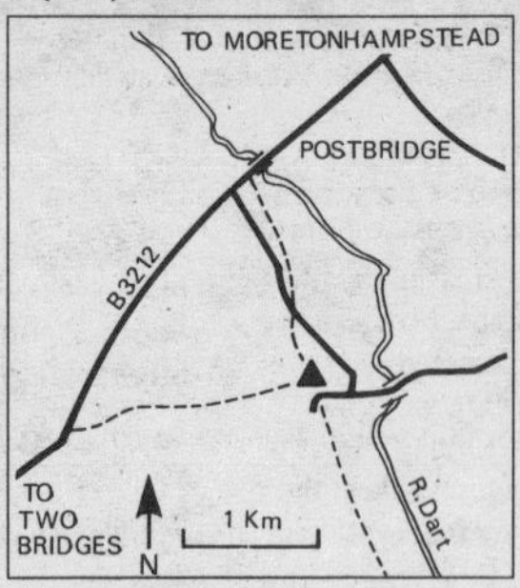

Overnight charge:
Young £3.80 Junior £4.70 Senior £5.90 Evening meal 19.00 hrs. Shop and PO Postbridge. ECD Thu. P Limited for cars. Hostel opens 17.00 hrs

Jan 1-Mar 26	Closed try Exeter
Mar 27-Jun 30	Open (except Mon)
Jul 1-Aug 31	Open
Sep 1-Nov 2	Open (except Mon)
Nov 3-Feb 29 92	Rent-a-Hostel*

During the Winter Closed Period, the Southern Region Booking Service will be pleased to help with bookings and enquiries: Rolfes House, 60 Milford St, Salisbury, Wilts SP1 2BP (0722 337494)

*Rent-a-Hostel: from 3 Nov 91, Hostel will be available during this period for the exclusive use of groups booked in advance

Once part of a barn belonging to a Royal Duchy farm and now converted to a Hostel of character in heart of Dartmoor National Park, it has recently been refurbished. 1m SE of Postbridge on W bank of River Dart. From Postbridge follow the tarmac road beginning 100 yds above petrol station. Keep the forest on your right. 1½m to Hostel

OS 191 GR 654773 Bart 2

Attractions: Postbridge clapper bridge. i Postbridge 1½m. Dartmeet 3m. Widecombe in the moor 6m. Cranmere pool 7m. L i (0822) 88272

Devon Services 359 from Exeter (passes close BR Exeter Central), alight Chagford, 9m (Devon CC Enquiry Line: 0392 272123)

Newton Abbot 19m

Next Youth Hostels: Steps Bridge 15m. Dartington 19m (15m over Dartmoor)

Administrative Region: South

DARTINGTON

36 BEDS

COMFORT IMPROVED yha

Youth Hostel, Lownard, Dartington, Totnes, Devon TQ9 6JJ
Totnes (0803) 862303
During Winter Closed Period:
(0722) 337494

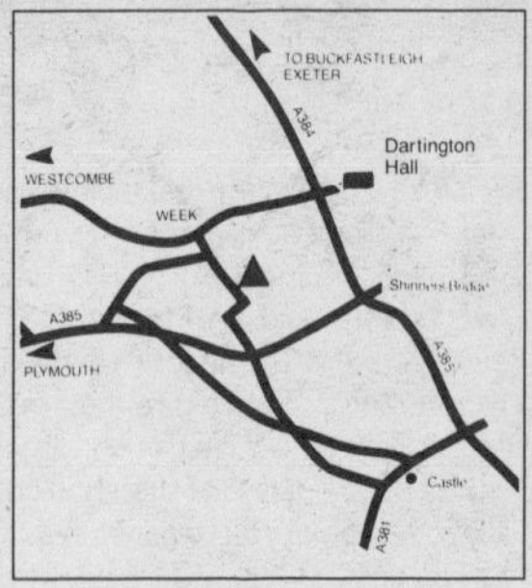

Overnight charge:
Young £3.50 Junior £4.40 Senior £5.50
Seasonal Prices Jul 1-Aug 31:
Young £3.80 Junior £4.70 Senior £5.90 Evening meal 19.00 hrs. Shop and PO Shinners Bridge ¼m. ECD Sat. Totnes, ECD Thu. P for cars. P coaches ¼m. Hostel opens 17.00 hrs

Jan 1-Mar 26	Closed
Mar 27-Jun 30	Open (except Thu)
Jul 1-Aug 31	Open
Sep 1-Oct 29	Open (except Thu)
Oct 30-Feb 29 92	Rent-a-Hostel*

When closed try Plymouth

During the Winter period Southern Region Booking Service will be pleased to help with bookings and enquiries: Rolfes House, 60 Milford St, Salisbury, Wilts SP1 2BP (0722 337494)

*Rent-a-Hostel: From Oct 30 91 Hostel is available during this period for the exclusive use of groups booked in advance

16th C low beamed cottage with annexe next to River Bidwell. From Shinners Bridge roundabout, take A385 Plymouth Road and look out for footpath opposite "Devon Garden Machinery". Follow path direct to Hostel on right hand side

OS 202 GR 782622 Bart 2

Attractions: Dartington Hall 1m. Waymarked footpaths by River Dart. Dart Valley Steam Railway 5m, Buckfast Abbey 5m. Dartmoor 5m. Cider Press Centre ¼m. Dartington Hall 1m — garden (free). Footpaths/trails by River Dart. Outdoor swimming pool ¼m. L i (0803) 863168

Western National/Devon General X80 Torquay — Plymouth (passes BR Paignton & Totnes), alight Shinner's Bridge, ½m (0803 63226)

Totnes 2m

Next Youth Hostels: Maypool 11m. Bellever 19m (15m by Dartmoor)

Administrative Region: South

EXETER

90 BEDS

Youth Hostel,
47 Countess Wear Road,
Exeter, Devon EX2 6LR
☎ Topsham (039287) 3329

Overnight charge:
Young £4.40 Junior £5.40 Senior £6.60
🅗🅐🄰④ Jul & Aug 🆂🅘🄾 Evening
meal 18.30 hrs for groups or other
time by prior arrangement. Cafeteria
service for individuals and families
17.00-20.00 hrs. 🆂 Shops and 🄿🄾
Countess Wear village ½m. 🄴🄾 Wed.
🄿 in Countess Wear Road only,
coaches — ask warden. Hostel
opens 17.00 hrs

Jan 1-Feb 28	Open (except Tue)
Mar 1-Oct 31	Open
Nov 1-30	Open (except Tue)
Dec 1-26	Closed
	try Plymouth
Dec 27-Feb 29 92	Open (except Tue)

Large house overlooking River Exe
on outskirts of ancient cathedral city.
2m SE of city towards Topsham.
From Exeter take B3182 direction
Exmouth and Topsham. Turn right
into School Lane at Countess Wear
🄿🄾 1¾m from city centre. Turn left
into Countess Wear Road at Tally Ho
pub

From Honiton A30 or M5 junction 30
follow signs to Exeter centre. Turn
right at Countess Wear roundabout
(motel) then 400 yds later turn left
into School Lane. From Plymouth/
Dawlish follow A379 signposted
Topsham. Turn left into Countess
Wear Road after crossing River Exe
by Bridge Stores

🄾🅂 192 🅶🅁 941897 🄱🅰🅁🅃 2, 3

Attractions: 11th century cathedral.
Maritime museum. 13th century
guildhall. Roman wall round city.
Topsham port. Nature reserves,
winter 🏊 leisure centre. 🄸 Dartmoor
10m. 🛶🄰🄻🄻🄲 (seats 25 people).
Exeter Museums. 🄸 (0392) 265297

🚌 Exeter City Services K,L,T (pass
close BR Exeter Central), alight
Countess Wear 🄿🄾, ⅓m
(☎ 0392 56231)

🚉 Topsham 2m; Exeter Central 3m;
Exeter St David's 4m

Next Youth Hostels: Steps Bridge
10m. Beer 24m. Bellever 25m.
Maypool 32m. Exford 40m. Instow
46m

Exeter Youth Hostel

MAYPOOL

96 BEDS

Youth Hostel, Maypool,
Galmpton, Brixham,
Devon TQ5 0ET
☎ Churston (0803) 842444

Overnight charge:
Young £3.80 Junior £4.70 Senior £5.90
Seasonal Prices Jul 1-Aug 31:
Young £4.00 Junior £5.10 Senior £6.30
🅗🅐②🆂🅘🄾🄲🔍🄾 Evening meal
19.00 hrs. 🆂 Shop and 🄿🄾 Galmpton.
🄴🄾 variable in Torbay area. 🄿 for cars
and coaches (not m/way). Hostel
opens 17.00 hrs

Jan 1-Feb 28	Closed
Mar 1-May 31	Open (except Sun)
	Open Bank Hol Sun
Jun 1-Aug 31	Open
Sep 1-Nov 2	Open (except Sun)
Nov 3-Dec 22	Closed
Dec 23-29	Open for Xmas
Dec 30-Feb 29 92	Closed

When closed try Plymouth or Exeter.
Alternatively when closed, bookings
may be accepted from parties: please
enquire

Built in 1883 for owner of local
boatyard, with view of Kingswear
and Dartmouth. Set in 3½ acre
grounds. 1m SW of Galmpton village.
Take the road to Greenway Ferry
and bear left at fork to Maypool

🄾🅂 202 🅶🅁 877546 🄱🅰🅁🅃 2

Attractions: Water sports facilities,
river or bay, can be arranged daily or
weekly. Moorings available for hire.
Guides for Torbay available from Torbay
Tourist Board, Tel: 0803 26244. 🄰
Beaches. 🏖 Paignton. Coastal path.
Marine biology, zoology, geographical
and geological study. Dartmouth Port
5m. Dart Valley steam. 🛶🄾🅄🄻
🄸 (0803) 558383

🚌 Devon General 22, Burton 118 BR
Paignton — Brixham, alight Churston
Pottery, 2m (☎ 0803 63226 long
distance, 0803 525555 local)

🚉 Paignton 5m; Churston (Dart
Valley Rly) 2m

Next Youth Hostels: Dartington
11m. Salcombe 26m

SOUTH DEVON AND DARTMOOR

26

PLYMOUTH

Youth Hostel, Belmont House,
Devonport Road, Stoke,
Plymouth PL3 4DW
📞 Plymouth (0752) 562189

NOT TO SCALE

Overnight charge:
Young £3.80 Junior £4.70 Senior £5.90
🏠🏠🏠🏠 ④ Jul & Aug 🔒 🍴
Evening meal 18.30 hrs (Groups).
Cafeteria meals. **S** Shop and **PO** near
Hostel. **ED** Wed. **P** for cars and
coaches. Hostel opens 17.00 hrs

Jan 1-7	Closed
Jan 8-Oct 31	Open
Nov 1-30	Closed
Dec 1-24	Open
Dec 25-27	Closed
Dec 28-Feb 29 92	Open (except Sun)

When closed, try Exeter or Penzance

Charles G Allen Memorial Hostel.
Classical Grecian Style house built
for wealthy banker in 1820, set in
own grounds within easy walking
distance of city centre. Adjacent to
Belmont Methodist Church, Stoke.
Motorists leave A38 at A386
intersection and follow signs for
Torpoint ferry until Stoke and
Devonport Road reached

OS 201 **GR** 461555 **Sat** 2

Attractions: Ferries to France and
Spain. Barbican. The Hoe. Mayflower
Steps — Pilgrim Fathers' connection.
Dartmoor 5m — **U** Mount
Edgcumbe Country park 2m. Saltram
House (NT) 4m. Buckland Abbey
(NT) home of Sir Francis Drake 10m.
Buckfast Abbey 15m. Devon and
Cornwall coastal footpath. Launch
trips to dockyard and up River Tamar
(⛴️). 🛶 🏕️ 🚲 and moped hire in city.
🛈 (0752) 264849/264851

🚌 Western National Buses 15, 15A,
81 from City Centre & Railway
Station (📞 0752 222221)

🚉 Plymouth 1½m

Next Youth Hostels: Bellever 21m.
Dartington 22m. Salcombe 25m.
Golant 38m via Fowey and Torpoint
Ferries

SALCOMBE

Youth Hostel, 'Overbecks', Sharpitor,
Salcombe, Devon TQ8 8LW
📞 Salcombe (054884) 2856
During Winter Closed Period:
📞 (0722) 337494

TO KINGSBRIDGE

MALBOROUGH

A381

SALCOMBE

South
Sands

1 Km

Bolt Head

Overnight charge:
Young £3.80 Junior £4.70 Senior £5.90
Seasonal Prices Jul 1-Aug 31:
Young £4.00 Junior £5.10 Senior £6.30
🏠🏠 ① 🍴 Evening meal 19.30 hrs. **S**
Shop and **PO** Salcombe 2m. **ED** Thu. **P**
for cars and minibuses. National Trust
Car Park (£1 per day; free overnight).
Coaches: Salcombe. Hostel opens
17.00 hrs

Jan 1-Mar 26	Closed
Mar 27-Jun 20	Open (except Fri)
	Open Bank Hol Fri
Jun 21-Aug 31	Open
Sep 1-Oct 31	Open (except Fri)
Nov 1-Feb 29 92	Closed

When closed try Plymouth

During the Winter Closed Period, the
Southern Region Booking Service
will be pleased to help with bookings
and enquiries: Rolfes House, 60
Milford St, Salisbury, Wilts SP1 2BP
(📞 0722 337494)

Large house in National Trust semi-
tropical gardens on cliff just below

Sharpitor Rocks, overlooking sea and
estuary in Area of Outstanding
Natural Beauty. 2m SW of Salcombe
along Cliffe Road passing North
Sands then South Sands or turn right
in Malborough and follow sign for
Overbecks NT Museum and
Gardens. Cliffpath from Bigbury ends
at Hostel. Accessible by minibus but
nearest approach by coach 1½m

OS 202 **GR** 728374 **Sat** 2

Attractions: Devon coastal
footpath. Sea bathing. Pleasant
coves. Clear water for underwater
swimming. 🏖️ 🌸 Wild flowers. 🌍
Geology. Open farm with rare
breeds 1½m. Marine biology. NT
Museum in same building. Small
maritime museum in town. Nature
trails. Holiday Aqualung Diving
(residential). Salcombe Regatta
Weeks (Aug). **L** 🛈 (0548) 853195

🚌 Tally Ho! from Kingsbridge
(connects from Plymouth,
Dartmouth and, for BR connections,
from Totnes), alight Salcombe, 2m
(📞 Devon CC Enquiry Line: 0392
272123)

🚉 Totnes 20m; Plymouth 25m

Ferries: Bantham-Bigbury (for
coastal footpath west). Summer only,
10-11am and 3-4pm, not Sun, no
bikes. Special arrangements for
parties.
Salcombe-East Portlemouth (for
coastal footpath east). All year,
frequent, until 5pm in winter, 7pm in
summer.
Salcombe-South Sands, 10am-5pm,
May-Sep.
Ferries across River Dart regular all
year

Next Youth Hostels: Dartington
21m. Plymouth 25m. Maypool 26m
via Dart ferry or Totnes

Salcombe Youth Hostel

26

START BAY

Youth Hostel, Parish Hall,
Strete, Dartmouth,
Devon TQ6 0RW
☎ Stoke Fleming (0803) 770013

We regret that this Youth Hostel is no longer open

Alternative Hostels in this area are Salcombe, Maypool and Dartington

---

STEPS BRIDGE

24 BEDS

Youth Hostel, Steps Bridge,
Dunsford, Exeter EX6 7EQ
☎ Christow (0647) 52435
During Winter Closed Period:
☎ (0722) 337494

Overnight charge:
Young £3.10 Junior £4.00 Senior £5.10
🅰 🅼 ① 🍴 Evening meal 19.00 hrs.
Small Ⓢ Shop and 🄿🄾 Dunsford 1m.
🄴🄳 Wed and Sat. 🄿 (Public) opposite
Hostel lane. No Smoking Hostel due
to its timber construction. Hostel
opens 17.00 hrs

Jan 1-Mar 26	Closed
Mar 27-Sep 30	Open (except Wed)
Oct 1-Feb 29 92	Closed

During the Winter Closed Period, the
Southern Region Booking Service
will be pleased to help with bookings
and enquiries: Rolfes House, 60
Milford St, Salisbury, Wilts SP1 2BP
(☎ 0722 337494)

Wooden chalet in woodland setting
in River Teign gorge, just inside
Dartmoor National Park. 1m SW of
Dunsford village on main Exeter-
Moretonhampstead Road. Entrance
opposite Dartmoor National Park
information and car park. Due to fire
risk, this is a No Smoking Hostel

🄾🄢 191 🄶🄡 802882 Dartmoor Tourist
🄼🄰🄿 2

Attractions: Woodland walks. 🏞
Fingle Bridge 5m. Heltor Rock 1½m.
Blackingstone Rock 2½m Kennick
Reservoirs 4m. Castle Drogo (NT)
7m. 🚴 at Hostel. Ⓛ 🅱 (0392)
265297

🚌 Devon Services 359 from Exeter
(passes close BR Exeter Central)
(☎ Devon CC Enquire Line: 0392
272123)

🚋 Exeter Central 9m; Exeter St
David's 9m

Next Youth Hostels: Exeter 10m.
Bellever 15m. Dartington 25m. Beer
32m

SOUTH DEVON AND DARTMOOR

26

27 CORNWALL

G ranite cliffs, picturesque fishing harbours and sandy coves are characteristic of the coastline. The atmosphere is romantic, with Celtic lore, legends of smugglers and old traditions. Historic castles are perched on the cliffs and old tin mine workings can be seen. Having a mild climate, the Southern Coast is known as the English Riviera. The stretch of the South West Peninsula Coast Path along the North Coast of Cornwall is probably the wildest and most spectacular on the whole path.

The inland countryside also has its attractions, with wooded valleys and high moors. Bodmin Moor at 1400ft, is an Area of Outstanding Natural Beauty.

Travel

Frequent Inter-City highspeed train services direct from London, Birmingham and many other areas of the country, serve all parts of Cornwall.

Useful Information

Scilly Isles — regular services from Penzace. Details from Isles of Scilly Steamship Co, Quay Street, Penzance PR18 4BD. Tel: (0736) 62909. British International Helicopters (0736) 63871.

South West Way Association Coastal Footpath information is available from: Mr E Wallis, "Windlestraw", Penquit, Ermington, Devon PL21 0LU.

For general advice and information (including Area and Hostel leaflets) about hostelling in this region, contact: South England Regional Office, Rolfes House, 60 Milford Street, Salisbury, Wiltshire SP1 2BP.

Winter closed Hostels

The new Southern Region Booking Service offers the opportunity to book in advance when the Hostel is closed during the winter. See individual Hostel entries for further details.

Parties of 10 or more wishing to stay during the winter closed period, with meals provided, should contact the individual Hostel as many wardens are happy to open for a booking made in advance.

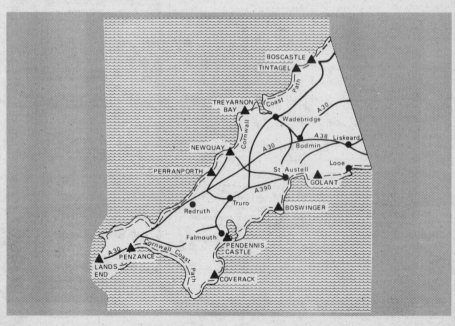

B OSCASTLE HARBOUR

24 BEDS

Youth Hostel, Palace Stables,
Boscastle, Cornwall PL35 0HD
☎ Boscastle (08405) 287 or from
Summer ☎ (0840) 250287 — During
Winter Closed Period: ☎ (0722) 337494

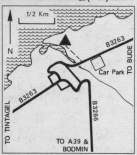

Overnight charge:
Young £3.80 Junior £4.70 Senior £5.90
Seasonal Prices Jul 1-Aug 31:
Young £4.00 Junior £5.10 Senior £6.30
👨‍👩‍👧 🏠 ① 🍴 Evening meal 19.00 hrs. S
Shop and P0 nearby. P for cars and
coaches overnight car park 250 yds.
No parking in harbour area. Hostel
opens 17.00 hrs

Jan 1-Mar 26	Rent-a-Hostel*
Mar 27-Jun 30	Open (except Mon)
	Open Bank Hol Mon
Jul 1-Aug 31	Open
Sep 1-Nov 2	Open (except Mon)
Nov 3-Feb 29 92	Rent-a-Hostel*

When closed try Plymouth or Exeter

During the Winter Closed Period, the
Southern Region Booking Service
will be pleased to help with bookings
and enquiries: Rolfes House, 60
Milford St, Salisbury, Wilts SP1 2BP
(☎ 0722 337494)

*Rent-a-Hostel: Hostel is available
during this period for the exclusive
use of groups booked in advance

In superb position on harbour edge
where Valency River enters National
Trust preserved fishing harbour. Hostel
at harbour. Last building on right, top
of slipway behind 'Pixie House'

OS 190 GR 096915 Ref 1

Attractions: In Area of Outstanding
Natural Beauty with Thomas Hardy
connection. 🚶 harbour and cliff
scenery (NT). On Cornwall Coast
footpath. Very old stone village with
16th C inn. Boat trips. Daily climbing
courses. U A 🖊 F 🍴 (0566) 2321

🚌 Fry's from Bodmin or Plymouth
(passes close BR Plymouth)
(infrequent) (☎ 0840 770256)

🚆 Bodmin Parkway 24m

Next Youth Hostels: Tintagel 5m.
Elmscott 28m. Treyarnon Bay 28m.
Golant 30m

B OSWINGER

32 BEDS

COMFORT IMPROVED YHA

Youth Hostel, Boswinger, Gorran,
St Austell, Cornwall PL26 6LL
☎ Mevagissey (0726) 843234
During Winter Closed Period:
☎ (0722) 337494

Overnight charge:
Young £3.80 Junior £4.70 Senior £5.90
Seasonal Prices Jul 1-Aug 31:
Young £4.00 Junior £5.10 Senior £6.30
👨‍👩‍👧 🏠 ② 🍴 Evening meal 19.00 hrs.
Hot snacks available until 20.00 hrs.
S Shop and P0 Gorran 1m. P0 Sat.
P for cars and coaches. Hostel
opens 17.00 hrs

Jan 1-Mar 26	Rent-a-Hostel*
Mar 27-Jun 30	Open (except Wed)
Jul 1-Aug 31	Open
Sep 1-Nov 2	Open (except Wed)
Nov 3-Feb 29 92	Rent-a-Hostel*

If closed try Pendennis or Penzance

During the Winter period Southern
Region Booking Service will be pleased
to help with bookings and enquiries:
Rolfes House, 60 Milford St, Salisbury,
Wilts SP1 2BP (☎ 0722 337494)

*Rent-a-Hostel: Hostel is available
during this period for the exclusive
use of groups booked in advance

Stone-built cottages and converted
barn in an area of outstanding
coastal scenery. 4m SW of
Mevagissey 1m SW of Gorran. Turn
down road at Sea View Caravan Park

OS 204 GR 991411 Ref 1

Attractions: Binocular and map
hire. Projector and slides of area on
loan. Bathing beach nearby. Cornish
coastal footpath. Boat trips at
Mevagissey 4m. 🚶 A 🏊
🛈 (0872) 74555. Painting holidays. L

🚌 Western National 26/A, Link
Services 7 from BR St Austell, alight
Mevagissey, 4½m (☎ 0872 40404 or
0726 883474). Minibus service daily
from Mevagissey to Boswinger —
contact warden

🚆 St Austell 10m

Next Youth Hostels: Golant 17m.
Newquay 23m. Pendennis Castle
24m (19m via ferry)

C OVERACK

36 BEDS

Youth Hostel, Parc Behan, School Hill,
Coverack, Helston, Cornwall TR12 6SA
☎ St Keverne (0326) 280687
During Winter Closed Period:
☎ (0722) 337494

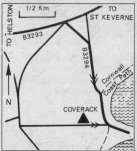

Overnight charge:
Young £3.80 Junior £4.70 Senior £5.90
Seasonal Prices Jul 1-Aug 31:
Young £4.00 Junior £5.10 Senior £6.30
👨‍👩‍👧 🏠 ② 🍴 Evening meal 19.00 hrs.
Small S Shop and P0 200 yds. P0
only, Sat. P for cars and mini buses
only. Coaches 200 yds. Hostel opens
17.00 hrs

Jan 1-Mar 26	Closed
Mar 27-May 31	Open (except Mon)
Jun 1-Sep 30	Open
Oct 1-Nov 2	Open (except Mon)
Nov 3-Feb 29 92	Closed

If closed try Pendennis or Penzance

During the Winter period Southern
Region Booking Service will be pleased
to help with bookings and enquiries:
Rolfes House, 60 Milford St, Salisbury,
Wilts SP1 2BP (☎ 0722 337494)

Large country house, with staircase
salvaged from SS Mohegan wrecked
on Manacles Rocks 1898. Situated
above old fishing village with views of
bay and coastline. 200 yds W of
village centre, take road opp turning
to harbour. Drive entrance next to
village school

OS 204 GR 782181 Ref 1

Attractions: Sea bathing ½m.
Cornish coastal footpath. Cliff
scenery. 🚶 and boating trips,
windsurfing R.Y.A. school (all at
reduced rates for YHA). Harbour.
Beaches. A 🖊 L 🛈 (0326) 312300

🚌 Truronian 311 from Helston
(outside Woolworths) with frequent
connections from BR Penzance (☎
0872 73453 or 0736 69469 for
connections)

🚆 Penryn or Penmere (not Sun,
except May-Sep), both 18m

Next Youth Hostels: Pendennis
Castle 20m (via Helford Passage
17m). Penzance 25m. Land's End 31m

27

GOLANT

94 BEDS

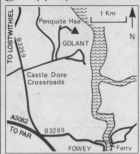

Youth Hostel, Penquite House,
Golant, Fowey,
Cornwall PL23 ILA
☎ Fowey (0726) 833507

Overnight charge:
Young £4.40 Junior £5.40 Senior £6.60
Seasonal Prices Jul 1-Aug 31:
Young £4.60 Junior £5.90 Senior £7.00
[icons] Evening meal 19.00
hrs. Vegetarian food always available.
Alcoholic drink available with meals.
Ⓢ Shop and ℗ Golant. 🚋 Wed
(Fowey) Sat (Golant). 🚆℗ for cars
and coaches. Hostel opens 17.00 hrs

Jan 1-Mar 26	Closed for major building works
Mar 27-Nov 14	Open
Nov 15-30	Closed
Dec 1-22	Open (except Wed & Thu)
Dec 23-29	Open for Xmas
Dec 30-Jan 31 92	Closed
Feb 1-29	Open (except Thu)

When closed, try Penzance,
Pendennis or Plymouth

Mansion built in 1847 on west bank
of Fowey River with views over
wooded estuary. From A390 take
B3269 1½m W of Lostwithiel,
signposted Fowey. After 1½m turn
left at Castle Dore crossroads,
signposted Golant. Drive entrance
½m on left, Hostel 1m down drive
taking right hand fork. From Par
station turn left, take 1st right and
continue to Castle Dore (2m)

Ⓞ 200 Ⓖ 118556 🚇 1

Attractions: Dinghy and canoe hire.
▲ 🚣 boat trips. Fowey 3½m. Cornish
coastal footpath 3m. [icons] (0726)
833616

🚌 Cornwall Busways 24 St Austell —
Fowey (passes BR Par), alight Castle
Dore Crossroads, 1½m (☎ 0872
40404)

🚉 Par (not Sun, except May-Sep)
3m; St Austell 7½m

Next Youth Hostels: Boswinger
17m. Newquay 24m. Tintagel 28m.
Boscastle Harbour 30m

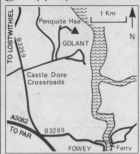

LAND'S END

46 BEDS

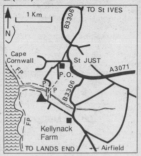

Youth Hostel, Letcha Vean, St Just-in-
Penwith, Penzance, Cornwall TR19 7NT
☎ Penzance (0736) 788437
During Winter Closed Period:
☎ (0722) 337494

Overnight charge:
Young £3.80 Junior £4.70 Senior £5.90
Seasonal Prices Jul 1-Aug 31:
Young £4.00 Junior £5.10 Senior £6.30
[icons] Evening meal 19.00
hrs. Ⓢ Shop, ℗ and launderette
St Just 1m. 🚋 Thu. ℗ for cars and
minibuses. Hostel opens 17.00 hrs

Jan 1-Mar 26	Closed
Mar 27-Jun 30	Open (except Sun)
Jul 1-Aug 31	Open
Sep 1-Nov 2	Open (except Sun)
Nov 3-Feb 29 92	Rent-a-Hostel*

When closed try Penzance

For bookings and enquiries during
Winter Closed Period: Southern
Region Booking Service, Rolfes House,
60 Milford St, Salisbury, Wilts SP1 2BP
(☎ 0722 337494)

*Rent-a-Hostel: From 3 Nov 91,
Hostel will be available during the
Winter Closed Period for the sole
use of groups booked in advance

House with sea views at end of
peaceful Cot Valley; path leading to
cove. 5m from Land's End by cliff
path or road 1m S of St Just. From
bus station (rear exit) turn left, follow
lane past chapel and farm to its end,
turn right down track to Hostel. From
B3306 (only access for cars) turn right
at Kelynack through farmyard and
down lane marked 'dead end'

Ⓞ 203 Ⓖ 364305

Attractions: By Cornwall coast
path surfing and sea bathing Sennen
Cove 3m. Land's End 5m. Airport 1m
— Scilly Isles. Geevor Mine 4m, Ⓤ
1m. Geology, 🎣 sea 🏖 Area famous
for 🌸 wild flowers and prehistoric
remains. [icons] (0736) 62207. 🚾

🚌 Cornwall Busways 1A, 10/A/B, 11
from Penzance (passes BR Penzance),
alight St Just, ¾m (☎ 0736 69469)

🚉 Penzance 8m

Next Youth Hostels: Penzance 7m.
Pendennis Castle 30m. Coverack 31m

NEWQUAY

70 BEDS

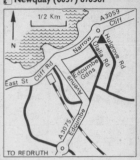

Youth Hostel, Alexandra Court,
Narrowcliff, Newquay,
Cornwall TR7 2QF
☎ Newquay (0637) 876381

Overnight charge:
Young £4.40 Junior £5.40 Senior £6.60
Seasonal Prices Jul 1-Aug 31:
Young £4.60 Junior £5.90 Senior £7.00
[icons] Evening meal 19.00
hrs. Ⓢ Shop 300 yds. 🚋 Wed. ℗ ½m.
℗ for cars and coaches.
Recommended for families ℗ for cars
and coaches. Hostel opens 17.00 hrs

Jan 1-31	Closed
Feb 1-Apr 30	Open (except Sun & Mon) Open Bank Hol
May 1-31	Open (except Sun) Open Bank Hol Sun
Jun 1-Sep 30	Open
Oct 1-Nov 30	Open (except Sun & Mon)
Dec 1-26	Closed
Dec 27-Jan 4 92	Open
Jan 5-Feb 29	Closed

When closed try Penzance or
Pendennis Castle

Alternatively, advance bookings for
parties accepted at wardens
discretion when Hostel would
otherwise be closed

Large house in prime position on seafront road into seaside resort. Facing
Barrowfields (open space), which
adjoins Tolcarne Beach

Ⓞ 200 Ⓖ 818619 🚇 1

Attractions: Cornish Coastal
footpath, beaches (patrolled in
summer), surfing, surfboard hire, sea
trips, swimming pools (indoor and
outdoor), 🐾 zoo, museum, sports
centre, golf course, cinema, 🚾 Ⓤ 2m,
Lappa Valley Steam Railway 5m, Dairy-
land Farm 3m. [icons] (0637) 871345

🚌 Frequent from surrounding areas
(☎ 0872 40404)

🚉 Newquay (not Sun, except May-
Sep) ¼m

Next Youth Hostels: Perranporth
10m. Treyarnon 10m. Boswinger 23m

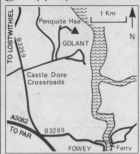
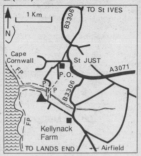
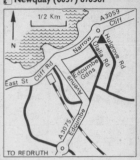

Administrative Region: South **Administrative Region: South** **Administrative Region: South**

PENDENNIS CASTLE

Youth Hostel,
Pendennis Castle, Falmouth,
Cornwall TR11 4LP
☎ **Falmouth (0326) 311435**

90 BEDS

Overnight charge:
Young £4.40 Junior £5.40 Senior £6.60
Seasonal Prices Jul 1-Aug 31:
Young £4.60 Junior £5.90 Senior £7.00
🏠🅰️◻️🅒🔲②📺 GSC 🔔 Evening
meal 19.00 hrs. Ⓢ Snack service.
Shop and ℗ ½m. 🔌 Wed. Ⓟ 100 yds.
Hostel opens 17.00 hrs

Jan 1-31	Closed try Penzance
Feb 1-Mar 25	Open (except Sun & Mon)
Mar 26-Sep 8	Open
Sep 9-Oct 30	Open (except Sun)
Nov 1-30	Open (except Sun & Mon)
Dec 1-26	Closed
Dec 27-Jan 4 92	Open
Jan 5-Feb 29	Open (except Sun & Mon)

A recently refurbished Victorian barrack building in grounds of 16th century castle, floodlit at night on promontory beyond Falmouth town, with views over Carrick Roads and Falmouth Bay. Hostel now offers smaller rooms and the use of a classroom, making it ideal for both groups and families. From town centre follow Market Street, past church, continue to and pass under railway bridge to small roundabout. Go straight across to reach sea front. Bear left to climb drive. Hostel in castle grounds

OS 204 GR 823319 Barf 1

Attractions: Bathing beaches ½m. 🅰️ Dockside taverns. Seal sanctuary. Riverboat trips. Maritime museum 1m. Cornish coastal footpath. Historical Re-enactments with The Sealed Knot Society🔌 ☑️ Ⓛ Sub-Aqua courses and holidays available

🚌 Frequent from surrounding areas (☎ 0872 40404)

🚍 Falmouth (not Sun, except May-Sep) ¾m

Ferries: Falmouth — St Mawes passenger only, shorter route to Boswinger & Golant (0326) 318534. Helford passage (0326) 250116. Easter-Sep on demand, subject to tide

Next Youth Hostels: Perranporth 19m. Coverack 20m (via Helford Passage 17m). Penzance 24m. Boswinger 24m (via ferry 19m)

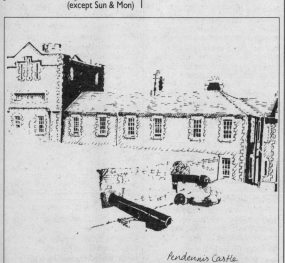

Pendennis Castle

PENZANCE

Youth Hostel, Castle Horneck,
Alverton, Penzance,
Cornwall TR20 8TF
☎ **Penzance (0736) 62666**

90 BEDS

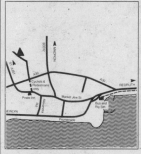

Overnight charge:
Young £4.60 Junior £5.90 Senior £7.00
🏠🅰️🅰️② 📺 Evening meal and cafeteria facilities 17.30-20.00 hrs. Ⓢ Shop and ℗ Alverton ½m. 🔌 Wed. Ⓟ for cars and coaches. Hostel opens 17.00 hrs

Jan 1-3	Closed
Jan 4-Dec 31	Open
Jan 1-Feb 29 92	Open

Mansion rebuilt in 18th Century (reputed to have smugglers' tunnel), on site of ancient fortification, on outskirts of busy market town. Pedestrians — West on Lands End road, through town, turn right at thatched cottage opposite Pirate Inn, cross new by-pass, take lane as signposted. Motorists take by-pass (A30) from outskirts of Penzance, turn at YHA signposts

OS 203 GR 457302 Barf 1

Attractions: Cornish coastal footpath. Mild climate. Old mine workings. Drift Dam nature reserve 3m. Harbour. Trengwainton Gardens (NT) 1½m. Maritime museum ½m. Mousehole village and harbour 3m. St Michael's Mount 3¼m. Sea bathing, 🔌 and boat trips 1m. 🅰️☑️Ⓤ Ⓛ Scilly Isles Ferry 1m — tickets available from Hostel. Helicopter Service 2½m. 🔳 (0736) 62207

🚌 Cornwall Busways A, B, 5, 10B from BR Penzance to within ¾m (☎ 0736 69469)

🚍 Penzance 2m

Next Youth Hostels: Land's End 7m. Pendennis Castle 24m. Coverack 25m. Perranporth 29m

---

Administrative Region: South

Administrative Region: South

CORNWALL

27

PERRANPORTH
24 BEDS

COMFORT IMPROVED yha

Youth Hostel, Droskyn Point,
Perranporth, Cornwall TR6 0DS
☎ Truro (0872) 573812
During Winter Closed Period:
☎ (0722) 337494

Overnight charge:
Young £3.50 Junior £4.40 Senior £5.50
Seasonal Prices Jul 1-Aug 31:
Young £3.80 Junior £4.70 Senior £5.90
⚠ ⊞ ⚠ ① Snack meals. Small Ⓢ
Shop and P0 ½m. ⒺⒹ Wed. Ⓟ — No
access for vehicles. Ⓟ 100 yds, 250
yds. Hostel opens 17.00 hrs

Jan 1-Mar 26	Rent-a-Hostel*
Mar 27-Jun 30	Open (except Tue)
Jul 1-Aug 31	Open
Sep 1-30	Open (except Tue)
Oct 1-Feb 29 92	Rent-a-Hostel*

When closed try Newquay or
Pendennis Castle

During the Winter period Southern
Region Booking Service will be pleased
to help with bookings and enquiries:
Rolfes House, 60 Milford St, Salisbury,
Wilts SP1 2BP (☎ 0722 337494)

*Rent-a-Hostel: Hostel is available
during this period for the exclusive
use of groups booked in advance

Single storey Hostel high on the cliffs
looking out over three miles of surf
beach to Ligger Point. On coastal
footpath, western edge of village. From
village centre take Beach Road to lower
car park, then Cliff Road to higher car
park. Hostel is beyond Droskyn Castle

ⓄⓈ 200, 204 ⒼⓇ 752544 Ⓑⓐⓡ 1

Attractions: North Cornish coastal
path. Bathing. Surfing. Wild flowers
on cliffs and sand dunes. Industrial
archaeology — St Agnes 3m. Truro
9m. ⚠ ⚠ ⚠ Ⓩ Ⓘ (0637) 871345

🚌 Cornwall Busways 87/A, 88A,
National Express 343, 705 Truro —
Newquay (pass close BR Truro &
Newquay) (☎ 0872 40404)

🚂 Truro 10m; Newquay (not Sun,
except May-Sep) 10m

Next Youth Hostels: Newquay 10m.
Pendennis Castle 19m. Penzance 29m.
Boswinger 25m. Land's End 36m

Administrative Region: South

TINTAGEL
27 BEDS

Youth Hostel, Dunderhole Point,
Tintagel, Cornwall PL34 0DW
☎ Tintagel (0840) 770334
During Winter Closed Period:
☎ (0722) 337494

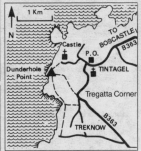

Overnight charge:
Young £3.80 Junior £4.70 Senior £5.90
Seasonal Prices Jul 1-Aug 31:
Young £4.00 Junior £5.10 Senior £6.30
⚠ ① ⓘⓞ Evening meal 19.00 hrs for
parties. Cafeteria facilities. Ⓢ Shop
and P0 Tintagel. ⒺⒹ Wed. Hostel
opens 17.00 hrs

Jan 1-Mar 26	Closed
Mar 27-Jun 30	Open (except Tue)
Jul 1-Aug 31	Open
Sep 1-Nov 2	Open (except Tue)
Nov 3-Feb 29 92	Closed

When closed try Plymouth,
Pendennis Castle or Boscastle

During the Winter period Southern
Region Booking Service will be pleased
to help with bookings and enquiries:
Rolfes House, 60 Milford St, Salisbury,
Wilts SP1 2BP (☎ 0722 337494)

150-yr-old slate quarry cottage now
owned by NT, in spectacular coast
setting on cliffs, with 18m view across
Port Isaac Bay. From village follow lane
to Tintagel Church (¼m) then follow
track by NT sign bearing left along
cliff top (Glebe Cliff). Hostel 300 yds
along track below cliff top. Take care
in approaching after dark; Hostel not
visible from Tintagel Church. Car
park at top of cliff

ⓄⓈ 200 ⒼⓇ 047881 Ⓑⓐⓡ 1

Attractions: NT cliff land (AONB).
Tintagel Castle ½m. On Cornwall
North Coast footpath. King Arthur's
Hall. Sandy beaches ½m. Rough Tor
and Brown Willy (Bodmin Moor) 8m.
Delabole Slate Quarry Museum 4m.
Surf board hire at Hostel. Ⓤ ⓦ Ⓕ ⚠
Ⓩ Ⓛ Ⓘ (020881) 3725

🚌 Fry's services from Bodmin or
Plymouth (daily), alight Tregatta
Corner, Hostel sign-posted thereon
(☎ 0840 770256)

🚂 Bodmin Parkway 20m

Next Hostels: Boscastle Harbour
5m. Treyarnon Bay 23m (via ferry 18m)

Administrative Region: South

TREYARNON BAY
45 BEDS

Youth Hostel, Tregonnan, Treyarnon,
Padstow, Cornwall PL28 8JR
☎ Padstow (0841) 520322
During Winter Closed Period:
☎ (0722) 337494

Overnight charge:
Young £3.80 Junior £4.70 Senior £5.90
Seasonal Prices Jul 1-Aug 31:
Young £4.00 Junior £5.10 Senior £6.30
⊞ ⚠ ① ⓘⓞ Evening meal 19.00 hrs. Ⓢ
Shop Constantine ½m. P0 St Merryn
2½m. ⒺⒹ Wed. Ⓟ for cars. Coaches
110 yds. Hostel opens 17.00 hrs

Jan 1-Mar 26	Closed
Mar 27-Jun 30	Open (except Fri)
	Open Good Fri
Jul 1-Aug 31	Open
Sep 1-Nov 3	Open (except Fri)
Nov 4-Feb 29 92	Rent-a-Hostel*

When closed try Newquay or
Pendennis Castle

During the Winter period Southern
Region Booking Service will be pleased
to help with bookings and enquiries:
Rolfes House, 60 Milford St, Salisbury,
Wilts SP1 2BP (☎ 0722 337494)

*Rent-a-Hostel: From Nov 4 91,
Hostel is available during this period
for the exclusive use of groups
booked in advance

House overlooking sandy cove, in
AONB. On the N cliffs just after the
hotels, along signposted private drive
ⓄⓈ 200 ⒼⓇ 859741 Ⓑⓐⓡ 1

Attractions: Sea bathing. Surfing.
Cornish coastal footpath. Lighthouse
at Trevose Head 2m, Padstow (5m).
Footpath & cycle path along River
Camel — 🚲 and old slate workings.
Cycle hire St Merryn 2m. Golf course
and tennis courts ½m. Ⓤ 3m. ⚠ ⓦ
Ⓘ (020881) 3725

🚌 Cornwall Busways 55 BR Bodmin
Parkway — Padstow, alight Padstow,
4½m, on most, but some extended to
Constantine, ½m (☎ 0872 40404)
Newquay-Padstow, summer service
inc. Sundays

🚂 Newquay (not Sun, except May-
Sep) 10m; Bodmin Parkway 21m

Next Youth Hostels: Newquay
10m. Tintagel 25m (via ferry 18m)

Administrative Region: South

The Best Way To Discover All That North America Offers Is To Pick Up Our New Hostel Handbook.

It's loaded with maps, photos and information
on 300 hostels in the USA and Canada.
Available May 1 at
YHA Adventure Shops everywhere.

INTERNATIONAL YOUTH HOSTEL FEDERATION
Canadian Hostelling Association
L'Association Canadienne de l'Ajisme
American Youth Hostels

BALLYGALLY

48 BEDS YHANI

Youth Hostel,
210 Coast Road, Ballygally,
Co. Antrim BT40 2QQ
☎ **Ballygally (0574) 583355**

Overnight charge:
Low season (Oct-Apr)
Junior £4.50 Senior (18+) £5.00
High season (May-Sep)
Junior £4.75 Senior (18+) £5.75
Bedlinen included
🚻 🚮 🅿️ SC P C SC 🍴 S and PO in
village. Hostel opens 17.00 hrs

Dec 22-Jan 6 92 Closed

Located on an elevated site above
shore with splendid views of Antrim
Coast. On main coast road just
south of Ballygally village. Good
location for travellers on ferry to and
from Scotland

OS Sheet 9, Ballymena, Larne 379079
🗺 Ireland Travel Map, Sheet 1,
Antrim-Donegal

Attractions: Beach opposite. Sea 🛶
Local walks on Antrim Plateau.
Glenarm Forest Park. Carnfunnock
Country Park, N.I. Maze, golf, 🛶
from shore and local boats (lines and
bait available), sea swimming, 'Ulster
Way' close by (long distance
footpath), U

🚌 North/South Coastal Route,
alight opposite

🚂 Larne 4m

Ferry: Larne – Stranraer (Scotland)
4m (25% discount). Taxis from
harbour to Hostel

Next Youth Hostels: Belfast 25m.
Cushendall 25m. Whitepark Bay 40m

Additional Information: Advance
booking to National Office,
56 Bradbury Place, Belfast BT7 1RU.
☎ (0232) 324733. Fax: (0232)
434699

Administration: N Ireland

BELFAST

60 BEDS YHANI

International Youth Hostel,
"Ardmore", 11 Saintfield Road,
Belfast BT8 4AE
☎ **Belfast (0232) 647865**

Fax: (0232) 640298

Overnight charge:
includes Continental breakfast
Low season (Oct-Apr)
Junior £5.50 Senior (18+) £6.50
Mid season (May, Jun & Sep)
Junior £6.50 Senior (18+) £7.50
High season (Jul-Aug)
Junior £7.00 Senior (18+) £8.00
Bedlinen included
🚻 🚮 🅿️ SC P S and PO 200m.
Hostel opens 17.00 hrs

Dec 22-Jan 6 92 Closed

Large detached town house in its
own grounds. Situated 2 miles south
from the city centre on main road to
Newcastle. Good location to visit
sights of Belfast and good access
points to the rest of Northern
Ireland. All day opening during
summer

OS Sheet 15, Belfast 351704 🗺 Ireland
Travel Map, Sheet 1, Antrim-Donegal

Attractions: Ulster Museum. Ulster
Folk and Transport Museum (50%
reduction). Queen's University. Grand
Opera House. Belfast City Hall.
Crown Liquor Saloon — National
Trust

🚌 84 or 38 from City Centre, alight
at hostel

🚂 3m to routes North & South

Ferry: Belfast – Liverpool 3m (25%
reduction)

Next Youth Hostels: Ballygally
25m. Newcastle 30m

Additional Information: Advance
booking to National Office,
56 Bradbury Place, Belfast BT7 1RU.
☎ (0232) 324733. Fax: (0232)
434699

Administration: N Ireland

CASTLE ARCHDALE

55 BEDS YHANI

Youth Hostel, Castle Archdale
Country Park, Irvinestown,
Co. Fermanagh BT94 1PP
☎ **Irvinestown (03656) 28118**

Overnight charge:
Low season (Oct-Apr)
Junior £4.00 Senior (18+) £5.00
High season (May-Sep)
Junior £4.50 Senior (18+) £5.50
Bedlinen included
🚻 🚮 🚮 U (groups only) SC FS C P
cars and coaches 🅰️ U L Hostel
opens 17.00 hrs

Dec 1-Jan 31 92 Closed
(except for advance booking groups)

Built in 1773 in the very heart of
Castle Archdale Country Park, 10m
N of Enniskillen on E shore of Lower
Lough Erne. The Youth Hostel
occupies a major wing of the old
courtyard complex; also Wildlife
Exhibition Centre, Museum and
D.O.E. Countryside & Wildlife
Branch Lecture Theatre and Field
Study Labs. Nearby is a modern
Marina, shops and cafe

OS Sheet 17, Lower Lough Erne
176588 🗺 Ireland Travel Map,
Sheet 1, Antrim-Donegal

Attractions: In courtyard complex:
Wartime History of Castle Archdale;
Wildlife Exhibition. In Castle
Archdale: Boat trips (max 9 in any
one trip) to White Island;
Cleanishgarve Island; Innishmakill
Island and Crevinshaughy Island
(barbecue facilities); Forest paths and
walks with permanent orienteering
course; U with Drumhoney stables
— traps available (YHA discounts);
Day boat hire from Marina; Crum-
Boat trips abroad 'Trasna' on Upper
Lough Erne (NT); Marble Arch
Caves; Belleek Pottery. Boat, canoe,
windsurfer and cycle hire.

Next Youth Hostel: Ball Hill,
Donegal 30m

Additional Information: Advance
booking to National Office,
56 Bradbury Place, Belfast BT7 1RU.
☎ (0232) 324733

Administration: N Ireland

C USHENDALL 56 BEDS YHANI

Youth Hostel,
Layde Road, Cushendall,
Co. Antrim BT44 0NQ
☎ **Cushendall (02667) 71344**

Overnight charge:
Low season (Oct-Apr)
Junior £4.00 Senior (18+) £5.00
High season (May-Sep)
Junior £4.50 Senior (18+) £5.50
Bedlinen included

🚿 🏠 ⊠ SC P L S and PO in village.
Hostel opens 17.00 hrs

Dec 1-Feb 29 92 Closed
(except for advance booking groups)

Situated 1 mile North of Cushendall
Village on the Layde Road towards
Cushendun. A large building set in its
own grounds on an elevated site
overlooking Cushendall Bay and
Garron Point

OS Sheet 5, Ballycastle 241286
🗺 Ireland Travel Map, Sheet 1,
Antrim-Donegal

Attractions: In Cushendall:
Swimming — beach ½m at golf
course; Sea ☒ off rocks — ¼m or
boats in Red Bay; Red Curfew Tower
— built 1809; Moyle Way Path; Layde
Church (13th century). Nearby:
Trostan — highest mountain in Co.
Antrim; Ossians Grave; Tieveragh
Hill (Fairy Hill); National Trust —
Cushendun Village; Glens of Antrim
— Glenarm, Glencoy, Glenariff,
Glenballyeamon, Glenann, Glencorp,
Glenshesk, Glentaisie and Glendun;
Glenariff Forest Park and Nature
Reserve; Ballypatrick Forest Park;
Pony Trekking — Loughareema
Trekking Centre; Torr Head Scenic
Drive; Loughareema — The
Vanishing Lake

🚌 North/South Coastal Route

Next Youth Hostels: Ballygally
18m. Whitepark Bay 25m

Additional Information: Advance
booking to National Office,
56 Bradbury Place, Belfast BT7 1RU.
☎ (0232) 324733. Fax: (0232)
434699

Administration: N Ireland

N EWCASTLE 40 BEDS YHANI

Youth Hostel,
30 Downs Road, Newcastle,
Co. Down BT33 0AG
☎ **Newcastle (03967) 22133**

Overnight charge:
Low season (Oct-Apr)
Junior £4.50 Senior (18+) £5.00
High season (May-Sep)
Junior £4.75 Senior (18+) £5.75
Bedlinen included

🚿 🏠 ⊠ SC L Hostel opens 17.00
hrs

Dec 1-Jan 31 92 Closed
(except for advance booking groups)

A large town house situated near the
seafront in Newcastle

OS Sheet 29, The Mournes 379314
🗺 Ireland Travel Map, Sheet 1,
Antrim-Donegal

Attractions: In Newcastle: Beach
and promenade; Donard Park and
Glen River Walks; Tropicana —
Newcastle Centre — swimming and
theatre; amusements and cafes;
Mourne Countryside Centre — local
walks and exhibition; Boating lake,
Pitch and Putt and tennis courts.
Nearby: Tollymore Forest Park;
Castlewellan Forest Park, Aboretum
and permanent orienteering course;
Ⓤ Castlewellan & Newcastle Riding
Centre; Mourne Mountains — Slieve
Donard and Brandy Pad. Seaforde
Butterfly Centre (Apr-Oct); Dundrum
Castle, Dundrum; Murlough Nature
Reserve; Bloody Bridge Coastal Path;
Annalong and working corn mill;
Kilkeel — fishing port; Silent Valley
Reservoir. Day trips: Strangford Ferry
to Portaferry Aquarium; NT —
Castleward; Down Cathedral, Saul
(St. Patrick); Down Museum —
Downpatrick; Quoile Pondage and
Inch Abbey — Downpatrick

🚌 Newcastle Bus Station 300 metres

Next Youth Hostel: Omeath 20m.
Belfast 30m

Additional Information: Advance
booking to National Office,
56 Bradbury Place, Belfast BT7 1RU.
☎ (0232) 324733

Administration: N Ireland

W HITEPARK BAY 44 BEDS YHANI

Youth Hostel, 157 Whitepark Road,
Ballintoy, Ballycastle,
Co. Antrim BT54 6NH
☎ **Ballycastle (02657) 31745**

Fax: (02657) 32034
Overnight charge:
Low season (Oct-Apr)
Junior £4.50 Senior (18+) £5.50
High season (May-Sep)
Junior £5.00 Senior (18+) £6.00
(£1 supplement for en-suite facilities)
Bedlinen included

🚿 🏠 SC P cars and coaches L
Hostel opens 17.00 hrs

Dec 22-Jan 6 92 Closed

The Hostel may close for building
work during 91, telephone in advance

The Hostel is situated in the very
heart of Antrim's Causeway Coast
between the famous Giants
Causeway and Carrick-a-Rede Rope
Bridge. Whitepark Bay itself, is a
natural moon-shaped bay, once
owned by the YHA but given to the
National Trust, it is now designated
as an Area of Natural Beauty

OS Sheet 5, Ballycastle 013436
🗺 Ireland Travel Map, Sheet 1,
Antrim-Donegal

Attractions: Whitepark Bay Nature
Trail — NT leaflet. Beach Walks and
coastal path from Port Bradden to
Giant's Causeway — World Heritage
Site. Causeway Visitor Centre. Carrick-
a-Rede Rope Bridge (May-Sep) 60 ft
chasm - 80 ft drop. Bushmills Distillery.
Ferry from Ballycastle to Rathlin Island
(walks and bird sanctuary). Portrush
Waterworld. Fair Head. Port Bradden
— smallest church in Ireland.
Dunseverick Castle. Port Ballintrae

🚌 North/South Coastal Route

🚆 Portrush 12m. Coleraine 17m

Next Youth Hostels: Cushendall
25m. Tra-na-Rossan, Donegal

Additional Information: Advance
booking: National Office, 56 Bradbury
Place, Belfast BT7 1RU. ☎ (0232)
324733. Fax: (0232) 434699

Administration: N Ireland

MAIL ORDER ITEMS

Ring with your VISA / ACCESS / AMEX / DINERS / YHA BUDGET ACCOUNT number on 071-836 8541. **Write with your order and payment to YHA Mail Order Department, YHA Adventure Shops Plc, 14 Southampton Street, London WC2E 7HY.**

Handbooks and Guides for Travel Abroad	Price (inc. p&p)	Total
EXPLORING EUROPE Touring routes through Western Europe and Scandinavia. Where to go, what to do type information. Written by Hostellers for Hostellers.	£8.99	
INTERNATIONAL YOUTH HOSTEL HANDBOOK Addresses and brief details of Youth Hostels. Revised in March. Each Volume includes a full pull-out Youth Hostel map.		
Volume 1: Europe, N. Africa and Israel.	£6.55	
Volume 2: Australasia, Americas, Asia and Africa (Sudan Southward).	£6.55	
INTERNATIONAL CONVERSATION BOOK FOR HOSTELLERS Words and phrases in English, French, German & Spanish.	£2.45	
SCOTTISH YH HANDBOOK Published annually in January.	£1.30	
IRISH YH HANDBOOK Irish Republic only, published annually in April.	£1.95	
ORDER YOUR SLEEPING BAG		
Sheet sleeping bag (8oz)	£13.95	
Sheet sleeping bag (12oz)	£10.95	
Total Amount Payable		

I enclose crossed cheque/postal order No: _____

Value £ _____ payable to YHA Adventure Shops Plc

I wish to pay by Visa/Access/Amex/Diners/YHA Budget Account *(delete as appropriate)*. Credit Card Orders on 071-836 8541.

My Credit Card number is: Expiry Date:

Name: _____

Address: _____

_____

N.B. Whilst every effort will be made to maintain these prices, YHA Adventure Shops reserve the right to alter the above prices if necessary.

YHA Adventure Shops are the professionals in modern adventure sport. For beginners or experts we offer a truly outstanding range of clothing and accessories that encompasses both state-of-the-art equipment and outdoor fashion.

That's why YHA Adventure Shops are the first choice for novices, as well as many of the best known names from the world of major expeditions. In fact YHA Adventure Shops have been involved in with every major British expedition mounted in the last 10 years.

And because we're the country's biggest specialist retailer, we can offer you the widest choice, at a price that is guaranteed to be unbeatable.

Nowhere else will you find more top British and international equipment under just one roof — including a vast array of camping and travel accessories, books, maps, climbing gear and specialist food, as well as those areas illustrated in our range of Fact Sheets.

And when you walk into any of our Adventure Shops you are assured of personal service and sound advice, because all of our staff are trained to ensure you get the most from your activity. We offer practical advice on every aspect of equipment and clothing — added to which most of our staff are enthusiasts themselves, regularly using new and established products.

This friendly advice, given in pleasant, comfortable surroundings, will enable you to make your choice from the world's biggest names in adventure gear. Safe in the knowledge that you have bought from YHA Adventure Shops a guarantee of top quality and reliability.

Plus, where else can you plan and book your travel requirements at the same time? Campus Travel can be found in our larger stores. They provide expert advice on places to go, how to get there and where to stay at excellent value for money.

Combine the YHA Adventure Shops choice of gear, clothing, maps and guide books for camping, climbing, backpacking and skiing and you can easily see why YHA Adventure Shops are the UK's biggest and best specialist retailer.

YHA Adventure Shops — really going places.

A personal invitation to 300,000+ enthusiasts from 183 others!

DOME TENTS • RIDGE TENTS • SLEEPING BAGS • DAYSACS • RUCSACS • WALKING JACKETS • WALKING BOOTS • WALKING SHOES • WATERPROOF CLOTHING • BREECHES & SHORTS • CLIMBING GEAR • CLIMBING BOOTS • ICE AXES & HARNESSES • STOVES & FUELS • EXPEDITION FOOD • YHA PUBLICATIONS • YHA MEMBERSHIP ENROLMENT • GUIDE BOOKS • TRAVEL BOOKS • ORDNANCE SURVEY MAPS • DOWNHILL SKI • SKI CLOTHING AND HARDWARE • SUNGLASSES & SUNHATS

YOUR ADVENTURE STARTS HERE ...

LONDON 174 KENSINGTON HIGH ST TEL: 071 938 2948 • **LONDON** 14 SOUTHAMPTON ST CO GARDEN TEL: 071 836 8541 • **MANCHESTER** 166 DEANSGATE TEL: 061 834 7119 • **BIRMINGHAM** CORPORATION ST (BULL ST SUBWAY) TEL: 021 236 7799 • **BRIGHTON** 126-127 QUEENS TEL: 0273 821554 • **BRISTOL** 10-12 FAIRFAX ST TEL: 0272 297141 • **CAMBRIDGE** 6-7 BRIDG TEL: 0223 353956 • **CARDIFF** 13 CASTLE ST TEL: 0222 399178 • **LEEDS** 80 BRIGGATE TEL: 0532 465 **OXFORD** 9-10 ST CLEMENTS (THE PLAIN) TEL: 0865 247948 • **LIVERPOOL** 25 BOLD ST TEL: 051 709 • **NOTTINGHAM** 20-22 WHEELER GATE TEL: 0602 475710 • **SHEFFIELD** 7-9 ROCKINGHAM TEL: 0742 765935 • **STAINES** 133 HIGH ST TEL: 0784 452987

*All items subject to availability. Whilst every effort will be made to maintain prices, some changes m necessary. YHA (E&W) members discount regrettably excludes books, maps, membership or YHA Adve Shops "Price Guaranteed" items. Information is compiled with all possible care, but YHA Adventure S plc cannot be held responsible for any errors or omissions.

A YHA membership card gives you special cut prices on a whole range of services and tourist attractions throughout England and Wales. Just show your validated 1991 YHA membership card at the places listed below and you will receive a very useful discount. There are all sorts of advantages, so make the most of them **NOW!**

ATTRACTION	NEAREST YOUTH HOSTEL

NORTHERN REGION

BORDER AND DALES

ATTRACTION	NEAREST YOUTH HOSTEL
Alnwick Castle Alnwick NORTHUMBERLAND	Rock Hall Wooler
Beamish North of England Open Air Museum Beamish Hall, Stanley CO DURHAM DH9 0RG (0207) 231811	Durham Edmundbyers Once Brewed Newcastle
Haltwhistle Swimming Pool and Leisure Centre 10% discount for YHA members	Once Brewed
North York Moors Railway Pickering Station, Pickering NORTH YORKSHIRE YO18 7AJ (0751) 72508 Talking timetable 73535 No discount Jun 28-Sep 5 or to Santa Special trains	Wheeldale
Outdoor World (Outdoor/Sports Equipment) 49 Ilfracombe Gardens Whitley Bay TYNE & WEAR NE26 3LZ (091) 2514388	Newcastle
Weardale Mountain Bikes Guided Tours/Hire 39/41 Front Street Frosterley COUNTY DURHAM DL13 2QP	Edmundbyers Langdon Beck

YORKSHIRE

ATTRACTION	NEAREST YOUTH HOSTEL
Embsay Steam Railway Embsay Station, Skipton NORTH YORKSHIRE BD23 6AY (0756) 794727	Linton 8m Earby 9m Malham 12m Kettlewell 15m
Keighley and Worth Valley Light Railway Haworth Station Haworth, Keighley WEST YORKSHIRE (0535) 45214	Haworth 1m
York Marine Services Ltd Ferry Lane Bishopthorpe, YORK YO2 1SB (0904) 704442	York

ATTRACTION	NEAREST YOUTH HOSTEL
YHA Adventure Shop 80 Briggate, LEEDS (0532) 465339	
YHA Adventure Shop 7-9 Rockingham Gate, SHEFFIELD (0742) 765935	

LAKES

ATTRACTION	NEAREST YOUTH HOSTEL
Ambleside Mountain Bikes c/o Scotts Café, Waterhead Ambleside, CUMBRIA	Ambleside 50 yds
Appleby Castle Appleby, CUMBRIA	Dufton 3m Kirkby Stephen 10m
The Dove Cottage & Wordsworth Museum Grasmere CUMBRIA	Grasmere (Butharlyp How) 1m Grasmere (Thorney How) 1½m
Hawkshead Sportswear The Square Hawkshead CUMBRIA	Hawkshead 1m
Levens Hall and Topiary Garden Kendal, CUMBRIA LA8 0PD (05395) 60321	Arnside 6m
Lowther Wildlife Adventure Park Lowther Penrith, CUMBRIA	Patterdale 12m Helvellyn 12m
Mirehouse Keswick, CUMBRIA CA12 4QE (0596) 72287	Keswick 4m
Rentacamp Cycle Hire Lakeland Leisure The Chalet, Station Precinct Windermere, CUMBRIA (09662) 4786	Windermere 2m Ambleside 4m
Rydal Mount Rydal Ambleside CUMBRIA (05394) 33002	Ambleside 2m High Close 2m Grasmere (Butharlyp How) 2m Grasmere (Thorney How) 2½m
Windermere Iron Steam Boat Co. Ltd Lakeside, Ulverston CUMBRIA, LA12 8AS	Steamer service on Windermere Lake
The Climber's Shop Ltd Compston Corner Ambleside, CUMBRIA	Ambleside 1m

TRACTION	NEAREST YOUTH HOSTEL	ATTRACTION	NEAREST YOUTH HOSTEL
e Keswick on rwentwater Launch Co. Ltd swick, CUMBRIA	Launch service around Derwentwater Lake	**Hitch'n'Hike** Mytham Bridge, Barmford DERBYSHIRE S30 2BH (0433) 51013	
e Ravenglass & Eskdale ilway Co. Ltd wenglass UMBRIA CA18 1SW 229) 717171	Eskdale 1½m Wastwater 6m	**Markfield Equestrian Centre** Scanton Lane Farm, Markfield LEICESTERSHIRE (0530) 242373	Copt Oak
lswater Navigation & ansit Co. Ltd Maude Street ndal, CUMBRIA	Steamer service on Ullswater Lake	**Midland Railway Centre** Butterley Station Ripley, DERBYSHIRE	Shining Cliff Matlock
		National Tramway Museum Crich DERBYSHIRE	Matlock Elton Shining Cliff

CENTRAL REGION

'AK			
rbyshire Day scoverer Tickets	Available from all wardened Peak District Hostels and Area Office	**Peak District Mining Museum** Matlock Bath DERBYSHIRE (0629) 3834	Matlock Elton Youlgrave Shining Cliff
gshaw Cavern adwell RBYSHIRE*	Castleton Edale Hathersage	**Peak Hang Gliding** 4 Abbey Units,Macclesfield Leek, STAFFORDSHIRE (0538) 383659	Ilam Hall Meerbrook Gradbach
eacon Cycles Derby Road ughborough CESTERSHIRE	Copt Oak	**Peak National Park Cycle Hire** (all centres)	All Hostels in and near National Park
xton Micrarium xton RBYSHIRE	Buxton Ravenstor Gradbach	**Peak Rail** Buxton, DERBYSHIRE	Buxton Ravenstor
aatterley Whitfield ining Museum nstall OKE-ON-TRENT 782) 813337	Gradbach Ilam Hall Meerbrook Dimmingsdale	**Peak School of Hang Gliding** c/o Ilam Hall Youth Hostel Ashbourne Derbyshire DE6 2AZ (033527) 257	
atsworth House kewell RBYSHIRE	Bakewell Youlgrave Elton	**Pooles Cavern** Green Lane Buxton, DERBYSHIRE	Buxton Ravenstor
rbar Riding and ekking Stables aberbrook Bar Road rbar, Calver ope Valley, DERBYSHIRE	Eyam Hathersage	**Riber Castle** Matlock DERBYSHIRE	Matlock Shining Cliff Youlgrave Elton
erbyshire Brass Rubbing entre ng Street, Ashbourne RBYSHIRE	Ilam	**Speedwell Cavern, Treak Cliff Cavern, Blue John Cavern and Peak Cavern** Castleton, DERBYSHIRE	Castleton Edale Hathersage
eo Supplies Station Road, Chapeltown, EFFIELD S30 4XH		**YHA Adventure Shop** 20-22 Wheeler Gate NOTTINGHAM (0602) 475710	
eat Central Railway ughborough CESTERSHIRE	Copt Oak	**EASTERN**	
		Museum of East Anglian Life Stowmarket, SUFFOLK IP14 1DL (0449) 612229	Alpheton 14m
ddon Hall kewell RBYSHIRE	Bakewell Youlgrave Elton Matlock	**Doug's Cycles** Norwich	Norwich
eights of Abraham tlock Bath RBYSHIRE	Matlock Elton Youlgrave Shining Cliff	**Beeston Hall** Beeston St Lawrence Norwich, NORFOLK NR12 9YS	Norwich 9m

ATTRACTION	NEAREST YOUTH HOSTEL
Belvoir Castle Grantham, LINCOLNSHIRE (0476) 870262	Thurlby Lincoln Copt Oak
Benington Lordship Stevenage HERTFORDSHIRE, SG2 7BS (043885) 668	St Albans 18m
Thrigby Hall Wildlife Gardens Near Filby, Great Yarmouth NORFOLK	Great Yarmouth 7m
Oasis Leisure Centre Hunstanton	Hunstanton
Haddenham Farmland Museum Haddenham	Ely
Park Farm Snettisham King's Lynn	King's Lynn
East of England Ice Rink Peterborough	Thurlby
Norfolk Shire Horse Centre Cromer	Sheringham
Lavenham Priory Lavenham	Castle Hedingham
Geoff's Bike Hire 65 Devonshire Road CAMBRIDGE (0223) 65629	Cambridge (adjacent)
Kentwell Hall Long Melford, SUFFOLK	Alpheton 3m
Rutland Water Cycle Hire	Thurlby
Terry Wright Cycles 2 Horsegate Deeping St James LINCOLNSHIRE	Thurlby
North Norfolk Railway SHERINGHAM	
Wetlands Wildlife Reserve Near Retford NOTTINGHAMSHIRE (0777) 818099	Lincoln Matlock

MIDLANDS

ATTRACTION	NEAREST YOUTH HOSTEL
Avoncraft Museum of Buildings Stoke Heath Bromsgrove, WORCS	Stratford-upon-Avon 20m Malvern Hills 20m
Broughton Castle Banbury, OXFORDSHIRE (0295) 2624	Stratford-upon-Avon 18m
Shropshire Country World Yockleton, SHREWSBURY	Shrewsbury 7m
Corinium Museum Park Street, Cirencester GLOS GL7 2BX	Duntisbourne Abbots 5m
Cosford Aerospace Museum Cosford, Wolverhampton WEST MIDLANDS WV7 3EX	Ironbridge 15m

ATTRACTION	NEAREST YOUTH HOSTE
Cotswold Farm Park **Rare Breeds Survival Centre** Guiting Power, Cheltenham, GLOS	Cleeve Hill 8m
The Falconry Centre Newent, GLOUCESTERSHIRE	Welsh Bicknor 13m
Guisborough Grange Wildlife Park Haddon Road, Guisborough NORTHAMPTONSHIRE	Badby 10m
Ironbridge Gorge Museums Ironbridge, Telford SHROPSHIRE TF8 7AW	Ironbridge 2m
Kingston Bagpuize House and Gardens Near Abingdon, OXFORDSHIRE (0865) 820259	Oxford 10m
Midland Motor Museum Stanmore Hall, Stourbridge Road Bridgnorth, SHROPSHIRE	Wilderhope 12m
Brass Rubbing Gallery University Church of St Mary the Virgin High Street, OXFORD	Oxford 1m
The Pack Age Revisited **The Robert Opie Collection** Albert Warehouse Gloucester Docks GLOUCESTERSHIRE	Slimbridge 13m
Painswick Rococo Garden Painswick, GLOUCESTERSHIRE	Duntisbourne Abbots 8m
Shipton Hall Much Wenlock, SHROPSHIRE	Wilderhope Manor 7m
Slimbridge Wildfowl Trust Slimbridge GLOUCESTERSHIRE GL2 7BT	Slimbridge 1m
Sudeley Castle Winchcombe, Cheltenham GLOUCESTERSHIRE GL54 4JD (0242) 602308	Cleeve Hill 4m
Stratford Brass Rubbing Centre The Summerhouse Avonbank Gardens Stratford-upon-Avon WARWICKSHIRE	Stratford-upon-Avon 2m
YHA Adventure Shop 90-98 Corporation Street (Bull Street Subway), BIRMINGHAM (021) 236 7799	
YHA Adventure Shop 6-7 Bridge Street, CAMBRIDGE (0223) 353956	
YHA Adventure Shop 9-10 St Clements (The Plain) OXFORD (0865) 247948	
YHA Adventure Shop 133 High Street, STAINES (0784) 452987	

WALES REGION

CHESTER AREA

Arley Hall and Gardens — Chester 18m
Near Northwich
CHESHIRE, CW9 6NA
(056585) 353

Sithells Boats — Chester ½m
The Groves, Chester

Boat Museum — Chester 8m
(National Waterways Museum)
Dockyard Road, Ellesmere Port
(051355) 5017

Gateway Theatre — Chester 1m
Hamilton Place, Chester

Toy Museum — Chester
3A Lower Bridge Street
The Rows, CHESTER

Grange Cavern — Chester 16m
Military Museum — Maeshafn 16m
Holywell (off A55) — Colwyn Bay 18m

YHA Adventure Shop
5 Bold Street, LIVERPOOL
(051) 709 8063

YHA Adventure Shop
166 Deansgate, MANCHESTER
(061) 834 7119

CONWY AREA

Aberconwy House (NT) — Penmaenmawr 3m
Castle Street/High Street — Colwyn Bay 4m
Conwy — Rowen 5m

Bodnant Garden (NT) — Rowen 4m
Tal-y-Cafn (A470) — Colwyn Bay 8m

The Conwy Butterfly House — Penmaenmawr 2½m
Bodlondeb Park, Conwy — Colwyn Bay 4½m
(0492) 593149 — Rowen 5m

Harlequin Marionette Theatre — Colwyn Bay
Rhos-on-Sea — Rowen 9m

Plas Mawr (Royal Cambrian — Penmaenmawr 3m
Academy of Art) — Colwyn Bay 4m
High Street, Conwy — Rowen 5m

River Cruises — Penmaenmawr 3m
Conwy Bay — Colwyn Bay 4m
— Rowen 5m

Trefriw Wells Roman Spa — Rowen 2½m
Trefriw, Gwynedd LL27 0JS — Penmaenmawr 10m
(0492) 640057 — Colwyn Bay 13m

Welsh Mountain Zoo — Colwyn Bay 2m
Colwyn Bay

West End Cycles — Colwyn Bay 1m
Conwy Road, Colwyn Bay — Rowen 8m

West End Cycles — Penmaenmawr 7m
Augusta Street, Llandudno — Rowen 9m

BANGOR AREA

Arvon's Mountaineering Stores — Bangor 4m
Camping and Sports Equipment — Idwal Cottage 4m
Bogwen Terrace, Bethesda

Anglesey Sea Zoo — Bangor 7m
Brynsiencyn — Llanberis 16m
ANGLESEY, (off A4080)

Crosville Wales Ltd — Express services:
Imperial Buildings — 700 Cardiff-Brecon-
Llandudno Junction — Newtown-Dolgellau-
GWYNEDD — Rhyl
(0492) 85115 — 701 Cardiff-Swansea-
— Aberystwyth-Dolgellau-
— Bangor
— 708 Aberystwyth-
— Chester-Manchester
— 709 Pwllheli-Chester-
— Liverpool

Museum of Childhood — Bangor 7m
1 Castle Street — Llanberis 12m
Beaumaris, ANGLESEY

Museum of Welsh Antiquities — Bangor 1m
University College — Idwal Cottage 10m
Ffordd Gwynedd, Bangor — Llanberis 10m

Penrhyn Castle (NT) — Bangor 1½m
Llandegai — Idwal Cottage 7m
Bangor (A5122)

Plas Newydd (NT) — Bangor 5m
Llanfairpwll — Llanberis 14m
ANGLESEY (A4080)

Theatr Gwynedd — Bangor 1m
Bangor — Idwal Cottage 10m
(0248) 351707 — Llanberis 10m

SNOWDONIA

Bryn Bras Castle — Llanberis 4m
Llanrug — Pen-y-Pass 9m
Near Caernarfon, (off A4086)

Ffestiniog Power Station — Ffestiniog 4m
(Hydro-Electric Pumped — Lledr Valley 6m
Storage Scheme) — Llanbedr 20m
Tan-y-Grisiau, (off A496)

Gwydir Castle — Lledr Valley 5m
Llanrwst — Rowen 8m
(B5106) — Capel Curig 9m

Llechwedd Slate Caverns — Ffestiniog 4m
Blaenau Ffestiniog (A470) — Lledr Valley 6m

Sygun Copper Mine — Bryn Gwynant 3m
near Beddgelert — Snowdon Ranger 6m
(A498) — Pen-y-Pass 7m

Ty Mawr (NT) — Lledr Valley 3m
Penmachno — Capel Curig 7m
Betwys-y-Coed

CAMBRIAN COAST

Centre for Alternative — Borth 17m
Technology — Kings 18m
Llwynygwern Quarry — Corris 3m
Machynlleth, POWYS
(0654) 2400

Joyrides Cycles — Corris 6m
(Cycle Hire & Shop) — Borth 14m
Yr Hen Orsaf, Machynlleth
Powys SY20 8TN
(0654) 3109

Llanfair Slate Caverns
Harlech (off A496)

Llanbedr 2m

Portmeirion Village
Minffordd
Penrhyndeudraeth (A487)

Ffestiniog 7m
Llanbedr 12½m

Plas Yn Rhiw (NT)
Near Aberdaron
(Lleyn Peninsula)

Bryn Gwynant 36m
Snowdon Ranger 37m
Llanbedr 37m

Rheidol Power Station
(Hydro-Electric Scheme)
Capel Bangor
Near Aberystwyth (off A44)

Borth 6m
Ystumtuen 9m
Corris 23m

Welsh Highland Railway
Porthmadog (A487)

Ffestiniog 10m
Bryn Gwynant 12m
Llanbedr 13m

DEE VALLEY

Bala Lake Railway
Llanuwchllyn (B4403)

Bala 1m
Cynwyd 12m

Chirk Castle (NT)
½m W of Chirk (off A5)

Llangollen 5m

Chwarel Wynne
Wynne Slate Mine
Glyn Ceiriog
Near Llangollen, (B4500)

Llangollen 4m
Cynwyd 16m

Erddig House (NT)
Near Wrexham (off A525)

Llangollen 11m
Maeshafn 12m

Llangollen Motor Museum
Pentrefelin
Near Llangollen (A542)

Llangollen 2m
Cynwyd 10m

Powis Castle (NT)
Near Welshpool (A483)

Llangollen 30m
Bala 30m

SOUTH WALES

Aberdulais Falls
Aberdulais
Neath, WEST GLAMORGAN
SA10 8EU
(0639) 636674

Llanddeusant 26m
Ystradfellte 13m

Cardigan Wildlife Park
Gilgerran
Cardigan, DYFED
(0239) 614449

Poppit Sands 6m

Dean Heritage Centre
Soudley, Cinderford
GLOUCESTERSHIRE
GL14 7UG
(0594) 22170

Welsh Bicknor 6m
St Briavels 11m

Dolrhanog Isaf Cilgwyn
Trefdraeth (Newport)
Pembrokeshire
DYFED, West Wales
(0239) 820432

Poppit Sands 15m
Pwll Deri 14m

Devils Bridge Falls
& Nature Trail
The Woodlands, Devils Bridge
Aberystwyth
DYFED, SY23 3JW
(097085) 233

Borth 20m
Ystumtuen 2m

Dolaucothi Goldmines
Near Pumpsaint
Llanwrda, DYFED, SA19 8RR
(05585) 359 or 605

Tyncornel 18m
Bryn Poeth Uchaf 13m

Gwili Railway
Bronwydd Arms
Near Carmarthen, DYFED
(0267) 230666

Pentlepoir 35m
Manorbier 43m

Gwent Rural Life Museum
The Malt Barn, Usk, GWENT
(02913) 3777

Chepstow 13m
St Briavels 20m
Monmouth 15m

Margam Country Park
Port Talbot
WEST GLAMORGAN SA13 2TJ
(0639) 881635

Llwynypia 21m
Port Eynon 23m
Cardiff 24m

Penhow Castle
(Personal stereo for Castle tour)
Near Newport, GWENT
(0633) 400800

Chepstow 8m
St Briavels 18m
Monmouth 24m
Welsh Bicknor 26m

Penscynor Wildlife Park
Cilfrew, Neath, SA10 8LS
(0639) 642189

Llwynypia 24m
Ystradfellte 14m
Llanddeusant 22m

Teifi Valley Railway
Henllan, Llandysul, DYFED
(0559) 371077

Poppit Sands 17m

Tredegar House and
Country Park
Newport, GWENT, NP1 9YW
(0633) 815880

Chepstow 18m
Cardiff 12m
Llwynypia 25m

Tudor Merchants House
Quay Hill, Tenby, DYFED
(0834) 2279

Manorbier 8m
Pentlepoir 5m

YHA Adventure Shop
13 Castle Street, CARDIFF
(0222) 399178

LONDON REGION

Streets of London
(Guided walking tours)
32 Grovelands Road
LONDON, N13 4RH
(071) 882 3414

London Hostels

YHA Adventure Shop
174 Kensington High St, LONDON
(071) 938 2948

YHA Adventure Shop
14 Southampton Street
Covent Garden, LONDON
(071) 836 8541

SOUTH OF ENGLAND REGION

SOUTHERN

West Dean Gardens
West Dean Estate, Near Chichester
WEST SUSSEX PO18 9QX
(024362) 301

Arundel 15m

YHA Adventure Shop
126-127 Queens Road, BRIGHTON
(0273) 821554

WESSEX

Cricket St Thomas Wildlife Park — Bridport 14m
Cricket St Thomas, SOMERSET — Beer 17m
(046030) 755

Combe Sydenham — Exford 14m
Country Park — Crowcombe
Monksilver, Taunton — Heathfield 7m
SOMERSET — Minehead 8m
(0984) 56284/56364 — Holford 10m

Devizes Museum — Bath 20m
41 Long Street, Devizes — Salisbury 24m
WILTSHIRE SN10 1NS
(0380) 2765

Heavy Horse Centre — Cranborne 2m
Brambles Farm, Edmonsham
Cranborne, DORSET

Poundisford Park — Crowcombe
Poundisford — Heathfield 13m
Taunton, SOMERSET, TA3 7AF — Street 22m
(082342) 244 — Holford 22m

Salisbury and South — Cranborne 14m
Wiltshire Museum — Salisbury ½m
The Kings House, 65 The Close
Salisbury, WILTSHIRE
(0722) 332151

Sealife Centre — Litton Cheney 13m
Greenhill, Weymouth — Lulworth Cove 14m
DORSET DT4 7SX — Swanage 29m
(0305) 788255

The Tropical Bird Gardens — Bath 10m
Rode, Bath, AVON — Bristol 20m
(0373) 830326 — Salisbury 29m

Wessexplore Evening Walks
Salisbury (2030 from TIC)
(0722) 26304

YHA Adventure Shop
0-12 Fairfax Street, BRISTOL
(0272) 297141

SOUTH WEST

Bickleigh Mill Craft Centre — Exeter 13m
and Farm — Steps Bridge 19m
Near Tiverton, DEVON EX16 8RG — Exford 26m
(08845) 419

Buckfast Abbey — Dartington 5m
Buckfastleigh — Bellever 10m
DEVON — Maypool (Torbay) 14m

Buckfast Butterfly Centre — Dartington 5m
Buckfastleigh, DEVON — Bellever 10m
(0364) 42916 — Maypool (Torbay) 14m

Carnglaze Slate Caverns — Golant 15m
St Neots, Liskeard, CORNWALL — Plymouth 21m
(0579) 20251

Coverack Windsurfing School — Coverack
Coverack — Pendennis Castle 20m
Helston, CORNWALL

Dartmoor Wildlife Park — Plymouth 9m
Sparkwell — Dartington 17m
Near Plymouth, DEVON
(075537) 209

Exeter Maritime Museum — Exeter 2m
The Quay, Exeter — Steps Bridge 8m
DEVON EX2 4AN
(0392) 58075

Falmouth Maritime Museum — Pendennis Castle 1m
Custom House Quay — Coverack 18m
Falmouth, CORNWALL — Boswinger 21m
(0326) 318107
ALSO AT:
Bells Court, off Market Street — Pendennis Castle
Falmouth, CORNWALL
(0326) 250507

Dobwalls Theme Park — Golant 15m
Dobwalls, Liskeard, CORNWALL — Plymouth 20m
(0579) 20325/21129

Geevor Tin Mine — Penzance 6m
Pendeen, Penzance — Lands End 4m
CORNWALL TR19 7EW — Coverack 31m

H. Martin Fishing Trips/ — Coverack
Boat Trips — Pendennis Castle 20m
Coverack Harbour
Coverack, CORNWALL
(0326) 280545

Lands End — Lands End 5m
CORNWALL — Penzance 9m

National Shire Horse Centre — Plymouth 8m
Dunstone, Yealmpton — Salcombe 16m
Plymouth, DEVON
(0752) 880268

Otterton Mill Museum — Exeter 10m
and Crafts — Beer 12m
Otterton, Near Budleigh
Salterton, DEVON

Paradise Park — Penzance 9m
Hayle, CORNWALL — Lands End 15m
(0736) 753365 — Pendennis Castle 20m

Parke Rare Breeds Farm — Steps Bridge 11m
Parke Estate, Bovey Tracey — Bellever 12m
DEVON TQ13 9JQ — Dartington 15m
(0626) 833909 — Exeter 15m

Poldark Mine & Heritage Centre — Pendennis Castle 11m
Wendron, Helston, CORNWALL — Coverack 12m
(0326) 573173 — Penzance 17m

G H Riddals and Sons — Maypool 4m
Pleasure Boat Proprietors
44 Above Town
Dartmouth
DEVON TQ6 9AG
(08043) 2109

St Agnes Leisure Park — Perranporth 4m
and World in Miniature — Newquay 7m
Duchy Parklands, St Agnes — Pendennis Castle 15m
CORNWALL
(087255) 2793

Sand Historic House — Beer 9m
Sidbury, Sidmouth — Exeter 14m
DEVON EX10 0QN

YHA ENROLMENT CENTRES

Please remember that those individual YHA members who offer a voluntary enrolment service are likely to be available only outside office hours. In addition to these Enrolment Centres, all Offices and most Local Groups can issue membership. Membership can also be taken out at a Hostel if you are staying there.

AVON

Bath University Student Travel
The Foyer 3W, Claverton Down, Bath, BA2 7AY.
Tel: (0225) 464263

Bristol Poly Travel Shop
Coldharbour Lane, Frenchay, Bristol, BS16 1QY.
Tel: (0272) 6561 Ext: 2578

Frank Martin
20 Cornwallis Avenue, Clifton, Bristol, BS8 4PP.
Tel: (0272) 292350 ☆ ◇

University of Bristol Union Travel Bureau
Queen's Road, Bristol, BS8 1LN.
Tel: (0272) 741178

BEDFORDSHIRE

Bedford Tourist Information Centre
10 St Paul's Square, Bedford, MK40 1SL.
Tel: (0234) 214344

BERKSHIRE

Mr Hedley Alcock
29 Lowther Road, Wokingham. Tel: (0734) 793904 ☆ ◇

Mrs J. Briggs
34 Scrivens Mead, Thatcham. Tel: (0635) 66616 ☆ ◇

R.U.S.U. Travel
Reading University Students Union, Whiteknights, Reading,
RG6 2AZ. Tel: (0734) 868030

BUCKINGHAMSHIRE

High Wycombe Tourist Information Centre
6 The Cornmarket. Tel: (0494) 461892

CAMBRIDGESHIRE

Oundle Tourist Information Centre
Market Hall, Market Place, Oundle, Nr Peterborough,
PE8 4BA. Tel: (0832) 274333

Campus Travel
5 Emmanuel Street, Cambridge, CB1 1NE.
Tel: (0223) 324283

CHESHIRE

Altrincham Tourist Information Centre
Stamford New Road, Altrincham, WA14 1EJ.
Tel: 061-941 7337

Chester Tourist Information Centre
Town Hall, Northgate Street, Chester, CH1 2HF.
Tel: (0244) 313126

Chester Visitors Centre
Vicars Lane, Chester, CH1 1QX. Tel: (0224) 351609

Helen Race
21 Empress Road, Stockport, SK4 2RW. Tel: 061-442 9998 ☆ ◇

Warrington Information Centre
21 Rylands Street, Warrington, WA1 1EJ. Tel: (0925) 36501

CLEVELAND

Mr D. Hartley
14 Auckland Street, Guisborough, TS14 6HT.
Tel: (0287) 635831 ☆ ◇

Hartlepool Tourist Information Centre
Leisure Services Department, Civic Centre, Hartlepool,
Cleveland, TS24 8AY. Tel: (0429) 266522

Middlesborough Tourist Information Centre
51 Corporation Road, Middlesborough, Cleveland, TS1 1LT.
Tel: (0642) 243425

Stockton on Tees Tourist Information Centre
Theatre Yard, Off High Street, TS18 1AT.
Tel: (0642) 615080

CUMBRIA

Barrow-in-Furness Tourist Information Centre
Town Hall, Duke Street, Barrow-in-Furness, Cumbria,
LA14 2LD. Tel: (0229) 870156

Carlisle Visitor Centre
The Old Town Hall, Carlisle, CA3 8JH. Tel: (0228) 512444

CO DURHAM

Peterlee Town and Tourist Information Centre
20 The Upper Chare, Peterlee, SR8 5TE.
Tel: 091-586 4450

Mr Alistair Taylor
Durham Unversity Local Group, College of St Hilda and
St Bede, The University, Durham.

DERBYSHIRE

Derby Local Group
c/o The Dolphin Inn, Queen Street, Derby.
(Enrolment facilities available alternate Tuesdays only)

Peacock Information Centre
Low Pavement, Chesterfield, S40 1PB. Tel: (0246) 207777

DEVON

Exeter University Guild of Students
Devonshire House, Stocker Road, Exeter, EX4 4PZ.
Tel: (0392) 263528

Mid Devon Tourist Information Association
Tiverton Tourist Information Centre, Phoenix Lane,
Tiverton, EX16 6LU. Tel: (0884) 255827

The Travel Centre
Polytechnic South West, Students Union, Drake Circus,
Plymouth, PL4 8AA. Tel: (0752) 663337

DORSET

S.E. Dorset Local Group
3 Tree Hamlets, Border Road, Poole. Tel: (0202) 624704 ☆

DYFED

Aberystwyth Student Travel
Students Union, Penglais, Aberystwyth, SY23 3DX.
Tel: (0970) 624758/624242

ESSEX

Mr Ian McHardy
4 Woodbine Close, Linford End, Harlow, CM19 4PA.
Tel: (0279) 443004 ☆ ◇

Colchester Tourist Information Centre
1 Queen Street, CO1 2PJ. Tel: (0206) 46379

Essex Tourist Information Centre
County Hall, Market Road, Chelmsford, CM1 1GG.
Tel: (0245) 283400

Harwich Tourist Information
Parkeston Quay, Harwich, CO12 4SP. Tel: (0255) 506139

Southend on Sea Tourist Information Centre
High Street Precinct, SS1 1DZ. Tel: (0702) 355120

Swallow Cycles
Stannetts, Laindon North Trade Centre, SS15 6DJ.
Tel: (0268) 41655

GLAMORGAN

Cardiff Student Travel
Student Union, Park Place, Cardiff, CF13 QN.
Tel: (0222) 382350

High Adventure
5 Wind Street, Swansea, SA1 1DF. Tel: (0792) 648712

GLOUCESTERSHIRE

Tewkesbury Tourist Information Centre
64 Barton Street, Tewkesbury, GL20 5PX.
Tel: (0684) 295027

GREATER MANCHESTER

Campus Travel
Manchester Polytechnic, Students Union, Mandela Building,
99 Oxford Road, Manchester. Tel: 061-273 1721

Manutech Travel Services
U.M.I.S.T. Student Union, Sackville Street, Manchester,
M60 1QD. Tel: 061-236 1382

GWYNEDD

Conway Visitors Centre
Rosehill Street, Conway, LL32 8LD. Tel: (0492) 596288

Student Travel Office
Students Union, U.C.N.W., Deiniol Road, Bangor, LLS7 2TH.
Tel: (0248) 364568

HAMPSHIRE

Basingstoke Tourist Information Centre
Willis Museum, Old Town Hall, Market Place, Basingstoke,
RG21 1QD. Tel: (0256) 817618

Fareham Tourist Information Centre
Fareham Museum, Westbury Manor, West Street, Fareham,
PO16 7DB. Tel: (0329) 221342

Farnborough and Camberley Local Group
130 Beta Road, Farnborough, Hampshire, GU14 8PH.
Tel: (0252) 543444

Fleet Tourist Information Centre
Gurkha Square, Fleet Road, GU13 8BX. Tel: (0252) 811151

Petersfield Tourist Information Centre
County Library, 27 The Square, Petersfield, GU32 3HH.
Tel: (0730) 68829

Southampton Tourist Information Centre
Above Bar Precinct, SO9 4XF. Tel: (0703) 221106

Southampton University Travel Centre
University Road, Highfield, SO9 5NH. Tel: (0703) 553533

Student and Youth Travel Centre PPSU
Alexandra House, Museum Road, Portsmouth, PO1 2QH.
Tel: (0705) 816645

HERTFORDSHIRE

Hatfield Polytechnic Students Union
Travel Office, College Lane, P.O. Box 109, Hatfield, AL10 9AB.
Tel: (0707) 272203

HUMBERSIDE

Hull Tourist Information Centres
1) Central Library, Albion Street, Hull, HU1 3TF.
   Tel: (0482) 223344
2) 75/76 Carr Lane, Hull. Tel: (0482) 223559

Hull University Union Travel
The University, Hull, HU6 7RX. Tel: (0482) 43608

Mr Brian Witty
8 Pickering Road, Kingston upon Hull, HU4 6TL.
Tel: (0482) 572712 ☆

Hull District Group
1) Mr G. Bolton, 99 Belvoir Street, Hull, HU5 3LP.
   Tel: (0482) 445009
2) Membership Secretary, 17 Mollison Road, Hull, HU4 7HB.
   Tel: (0482) 644356 ☆
3) YHA Clubroom, North Hull Community Centre,
   37th Avenue, Hull. (Wednesdays 8pm to 10pm only)

C. Hursey
6 Kedlington Road, Howden, Nr Goole, DN14 7DG.
Tel: (0430) 431631 (eve), (0430) 430904 (day)

KENT

Dover Tourist Information Centre
Townwall Street, Dover, CT16 1JR. Tel: (0304) 205108

June Jordan
Berwyn Kits Coty, Aylesford, Maidstone. Tel: (0634) 861348

Derek Baker
9 Pine Ridge, Tonbridge. Tel: (0732) 353246 ☆ ◇

Tonbridge Castle Tourist Information Centre
Castle Street, Tonbridge, Kent, TN9 1BG.
Tel: (0732) 770929

LANCASHIRE

Blackburn and District CTC
1 School Cottages, Bashall Eaves, Clitheroe, BB7 3DA.

Burnley Tourist Information Centre
Burnley Mechanics, Manchester Road. Tel: (0282) 30055

Kendal Local Group
24 Holme Mills, Holme, Via Carnforth, LA6 1RD.
Tel: (0524) 781806

Fylde Local Group
4 Holly Road, Thornton, Cleveleys, Lancs, FY5 4HH.
Tel: (0253) 866085 ☆ ◇

Preston Tourist Information Centre
At Leisure Shop, Guildhall, Lancaster Road, PR1 1HT.
Tel: (0772) 53731

Saddleworth Tourist Information Centre
Saddleworth Museum, High Street, Uppermill, Oldham,
OL3 6HS. Tel: (0457) 874093/870336

Salford University Travel Bureau
University House, The Crescent, Salford, M5 4WT.
Tel: 061-736 7811 Ext: 232

Uni-Travel
Alexandra Square, University of Lancaster, Lancaster,
LA1 4YW. Tel: (0524) 37675

Voyager
B.I.H.E., Deane Road, Bolton, BL3 5AB. Tel: (0204) 386650

Wigan Tourist Information Centre
Trencherfield Mill, Wigan Pier, Wigan, WN3 4EL.
Tel: (0942) 825677

LEICESTERSHIRE

Copt Oak Local Group
38 Nottingham Road, Barrow Upon Soar, Loughborough.
Tel: (0509) 413901 ☆

Polytech Travel
Leicester Polytechnic Students Union, 4 Newarke Close,
Leicester, LE2 7BJ. Tel: (0533) 555576

Leicester City Tourism & Information
2-6 St Martin's Walk, St Martin's Square, Leicester, LE1 5DG.
Tel: (0553) 511300

L.U.S.U. Travel
University, Leicester, LE1 7RH. Tel: (0533) 556282

LINCOLNSHIRE

Mr Andrew Widd
Orchard Cottage, Worthington Lane, Woolsthorpe by
Belvoir, Grantham, NG32 1LY. Tel: (0476) 870381 ☆ ◇

LONDON

Ealing Local Group
St Matthews Church Hall, North Common Road, Ealing, W5.
Tel: 081-992 8923
(Enrolment facilities available 8pm - 10pm Tuesdays only)

Ian McElvenney
18 Ansell Road, Tooting, London, SW17 7LS.
Tel: 081-672 3990 ☆ ◇

Harrow and Wembley Local Group
Perrin Road Junior School, Perrin Road, Sudbury Town.
Tel: none

MERSEYSIDE

Merseyside Welcome Centre
Clayton Square, Liverpool. Tel: 051-709 3631

Campus Travel
Haigh Building, Maryland Street, Liverpool, L1 9DE.
Tel: 051-709 2474

Campus Travel
Students Union Building, Liverpool University, 2 Bedford
Street North, Liverpool, L7 7BD. Tel: 051-708 0721

Southport Tourist Information Centre
112 Lord Street, Southport, PR8 1NY. Tel: none

MIDDLESEX

Graham Lee
54a Brixham Crescent, Ruislip Manor, HA4 8TX.
Tel: (0895) 673188

NORFOLK

Mr Chris Merry
50 Lindley Close, Old Catton, Norwich, NR6 7LL.
Tel: (0603) 788346 ☆

Tourist Information Centre
Guildhall, Gaol Hill, Norwich, NR2 1NF. Tel: (0603) 666071

NORTHAMPTONSHIRE

Northampton Tourist Information Centre
21 St Giles Street, NN1 1JA. Tel: (0604) 22677

NORTHUMBERLAND

Morpeth Tourist Office
The Chantry, Bridge Street, Morpeth, NE61 1PJ.
Tel: (0670) 511323

NOTTINGHAMSHIRE

Pioneer Travel
University Park, Nottingham. Tel: (0602) 502975/586096

Trent Union Travel
Byron House, Shakespeare Street, Nottingham.
Tel: (0602) 411018

OXFORDSHIRE

Campus Travel
13 High Street, Oxford, OX1 4DB. Tel: (0865) 242067

SHROPSHIRE

Shrewsbury Tourist Information Centre
The Square, SY1 1LH. Tel: (0743) 50762

Mr N. Montgomery
67 Watling Street, Church Stretton, SY6 7BQ.
Tel: (0694) 722536 ☆ ◇

STAFFORDSHIRE

Keele Travel Bureau
Students Union, Keele University, Newcastle under Lyme.
Tel: (0782) 622069

Leek Tourist Information Centre
1 Market Place, Leek, ST13 5HH. Tel: (0538) 381000

Student Travel
Staffordshire Polytechnic, Students Union, College Road,
Stoke on Trent, ST4 2DE. Tel: (0782) 413674

Mr Nick Rutter
Heath View, Cannock Road, Heath Hayes, Cannock,
WS12 5HS. Tel: (0534) 74314

Stafford Local Group
Room 1, Trinity Church, Broad Street, Stafford. Tel: none
Alternate Wednesdays 8pm - 9.30pm)

Bury St Edmunds Tourist Information Centre
Atheneum, 6 Angel Hill, Bury St Edmunds, IP33 1U2.
Tel: (0284) 763233

Ipswich Tourist Information Centre
Town Hall, Princes Street, IP1 1BZ. Tel: none

John Annett
3 The Ridgeway, Croydon, CR0 4AD. Tel: 081-688 5051

Knights Park Travel
Kingston Polytechnic, Grange Road, Kingston, KT1 2Q3.
Tel: 081-546 6972

Surrey Student Travel
Union House, Surrey University, Guildford, GU2 5XH.
Tel: (0483) 509224

Chichester Tourist Information Centre
West Street, Chichester, PO19 1AH. Tel: (0243) 775888

South Coast Student Travel
1 Ditchling Road, Brighton, BN1 4SD. Tel: (0273) 570226

Sussex Student Travel
University of Sussex, Falmer House, Brighton, BN1 9QF.
Tel: (0273) 604134

Gateshead Tourist Information Centre
'Portcullis', 74 Russell Way, Metrocentre.
Tel: 091-460 6345

Morpeth Tourist Information Centre
The Chantry, Bridge Street, Northumberland, NE61 1PJ.
Tel: (0670) 511323

Newcastle City and Tourist Information Services
1) Central Library, Princess Square, Newcastle upon Tyne,
NE99 1DX. Tel: 091-261 0691
2) Main Concourse, Central Station, Neville Street,
Newcastle upon Tyne, NE1 5DL. Tel: 091-230 0030

Campus Travel
Student Union Building, Newcastle University, Kings Walk,
Newcastle upon Tyne. Tel: 091-232 1798/232 2881

Student Travel Office
Sunderland Polytechnic, Wearmouth Hall, Chester Road,
Sunderland, SR1 3SD. Tel: 091-565 7810

Warwick Travel
Union Building, University of Warwick, Coventry, CV4 7AL.
Tel: (0203) 523677

Warwick Travel
Students' Union, Coventry Polytechnic, Priory Street,
Coventry, CV1 5FB. Tel: (0203) 228263

Campus Travel
Bristol Road, Selly Oak, Birmingham, B29 6AU.
Tel: 021-414 1848

Campus Travel
Birmingham Polytechnic, Students Union, Franchise Street,
Perry Barr, Birmingham, B42 2SU. Tel: 021-344 4442

**Wolverhampton Polytechnic Students' Union
Travel Shop**
1 Wolfruna Street, Wolverhampton WV1 1LY.
Tel: (0902) 23863

University of Bradford Union Travel
Communal Building, Longside Lane, Bradford, 7.
Tel: (0274) 392404

Mr K. Lightowle
1 Rydal Avenue, Higher Coach Road, Baildon, W. Yorks,
BD17 5SD. Tel: (0274) 595074 ☆ ◇

Mr Jon Crowther
Halifax and District Local Group, 15 Lindrick Way, Bradshaw,
Halifax, W. Yorks, HX2 9QG. Tel: (0422) 247202 ☆ ◇

Progress Travel
Linden Mill, Linden Road, Hebden Bridge, W. Yorks,
HX7 7DN. Tel: (0422) 844028

Huddersfield Tourist Information Centre
3-5 Albion Street, HD1 2HW. Tel: (0484) 430808

H.P.U. Travel
Huddersfield Polytechnic Students Union, Queensgate,
Huddersfield, HD1 3D4. Tel: (0484) 538156

University of Leeds Travel Company
Union Buildings, P.O. Box 157, Leeds, LS1 1UH.
Tel: (0532) 448877/8/9

Leeds YHA Local Group
6 Westbourne Avenue, Garforth, Leeds, LS25 1BU.
Tel: (0532) 865155 ☆

Campus Travel
Nelson Mandela Building, Pond Street, Sheffield, S1 2BW.
Tel: (0742) 758366

Geo Supplies Ltd
16 Station Road, Chapeltown, Sheffield, S30 4XH.
Tel: (0742) 455746

S.U.S.U. Travel
Sheffield University Students' Union, Western Bank,
Sheffield, S10 2TG. Tel: (0742) 730733

Sheffield Tourist Information Centre
Town Hall Extension, Union Street, Sheffield, S1 2H4.
Tel: (0742) 734671

☆ PLEASE TELEPHONE IN ADVANCE.
◇ INDIVIDUAL YHA MEMBERS WHO OFFER VOLUNTARY ENROLMENT
SERVICE USUALLY AVAILABLE ONLY OUTSIDE OFFICE HOURS.

Andover and District
Julie Taylor, 22 Conholt Road, Andover, Hants, SP10 2HR.
Tel: (0264) 52962

Aylesbury and District
Sandra Macdonald, 49 Stratton Road, Princes Risborough,
Bucks. Tel: (08444) 4721

Barnet
Jane Lauder, 20 Sutherland Close, Barnet, Herts, EN5 2JL.
Tel: 081-449 1553

Barrow and South Lakeland
Gillian Lawson, 60 Victoria Road, Barrow-in-Furness,
Cumbria. Tel: (0229) 824097

Birmingham (North)
Louise Brealey, 76 Lavendon Road, Great Barr, Birmingham,
B42 1QG. Tel: 021-356 5223

Blackburn and District
Carina Wilson, 45 Eldon Road, Blackburn, Lancs, BB1 8BE.
Tel: (0254) 56565

Bolton
Ronald Ritchie, 82 New Drake Green, Westhoughton,
Bolton, BL5 2RF. Tel: (0942) 819412

Brighton
Tessa Clark, 124 Windmill Drive, Westdene, Brighton,
BN1 5HJ. Tel: (0273) 504453

Bristol
Geoff Parsons, Top Flat, 30 Studley Rise, Trowbridge, Wilts.
Tel: none

Bromley
Barbara Wells, 8 Downderry Road, Bromley, Kent.
Tel: 081-698 1453

Bucks/Berks Border
Jacqui Ward, 21 Stompits Road, Holyport, Maidenhead,
Berks, SL6 2LD. Tel: (0628) 782946

Cambridge and District
Tim Long, 35 Saffron Road, Histon, Cambridge, CB4 4LJ.
Tel: (0223) 237046

Canterbury
Alan Walkeden, 24 North Holmes Road, Canterbury, Kent.
Tel: (0227) 768959

Cardiff
Brian Dane, 15 Grove Park Drive, Malpas, Newport, NP9 6YZ.
Tel: (0633) 859122

Chelmsford
Colin Press, 1 Wash Road, Hutton, Brentwood, Essex,
CM13 1BS. Tel: (0277) 210429

Cheltenham and Gloucester
Roger Bailey, 29 Moorfield Road, Brockworth, Gloucester.
Tel: (0452) 863431

Chester
Rita Cothier, 18 Greystone Road, Chester.
Tel: (0244) 33694

Cornwall
Annette Hawkins, 19 Daniel Place, Penzance, TR18 4DU.
Tel: none

Coventry
Helen Bridges, 147 Holyhead Road, Coventry, CV1 3AD.
Tel: (0203) 630448

Crawley
Michael Heeley, 12 Osney Close, Southgate, Crawley,
West Sussex, RH11 8JW. Tel: (0293) 34362

Croydon
Philip Manning, 47A Friends Road, Croydon, Surrey,
CR0 1ED. Tel: 081-667 9585

Derby and District
Jane Pointon, 26 Overdale Road, Derby, DE3 6AT.
Tel: (0332) 766766

Doncaster
Patricia Tremain, 51 Cheriton Avenue, Adwick-le-Street,
Doncaster, DN6 7BU. Tel: (0302) 721347

Dorset, South East
Bob Hucklesby, Flat 6, Bracken Court, 16 Dean Park Road,
Bournemouth, BH1 1HX. Tel: (0202) 551401

Dunstable
Don Snoad, 2 Chiltern Road, Dunstable, Beds, LU6 1ER.
Tel: (0582) 601852

Durham, North
Mike Ellison, 5 North Crescent, North End, Durham.
Tel: 091-386 3746

Ealing and District
Sally Lovelock, 2 New Pond Cottages, Oxford Road,
Gerrards Cross, Bucks, SL9 7RL. Tel: (0753) 889365

Eastbourne
Fred Penfold, 28 Frenchgate Road, Hampden Park, East
Sussex, BN22 9ES. Tel: (0323) 504091

Eltham and Sidcup
Reg Hallett, 15 Cedar Avenue, Sidcup, Kent, DA15 8NL.
Tel: 081-302 7001

Essex Sailing Group
Eric Rolfe, 63 Sketty Road, Enfield, Middx, EN1 3SF.
Tel: 081-366 0968

Fylde
Frank Bilsborrow, 4 Holly Road, Thornton-Cleveleys,
Blackpool, Lancs, FY5 4HH. Tel: (0253) 866085

Grantham
Andrew Widd, Orchard Cottage, Worthington Lane,
Woolsthorpe-by-Belvoir, Grantham, Lincs. Tel: (0476) 870381

Guildford
Helen Brockis, 2 The Gardens, Marshall Road, Farncombe,
Surrey, GU7 3AU. Tel: (04868) 27218

Halifax
Jon Crowther, 15 Lindrick Way, Bradshaw, Halifax,
HX2 9QG. Tel: (0422) 247202

Harlow
Mike Haladij, 80 Canons Gate, Harlow, Essex, CM20 1QF.
Tel: (0279) 418164

Harrow & Wembley
Andrew Clarke, 46 Wedmore Road, Greenford, Middx.
Tel: 081-578 6637

Hornchurch
Gavin Roberts, 645 London Road, West Thurrock, Grays,
Essex, RM16 1HD. Tel: (0708) 867904

Hull District
Rachel Hartley, 197 Blenheim Street, Princes Avenue, Hull,
HU5 3PL. Tel: (0482) 491921

Ipswich
Pauline Jordan, 7 Burnham Close, Trimley, Ipswich, IP10 0XJ.
Tel: (0394) 278763

Kendal
Mike Daly, 61 Calder Drive, Kendal, Cumbria, LA9 7AE.
Tel: (0539) 732781

Kingston
Jacqui Cavanagh, 30 Colebrook Close, West Hill, Putney.
Tel: 081-788 3919

Lancaster and Morecambe
Bernadette Coyle, 7 Longlands Road, Vale, Lancaster.
Tel: none

Leeds
Tim Harvey, 17 Highfield Drive, Garforth, Leeds, LS25 1JY.
Tel: (0532) 863646

Leicester
Pete Coller, 3 St Helens Drive, Leicester, LE4 0GS.
Tel: (0533) 539162

Lincoln
Sue Jones, 50 Cotman Road, Lincoln LN6 7NU.
Tel: (0522) 689130

London (Central)
Jane Scoby-Smith, Flat 5, 6 Vanbrugh Park Road West,
London, SE3 7QD. Tel: 081-305 0522

London (South Bank)
Jean Amas, 14 Westfield Road, London, W13 9JR.
Tel: 081-567 6091

Luton
Ann Pennifold, 34 Ravenbank Road, Luton, Beds, LU2 8EJ.
Tel: (0582) 31886

Medway and Maidstone
Judi Bell, 4 Barn Meadow Cottages, Forge Lane, Boxley,
Maidstone, Kent, ME14 3DU. Tel: (0622) 683396

Newcastle
Gordon Hall, 161 Victoria Road West, Hebburn,
Tyne & Wear. Tel: 091-483 5967

Northampton
Jackie Fallon, 76 St Leonards Road, Northampton.
Tel: (0604) 705937

Norwich
Phyll Hardie, 24 Booty Road, Thorpe St Andrew, Norwich,
NR7 0NE. Tel: (0603) 35547

Notts Outdoor
Rob Baxter, 75 Central Avenue, New Basford, Nottingham,
NG7 7AG. Tel: (0602) 625015

Oxford
Martin Blackwell, 37 Hugh Allen Crescent, Marston, Oxford,
OX3 0HL. Tel: (0865) 723003

Portsmouth
Mark Gee, 42 Christopher Way, Emsworth, Hants,
PO10 7QZ. Tel: (0243) 378371

Postellers
Rosie Bland, Ravensdal, Rabley Heath, Welwyn, Herts.
Tel: (0438) 870222

Potteries
Nigel Lee, 93 Lockwood Street, Newcastle-under-Lyme,
Staffs. Tel: (0782) 616278

Preston
Alan Stirzaker, 24 Wellington Street, Preston, PR1 8TP.
Tel: (0772) 561824

Reading
Tom Stagles, 86 Cumberland Road, Reading, RG1 3JT.
Tel: (0734) 64753

Redhill & Reigate
Judith Bourne, 134 Croydon Road, Reigate, Surrey,
RH2 0NQ. Tel: (0737) 246074

St Albans
Shirley Welch, 32 High Firs Crescent, Harpenden, Herts.
AL5 1NA. Tel: (0582) 715451

Sale
Beryl Kuse, 14 Homewood Road, Northenden, Manchester.
Tel: 061-962 3826

Salisbury
Fenella Cohen, 33 Nursery Road, Salisbury, SP2 7HX.
Tel: (0722) 332933

Sheffield
John Woolston, 90 Park Grange Croft, Sheffield, S2 3QL.
Tel: (0742) 738498

South Middlesex (Hounslow)
Ann Field, 286 Ellerdine Road, Hounslow, Middx, TW3 2PY.
Tel: 081-568 7105

Stafford
Chris Moyle, 47 Tenbutts Crescent, Stafford, ST17 9HP.
Tel: (0785) 47600

Stockport
Pete Hudson, 32 Borrowdale Road, Heaviley, Stockport,
SK2 6DX. Tel: 061-487 2478

Sunderland
David Ritchie, 42 Weymouth Drive, Dalton Grange, Seaham,
Co Durham, SR7 8HG. Tel: 091-581 0490

Sutton
David Horton, 21 Summerfield, West Farm Avenue, Ashtead,
Surrey, KT21 2LF. Tel: none

Swansea and District
Chris Lewis, 25 Heol Fach, Treboeth, Swansea, SA5 9DQ.
Tel: (0792) 771614

Taunton and District
Frances Wade, 17 Clifford Terrace, Wellington, Somerset.
Tel: (0823) 663658

Telford and Shropshire
Bill Braiden, 1 Claverley Drive, Stirchley, Telford, TF3 1EU.
Tel: (0952) 598002

Wakefield
Jackie Richardson, 6 Shelley Walk, Stanley, Wakefield.
Tel: (0924) 829096

Walthamstow and Chingford
Marcus New, 22 Groveside Road, Chingford, London, E4 6HG.
Tel: 081-529 8756

Watford and District
Nicholas Coe, 44 Oak Green, Abbots Langley, Watford,
Herts, WD5 0PH. Tel: (0923) 260484

Wolverhampton
Erica Edwards, 24 Wynn Road, Wolverhampton,
West Midlands. Tel: (0902) 340809

Worcester
Anne Bendall, 11 Blakefield Walk, St Johns, Worcester,
WR2 5DW. Tel: (0905) 427974

York and District
Joanne Foster, 52 Horner Street, Burton Stone Lane, York.
Tel: (0904) 641444

UNIVERSITY GROUPS

Cambridge University
David Grainger, Magdalene College, Cambridge.
Tel: (0223) 333635 (work)

Cardiff University
Sarah Young, Flat J7, Room 3, Senghennydd House, PO Box
8, Cardiff, CF1 1UJ. Tel: none

Durham University
John Cloke, Hatfield College, Durham University, Durham.
Tel: none

Imperial College
Brian Dorricott, Imperial College Union, Prince Consort
Road, London, SW7 2BT. Tel: 071-589 5111 (ext. 3500)

London University
Liz Elliott, London University Students Union, Malet Street,
London, WC1. Tel: none

Loughborough University
Deborah McIntosh, Loughborough University Students
Union Building, Loughborough, Leics, LE11 3TT.
Tel: (0509) 217766 (work)

MAP OF YHA
LOCAL GROUPS IN
ENGLAND & WALES

KEY: ▲ Local Groups   ▼ University Groups

VOLUNTARY AREAS

Voluntary activities are organised on an area basis and Voluntary Areas are defined by the dotted lines on the map below. See page 17 for details of the YHA Democracy.

1 BORDER & DALES
2 YORKSHIRE
3 EAST OF ENGLAND
4 SOUTH OF ENGLAND 7
5 SOUTH OF ENGLAND 6
6 SOUTH OF ENGLAND 5
7 SOUTH OF ENGLAND 4
8 SOUTH OF ENGLAND 3
9 SOUTH OF ENGLAND 2
10 SOUTH OF ENGLAND 1
11 MIDLAND
12 SOUTH WALES
13 NORTH WALES
14 PEAK
15 LAKELAND

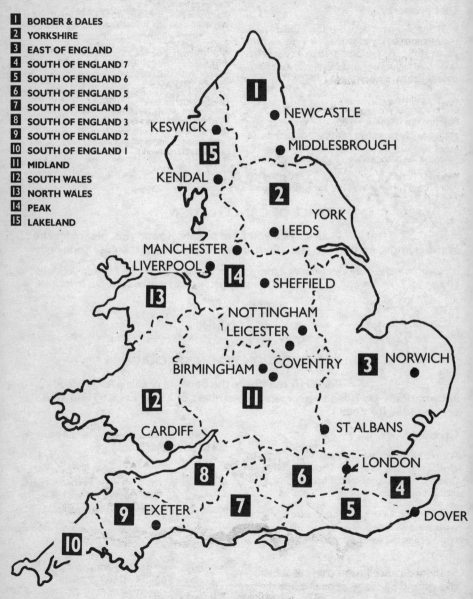

YOU AND YOUR BELONGINGS

Please remember that you are responsible for insuring yourself and all your property when you go on holiday in Britain or abroad. Keep valuable items such as money, jewellery and cameras with you.

Lost property

Anything you leave behind at the Youth Hostel will be returned if you send the Warden brown paper, string and sufficient stamps. For articles likely to weigh over 1 kg (2.2 lb) please send enough for parcel postage.

Notice

Neither the Association nor its employees accept any responsibility arising from any cause whatever for loss of or damage to property left anywhere on any premises owned, occupied or maintained whether temporarily or permanently by the Association, or by any private individual either for, and on behalf of, or jointly, with the Association. Bicycles must be locked. The Association retains the right to dispose of and to retain any proceeds of sale of property left unclaimed for three months.

CANCELLATIONS

NOTICE OF CANCELLATION

In all cases if you have to cancel your visit, please let the Warden know, even at the last minute; someone else can then use your bed.

In mountain and remote areas, it is vital that you contact the Youth Hostel if you do decide not to take up your reservation. Otherwise, the police or rescue teams may be called out to look for you.

REFUNDS

CANCELLATION REFUND PACKAGE

For YHA members the benefits of this package are automatically provided as a service to members of YHA (England and Wales), see page 188 for details.

Groups

A similar package is available at a low charge to groups travelling under the Group Membership Concession. Please contact National Office for more information.

Payments for Adventure Holidays are subject to separate insurance policies and details will be sent to all participants prior to the holiday.

Standard cancellation charges where the refund package does not apply

YHA (England and Wales) MEMBERS (in circumstances not covered by refund package) and NON-MEMBERS:

A refund may be claimed provided 7 days notice of cancellation has been given to the Hostel(s). A cancellation fee is charged, of one half of the total overnight fees which have been paid.

Group cancellation

See YHA Group Booking Forms for conditions — available from the Hostel Warden.

Details of members cancellation refund package

YHA will refund the member in respect of loss of charges paid to the Association (up to £100) for the member's accommodation and/or meals not used if the member is forced to cancel or cut short the booked Youth Hostel journey as a direct and necessary result of:

A Accidental bodily injury to or illness or death of:

1) The member or any person with whom the member intends to travel.

2) A relative, close friend or business colleague of the member or of any person with whom the member intends to travel.

B The member or the person with whom the member intends to travel being placed in quarantine, being summoned for jury service or being made redundant, provided that such redundancy qualified for payment under the Employment Protection Act or any subsequent employment legislation.

C The member being required to remain at home or to return home because of major accidental damage or burglary at his permanent residence or place of business.

D Cancellation or curtailment of scheduled public transport services consequent upon industrial action, strike, riot or civil commotion.

E The motor car, motor cycle or pedal cycle by which the member intends to travel being stolen or immobilised by accidental damage or fire (the theft of any pedal cycle not securely locked is excluded).

The first £5.00 of every claim will be met by the claimant. (The £5.00 excess should not apply to groups who take out the full insurance cover.)

COMPLAINTS

We hope you will enjoy using our Youth Hostels. However, if you do have a complaint and it is something the Warden can deal with, please consult him/her first.

Otherwise, write to the Regional Office concerned, or to National Office at St Albans if you consider that the complaint should be drawn to our attention.

LOST CARDS

If you lose your membership card, you can get a replacement from National Office. Send £1.00 with your name, address and membership number (if known). A member who arrives at a Youth Hostel without his card will be admitted only on payment of a new membership fee, for which a replacement card will be issued.

One of the membership fees will be refunded by YHA National Office if you return one card and quote the membership number of the other. An administration charge may be made in certain circumstances.

YHA ENROLMENT FORM

To YHA, TREVELYAN HOUSE, ST ALBANS, HERTS, AL1 2DY

Please enrol me as a member of the Association.
I have been resident in England or Wales for at least 12 months.

PLEASE COMPLETE IN BLOCK CAPITALS

Title	Surname	First Names	Date of Birth	Membership No. (if already a member)

We now offer our members the opportunity to receive mailings and offers from a few carefully selected Companies, whose products and services are particularly appropriate to the interests of YHA members.

If you do not wish to receive such mailings, please indicate by placing a tick in the box provided. ☐

Address _____

Post Code _____

I enclose £ _____ (for prices see inside front cover). PLEASE MAKE CHEQUES PAYABLE TO YHA.

Signature _____

Date _____

Please note that membership prices are valid between 1st October 1990 and 30th September 1991.

For applicants under 16 a signature from a parent/guardian is required.

HOSTEL BOOKING LETTER

(Please complete in BLOCK LETTERS)

To the Warden of _____ Youth Hostel.

Please reserve the following for the nights of:

Date Month _____ 1991 to _____ 1991 Date Month

Number of nights _____ If you require a family room please telephone the Youth Hostel to check availability.

For additional nights, continue on separate sheet	Please enter number under each date				Price		Total	
	Date	Date	Date	Date	£	p	£	p
Beds								
Seniors								
Juniors								
Young								
Total								
Male								
Female								
Meals								
Evening					3	00		
Breakfast †					2	30		
Packed Lunch †					1	60		
Sheet Sleeping Bags (for total stay)					0	80		
					TOTAL COST			

† for following morning   (cont'd over)

HOSTEL BOOKING LETTER

(Please complete in BLOCK LETTERS)

To the Warden of _____ Youth Hostel.

Please reserve the following for the nights of:

Date Month _____ 1991 to _____ 1991 Date Month

Number of nights _____ If you require a family room please telephone the Youth Hostel to check availability.

For additional nights, continue on separate sheet	Please enter number under each date				Price		Total	
	Date	Date	Date	Date	£	p	£	p
Beds								
Seniors								
Juniors								
Young								
Total								
Male								
Female								
Meals								
Evening					3	00		
Breakfast †					2	30		
Packed Lunch †					1	60		
Sheet Sleeping Bags (for total stay)					0	80		
					TOTAL COST			

† for following morning   (cont'd over)

✂

Please provide on each day:

	Pints of milk	Large loaves	Small loaves
Pints of milk			
Large loaves			
Small loaves			

(Payment for milk and bread on arrival.)

I wish to pay by Cheque/Postal Order/Credit Card* payable to YHA:

Visa ☐   Access ☐

My Credit Card number is:

Expiry date _____

Name _____

Credit card holder's name _____

Address _____

_____

_____

_____

Post Code _____

Tel Numbers: Home _____

Work _____

Signature _____ Date _____

*Notes: Family rooms and Credit Card facilities are not always available, please check in advance. Please help the Warden by enclosing a S.A.E. for acknowledgement.

✂

Please provide on each day:

	Pints of milk	Large loaves	Small loaves
Pints of milk			
Large loaves			
Small loaves			

(Payment for milk and bread on arrival.)

I wish to pay by Cheque/Postal Order/Credit Card* payable to YHA:

Visa ☐   Access ☐

My Credit Card number is:

Expiry date _____

Name _____

Credit card holder's name _____

Address _____

_____

_____

_____

Post Code _____

Tel Numbers: Home _____

Work _____

Signature _____ Date _____

*Notes: Family rooms and Credit Card facilities are not always available, please check in advance. Please help the Warden by enclosing a S.A.E. for acknowledgement.

DETAILS OF CANCELLATIONS

When returning this form, please attach copies of the following, if available — Youth Hostel Receipts, Invoices, Group Booking Forms, relevant Medical Notes/Certificates, and other documents or notes relevant to your claim.

Dates of Visit	Hostel Name(s)	Numbers Cancelled				Amount of Unclaimed Booking
		Beds	Evening Meals	Break-fasts	Lunch Packs	£ p

I hereby declare that the answers given to the above questions are true in every respect and I have not withheld from the YHA any material information in connection with this application.

Date _____ Signature _____

APPLICATION FOR A REFUND

For money outstanding in respect of a cancelled booking.

Refunds are dealt with by the Region in which the hostel is situated, if your cancellation covers Youth Hostels in more than one Region, please send your application to the office of the first Region on your tour. Regional Office addresses are shown on page 17.

Note:- If you did not book directly with the Youth Hostels you should contact the office,

organisation, or agency that dealt with your booking, eg YHA Adventure Holidays or the Pennine Way Booking Bureau.

Please complete this form fully as this will help us to deal with your application as quickly as possible. (Applications are usually processed within four weeks of receipt).

1. **Name of Claimant** _____

    Address _____

    _____

    _____

    _____

    Name in which booking made, if different from claimant:

    _____

2. **YHA Membership**

    What is your current YHA Membership Number? _____

    What age category are you? (Young, Junior, Senior) _____

    (If several members are involved, please attach a list giving names and the above information).

3. **Groups**

    If your claim is in respect of a group booking did you complete a
    YHA Group Booking Form?   **Yes / No**

    Did you take the Group Cancellation Refund Package?   **Yes / No**

4. **Reasons for Cancellation(s)**

5. **Date Warden(s) advised of Cancellation** _____ / _____ / _____

ADVERTISERS' INDEX

DONATIONS

We are grateful for donations from:
Tarmac Plc
Ocean Group Plc (PH Holt Trust)

John Laing Plc
W R Grace Ltd
Lucas Industries Plc
W H Smith Ltd

CALENDAR 1991

January

M	T	W	T	F	S	S
	1	2	3	4	5	6
7	8	9	10	11	12	13
14	15	16	17	18	19	20
21	22	23	24	25	26	27
28	29	30	31			

February

M	T	W	T	F	S	S
				1	2	3
4	5	6	7	8	9	10
11	12	13	14	15	16	17
18	19	20	21	22	23	24
25	26	27	28			

March

M	T	W	T	F	S	S
				1	2	3
4	5	6	7	8	9	10
11	12	13	14	15	16	17
18	19	20	21	22	23	24
25	26	27	28	29	30	31

April

M	T	W	T	F	S	S
1	2	3	4	5	6	7
8	9	10	11	12	13	14
15	16	17	18	19	20	21
22	23	24	25	26	27	28
29	30					

May

M	T	W	T	F	S	S
		1	2	3	4	5
6	7	8	9	10	11	12
13	14	15	16	17	18	19
20	21	22	23	24	25	26
27	28	29	30	31		

June

M	T	W	T	F	S	S
					1	2
3	4	5	6	7	8	9
10	11	12	13	14	15	16
17	18	19	20	21	22	23
24	25	26	27	28	29	30

July

M	T	W	T	F	S	S
1	2	3	4	5	6	7
8	9	10	11	12	13	14
15	16	17	18	19	20	21
22	23	24	25	26	27	28
29	30	31				

August

M	T	W	T	F	S	S
			1	2	3	4
5	6	7	8	9	10	11
12	13	14	15	16	17	18
19	20	21	22	23	24	25
26	27	28	29	30	31	

September

M	T	W	T	F	S	S
30						1
2	3	4	5	6	7	8
9	10	11	12	13	14	15
16	17	18	19	20	21	22
23	24	25	26	27	28	29

October

M	T	W	T	F	S	S
	1	2	3	4	5	6
7	8	9	10	11	12	13
14	15	16	17	18	19	20
21	22	23	24	25	26	27
28	29	30	31			

November

M	T	W	T	F	S	S
				1	2	3
4	5	6	7	8	9	10
11	12	13	14	15	16	17
18	19	20	21	22	23	24
25	26	27	28	29	30	

December

M	T	W	T	F	S	S
30	31					1
2	3	4	5	6	7	8
9	10	11	12	13	14	15
16	17	18	19	20	21	22
23	24	25	26	27	28	29

Published by Youth Hostels Association (England & Wales) ISBN 0-904530-14-0
Front cover design by In-Touch, Hatfield
Designed and phototypeset by Turners Creative Services Limited, Dunstable
Reproduced, printed and bound in Sweden by Elanders

GENERAL INDEX

HOSTEL INDEX